The Catholic University
A MODERN APPRAISAL

CONTRIBUTORS

Preface: Theodore M. Hesburgh, C.S.C.

Thomas E. Ambrogi	William J. Richardson, S.J.
John Cogley	Lorenzo Roy
John Tracy Ellis	Edward Schillebeeckx, O.P.
Norbert A. Luyten, O.P.	George N. Shuster
Neil G. McCluskey, S.J.	Lucien Vachon
Ladislas M. Orsy, S.J.	John E. Walsh, C.S.C.
Paul C. Reinert, S.J.	Michael P. Walsh, S.J.

The

Catholic University

A MODERN APPRAISAL

Neil G. McCluskey, S.J.

Editor

UNIVERSITY OF NOTRE DAME PRESS
Notre Dame
London

"Problem and Promise," and "Why a Catholic University?" are translated and reprinted with permission by N. A. Luyten, ed., *Recherche et Culture* (Fribourg: Editions Universitaires, 1965).

Library of Congress Catalog Card Number: 70–85353
Manufactured in the United States of America by
NAPCO Graphic Arts, Inc.

BIOGRAPHICAL NOTES

THOMAS AMBROGI, former professor of theology at Woodstock College, Maryland, is currently on the faculty of the University of the Pacific. He has had a long-time interest in ecumenical theology.

JOHN COGLEY entered the field of journalism in his native Chicago as founding editor of *Today*. He has served as executive editor of *Commonweal* and senior writer on religious affairs for the *New York Times*. He is presently editor of *The Center Magazine* published by the Center for the Study of Democratic Institutions, Santa Barbara, California.

JOHN TRACY ELLIS, priest of the Archdiocese of Washington, has taught church history for over thirty years, most notably at The Catholic University of America and presently at the University of San Francisco. Author of a dozen volumes, he also was managing editor of the *Catholic Historical Review* between 1941 and 1963.

NORBERT ALFONS LUYTEN, O.P., is professor of philosophy at the University of Fribourg in Switzerland, where he was also dean of the faculty of letters and rector from 1956 to 1958. He has edited *Recherche et Culture: Tâches d'une Université Catholique*.

NEIL G. MCCLUSKEY, S.J., is dean-director of Notre Dame's Institute for Educational Studies. Prior to his loan to Notre Dame, he was academic vice president at Gonzaga University in Spokane, Washington. He also served for five years as education editor of *America,* and is presently a contributing editor to that magazine.

LADISLAS M. ORSY, S.J., Hungarian by birth, is professor of theology and chairman of the theology department at Fordham University. He received his M.A. in jurisprudence from Oxford University and his doctorate in canon law from the Gregorian University, Rome. His major work, *Open to the Spirit: Religious Life After Vatican II,* appeared in 1968.

PAUL C. REINERT, S.J., for twenty years has served as president of St. Louis University following several years as dean of the College

v

of Arts and Letters. Additionally, he has exercised national leadership as president of the North Central Association of Colleges and Secondary Schools, and the College and University Department of the National Catholic Educational Association.

WILLIAM J. RICHARDSON, S.J., is an associate professor of philosophy at Fordham University. He is an alumnus of Holy Cross College and holds advanced degrees from Louvain University. Father's major book is *Heidegger: Through Phenomenology to Thought* (1963).

LORENZO ROY over a twenty-year period has filled several roles at Laval University in Quebec, where since 1963 he has been vice-rector. He is the author of *La Certitude de la Doctrine Morale*. During the Second Vatican Council he served as a theological counsellor.

EDWARD C.F.A. SCHILLEBEECKX, O.P., was born during World War I in Belgium. Since 1958 he has occupied a chair of dogmatic theology at the University of Nijmegen in Holland. Since Vatican II he has emerged as one of the world's innovative theologians.

GEORGE N. SHUSTER was managing editor and a founder of *Commonweal*. For twenty-one years he was president of Hunter College of the City of New York. He has written sixteen books in the fields of religion, education, and history. At present he is assistant to the president of the University of Notre Dame.

LUCIEN VACHON is dean of the faculty of theology at the University of Sherbrooke in Quebec. He received his Ph.D. in theology at the Angelicum University, Rome, in 1964. His book, *Diocesan Priests: Spirituality*, was published in 1965.

JOHN E. WALSH, C.S.C., is currently vice president for academic affairs at the University of Notre Dame with previous experiences at the same institution as vice president for public relations and as chairman of the department of education. Father Walsh is the author of *Education and Power*.

MICHAEL P. WALSH, S.J., was president of Boston College for the ten years immediately preceding the assumption in 1968 of the presidency of Fordham University. A biologist by profession, he has also served as president of the N.C.E.A.'s College and University Department.

PREFACE

In a world of rapid change, it is always difficult to compute absolute gain or absolute loss. One can be alternately optimistic and pessimistic about the present status of the Catholic university. Some think that the Catholic university is dying out on a worldwide basis, either through the onslaught of secularism, imminent bankruptcy, take-over by students, or the sheer impossibility of a Catholic university ever being what it purports to be: a true full-fledged university that is also Catholic; a university that is at once committed and free.

Others think that Catholic universities are entering a second spring of rebirth, comparable in importance to that first spring in the Middle Ages when universities came into being under the sponsorship of the Church. The reasons for optimism are also varied: the new interest of the Church in the temporal problems of the modern world, problems that can only find an intellectual solution in the climate of variegated disciplines that characterize the modern Catholic university that is also free and autonomous. New institutional structures, with much greater involvement of the laity in university governance, also give reason for renewed hope. The new strength of our International Federation of Catholic Universities is another legitimate cause for hope. One does not federate the dying.

I see many valid reasons for both optimism and pessimism as I look at Catholic universities on a worldwide scale. There is reason for hope and some fear, too. This is only to say that the total situation of the Catholic university in the world today is quite ambiguous, with an ambiguity born of many new opportunities and as many new pressures that could, if not successfully countered, easily push our institutions into irrelevancy, if not extinction. There are no easy answers available to a would-be prophet. A gaze into the crystal ball of the future shows many conflicting currents, productive and counterproductive, good and bad, hopeful and fearful. To be realistic about the future of our Catholic universities, we must take all of these currents into account, in the spirit of the Chinese ideograph that signifies both crisis and opportunity.

The history of Catholic universities somewhat parallels the history of theology, and this is also a reason for hope today as theology is certainly entering a second spring of rebirth. Theology also had its first spring in the Middle Ages when the great syntheses were being created, mainly in a university context. When the first great Catholic universities founded in the Middle Ages were secularized following the Reformation and the French Revolution, theology was relegated to the seminaries, outside the universities.

It was really not until theology reentered the university that theology began to enter its second spring which flowered with the fruitful activity of university theologians during Vatican Council II. It would be impossible to imagine the results of this council without the creative theology and active presence of the periti from university faculties of theology. Conversely, most of the difficulty in elaborating new and creative theological texts in the council came precisely from those theologians who were wedded to an outdated, repetitive, and uncreative theology that, unfortunately, had largely characterized seminary teaching for some centuries.

This parallel birth and rebirth of theology and the Catholic university should tell us something about the future growth or demise of Catholic universities. However, we cannot make a simple comparison of the situation in the Middle Ages and today. History has not stood still in the meanwhile; indeed, the world has undergone cataclysmic change that has affected both the university and theology in the modern context.

In the Middle Ages, theology was the acknowledged queen of the sciences within the university which comprised mainly only two other professional faculties of law and medicine. As we have noted above, with the secularization of the universities, theology was largely dropped from the university scene. But much more happened. The totality of knowledge which by then had taken centuries to develop, now is doubling in content every fifteen years, particularly in the natural, physical, and social sciences.

Many intellectuals today do not even recognize theology as a true science. If theology is to reenter the university, even the great Catholic university, in strength, it will only be accepted as a true university discipline if it proves itself to be relevant to the total scene of knowledge, and if it operates under the same kinds of university conditions of freedom and autonomy as the other disciplines do. Theology simply cannot be forced in, unless the university is by name Catholic and, in fact, not much of a university, which is to say that the secular disciplines there are either nonexistent or very weak. Theology, as a university discipline must be strong and free, among other strong and free university disciplines, and in living conversation and discourse with all the others.

Once reinstated in a strong and vital university, theology will not enjoy its ancient position of mistress or queen of all else taught there. Indeed, if theology does not dialogue with all the other knowledges, and bring some special new dimension of meaning and direction to all of the other disciplines, it will simply *be located* in the university. It will not *exist* and *thrive* there, and it will contribute nothing to the Catholicity of the university, which, without vital theology, will in fact not be Catholic, whatever its name or sponsorship.

I submit to you, in all frankness, that this has been the sad state of theology in many of our Catholic universities today which, therefore, are not very distinctive as Catholic, and which, consequently, have made all too little intellectual contribution to the Church or the world in that precise task which faces the university as Catholic.

We take pride in the fact that the Church sponsored the first universities in the Middle Ages, but have noted that most of these great mediaeval universities, Louvain excepted, are no longer Catholic. The re-creation of Catholic universities in North America—thanks to a climate of political freedom for higher education—began more than a century ago. In Europe and in Latin America, which shared much of Europe's experience in the early founding and subsequent losing of Catholic universities, the re-creation of Catholic universities came either late in the last century or, for the majority, during this century. All of the Catholic universities in the third world of former colonies are also of relatively recent vintage, with the exception of Santo Tomas in the Philippines. What can one say of this effort to re-create the mediaeval tradition of Catholic universities in modern times?

First of all, we must admit that while the Church sponsored the first great mediaeval universities, it soon enough lost them to the state and the secular world, which for the last several centuries have been the forces that have determined the rules governing the university world. The Church does not have to reenter this world but, if it wishes to do so, it must follow these established university rules of freedom and autonomy. It must be dedicated to all the varieties of knowledge and all the varied ways of knowing which constitute in the modern mind the very conditions of life for the university. The Catholic university can contribute to the variety of the worldwide university spectrum of knowledge another way of knowing, theology. Theology which has been largely lost to this world that, by the word *universitas,* is by its nature committed to universal knowledge which it will not really have without theology.

We must be perfectly clear, however, in realizing that theology cannot expect special treatment and exceptional existence in this university world which it did not create during these past centuries. Theology, too, must enjoy the full privileges of this world, if it is to be an accepted part of the total university life and experience and not exist in a world apart. The Catholic university has too often been looked upon by many Catholics as Catholic first and university second. University is the substantive noun in this combination, and the world judges clearly enough whether or not an institution, whatever else it claims to be, is in fact a university in the commonly accepted meaning of this word. One can similarly speak of a Catholic person, but he must be a person before he can become a Catholic. Catholic here is an adjective. So, too, in the case of the Catholic university. By reversing the order, putting Catholic before university, we have often created a Catholic something that lacked the essentials of what the secular university world considers necessary for a university; a combination of many strong, free, and autonomous faculties. If, in addition, there was the added defect of no strong, vital and creative theological faculty within it, the so-called Catholic university was neither a university nor Catholic.

This is not to say that the Catholic institutions of higher learning have a monopoly on weakness. But it is no compliment to God's honor and glory to say that Catholic universities are no better or no worse than the secular institutions around them. It does derogate from God's glory to find some Catholic universities judged commonly as much worse than the best of their kind in the secular world around them. And it is a real disgrace to God and to the Church when the most obvious weakness in many Catholic universities is their faculty of theology, which should be their greatest strength, particularly in the complicated and problematic world of post-Vatican Council II, so needful of theological insights from the university.

All this, perhaps too strongly said and too negatively sounding, brings us to the great challenge that faces the Catholic university in the world today, its special and proper mission.

Our central role in the modern world is to be among the best of universities, in the full meaning of the word, and to be Catholic in the full contemporary sweep of the Church's concern for worldwide human development in its ultimate personal, social, cultural, spiritual, and even material dimensions. One need only scan the long list of human problematics in Vatican Council II's Constitution on the Church in the Modern World to perceive the magnitude of our task.

The opening paragraphs of this Constitution provide a setting for this task:

> *The joys and hopes, and griefs and the anxieties of the men of this age, especially those who are poor or in any way afflicted, these too are the joys and hopes, the griefs and anxieties of the followers of Christ. Indeed, nothing genuinely human fails to raise an echo in their hearts. . . . This*

community realizes that it is truly and intimately linked with mankind and its history. . . . Though mankind today is struck with wonder at its own discoveries and its power, it often raises anxious questions about the place and role of man in the universe, about the meaning of his individual and collective strivings, and about the ultimate destiny of reality and of humanity. . . .

This Council can provide no more eloquent proof of its solidarity with the entire human family with which it is bound up, as well as its respect and love for that family, than by engaging with it in conversation about these various problems. . . .

To carry out such a task the Church has always had the duty of scrutinizing the signs of the times, and of interpreting them in the light of the Gospel. Thus, in language intelligible to each generation, she can respond to the perennial questions which men ask about this present life and the life to come, and about the relationship of the one to the other. We must, therefore, understand the world in which we live, its expectations, its longings, and its often dramatic characteristics. . . .

The Church as Church is not organized in a way that permits the deep and persistent and scientific study of realistic solutions to this vast panoply of human problems, such as war and peace; human rights in the social, cultural, economic, and political orders; world poverty and hunger and population; illiteracy and race and neo-nationalism; ecumenism both between and among Christian communities and nonbelievers; the personal and moral implications of the technological, atomic, space, agricultural, communications, and knowledge revolutions. The Church has declared itself concerned about all of these problems—but only in first-rate Catholic universities can the Church confront these problems with the necessary intellectual resources to seek solutions that are at once meaningful and humane and in keeping with Christian traditions of optimism and concern for the temporal and eternal dignity and destiny of the human person.

The university is the very quintessence of the pilgrim Church in the intellectual order, seeking answers to ultimate questions in concert with all men of intelligence and good will, drawing on all knowledges and every way of knowing and, especially bringing every philosophical and theological insight to bear upon the monumental task at hand, whatever the source of these insights.

This is no task for amateurs or dilettantes, nor for second-rate scholars or institutions less than first class. It is not a task that can be done without that intellectual climate of freedom that is the essential atmosphere of a university's research program, especially in theology. It is not something that can be accomplished in the face of arbitrary controls from outside the university's professional community of researchers and scholars.

Under the best of conditions, the task of the modern Catholic university and, especially, of the research theologians in it, is well nigh impossible. Under less than the best conditions, it would be better not to begin, for we serve both God and the Church badly by mediocrity in any order, but doubly so in the order of God's great gift to man called intelligence, intelligence that works best in function of God's other great gift of freedom. Let us renew our efforts in a manner commensurate with the noble and demanding task facing our Catholic universities in the world today: to bring Christian wisdom to bear upon the problems and opportunities facing all men in our times.

Theodore M. Hesburgh, C.S.C.

CONTENTS

xvi   *Contents*

Introduction

THIS IS HOW IT HAPPENED

NEIL G. McCLUSKEY, S.J.

Of necessity the university leads a precarious life. If it responds too easily to social pressures, the university loses its leadership muscle. If it is impervious to the needs of the times, it becomes arteriosclerotic and is by-passed. It cannot be too far out in front; it dare not fall behind. One world leader has likened it to "a city of the mind, a vast classroom of instruction, a laboratory of discovery and research, an infinity of small rooms containing solitary scholars and writers, a studio of artistic production, an endless conversation, a meeting place for scholars and a home for its students."[1]

Indeed, replete with its own priesthood, ritual, creed, and dogma today's university has become a kind of church. It has undoubtedly replaced the church as the fulcrum of influence in the contemporary world. Increasingly, government, industry, commerce, diplomacy, labor and management—the churches themselves—turn to the modern university for knowledge and direction.

What of the church-related university. Can it exist? What should it be? Who needs it? The immediate reply is: No one more than the Church itself. Looking at the frailty of the Church of the last century, Philip Hughes has written of the grave loss resulting from the disappearance of the universities, which had been Catholic and often papal in their founding. In all of them

[1] Pope Paul VI, Letter to the president of the International Federation of Catholic Universities on the opening of the 1965 General Conference in Tokyo, dated August 24, 1965.

there had been a faculty of theology, and "round this mistress science their whole intellectual life had turned." When restored they came back as universities under the state, dedicated to natural truth alone. His poignant summation continues:

> *Education, the formation of the Catholic mind and the new Catholic Europe, would suffer immeasurably, and religious formation be to its intellectual development an extra something added on. There would be the further mischievous effect that henceforth not universities but seminaries would set the tone of theological life. The leaders of Catholic thought would not be the professional thinkers whom a university produces, but technicians, those to whom the important work of training the future clergy is committed and who, among other things, teach them theology. The effect of this destruction of the faculties of theology in the universities of Catholic Europe, the disappearnce of the old Salamanca, Alcala, Coimbra, Bologna, Douai, Louvain, and Paris, is a theme that still awaits its historian.*[2]

During that crucial nineteenth century which so largely has shaped the present one, the Church was too intellectually impoverished to cope with the progressive and liberating ideas which remade the world. Lacking "the healthy interplay of the theological intellects of half a score of Catholic universities," again to borrow from Hughes, the Church could only look on helplessly as the world became modern.[3]

The current malaise in the university world has forced institutions everywhere to study themselves. In what might be termed the university's Protestant Reformation or French Revolution, like never before has today's university had to examine its goals and structures, its means and resources. The glories of yesteryear are not absolving any institution of higher learning from the serious *autocritique* called for by the times. In recent years the major Catholic universities of the world, linked in the Interna-

---

[2] Philip Hughes, *A Popular History of the Catholic Church* (New York: Macmillan, 1947), pp. 238–239.
  [3] *Ibid.*

tional Federation of Catholic Universities, have also begun to face the challenge of the contemporary.[4]

This book is about the Catholic university and its search for a modern identity. It pulls together much of the best thought that is revitalizing contemporary Catholic higher education. The idea for this volume was conceived in Tokyo, grew in the lake country of Northern Wisconsin and on a hill near the capital of the Congo, and came to term in a venerable palace of the Vatican. This introduction is to tell the reader what happened between Tokyo and Rome and to indicate its meaning.

At the close of the Tokyo meeting of the International Federation of Catholic Universities (IFCU) in late August, 1965, the assembled delegates adopted as their theme for the next meeting the nature and role of the contemporary Catholic university. In preparation for that meeting, planned for the Lovanium University at Kinshasa, Democratic Republic of the Congo, seminars were to be held in each of the four regions of the IFCU.

In mid-March of 1967, a planning committee of sixteen persons from major Catholic universities met at the University of Notre Dame to discuss what approach should be taken by the North American region. There were several side-products which came out of this historic two-day encounter. One was a new sense of institutional friendliness. Hostility and jealousy have not been exactly unknown among Catholic universities, even among those conducted by the same religious order, to say nothing of those operated by rival congregations.

The major outcome, however, was the decision to convene an invitational seminar the following July at Notre Dame's ecological center, Land O'Lakes, Wisconsin. A number of background papers were to be commissioned. A somewhat larger group would be invited, including high level authorities from Rome and representatives of the American bishops. The final number of those in attendance was twenty-six.

It was an unusual group which met that bright July day at

[4] There are about 600 institutions of higher learning in the world which are "Catholic" in one or other ways. This total includes 143 universities; 240 university colleges; 86 separate faculties on the university level; some 80 colleges as constituent members of state universities. There are 71 members of the IFCU, whose membership is restricted to university-type institutions.

Chicago's O'Hare Field to board the charter plane that was to wing them to the fabled lake country of Northern Wisconsin and Michigan. From Rome came the superior general of the Holy Cross Fathers and the American assistant general of the Jesuits, himself a former president of Fordham University. The scholarly Archbishop Paul J. Hallinan of Atlanta, now mourned, and Bishop John J. Dougherty, then president of Seton Hall University and chairman of the American bishops' committee for Catholic higher education, both graced the meeting. Several leaders of Catholic higher education in Canada were in attendance, as were the presidents of Boston College, Fordham, Georgetown, Notre Dame, and St. Louis. Neither the then rector of The Catholic University of America nor any of the vice rectors accepted the invitation to attend, but the rector-bishop did give permission to the assistant to the vice rector for development to go to Land O'Lakes as an "observer." Four distinguished laymen, including the chairmen of the boards of trustees of both St. Louis and Notre Dame, were soon an indistinguishable part of the summer-shirted clerical group.

Despite the allure of the magnificent sylvan surroundings, the twenty-six seminar participants had come great distances prepared to work, and work they did. In small groups and in plenary sessions, informally and formally, morning, noon, and night for four days these men attempted to bring their own experience, study, and expertise to confront various angles of two simple but all-important questions: What makes a modern university Catholic? How does a modern university act Catholic?

An observer of the contemporary scene has hinted at the implications of the first query, writing:

> *In what sense is a Catholic university Catholic if it is composed predominantly of lay professors who employ, in their teaching and research, the same methods and norms as their counterparts in secular universities, and who are engaged in the pursuit of knowledge in autonomous spheres that are in no way dependent upon any over-all*

"Catholic position"? What, in short, is the reason for being of the Catholic *college or university.*[5]

The North American group agreed that the Catholic university is and has been rapidly evolving and that some distinctive characteristics of this evolving institution should be carefully identified and described. These had not been clearly articulated, at least in the modern context, by any authoritative group. The "Land O'Lakes" statement attempted to call attention to some of these characteristics which are particularly relevant to the contemporary problems facing the Catholic universities of the world and with special reference to the United States and Canada. Accordingly, the group statement did not pretend to present a full philosophy or description of the Catholic university. It was selectively and deliberately incomplete. Furthermore, since the seminar discussions were under the sponsorship of the International Federation of Catholic Universities and centered primarily on university-level problems, the nature and role of the Catholic liberal arts college or of the smaller university were only indirectly considered.

Another important limitation of the statement was noted in the preamble. The group clearly recognized that the presence of and active participation by persons who are not Catholics in the Catholic university community are both desirable and necessary to bring authentic universality to the Catholic university itself. It should hardly need stating but those of other views, whether students, faculty members, or administrators, bring rich contributions from their own traditions. Moreover, seriousness and integrity in the search for understanding and commitment are guaranteed by their presence. However, the document did not attempt to describe how this desirable participation of others than Catholics can be integrated with the Catholic community, so that, in fact, their participation would make the Catholic university a Catholic-sponsored pluralistic society in microcosm.

[5] J. Philip Gleason, "A Historical Perspective," *The Shape of Catholic Higher Education,* ed. Robert Hassenger (Chicago: University of Chicago Press, 1967), p. 52.

There was an excitement among the group as awareness grew that a consensus was bringing them to the point where they could put their convictions on paper. The document that came out of that meeting is known now throughout the world as the "Land O'Lakes Statement" and it has a firm place in the literature.[6] Despite the general awareness that what they had done was important, some of the group had an initial timidity about releasing the statement to the public. At this interval the veteran journalist John Cogley pointedly reminded the group that a gathering of this kind just could not escape the sharp eyes of the media world. (Already the news magazines and several newspapers had attempted to find out why such an eminent group was assembling in Northern Wisconsin.) Rather than risk partial or slanted disclosures, it was decided that the complete statement would be made public along with the list of the signatories. All agreed.

Several thousand printed copies were circulated. The Land O'Lakes statement was not issued as holy writ but in the hope, as the preface put it, of "widening and deepening the discussion," and comments from all quarters were invited. The document was reprinted in its entirety in *America* and several other journals. It served as a basis for discussion by faculties in dozens of institutions and, as was hoped for from the beginning, led to important refinements. Members of the hierarchy wrote to congratulate its authors. One cardinal-archbishop said of the document that it reflected "convictions with which most persons I think would be in substantial agreement."

Understandably but somewhat regretfully, the secular press played up those sections of the statement which spoke of the Catholic university's need for autonomy and academic freedom "in the face of authority of whatever kind, lay or clerical, external to the academic community itself," in order to best serve the church. (The memory was still fresh of incidents at St. John's, Dayton, and The Catholic University.) Casually touched upon were the ringing affirmations of the centrality of theology and of Christian inspiration to validate the existence of the institution ascribing to the proud title of "Catholic university."

[6] The complete statement is reprinted as an appendix to this volume.

The document proved too heady for a portion of the Catholic press. A number of diocesan papers clucked their tongues editorially at its bold "declaration of independence" from the hierarchy. The bishop-rector of The Catholic University of America categorically denounced the statement and attempted without success to force the institution's representative to join in his public denunciation. The document shocked some of the Roman bureaucracy and delighted others. Privately a number of prelates let their distress be known and their fears over American *liberalismo*.

*   *   *   *   *   *

Twelve months and ten thousand miles later came the next important phase. In early September of 1968 a group of roughly one hundred delegates and observers from some fifty Catholic institutions of higher learning gathered in Kinshasa, capital of the Democratic Republic of the Congo, for the Eighth Triennial Congress of the International Federation of Catholic Universities.

The host institution, the Lovanium University, daughter of Belgium's venerable University of Louvain, provided gracious and generous hospitality in a colorful Congolese setting. First-time visitors to the Lovanium were amazed by the spaciousness and modernity of the plant. This writer, a visitor on the eve of the demise of the old Belgian Congo nine years earlier, even then impressed with the promise of the young institution, was overwhelmed by the clusters of imposing buildings, the beautiful gardens and residences that are today's Lovanium. Thanks to Belgian and American largess, in addition to generous support from the Congolese government, in its fifteen-year life the Lovanium has gone from 300 to 2,200 students spread among eight faculties including law and medicine, engineering and agronomy. The opening ceremonies and festivities, the hospitality and organization of the congress met the finest standards established for major educational gatherings anywhere. Because of the Lovanium's storied remoteness in "darkest" Africa all these things were doubly impressive.

On September 9 the congress officially opened in the central air-conditioned aula of the university equipped with facilities for simultaneous translation in English, French, and Spanish. It became almost immediately apparent that with this congress the International Federation of Catholic Universities had come to maturity. The quality of the papers, the level of the discussion, the frankness of the exchange, the skillful organization, the presence of the cardinal-prefect of the Congregation for Catholic Education, all signaled the end of IFCU's twenty-year adolescence and the start of adulthood.

The Land O'Lakes statement by the North American group was not the only document ready for the hands of participants. Similar seminars and meetings had been held in Buga (Colombia), in Manila, and in Paris for the other three regions of the Federation. Moreover, a mountain of material had been prepared to provide background information and data about each of the four regions of the Federation under three headings. The first concerned the present situation of Catholic universities in the world and its significance. The next was the justification and mission of the Catholic university in the modern world, while the third treated of the means and conditions necessary to realize that mission.

A certain polarization quickly became apparent, a confrontation between those defending the classic, post-Reformation, church-controlled institution and advocates of the contemporary, open, and autonomous institution. In the discussions the apologetic of Trent often seemed to clash with the ecumenism of Vatican II, and at times the debate seemed to be between men of different centuries. The delegates, sometimes even from the same country, were divided on such basic points as the nature of the university, its responsibility to serve society, and above all its relationships to church authority.

During the discussion of the items in the first two categories, considerable agreement was reached. All agreed to the centrality of the theological inspiration and the need for some type of Catholic "character" within the university community though there were different interpretations of what these things meant in practice. There was agreement that the Catholic university had a unique role to play in the developing or emerging nations but the agreement foundered in discussing specific countries. It was agreed that the reckless proliferation of institutions of higher learning under Catholic sponsorship had to cease. A much stronger resolution on the point was watered down in favor of one which simply urged that "to achieve any significant influence on contemporary society, an institution of higher learning must possess a certain quality of excellence recognizable throughout the academic world." Accordingly, careful planning was urged with an additional good word thrown in for affiliation and sharing of facilities, both among Catholic schools and with others. But after these points unanimity fled and returned only briefly to the floor.

What are the means and conditions needed for a Catholic university to achieve its mission? Nearly everybody thought he had some ideas here. Several speakers trotted out dire warnings about the secularizing trends in Catholic higher education. A few of them strained the congress' patience by equating "secularization" and "laicization."[7]

The ideas in the Land O'Lakes statement regarding autonomy and academic freedom were considered by many as outlandish and dangerous. "True autonomy and academic freedom in the face of authority of whatever kind, lay or clerical, external to the academic community itself" was a huge morsel to swallow for a number of the assembled brethren whose philosophy of education was shaped in a more traditional context. Speaker followed speaker to warn (frequently in Latin) against "false" autonomy or "absolute" autonomy and to defend the need of the Catholic university to depend on the magisterium of the church. At least twice the topic was labeled a false problem on the score that it involved clerics and religious and so was merely a question of church discipline.

However, seeds of thought were being planted. The more perspicacious of the traditionalist group could at least grant that in the American milieu such freedom might be necessary

---

[7] For the writer this recalled a memory of the 1965 Tokyo congress of the IFCU, at which the rector of an ancient Catholic institution of higher learning solemnly avowed to the group that only a priest could truly and ideally fill a Catholic university presidency because only he fulfilled in his person the union of secular and sacred learning. No doubt a new version of the hypostatic union!

but, they asked, would this kind of institution, independent of ecclesiastical guidance, be any longer *Catholic*? This question, of course, led to another more basic one which became the most discussed topic of the week: What essentially constitutes a Catholic university? Is it the university's juridical link with the ecclesiastical authorities or the animating presence of the Catholic faith? Or both? The group was hopelessly split.

It was proposed that the group come up with some kind of final declaration embodying the group thought on the nature and role of the Catholic university. Accordingly, a nine-man representative committee was appointed: two Americans, two Latino-Americans, three Europeans, and two Canadians, including the rector of the Pontifical Gregorian University in Rome. As chairman, the present writer attempted to collect the ideas which commanded a consensus or near consensus. This proved fairly simple. The difficult—ultimately impossible—task was to find a consensus or compromise expression of the meaning of autonomy and academic freedom. The committee did agree that autonomy was vital to the life of the university but since the understanding of autonomy differed as much as the Russian meaning of democracy does from the Swiss, this topic along with its correlative "academic freedom" were not included in the committee statement.

After prolonged debate and much soul-searching for some, the committee reached a consensus that non-Catholic participation was vital for the future of Catholic higher education. The committee struggle mirrored precisely the mixed feelings of the larger group and it was only the statement in its fifth revision which reached the floor. Speaking of the appropriate endeavors of a Catholic university, the committee wording paralleled Land O'Lakes: One endeavor is "to create a Christian community of learners, in which, because of its authentic universality, non-Catholics as well as Catholics may participate and cooperate, thus bringing to the Catholic university the ideas and values of many traditions."[8] There were a few delegates, however, who still argued that by definition a non-Catholic pro-

---

[8] The complete statement is reprinted as an appendix to this volume.

fessor or student belonged to an inferior category and hence could not share the full rights and status of the Catholic. Though there was no minority effort to include this enlightened piece of sixteenth-century apologetics in the statement, the finally approved version above passed by only a slender majority.

The relation between a university and church authority proved another impossible point of agreement. The committee had attempted to satisfy everybody by simply stating that there were different interpretations here, and proposed this draft to the floor: "In addition to the theological inspiration which distinctly characterizes the Catholic university, some of the group judge that there must also be a juridical relationship which constitutes a university as Catholic, exercised either through papal charter or through a religious congregation approved by the Holy See." By a two-to-one vote this simple statement of division had to be deleted from the final document. The traditionalists would not allow even the possibility that an institution could be constituted Catholic without juridical relationship to church authority.

Another clash came over the understanding of the phrase "institutional commitment." Over and above the personal commitment to the Church which an individual as Catholic might have, does the institution *as such* have a commitment to the Church? How does it discharge such a commitment? If the phrase were to mean a joint respect for and fidelity to the ideals of the Church, this would be one thing. But if commitment were translated in action to be a kind of uncritical obedience by the entire university toward every level of ecclesiastical authority, that would decidedly be another. How does one properly speak of autonomy and academic freedom if an institution *as such* is committed in obedience to the teaching authority of the Church? Given this latent ambiguity and given the then raging controversy between the Archbishop of Washington and the theological faculty of The Catholic University of America, many American representatives argued against the use of the phrase.

The draft committee attempted to satisfy both sides and at the conclusion of the list of distinctive tasks of the Catholic university proposed this phrasing:

To these special tasks Catholic universities are dedicated by an institutional commitment which includes a respect for and voluntary acceptance of the church's teaching authority. This commitment may be insured either by canonical erection, by dependence upon the Sacred Congregation for Catholic Education, by juridical dependence upon some ecclesiastical authority, or by determination by the founders and promoters, or by incorporation in the basic documents of the university, or by self-determination within the institution itself or by its own internal authority.

After what seemed interminable wrangling, the vote was called. Only the first sentence with the disputed phrase, "Institutional commitment" survived. The next words, which tried to explain the optional ways this commitment could be exercised, failed to rally the necessary votes. It was deleted. Wearily the delegates adjourned from the final session with a document many felt said little and in some places was liable to harmful interpretation.

Was the Kinshasa congress a disaster? Despite the negative coloring to much of what has been here narrated, the total result of the meeting comes out a big plus. Four factors can be listed upon which this statement is based—and a fifth, the meeting in Rome within eight months called by the Congregation for Catholic Education perhaps the best of all evidence. What were these?

1. The goodwill and native intelligence of the delegates, even from fragile institutions under the fist of Latin-American military dictatorships who consider themselves Catholic because the charter says they are. Even the most reactionary and conservative were impressed by their ten days of contact with scholars and administrators from other parts of the world. Everyone learned. The Church is *Catholic.*

2. The stellar performance of the distinguished lay participants who made it patent that a layman can be as dedicated and competent in the things of Catholic higher education as anyone who bears priestly or episcopal anointing. One cannot forget the morning session presided over by Mr. Edmund Stephan and

Mr. Daniel Schlafly, chairmen (respectively) of the boards of trustees of the University of Notre Dame and St. Louis University. Neither will any Paraguan, Italian, or Spanish delegate who witnessed their performance.

3. The superlative opening paper of Père Norbert Luyten, O.P., former rector and now professor of philosophy at the University of Fribourg. In response to questioning, he could explain that his magnificent conception of the Catholic university was not sheer theory out of canon law or scholastic theology or a working hypothesis but was drawn from a lived experience of Fribourg—which had not the slightest juridical or official tie to any church governing group but was proudly known as Catholic.

4. The Lovanium itself was a constant reminder of how far an institution can move, given the evolution of circumstances. Now almost totally state-supported and influenced, it has provided the cadre for service to the Congolese state in every professional and leadership area. Yet it considers itself and *acts* Catholic without the slightest juridical or other formal link to a church group. The classical "churchy" institution which might have been imposed and guided from Europe by now would have been buried in jungle overgrowth—and forgotten—because it would have been helpless to adapt.

And so the day for departure came and amid happy African confusion at the airport we boarded the Air Congo Boeing 707 for Brussels with our new friendships, memories, and souvenirs. As the giant jet lazily circled its way into pattern over the river and town and university below, the realization began that something important had happened there for the future of Catholic higher education in this wobbly world.

*   *   *   *   *   *

Some delegates returned from Kinshasa disappointed that more had not been accomplished. There was, however, one man determined to make sure that more would be done and as Cardinal Prefect of the Congregation for Catholic Education, he was in a position to do so. Since his appointment, Gabriel-Marie Garrone had impressed observers with his open mind, ready ear, and eagerness to learn—new qualities in what had become one of the most autocratic of the Roman congregations. In early January, 1969, the congregation proposed to Catholic universities throughout the world a detailed series of questions relating to their own aggiornamento in the light of Vatican II. The bulk of the questionnaire was based upon the discussions and final position paper of the Kinshasa congress. Every bishop within whose diocese there was a Catholic university also received it.

Among the questions were unresolved veterans of Kinshasa such as: "What should be the position of non-Catholic professors and students in the Catholic university?" "What should be the role of the laity in the direction of the Catholic university?" "Can one conceive of and define different kinds of Catholic universities?" "What can or should be the relations of the Catholic university to the local bishop or episcopal conference, or to the Holy See relative to its establishment, approval and governance?"

The compiled answers from 79 institutions came to 553 mimeographed pages and, predictably enough, span the spectrum of philosophies and theologies of education. Along with the questionnaire was sent a covering letter inviting the universities to elect representatives who would come to Rome in the spring for a meeting with officials of the congregation—a meeting, one hastens to add, without precedent. Six places were assigned to the United States and forty American institutions were asked to vote. Nine persons received practically all of the votes of the thirty-two schools which returned ballots, while the remainder were scattered among twenty-eight other choices. These nine names, including three alternates, were sent to the Apostolic Delegate's office. Apparently consternation rose over the results so that someone in Washington or Rome decided that the list should be improved on by quietly substituting four new names for four elected delegates—men all known for their strong views on autonomy and academic freedom. The scheme might have worked except for one thing. The outcome of the election had been circulated to all the balloting institutions. Any attempt to falsify the results of an open election would have resulted in a storm of unpleasant publicity. When this possibility was pointed out, the four names were restored.

In any event, the thirty-nine delegates and observers from twenty-two countries assembled in Rome for the week-long congress, beginning April 25. Though the color and pageantry surrounding the creation of thirty-one new cardinals that same week overshadowed this congress, it may have at least an equal importance for the future of the Church. The meeting was an important first: a first modern attempt to hold a frank exchange of views on the critical questions confronting higher education; a first attempt by Rome to listen at length to what elected representatives of the Catholic universities had to say; a first unstructured meeting whose agenda was left entirely up to the delegates; a first welcoming of a position paper as the basis of further dialogue between Rome and the Catholic universities of the world.

At the opening session in the same aula which houses the world synod of the bishops, Cardinal Garrone and Archbishop Joseph Schroeffer, the congregation's genial German secretary, turned the meeting over to the delegates to fix their own rules of procedure and agenda. As at Kinshasa, here began a mutual education which bared the same astonishing differences in educational philosophy. It likewise became increasingly clear why serious misunderstandings between Vatican bureaucracy and certain American Catholic universities in the area of academic freedom were simply inevitable.

Mindful of Pope Paul's injunction during his reception of the group that they "open up the paths of the future with boldness and firmness," the delegates rolled up their sleeves. After discussing various approaches, an ad hoc committee on agenda and procedures was selected. On their recommendation the group divided itself into three commissions to tackle the large issues raised by the questionnaire answers. Each commission was to meet apart for three days and attempt to state the question and formalize a consensus where possible. The last four days would be devoted to general assemblies in which the texts would be discussed and voted on.

Important as was the work of the other two commissions, particularly in respect to statements on the internal life of the Catholic university and its present position in world society, the strongest attention was focused on the work of Commission III which dealt with the Catholic university's distinguishing characteristics and its relationships with church authority. Most of the periti and staff of the congregation attended these sessions and, in fact, were quite active in the debates.

The commission was able to build on work done at Land O'Lakes and at Kinshasa and with relative ease came up with this affirmation of the essential characteristics of a Catholic university.

> *Since the objective of the Catholic university, precisely as Catholic, is to assure in an institutional manner a Christian presence in the university world confronting the great problems of contemporary society, the following are its essential characteristics:*
>
> *(1) a Christian inspiration not only of individuals but of the community as well;*
>
> *(2) a continuing reflection in the light of Christian faith upon the growing treasure of human knowledge;*
>
> *(3) fidelity to the Christian message as it comes to us through the Church;*
>
> *(4) an institutional commitment to the service of Christian thought and education.[9]*

So far so good. The first problem to raise the temperature, both in the commission and later in the larger assembly, was, as might be anticipated, the problem of the "link." In other words, to be *Catholic* in the fullest and truest sense of the word, must there not be a juridical relation to the "official" church? In the American context, can institutions like the University of Notre Dame and St. Louis University, which in 1967 transferred legal ownership and ultimate goverance to a board of trustees whose composition no longer gave the Holy Cross or Jesuit Fathers control, continue to style themselves *Catholic?*[10]

---

[9] The complete statement is reprinted as an appendix to this volume.

[10] See Neil G. McCluskey, "The New Catholic College," *America*, March 25, 1967, pp. 414–417.

Neither possesses a papal charter nor has any other legal connection with the local diocese or the religious order which founded and continues to support them. They are legally constituted by charters from the States of Indiana and Missouri which do not recognize their catholicity but only their "university-ness."

As will be recalled, less than eight months earlier at Kinshasa, a similar proposal which would have omitted juridical relationship as an essential characteristic of a Catholic university was voted down. All the more remarkable then was the section adopted unanimously during the Rome meeting which unequivocally stated: "All universities that realize these conditions [the four earlier enumerated] are Catholic universities, whether canonically erected or not." Of equal meaning was the statement in a neighboring passage: ". . . there are various categories into which fall Catholic institutions of higher learning. Two basic categories can immediately be discerned: those institutions which have a juridical bond to church authorities in one form or another and those which do not."

Did this signify a mass conversion or change of heart among the Rome delegates, fifteen of whom were present at this and the Kinshasa meetings? Probably not, despite the unanimous approbation these passages received. What did grow was an awareness, as the document put it, that "the purposes of the Catholic university can be pursued by different means and modalities according to diverse situations of time and place." Moreover, that "given the different stages of development of higher education under Catholic auspices in various parts of the world, and even of institutions within the same country, it would be futile to attempt a univocal approach to the contemporary challenges and problems of our institutions of higher learning." Here then is the key to resolving the complex problems surrounding the relationships between the Catholic university and the Church's magisterium and nothing done during the Roman meeting was of greater significance than the agreement on this point. Before the close of this chapter the reader hopefully will understand why.

To their credit most European and Latin American dele-

gates to the Roman congress broadened their minds to allow
equal legitimacy to a new category of Catholic university, even
though they probably judged that their own institutions were
closer to the ideal or at least were better suited to their own
contexts. Moreover, they and, in fact, all the delegates were
undoubtedly influenced by the general and profound dissatisfaction in the university world with its professed functions and
goals. The congress here expressed its concern in these words:

> *Everywhere, but especially in developing countries, there*
> *is a feeling that a new age has begun. The age of unques-*
> *tioning subservience, of colonial dependence, has passed.*
> *The times demand the assertion of individuality, the devel-*
> *opment of personality, the exercise of an inalienable right*
> *to equality of opportunity and status. From the obstruction*
> *of these ambitions there develops among some students a*
> *conviction that the universities are outdated embodiments*
> *of traditions which ignored these ambitions in the past, and*
> *that they are still too closely allied today with forms of*
> *government, or structures of society, that are violations of*
> *democracy in practice.*

In trying to make precise the nature of the university's
autonomy, the group divided initially along traditionalist and
contemporary lines. While everyone could agree that "to perform its teaching and research functions effectively the Catholic
university must have a true autonomy and academic freedom,"
and that autonomy and freedom cannot exist in absolute independence of the society which "created and sustains the university," each camp had its own interpretation of these words,
as the discussion brought out.

The classical point of view is that a Catholic university exercises its true autonomy and freedom within the perimeters of
the dogmatic and moral definitions laid down by the Church,
often in practice meaning the local bishop or the provincial
superior.

The other interpretation is that, like any other true university, the Catholic university can serve the total community only
if it is able "without restrictions to follow the imperatives which

flow from its very nature: pursuit of the truth without conditions." In other words, the university is limited by no other factor than the "truth it pursues." Moreover, every limitation imposed on the university which would clash with "this unconditioned attitude for pursuing truth would be intolerable and contrary to the very nature of the university."

Somewhat surprisingly the entire group went on record adopting these lines, some no doubt giving them a traditional meaning. What brought some of them around possibly was that the document tried earnestly to express in the paragraphs which immediately followed, the delicate balance between the right to self-government of the university and the right of *accountability* which belongs to the society from which the university takes its origin and in which it exists. It is simply a myth that any university anywhere is absolutely autonomous or that its professors enjoy complete academic freedom. No university anywhere operates in an influence-free vacuum or without accountability. Values, whether of Catholicism or secularism or Marxism very much qualify the exercise of true autonomy and academic freedom in any university because it is of and in a society with values.

Moreover, the presence of the Christian message makes for a special element in the domain of academic autonomy including freedom of teaching and research. To quote from the Roman document:

> *Though all natural truth is directly accessible to us through the exercise of our innate ability to grasp and to understand reality, the authentic Christian message is not available to us except with a guarantee of doctrinal authority, which is the magisterium of the Church. The datum from which theological reflection arises is not a datum of reality fully accessible to the human intelligence, but a revealed message entrusted to the Church. The freedom of the theological researcher, at the risk of basic self-destruction, rests on the foundation of revelation.*

Given the unique nature of the theological deposit with its protected-from-error-by-the-Giver status, at times when the truth

of the revealed message is clearly at stake, authoritative intervention may be called for. However, as the final document
phrased it: "In every case the intervention of the competent
ecclesiastical authority should respect the statutes of the institution as well as the academic procedures and customs of the
particular country."

Since the touchstone of academic freedom is that accorded
the theological scholar, the document attempted to illuminate
this highly nuanced point. All Catholics, as such, come under
the authority of the magisterium, whether lay or cleric, preacher
of theologian. However, the theological scholar, in taking his
place in the university must be able to pursue his discipline
in the same manner as other research scholars. "He must be
allowed," continues the Rome document, "to question, to develop new hypotheses, to work toward new understandings and
formulations to publish and defend his views, and to approach
the theological sources, including pronouncements of the teaching church, with the full play of modern scholarship. His work
should normally be reviewed and evaluated by his scholarly
peers as is the case in other disciplines."

With candor, the statement adopted in Rome mentioned how
history has taught us how much the influence of the Church has
been limited because of "certain ecclesiastical or religious
authorities who, overzealous to defend certain established positions, have precipitously and arbitrarily blocked the diffusion
of scholarly research." Yes, the reader's surmise that this wording
was much struggled over is correct. There were those delegates
who had to be reminded that the Church is a divine idea incar-
nated in time and space and, therefore, at times in its leaders
very much subject to the limitations of the human condition—
stupidity, ambition, greed, and pride—and that to admit this
fact is not attacking the Church. Several wanted to delete the
passage or to indicate that since Vatican II the bad old days
are gone forever. After much discussion a big majority agreed
that the phrasing should be adopted to help prevent the harass-
ment of future John Courtney Murrays and Henri de Lubacs.
In his teaching the theologian must of course present the authentic teaching of the Church, whether he is in perfect agreement

or not, but he should at the same time, continued the document, form his students to an intelligent and critical understanding of the faith, "prudent account being taken of the maturity and previous preparation of the students."

Another critical phase of the same basic question of autonomy was a large topic of discussion—the relation of the theologian, lay or clerical, to ecclesiastical and religious authorities. This is in essence the problem of the possibility of professionalism in a Catholic university. Does the fact that a scholar is a priest or that a lay scholar is in a Catholic university limit him as a professional person? As a scholar or professor how does he come under ecclesiastical discipline? Does the "priest" or "Catholic" factor create a new *direct* relationship? The congress finally agreed to the following understanding. The relationship, says the document, will vary in accordance with the type of Catholic institution. A seminary and a university are in different categories. A bishop obviously does have the right to oversee directly the orthodoxy of what is taught in the diocesan seminary because for clerics it is the professional and technical school.

There are institutions, in addition to seminaries, more closely linked to church authorities which come directly and immediately under episcopal jurisdiction. An example would be the Catholic Institute of Paris which has been established and is supported by the French bishops. Here the statutes themselves give the power of appointment and removal of faculty members to the committee of bishops. Even here, though, the document cautions that "any action taken by ecclesiastical or religious superiors should conform exactly to their authority as established in the statutes and recognized as general university common law in the geographical region of the particular university."

The heart of the issue, however, is not the seminary nor an institute but the university without statutory relationships with ecclesiastical or religious authorities, which is actually the case with many, if not most, U. S. Catholic colleges and universities because of their state-granted charters. The commission draft proposed to the whole group for voting that church authorities deal with the theologian in such institutions *as an individual member of the church*. If a bishop feels that certain theologizing activity on a given campus is harmful, then he has the right and the duty to advise the man, to inform the administration, and if called for, even to warn the faithful that, in his considered judgment, the institution itself has departed from orthodox teaching. However, this is the limit of his competence. According to the document, any *juridical* intervention in university affairs by ecclesiastical authority must be excluded. The delegates approved.

Remarkably enough, the final document was accepted without a voiced dissent. Though the document under discussion carried only the authority of the delegates, it was bound to have impact. In closing the congress, Cardinal Garrone warmly thanked the delegates and said that he "gratefully welcomed" the document as a basis for continued dialogue. He promised that it would be circulated to all the Catholic universities of the world.

There was a certain nervousness among congregation officials about the publicity the document might gain but objection disappeared after it was agreed that its nonofficial nature would be stressed.

There was a sense of achievement among the delegates as they prepared to return to their own countries, but any elation they might have had was tempered by the almost certain surmise that the sections of their work which treated of relationships to church authority would be unacceptable to most of the forty-three cardinals and eight bishops, who were to meet in October for the plenary session of the congregation. The important advance, however, was that Vatican officials had begun to listen. They may not have always heard; they may not have always understood. But they now were listening. Moreover, the new leadership of the Congregation for Catholic Education had demonstrated a genuine desire for dialogue. The North American group of delegates were satisfied that their colleagues from other parts of the world could be (and in fact now were) convinced that the Catholic university which had evolved in Canada and the States was both a legitimately different and equally valid realization of the idea of a Catholic university.

*   *   *   *   *   *

The plenary session met in October, just before the world synod of the bishops. The session limited itself to more general observations, as the letter of transmittal of the Results said, "with a view to further soliciting the collaboration of the various Catholic universities of the world before proceeding at some future date to lay down the principles and suitable norms which should regulate Catholic university structure and life today."

When the work of the plenary session was completed, Cardinal Garrone submitted the Results to the pope in an audience on November 13, who approved them and "ordered that they be sent to all the directors of Catholic universities throughout the world." The transmittal letter conveyed sincere gratitude to all the institutions and especially to the delegates who participated in the Rome congress. Finally, the congregation cordially invited the directors of all Catholic universities to send in their proposals, amendments, and suggestions within three months, so that "the work on the document on which the delegates labored so arduously might be completed with the collaboration and agreement of all."

The responses given in the Results of the plenary session are friendly and sincere, tactful and intelligent, pastoral and paternal. Happily gone is the old tone of condemnation, reproof, and threat. Unhappily, on the critical issues of autonomy and academic freedom the responses are in direct opposition to the position paper unanimously adopted by the delegates to the Rome Congress.

One need only read the next lines to see little chance for autonomy and rejection of any other kind of Catholic university than that in which ecclesiastical authority is central.

To fulfill [its] mission, a Catholic university must be seen as existing not only in the world, but also in the Catholic community and therefore it is related to those who preside over the Catholic community: the Catholic hierarchy. Obviously, the specific purpose of the Catholic university cannot be realized if those whose proper function it is to be the authentic guardians of the deposit of faith are relegated to a marginal place in its life and activity.

On the specific problem of the relationship between the magisterium and the university, "the fathers were favorably impressed by the new and useful points of view presented in the document." However, there followed an almost hurt reminder to those concerned of "the obvious presupposition fundamental to every Catholic university; namely,

> *that the exigencies of scientific freedom are not opposed to the mission of the Church's magisterium to announce and safeguard Catholic doctrine with appropriate means. The doctrinal and moral guidance which the Church gives in higher studies, both through the faith of the individuals involved and through the intervention of the magisterium, not only does not limit the horizon and activity of such studies, but, as a matter of fact, protects and assists them."*

Yes, that is the textbook theory but frequently it is not a matter of fact. The theory is put into practice by men, whether of the magisterium or of the university, who have to grope for truth and understanding in the shadows which only on the rarest occasions are perfectly illumined for us. That the Church's effort to furnish doctrinal and moral guidance in higher studies has not always achieved its lofty purpose of protecting and assisting is a matter of record, part of which is narrated in this volume.[11]

The fathers of the plenary session expressed several reservations about the way some of the assertions in the document were formulated, relative to the modes of harmonizing academic freedom and the function of the magisterium. Their doubts are:

(1) that research in the field of theology can be conducted with the same freedom as in any other field;

(2) that the judgment about the value of a doctrine in theology can be normally left to fellow theologians;

(3) that a critical attitude towards the truths of the faith can be assumed;

(4) that a diverse relationship with the magisterium can exist depending upon the various types of Catholic universities.

Moreover, they immediately add, in order that there be a

---

[11] See "A Tradition of Autonomy?" p. 206.

"correct harmonization of the laws of freedom in research and teaching with the duty of the magisterium," the prelates request that these two principles be adhered to:

(1) that the competence of the magisterium extends not only to the truths of faith, but also to those matters connected with the truths of faith;

(2) that freedom in doing research be distinguished from freedom to teach or diffuse the fruits of research, to avoid confusing and bewildering the minds of the faithful.

Finally, the full session of the congregation urge consultation as soon as possible with the International Theological Commission on the delicate problem of the "development of doctrine" and the practices of the magisterium in general. They emphasized that in order to safeguard the reciprocal rights and obligations of the university and the magisterium, their relationship should be marked "by the highest possible goodwill and the greatest mutual respect." The fathers close this section by saying that this amicable relationship "should be possible, provided that both sides do their part to create and maintain a climate of cordial trust, to better their continual contacts."

At the risk of appearing to patronize, it must be pointed out that the educational background and seminary experiences of the group of forty-three cardinals and eight bishops make the four-page Results predictable, relative to any proposal to lessen church authority over—what for centuries churchmen generally have been mistrustful, suspicious, and disturbed—the university. A seminary education completed before 1930 even with advanced work in theology or canon law in as eminent an institution as Rome's Gregorian University (which bears small resemblance to universities in America or anywhere else) is not the broadest possible university experience. More significant still, the staff of the Congregation for Catholic Education, as is hinted at in the name it bore until 1968, Sacred Congregation for *Seminaries* and Universities, has always been oriented toward the seminary.[12] Though efforts are being made to give greater breadth to the staff, with perhaps one or two exceptions they are seminary-trained and seminary-experienced. This situation

12 My emphasis.

creates some doubt as to the kind of collaboration the congregation might be able to offer in the attempt "to lay down the principles and suitable norms which should regulate Catholic university structure and life today."

What is basically in conflict here of course are widely different conceptions of the Catholic university. For many ecclesiastics, particularly in the Latin countries of Europe and South America, the Catholic university is simply an extension of the true Church into academe. It is founded by a bishop or a religious group and is granted a papal charter. The administration and faculty are predominantly clerical. The rector or head is a priest, appointed and accountable to ecclesiastical authorities. The environment is ecclesial. Supervision over the quality of life and the orthodoxy of teaching are, in descending degrees, the concern of the local bishop or religious superior (sometimes both), the provincial or regional superior, the general superior of the religious order in Rome, and eventually, through the Sacred Congregation for Catholic Education, the pope. Canon Law forbids the alienation of any university property without Rome's approval, for property rights are ultimately vested in the Holy See. Since priests are under obedience to their bishop and religious to their superior, it is normal that their work as professors and scholars and administrators be supervised by church authority.

And what of the layman, how does he fit into this clerical picture? If the responses to the questionnaire are to be believed, in a number of Catholic institutions, just barely. Repeatedly it was stated that only laymen whose orthodoxy was unimpeachable should be hired, and that non-Catholics could be tolerated only where there was an insufficient number of qualified clerics or Catholic laymen—and then only in less sensitive areas like mathematics or engineering.[13] Clerical presence and ecclesias-

---

[13] Indeed, some American ecclesiastics seem to share almost fully this same conception. One diocesan university official in a very large Southern State dismissed the whole discussion of these items in the questionnaire as part of the contemporary rebellion against law and order, and thought the current attempts by Catholic educators to clarify the concepts of academic freedom and autonomy reducible to what he styled "the theological category of pride."

tical control are assumed to guarantee the Catholic character of the institution.

Historically, the university and the university college were offspring of the Church. Even in Colonial America, without exception the earliest foundations were under church sponsorship and clerical control. The churches supported the institutions and used them to prepare their clergy. Generally speaking, only the clergy were prepared in fields like philosophy, theology, Latin and Greek—most of the traditional curriculum. Traditionally the early collegiate institutions felt seriously responsible for the moral and religious formation of their students. Yet there is still nothing in the nature of higher education which makes it clear that clerics or churchmen can do the job better or worse than nonclerics and nonchurchmen.

The era of the clerically-dominated Catholic university is over in more and more countries. Just as the fields of nursing and hospital care, organized charity and relief, mental care and geriatrics no longer remain the exclusive domain of churches and church people, so higher education.

In concluding this introduction, several observations remain to be made.

First of all, one might wonder if, because of the ideological distance separating the congregation and at least the representatives of the Catholic universities in attendance at the Rome congress, there is any useful purpose in continuing the dialogue. Most emphatically, there is.

The university of the twelfth and thirteenth centuries was a child of the Church and was nurtured within the sacral environment of Christendom. The Christian faith gave it vigor and vitality even as it, in turn, was ennobled and enriched. Rome must be helped to realize that the academic community is no longer the faith community. The Catholic university of today cannot be secular but it must operate in a secular society. To be Catholic the university must be inspired by Christ and His Word but to be a university it must be free and autonomous. It would be incomplete without its theological inspiration and to make this idea more precise it needs Rome. A deeper understanding of institutional commitment is needed in order to make theological inspiration operative while respecting the valid autonomy of the secular order. The formulations concerning theological scholarship and academic freedom can be profitably studied together.

The current impasse involving academic freedom and institutional autonomy might be settled within the framework of one of the great monuments to the Second Vatican Council. If freedom is one and indivisible, academic freedom is not so diverse from religious freedom. The Declaration on Religious Freedom says:

> *It is in accordance with their dignity as persons—that is, beings endowed with reason and free will and therefore privileged to bear personal responsibility—that all men should be at once impelled by nature and also bound by a moral obligation to seek the truth, especially religious truth. They are also bound to adhere to the truth, once it is known, and to order their whole lives in accord with the demands of truth.*
>
> *However, men cannot discharge these obligations in a manner in keeping with their own nature unless they enjoy immunity from external coercion as well as psychological freedom. Therefore, the right to religious freedom has its foundation, not in the subjective disposition of the person, but in his very nature. In consequence, the right to this immunity continues to exist even in those who do not live up to their obligation of seeking truth and adhering to it.*[14]

In the absence of dialogue, it took many years of strain before the issue of religious freedom was satisfactorily settled. With continued dialogue clearer understanding on these other points will arrive the sooner.

Let the dialogue continue.

[14] "Declaration on Religious Freedom," *The Documents of Vatican II,* ed. Walter M. Abbott (New York: The America Press, 1966), p. 679.

Why a Catholic University?

NORBERT A. LUYTEN, O.P.

Is not the mere fact of asking this question at the very beginning of our study an admission of the questionable nature of the Catholic university? Does it not betray a certain lack of conviction? One does not call in question an institution whose merits are obvious. Does not the fact that it seems necessary to justify the existence of Catholic universities amount to admitting that they do not really succeed in convincing us of their right to exist?

Some may think so. They will see in this work merely a new proof of the highly problematic nature of the Catholic university. Without the slightest intention of ignoring or minimizing the problems arising from such a university, we wish to take issue from the very beginning with the somewhat shortsighted "wisdom" which equates the mere fact of setting a problem with lack of conviction. Man is by nature a being who questions both himself and the reality around him. The man who never asks questions is a man who has lost interest in everything. If a man believes that everything is clear and simple, then everything is all wrong on the truly human level, for it is in the very nature of man to think and thus to ask questions. It is only when he allows himself to drift along with life that all questions vanish out of sight—not because they no longer exist but because he has neither the inclination nor the courage to see them.

In this perspective, an institution which no longer gives rise to problems is very often an institution which is no longer of interest. Needless to say, this situation can be more harmful than all the questions that might be asked.

We are therefore not afraid to ask the question stated in the title of our contribution: Why a Catholic university? There is no need to be embarrassed just because we are asked to justify our existence. On the contrary, we should rejoice that the questions we are asked give us a better understanding of our role.

But let there be no mistake. The optimism in this position is in no way due to illusions. We are well aware that if the Catholic university is called into question by many people—including Catholics—it is by no means to allow us to better understand its purpose. Our "opponents" are convinced of the righteousness of their claims, and it would be unfair to minimize their objections. Besides, we would only be doing ourselves a bad turn; it never pays to act the ostrich! It is only by looking these objections straight in the face that we can prove to ourselves—and to others—the value of our convictions. And this test will be of value only if we begin by granting to others what we claim for ourselves: a sincere thirst for truth.

We will of course be led to challenge the convictions of our contradictors. Let it be clear, however, that this will never be merely for the sake of fruitless polemics, nor will we ever want to make our views triumph at all cost. Truth is seldom rigid in human matters, since human realities are far too complex to be cast into simple formulas. A discussion such as we will be led to wage here bears within itself the danger of hardening the conflicting positions. All the more reason for avoiding harsh opinions and rash pronouncements. To be more specific, we will not relax our position in any way or abandon strong convictions in order to take refuge in compromises that would be as vague as they are ineffective. But one can be faithful to one's principles and firm in one's positions and still take the nuances and the contingencies of human realities into account.

This means—in our case—that defending the Catholic university is not equivalent to condemning all non-Catholic universities. To say that the Catholic university is a valid institution is not to say that it is the only one. It is not enough that an institution be justified in its idea and in its realization; it must satisfy concrete needs and take root in a favorable environment. Historical, political, administrative, or other reasons may make it impossible to realize an idea, however great it may be. So let there be no misunderstanding on this point. Though we will be defending the idea of a Catholic university, this does not mean we believe it is the type of university that should prevail everywhere and under all circumstances. Not merely because Catholic universities form but a tiny minority in the modern academic world, but because we are thoroughly convinced of the merits of other types of universities which are better suited to existing concrete situations.

Before dealing with the objections raised against the idea of a Catholic university, we hasten to clear up a possible misunderstanding. In our view, "Catholic university" is in no way synonymous with "ecclesiastical university." These two characters coincide in most existing cases, but this is merely due to the way things happened; it is not an intrinsic requirement. For instance, the University of Fribourg (to which I belong), is both a Catholic and a state university. This may be exceptional nowadays, but it was the normal situation in those times when nationalism and Catholicism went hand in hand in many countries. The Catholic nature of a university is not mainly determined by an institutional tie with the ecclesiastical hierarchy. What matters is that a vision of the world inspired by the Catholic faith be the basic concept founding and supporting the whole university structure. Whether the institution opting for this Catholic inspiration and aiming at ensuring its concrete realization is an ecclesiastical institution, a state, or even a private organization, is only of secondary importance in the perspective we adopt in this study.

After clarifying these points, we now turn to the arguments which are most commonly used against the idea of a Catholic university.

IT IS OUT-OF-DATE

The first objection does not deal directly with the idea of a Catholic university as such, but with the anachronic nature of this idea in modern society. A Catholic university makes sense in a world that is uniformly Catholic, as during the Middle Ages for instance. The university was Catholic then, because everything was Catholic—the army, the law, even the taxes.

But this situation has been replaced by a fundamentally lay society which refuses to endorse any one religious view and opts for a pluralism that is determined to respect everyone's freedom of opinion. A Catholic university is out of place in this modern world. It is definitely an anachronism since it is contrary to the very principles governing our modern societies.

This opposition to the very idea of a Catholic university becomes even more obvious as the objections become more concrete. Thus, according to J. Leclercq, the Catholic university is a phenomenon which is typical of the nineteenth century and which he defines by means of the concept of the *ghetto*.[1]

The idea that led to the foundation of these Catholic universities is no other than to isolate the Catholic students in a closed environment, to better protect them from the injurious influence of "the world." One locks oneself up in a ghetto in order to manufacture Catholic "intellectuals" in a carefully sterilized and immunized environment.

These institutions, which owe their origins to apologetics rather than to a genuine desire for a university, never succeeded in becoming anything more than "higher technical schools" which were scarcely adequate for the formation of Catholic lawyers, doctors, and engineers. But they played an almost negligible role in the realm of science. If we add, following J. Leclercq, that the influence of these universities on Catholicism has been insignificant—if not paralyzing—it becomes obvious why the author sees how incongruous is even the *idea* of the Catholic university.

We also note that in his view, isolation in the ghetto is not only the expression of a purely defensive attitude, but also the eloquent index of a feeling of self-sufficiency contrary to the spirit of research so essential to a university worthy of the name. The author freely levels his sarcasm at these universities which

[1] Cf. J. Leclercq, "De katholieke Universiteit," *De Maand* VII, 5 (1964), 176–288. Our exposition of the objections raised against the Catholic university relies heavily on this article.

see no need to promote research since they already possess eternal truth. We can see, then, to what extent the very essence of the Catholic university is being called in question.

IT DOES NOT FIT INTO THE MODERN WORLD

A rather similar objection is often heard concerning the opportuneness of Catholic universities in the present spiritual climate.

The argument goes as follows: First of all, we are living in a definitely pluralistic world, in which the confrontation and mutual fertilization of the most varied convictions plays an essential part. Why then, in such an environment, refuse to play the game and stick to one's own clique by keeping the Catholic university away from this mingling of ideas? Is this not a great disservice to both young Catholic intellectuals and to the entire Church? By shielding them from all contact with other ideas during their period of formation, one makes them unable to hold their ground when the unavoidable confrontation in real life occurs. Raising plants in a green house never was the best way of increasing their resistance to bad weather! To form a carefully shielded elite which has never faced the problems of real life, is to form a generation of misfits who will be unable to affirm their authority in the struggle for life. Coming from a religion that claims to be apostolic, this is more than just peculiar: it is desertion. In fact, it is an absurdity and a scandal.

The argument becomes even stronger in these times that are marked by the *aggiornamento* of the Council. Is not the Church, through its most eminent representatives, promoting the spirit of ecumenism? We should be more concerned with meeting people than in relishing our sense of security. Is not the Catholic university a blatant contradiction to the most authentic spirit of ecumenism? Instead of meeting others, one cuts oneself off; instead of seeking dialog, one folds back upon oneself, obstinately preferring security (a rather dubious security indeed!), to the openness to others we are so sadly lacking. We see now that it is not so much the opportuneness of a Catholic university at this time of history that is in question, but the very concept which is said to be contrary to what it claims to be. For the more the university wants to be Catholic by closing in upon itself, the less it will be Catholic in the true sense of the word.

These objections, though already quite formidable, do not form the complete arsenal of arguments raised against us. In fact, the preceding considerations scarcely broach the problem. We therefore now try to go to the root of the matter.

A first complaint which attacks the Catholic universiy in its very essence, reproaches it with committing a crime against the true scientific spirit in its claim to denominationalize science. This is, critics tell us, absurd; there is no such thing as Protestant or Catholic chemistry or physics. Science is above the religious quarrels dividing mankind. It is objective, the same for all, and thus a uniting factor among men. Separating scientists according to their religious beliefs is therefore not only a sin against scientific spirit—which should be sheltered from these religious divisions—it is also a sin against mankind, which is thus maintained in a state of dissension instead of unity. If there are no Catholic sciences, but simply sciences, is it not logical to conclude that a Catholic university is as absurd as a Catholic chemistry or a Catholic physics?

It is even more so, not only because it embraces a large number of sciences and thus, in its desire to be Catholic in all these fields, accumulates absurdities. But more importantly, because precisely in its claim to be Catholic it rejects the universality to which—as a university—it should aspire. By virtue of its deepest aspirations, the university strives toward universality. It is not only the *universitas magistrorum et scholarium* but also the *universitas scientiarum*. It has always been characterized by its spirit of universality, the condition as well as the result of the universal openness of the human mind in its quest for truth. Does all denominationalism not appear in this perspective as an infringement upon this will to universality? Is not the very essence of the university threatened by this "compartmentation"? This thought leads to another, putting the Catholic university even more radically in question, and coming ever closer to the core of the problem.

Faith, and more especially the Catholic faith, imposes a certain number of truths upon the mind. These dogmas are by their very nature beyond all scientific verification, and claim to subjugate the mind with an absolute, unalterable truth which is fixed once for all by the authority of the Church. Is this not an intolerable claim which undermines what a university should hold most essential and most sacred?

To begin with the most serious, the human mind (which cannot unfold freely unless it can assert its absolute autonomy in its quest for truth), is being controlled by an institution which imposes norms and restrictions upon it. This amounts to subjecting the university, which has always—and with good reason—defended its autonomy, to a relentless heteronomy, which makes no secret of its unbounded claims.

Moreover, even if the absolute freedom of research—the deliberate will to always remain open to new discoveries—were to question what had hitherto appeared most definitively certain, will not the acceptance of dogmas endanger this ever total availability which is so characteristic of science and lies at the root of all its progress? Will not dogmas, in their claim to definitive truth, bar all further research, and hence all progress? Once more, we seem to be faced with an intolerable pretention—one that is thoroughly incompatible with true scientific spirit.

But there is more. Precisely because of this claim to "definitiveness," will the dogma not destroy the very stimulus of all scientific research and paralyze this noble striving of the human mind toward ever greater knowledge and truth? Why search for the truth if we already possess it? Besides, the danger is even greater. The scientist cannot help seeing this claim to definitive truth as an outrageous injustice and almost as a personal insult. He who knows by experience the cost of arduously searching for truth, finds himself faced with people who, without the slightest bit of research to their credit, without the slightest effort, claim to be in possession of a truth that is literally a godsend. Is it not an insult, this easy victory of easily satisfied minds over men who devote their entire life to the service of knowledge? Is it surprising that the true scientist rebels against the mere idea of this "unfair competition"?

This brings us to the last aspect of this "conflict" between science and dogma. Can the true scientist admit that there are truths he cannot verify, which he cannot hope to recover by scientific investigation? Is this not to surrender on a matter of principle which would immediately call the universal value of science in question? The ancients already used to say that all truth is intelligible. Since science is the search for the intelligible, does it not have the sacred duty of letting no realm of reality escape beyond its reach? Must it not therefore stand up against the pretention of dogma, which loudly proclaims its sovereignty in important areas of the truth?

However we look at it, the opposition between dogma and science appears to be as total as it is unyielding. How then can we not see the futility of the role of the Catholic university which rests precisely on the idea of making dogma and science cohabitate? Oil and water have never mixed. Would it not be better therefore to abandon once for all the idea of a Catholic university which—as we have seen—appears to be in the grip of internal contradictions? If we add that it goes against the stream of the most justified trends in our modern world (as was shown by the first objections), should we not conclude that, if the idea of a Catholic university was ever a valid one, this is certainly no longer the case today?

After listening at length to those who do not believe in the idea of a Catholic university in the middle of this twentieth century, we now sit down to a more positive task. This does not mean, of course, that our work so far has been useless. By carefully listening to the arguments of our opponents, we have better understood to what extent the Catholic university might seem a questionable institution to minds which are undeniably in good faith. It is therefore no luxury to begin a study of the problems of the Catholic university by asking the fundamental question: Why? In a sense we have made our work easier by first exposing—without coaxing them but also without hardening them—the views of the opponents of the Catholic university, even if this exposition almost seemed to be an indictment. By answering the various objections, we will at the same time bring to light the purpose of a Catholic university. We repeat that we are striving to be unprejudiced when dealing with these arguments. We do not wish to strike down our opponents, to ridicule their views or denounce ineptitudes. But we sincerely believe that, while containing a share of truth, their objections miss their mark and do not succeed in seriously upsetting the idea of a Catholic university. They will rather help us to clarify and purify this idea. It will not be the least merit of our opponents that they compel us to better understand ourselves. We should be grateful to them.

THE CATHOLIC UNIVERSITY IS NOT OUT-OF-DATE

A first series of objections tried to show that the Catholic university is a thing of the past. Without spending too much time on this aspect of the question—their very exaggeration already partially refutes them—we will try to clarify the situation.

Father Leclercq is probably not wrong in viewing a certain form of Catholic university as a typical product of a mentality that is now obsolete. But I believe he is somewhat too hasty in condemning this poor nineteenth century which he makes the scapegoat on whose back all faults and mistakes are wantonly heaped. It is true that we must learn from the mistakes as well as from the achievements of our forefathers. But we must not try to judge them, especially in their intentions. It is hard enough to make a somewhat accurate diagnosis! Leclercq's judgment of the nineteenth century, the cause of all our troubles, strikes me as not exactly impartial. There is, of course, some truth in the accusations he levels at the concepts which inspired the foundation of some Catholic universities in the nineteenth century. But let us be a little magnanimous, allowing some errors to each period; we will find it hard enough to bear our own! Above all, we must not only look at the mistakes of our predecessors; if they formed groups to better defend themselves, is it not also and mostly because powerful opponents had leagued against them? If there was a ghetto, the Catholics certainly did not build it entirely with their own hands! To a large extent they had been driven to it. And if we can now—with calm self-assurance—leave these spiritual ghettos in which we undeniably sought shelter for too long, is it not mostly thanks to these forefathers who, by withdrawing to their entrenched positions, preserved the values of the past and thus succeeded in preparing the future? Let there be no mistake. We have no intention of exaggerating in the opposite direction, and of seeing only the positive aspects in this attitude of our ancestors. As for all human matters, they had their merits and their faults. And if we want to judge them, the most elementary sense of justice demands that we consider both good and bad points.

But we are not concerned here with a spiritual bookkeeping of the nineteenth century; we are only interested in the Catholic university. One need not be a great scholar to see that the idea of a Catholic university is not necessarily called in question by some less laudable motives which may have played a role in their foundation during the nineteenth century. Earlier centuries, to which the ghetto idea was absolutely foreign, witnessed a fantastic bloom of the Catholic universities. Is this not sufficient to show the fallacy in considering the Catholic university as the typical result of a reflex of self-defense through isolation? To discredit the Catholic university by presenting it as an intellectual ghetto is as untrue as it is unfair, not to say outrageous. Who would not agree the ghetto mentality should be opposed and destroyed in our universities? But for God's sake, let us not be so naïve as to eagerly sacrifice an institution with a long and glorious tradition just because some errors of judgement were committed during a certain period! One might as well abolish the Catholic Church itself, because the ghetto mentality prevailed for some time among quite a few of its foremost spokesmen.

What we are after saying about the ghetto mentality can be applied, *servatis servandis,* to the accusation of self-sufficiency which is leveled somewhat offhandedly at Catholic universities. It is always despicable strategy to caricature what one is fighting. No one will deny that in some Catholic university environments there has been some degree of smugness, or perhaps a sense of superiority. Even then, one should emphasize that this is mostly in philosophical and theological milieu where, in spite of an undeniable stagnation and sclerosis, one was not

altogether wrong in believing oneself the depositary of ideas
and concepts that were sounder than those that prevailed in
other universities. But unfortunately, one visualized oneself
more as the depositary of a perfected system than as the heir to
a living thought. This is where the mistake lies in the interpretation of the meaning of teaching and research in the field of
philosophy and of theology. We must not think, however, that
this mentality was the general rule in all faculties of philosophy
and theology. Remember, for instance, the obstinate efforts of
Cardinal Mercier and his team to confront philosophy with the
data of modern science.[2] It is not unlikely that a more thorough
psychoanalysis of the Catholic university during the nineteenth
century would reveal more inferiority complexes than feelings
of self-sufficiency and the corresponding superiority complexes.
But once more, let us not judge the past. Let us rather turn to
the objections raised against the present situation of Catholic
universities.

THE CATHOLIC UNIVERSITY AND
OUR MODERN MENTALITY

We now recall those arguments which aim at showing to
what extent a Catholic university is in conflict with the deepest
aspirations of our times. We first note that these deep aspirations, while implying objective elements which it is relatively
easy to see, also call upon emotions which it is much more
difficult to evaluate. Expressions such as "pluralistic society,"
and "ecumenism" are often so loaded with affectivity that it is
difficult to discuss them objectively. No sooner do these expressions crop up in a discussion than one spontaneously takes sides
for or against anything that appears to be in any way related to
them. And indeed this is a bit what the objections quoted above
are doing. All the more reason for examining them closely.

The Catholic university, because of its denominationalism,
would be contrary to the spirit of our pluralistic society. If one
only stops to think about it, this objection is self-refuting. For

[2] See the special issue of the *R P L* 49 (November 1952), on the occasion of the
centenary of Cardinal Mercier's birth.

anyone who understands the word, a pluralistic society is one in which various visions of the world, various religious or philosophical beliefs, can coexist in peace without hindering one another, without any one of them wishing to eliminate or destroy another. Since this pluralism proclaims the right of all different institutions to exist—no matter their inspiration—should the Catholic university be denied the right to exist? A strange pluralism indeed, which strives to reduce everything to a single form! The contradiction is too blatant to be dwelt upon any longer.

The claim that the Catholic university is incompatible with the current climate of ecumenism is hardly better founded than that of its being contrary to pluralism. For "meeting" is the key word of ecumenism. Now is it not clear that in order to meet others in the full sense of the word, one must first be one-self? A meeting involving the self-effacement of one of the interlocutors is no real meeting. To ask Catholics to renounce their characteristic physiognomy, to efface the dominant features of their personality, is to rate them as rather stupid and to have a strange idea of what a meeting really is.

This would be an ecumenism of fools. To swallow it (or rather to be swallowed up by it), would call for an uncommonly large dose of thoughtlessness or blindness. True ecumenic dialog presupposes sound interlocutors, with a sufficiently extensive culture and a sufficiently strong personality to engage in a meaningful discussion. The more the Catholic universities will leave their mark on their students—and their teachers—the more such acceptable interlocutors there will be, capable of engaging in dialog in the name of true Catholicism. It would be paradoxical, almost to the point of bad faith, to claim that the ecumenical dialog would be better handled by intellectuals who received their formation in an environment that claims to be neutral (and most of all to ignore the problem of religion), than by students who have been made aware—throughout their whole formation—of the religious dimensions of human problems.

The old story of the narrow-mindedness which, according to our opponents, is bound to prevail in Catholic universities, will naturally have to be dragged up again. And what, may I ask, are the grounds for such a monstrous calumny? It is of course quite true that there are among us some narrow-minded people with limited horizons, but Catholic universities have no monopoly on such people. The ailment spreads pretty evenly over the whole of mankind. And indeed, narrow-mindedness and intolerance are often not found where they are said to be. How often do we not see non-Catholic students at the University of Fribourg expressing their amazement at the openness, the broad-mindedness, the amount of information which they find there and to which they had not been accustomed in their earlier studies!

I do not wish to be chauvinistic, but allow me at least to set what I know from experience against these monstrous and gratuitous accusations by people who do not know what we really are—if they are not allowing themselves to be guided by prejudice. We shall say no more on this subject or we might drift into controversy, which we had firmly decided to avoid.

We now tackle the much more essential problems covered by the objections against the very idea of a Catholic university. Since all these objections question even the concept of a Catholic university, it seems a good idea to begin our discussion with as clear and as convincing as possible a presentation of what we mean by the term "Catholic university."

Indeed, if all these objections led to the rejection of the Catholic university, it is because they claimed to be able to denounce internal contradictions in the very concept, catholicity being incompatible with the immanent requirements of a university. In our view, here is a misunderstanding which we are anxious to clear up. Oddly enough, the misunderstanding does not bear primarily on what is meant by *Catholic,* but rather on what is meant and implied by a *university.*

Owing to a faulty interpretation of the notion of science—due mostly to the prestige of physics—we have reached the rather paradoxical concept of a science that is completely independent of its human context.[3] From the postulate (which is

[3] For a more detailed study of this point, cf. N. Luyten, "Das Verhältnis zwischen Wissenschaftskritik und Naturphilosophie," *Naturwissenschaft und Theologie* 5, pp. 130–135.

once more misunderstood) that science must be objective, the conclusion has been drawn that all human implications must be eliminated from science, since man always carries within himself a dimension of subjectivity. It is not too difficult to see how such an ideal of "disanthropomorphization"[4]—which is in fact dehumanization—would lead straight to depriving science and scientific research of its true meaning. Science is born from man; it is meaningful only through him. To try to immunize it against all human "contamination" is to cut off its roots and thus condemn it to die. We stress this point since it is of the utmost importance for the question under examination.

That science—and more especially positive science—should make use of the objective data provided by verifiable instruments without intermingling them with the subjective impressions of any one scientist, is only natural; but this inherently sound idea somehow got misled along the way. This rule of "objectivity" which originates in the human yearning for truth pre-existent to all science (and thus presupposed to it), has been set up as an absolute principle. No one noticed that this was literally cutting the branch on which one was sitting. For this principle derives its validity exclusively from man's aspiration to truth. By setting up method as an absolute principle, and declaring that all that cannot be justified within the frame of science should be excluded from its preoccupations, one has implicitly banished from science the very foundation that gave it its substance. Man is a being yearning for truth; he knows he is compelled to recognize truth wherever he sees it, and he is faced with a reality he cannot shun and whose laws he must respect. These are so many presuppositions to science, and thus literally prescientific data—which the scientist cannot overlook, under pain of drying up the source from which his science flows. A science that is not integrated within a human context, a science that develops independently of all concepts of man

---

[4] F. Renoirte uses this term in *Eléments de critique des sciences et de cosmologie*, p. 116. The text reads as follows: "Physics then consists of 'depersonalizing' the information we have on the material world, of trying to 'disanthropomorphize' our statements and make them more objective."

and of the world, is basically an absurdity.[5] And if modern science sometimes gives the opposite impression, this is because it unwittingly lives on the human values which it mistakenly believes to have banished from its realm.

What we have just said about science is true a fortiori of the university. And again not only because a multitude of sciences cohabit inside the walls of a university and multiply, through their diversity, their ties with their common human source, but also because the university is the human environment in which science is elaborated and scientific research developed.

We can see that if the human climate must be propitious there to the practice and the development of science, this cannot possibly be ensured by the laws of scientific method alone. A thorough prescientific human conditioning is necessary and even determinant for the good working and the effectiveness of scientific activity. The scientist must take seriously his dignity and responsibility as a man, submitting to the laws of reality which his mind perceives. The whole human context is of importance in a university. Now, is it not clear that the climate created by the Catholic faith (which combines a high vision of man promised to an eternal destiny, with a deep respect for reality created by a good and all-powerful God), is such as to promote scientific research to the highest degree? It is probably not a mere coincidence that the concept of a university, as we know it, first appeared in an environment saturated with Catholicism. It is not this same Catholicism that is now going to destroy the idea of a university.

We are therefore not dealing with a denominalization of science, as some superficial minds would have it. Each science must enjoy its own autonomy, dictated by the laws inherent to its nature, without which it would no longer be a science. But as we have shown, science by its very nature has its roots in man and in the human world. No autonomy could overlook this fact. It is this human frame that the Catholic climate strives to ensure in the Catholic university.[6] Let there be no mistake:

[5] Cf. N. Luyten, *Universität und Weltanschauung* (Freiburg, 1958).
[6] E. Schillebeeckx' contribution will stress this point even more.

this necessity of human roots is not the exclusive property of Catholic universities. Each scientist practices his science in terms of human presuppositions which are more fundamental than the laws of scientific method. In a "neutral" university, each one contributes his own vision of the world—often without being explicitly aware of it. In this respect, the Catholic university with its explicitly stated common vision of the world will score higher rather than lower.

We also see how wrong it is to think of catholicity as a violation of universality. We will not dwell on the close relationship between the two words, which actually mean the same thing. The spirit of universality does not in any way mean that one gives up all opinions and beliefs. This would be a very nebulous universality indeed, one which it would be quite impossible to realize. To try to envisage the world and our human existence without forming any convictions or opinions would be absurd. Each scientist is bound to have his own vision of the world—and of himself. Complete abstention from taking a stand would automatically imply instantaneous cessation of all thought, and thus of all science. Why reproach only the Catholic scientist with having a vision of the world? Because they are the only ones to proclaim it?[7] What a strange reward for sincerity!

SUPERNATURE IMPERVIOUS TO SCIENCE

One might say that what is a scandal in a Catholic university is that the basic conviction on which it rests and which claims to be supernatural, sets it immediately on a level that is not accessible to science. Here lies the basic incompatibility between the university and Catholic faith.

Once more we cannot accept the objection. We have spoken about the human "substructure" prerequisite to all science. One of the most fundamental and characteristic features of our human nature is what we could call its transcendental dimension. Whether man likes it or not, his mind opens up onto the

---

[7] We are, of course, not saying that *only* Catholic universities can claim a well-determined vision of the world.

transcendent. Supernatural truth does not enter into the human mind as a foreign body that does not belong there. However supernatural it may be, Catholic faith claims to meet the deepest aspirations to the knowledge of truth and the acquisition of happiness which dwell in the heart of man. Though they operate at different levels, science and faith meet in the human mind. Mankind, as it actually exists, is a mankind to which God has entrusted a message, unveiling the ultimate answers to the most fundamental and most existential questions man asks himself. Do not these ultimate truths belong in the university, whose most authentic vocation is the search for all truth? Will it be said that they should not be allowed in the university because—as a human institution—it has no need for a truth that was revealed by God? One would then be forgetting that revelation consists precisely in that the truth of God is entrusted to man. It therefore becomes human in the true sense of the word and should not be excluded from the university in which man is questioning both himself and reality.

And this is how the university saw it from the very beginning. The faculty of theology, especially dedicated to the study of this divine message entrusted to man, traditionally ranks first in the university structure. This is more than mere politeness toward the sacred. It is an acknowledgment of the fact that wherever human knowledge is organized, the study and the thorough analysis of the knowledge entrusted to us by God himself are the most urgent and the most important duties.

It is only natural that those who do not share our belief in a divine revelation should feel otherwise. No one will force a faculty of theology upon them. But it should not be difficult for them to understand how it would be unnatural for those who do admit this revelation—and this is the case for Catholics —not to give it suitable emphasis there where human knowledge is elaborated and taught to the highest degree, namely in the universities. And indeed, it is not merely a question of setting aside a small compartment in the university—even if it is the first one—for the study of the revealed message; that is, for theology. The university is not a mere juxtaposition of various disciplines. Its universality is not above all extensive but intensive. The various branches which are taught there must come together and enrich one another in a permanent dialog if the university really wishes to fulfill the vocation indicated by its very name.

It is obvious to the believer that theology, as the science of the knowledge that is most fundamental and most important to man, should partake in this concert of all disciplines. We see, thus, how the Catholic university combines, in this respect, the ideal conditions for the interpenetration of all branches of knowledge based on a vision of the world which is vouched for by God himself, is shared by all scholars in the university, and systematically studied by those who are more especially devoted to the study of theology.

But our opponents are waiting for us here. Is scientific research not warped, if not paralyzed, by these revealed preliminary data which are established as absolute truths, independently of all scientific research? And are we not faced once more with all the objections pertaining to the incompatibility of dogma and scientific research?[8] After all we have said, it should not be too difficult to show once more that these objections rest on a misunderstanding and do not affect the true concept of a Catholic university.[9]

To speak of *heteronomy* in connection with revelation, dogma, or theology, is to set the problem very badly indeed. Physics, for example, can profit from the knowledge acquired by mathematics and there will be no mention of humiliating enslavement or intolerable heteronomy! All knowledge is inter-dependent with all other knowledge. The more we know, the more we realize this. Why should this rule not be valid for revealed knowledge, which deals precisely with the most fundamental and most vital questions that arise in the human mind?

One might say that it is then the authority of God and not the ingenuity of man that guarantees truth. And naturally, the guarantee of a God in which he does not believe by definition

---

[8] I see an almost funny paradox here, which I will mention in passing. On the one hand one claims that dogma has nothing to do with science; while on the other, one resents the unfair competition!

[9] See N. Luyten, *Wetenschap en Geloof* (Tielt, 1965).

tional arm of the Church is to engage in similar futility. At the present time (and under the present laws) the Catholic university often does not even belong to the Catholic Church. It is an academic community chartered as a civil corporation directed by the board of trustees, whose religious affiliation does not matter.

If the trustees and the higher echelons of the administration are members of religious congregations, the institutional Church may be able to exert some control through their vows and according to canon law, but even this is very doubtful. Though this may seem comforting to some, the fact is that there is a quickening trend toward putting laymen and non-Catholics on the board of trustees and into top administrative posts. Even the Catholics and many religious among the trustees feel that by now they have attained their intellectual majority and have outgrown the maternal solicitude of the Church. Like grown sons and daughters they respect their mother deeply but feel no obligation to comply with her academic demands. Their affection and respect bring sadness when they feel they must resist a mother who cannot understand her children's independence.

One may reject the part of the analogy that presupposes that such independence results from growing up. Still, the point remains that the Church will maintain its influence in the Catholic university not through constraint, but through commitment; not through laws and edicts, but through the convictions and professional dedication of her members and her friends. Whether one applauds this or is appalled by it, the fact remains that this appears to be the inexorable trend. It exists and it is forming the nature of the Catholic university of tomorrow. One can only realistically recognize it and then act accordingly.

There have been several recent cases in the United States where both members of the hierarchy and of the academic community have attempted to resist this trend, with results hardly complimentary to the Church. In such a period of transition there will continue to be such pain as long as bishops, religious superiors and laity will not acknowledge the reality. Eventually all may see that the Catholic university is not merely the exten-

sion of the teaching function of the episcopacy. Possibly a case
could be made that a seminary or at least a theologate is precisely such an extension. But the Catholic university has now
evolved far beyond that ideal. Its role is not merely to present
safe doctrine as propounded by accepted commentators, within
an environment designed to protect young people from dangers.
This observation leads now to some reflections on the second
major trend affecting the nature of the contemporary Catholic
university.

RESPONSIBILITY TO THE COMMON GOOD OF SOCIETY

The very fact that all Catholic universities must obtain a
charter from the state indicates that the good of society as a
whole is involved. At the founding of any Catholic university
a group of persons made a contract with the state to set up a
kind of public trust for the betterment of the commonweal.
Trustees were appointed with the serious civil and moral obligation of seeing that that trust was carried out. What goes on
in the Catholic university, then, is not an exclusively intramural affair. The state has understood that the institution is to
be a real university, and the bishop or religious congregation
has publicly agreed to this. Undoubtedly much leeway has
been given here, and restrictions for purely religious purposes
have been accepted before the law. Yet in the minds of the
public, the term "university" means at the least that the institution be academically respectable and that it strive to some
degree toward academic excellence. Today's Catholic universities have not been content with that minimum. If one can
believe publicity releases, each one is straining to be among the
best universities in the country. Each one says that it is in every
way a true university. Insofar as it can be done, the adminis-
trations are deliberately heading toward that goal. Here the
process of evolution appears to be in hand; consequently, well-
defined changes are being initiated. This one aspect of the
nature of the Catholic university cannot be denied.

In setting its academic goal as identical with that of the best
institutions in the country, the Catholic university is becoming

more and more reluctant to deny itself the means to reach that goal. The great universities of America claim that their attainments are due to the free spirit of inquiry, the ability to challenge every settled opinion, the possibility of creative dialogue, the atmosphere of unthreatened academic freedom. Such a rationale of their claim to be excellent has left many Catholic educators embarrassed, for they have accepted the goal but feel guilty about accepting the means to attain it. Elaborate and agonized attempts have been made to reconcile academic freedom and institutional commitment. The fact that they have not wholly succeeded leads one to suspect that the concept of institutional commitment may have been taken in too narrow a sense.

Perhaps for too long the Catholic university has considered her proper public to be the members of the Catholic faith; she has not considered sufficiently her nature as an institution set up by contract to serve society as a whole. Perhaps for too long the Catholic university has justified her service primarily in terms of directly improving the faith and morals of Catholics, and for such improvement a good education was seen as extremely helpful. *Fides quaerens intellectum* expresses a mighty impulse for learning, and certainly may be one reason for pursuing theology and philosophy. It seems inadequate, however, to explain the present existence of the gigantic apparatus of the Catholic university. No matter what the motives of the founding fathers were, this complex institution exists today for other reasons as well. They may be related only indirectly to the teaching of theology or to the elevation of moral life, but they are good reasons. It is a good thing to educate members of society. It is a good thing to encourage research and publication. It is a good thing to promote understanding through dialogue. It is a good thing to seek a better and more relevant formulation of old truths.

There has been a radical shift in priorities and it embarrasses the spokesmen of the Catholic university to admit it. The founding fathers sought primarily and directly the growth in faith and morals, and only secondarily did they aim at growth in learning. The Catholic university today seeks growth in learning as its immediate goal, and while maintaining a con-

cern for faith and morals, it is clearly a less direct though ultimate concern. Perhaps it is too early to admit this publicly,
but academic men should be the first to evaluate the evidence
calmly. Furthermore, there is no need for qualms of conscience
about changing the priorities set by the founding fathers. The
Catholic university can be justly proud of the good that it is
doing. Other Catholic institutions do not feel called upon to
apologize because their aim is to aid the poor, train the blind,
help faltering marriages, or send food and clothing to underdeveloped countries. People have easily accepted the fact that
they are fulfilling a responsibility and are serving society and
its needs. For though their concern for faith and morals is
mediate it is still the ultimate concern, and the same acceptance should be granted to the Catholic university.

Once this is accepted, and once it is admitted that it is of
the nature of the Catholic university to be as totally academic
and professional as possible, then it would seem that the problem of academic freedom does not pose istelf any differently
here than at a non-Catholic university. As mentioned in the
discussion of the trend away from ecclesiastical control, the
Catholic university is not merely an extension of the teaching
function of the Church. Without any criticism of the hierarchy intended, it may be said that historically speaking the
first trend is the reciprocal of the second: as ecclesiastical control wanes, the Catholic university more fully becomes a true
university serving society as a whole.

A brief word might be added concerning this broader concept of service. First of all, the student body and the faculty no
longer need to be largely Catholic, because the public at large
is more involved now. Secondly, the Catholic university is becoming more aware of its possible impact on the surrounding
community. Service to the community was formerly a work
distinctive of state universities, while Catholic higher education concentrated almost exclusively on its own students. For-
tunately that day is passing and the Catholic university is more
committed to directly sharing its insights, its knowledge, and
its values with the community beyond the campus.

At this point one may justifiably wonder what exactly *is*

distinctive of the Catholic university. This brings up the consideration of the third major trend affecting the nature and role of the Catholic university.

MAKING CATHOLICISM RELEVANT TODAY

If it is by now a truism to say that a Catholic university should be a real university, it ought also to be a truism to say a Catholic university should be really Catholic. Though the structural bonds holding it to the institutional Church may be wearing thin, the Catholic university shares in the incarnational nature of the Church. Here Christ (through His Church) is present in the academic life of the nation. The Catholic university by its commitment to the Church testifies to the redemption of the noblest potentialities of man.

The force of such witness before the intellectual world would appear to come as a result of institutional commitment as such. Individual Catholic scholars on secular campuses undoubtedly give similar witness, but in their cases the sign is not so clearly and unmistakably legible. In the light of what was said regarding the trend away from ecclesiastical control, however, it seems possible that this institutional commitment could evolve out of existence. The Catholic university which has no legal ties to the hierarchy nor with a religious congregation, and which has no clearly religious goal identified in its charter, would appear to be most open to this danger. Aware of this, some institutions have planned intricate steps to ensure continued effective control by the religious members of the board of trustees. Aside from the derogatory inferences that might be drawn about the Catholicism of the lay members of the board, it might be more to the point to attempt to formalize in some enduring way the institutional commitment of the Catholic university. This might be done by a change in the bylaws of the corporation or perhaps by demanding that the qualifications for trusteeship be very explicit on this matter. Thus the evident presence of Catholicism in the rapidly evolving world of contemporary higher education would be more firmly guaranteed. Since such clear institutional commitment is possible and since this will be taking place in a Catholic university that is more professionally academic than in the past, the opportunity to give witness to the presence of Catholicism is greater than ever before.

As the Catholic university evolves away from the seminary model and concentrates more fully on scholarship, it provides a unique opportunity for reflection and dialogue on Catholic theology. With a freedom not found in any other type of academic institution to specialize in this field, the Catholic university can pursue the frontiers of theological thought with great concentration. It can bring together scholars of many religious persuasions to share their insights and fruits of research. Here the body corporate of Christianity can bring its faith to self-reflective understanding. This means of course that the Catholic university must be free to analyze and to critically evaluate the formulations, policies and practical orientations of the Church. As the universities of the middle ages prepared the great advances in theology of the times, so today a similar possibility opens up before the contemporary Catholic university.

A third opportunity developing is that of bringing together the sacred and secular orders. The Second Vatican Council has given Catholics a new understanding and appreciation of the strengths, values, and proper integrity of the secular order. With this new understanding the Catholic university is in a strategic position to fashion a unity of the two orders, to point to a new synthesis of sacred and secular. This means demonstrating in theory and practice that the religious and secular orders can both prosper by mutual interaction and cooperation without either sacrificing its own function. It means that here of all places secular scholarship can find both meaning and increased depth in a religious milieu.

One other opportunity that is emerging in the contemporaneous Catholic university is that of creating a community of life, work and worship. A community must be self-conscious, with its members aware that they lead a shared life for a common goal. This awareness is growing in Catholic higher education today. In fact it is growing in most alert colleges and universities throughout the country, as dialogue and decision-making are spreading to the faculty and student body. Both groups are becoming more responsibly involved in their life of learning together. In the Catholic university this sense of community has several additional dimensions. The relationship of many persons can be more specifically characterized by the love of Christ and can be a reflection of the vital relationships between theology, faith and actual living. Intimately connected with this is the liturgical aspect which makes this a community of worship as well. This movement is well under way already and, it seems, should be pursued with a deliberateness that seizes upon the opportunities opening up.

The opening up of possibilities for more valuable institutional witness, for the free advancement of Catholic theology, for preparing a synthesis of the secular and sacred, and finally for establishing true community appear to be the trends that might characterize the nature and role of the Catholic university. The word "might" is used here since, of all the trends mentioned, these immediately above are in the greatest danger of being neglected. For this reason they have been categorized more as "opportunities." So far the Catholic university has neglected them to some degree. To do so in the future is to court suicide, for by their extinction the Catholic university will have ceased to be Catholic. The other trends are already strong. Their direction is already clear; they will not be stopped. But unless the opportunity for making Catholicism relevant is firmly seized upon, these other trends will reduce the visible Catholic presence to the status of a Newman club and the Catholic university will be no more.

To summarize the entire paper it might be said that at the moment the nature of the Catholic university is in the state of becoming. While the future is uncertain (due to the many forces at work) trends can at least be identified, indicating the shape that the nature is taking. These trends seem to indicate that the Catholic university is totally free from legal bonds with the institutional Church. It will be a university with the freedom of inquiry and the ecumenism of dialogue that should characterize the best educational institutions. At the same time it can provide an ideal location for the Church to meet the contemporary world in Christian witness, in theological inquiry, in cultural synthesis and in community.

Problems and Promise

EDWARD SCHILLEBEECKX, O.P.

When we see the attempts in all countries since the last war to find a new status for university education, whether academic or scientific, and when we see all that has been published in recent years—much of it showing signs of panic—on the "idea of a university,"[1] it seems obvious that the university is at present going through a rather critical phase. Some even go so far as to wonder if the university has not lost its essential meaning as a factor of culture and humanization: it has become a heterogeneous compound of specialties and laboratories in which everyone goes his own way, while current human problems and the destiny of mankind in our present situation—as full of promise as it is critical—are settled outside the walls of the universities. It had been thought for at least half a century that a committed science would be the end of all science. The "dehumanization" and in this sense the "objectification" of science—of which the natural sciences provided the model—was dealt a severe blow when quite a few atomic physicists found themselves compelled to raise the question of the human meaning of their discoveries. They suddenly realized that the practice of the "pure" science they had been recognizing was but a cog in a military strategy. Their science was committed

---

[1] For Germany we are especially thinking of the monumental collective work *Universität und moderne Welt: Ein internationales Symposion*, R. Schwarz, ed. (Berlin, 1962). For the Netherlands, see the journal *Universiteit en Hogeschool* published by the combined Dutch Universities and Hogescholen; it has been published now for over fifteen years.

after all—not to a grandiose task of humanization but to military strategy. The Oppenheimer affair was a hard jolt which made one think. This was but one of the many elements which raised the question of the humanizing value of science and made one acutely aware of the fact that man cannot live on the scientific ideal alone, which is but a *factor* in the great scheme to found a world that will be more worthy of man and in the "εὐ-ανθρωπεύεσθαι."[2]

The objectification of science does not prevent man from remaining the *subject* of all scientific work. The "man-being" is always involved: it is always finally a question of man as a being-in-the-world, knowing and controlling the world. The civilized man who landed among a baffled primitive people and explained that his plane had carried him in a day over a distance which they would need a month to cover, met with the following retort: "And what do you do with the other thirty days?" This is indeed the core of the matter.

PRESCIENCE FORESHADOWS SCIENCE

All science refers beyond itself to the "man-being," and even anthropology—together with all other sciences—rests on this initial metaphysical principle: the real exists and is intelligible. All science is preceded by a prescientific *Weltanschauung* without which it cannot exist. For before he ever engages in reflective thought or scientific action, man already is aware of himself as living in the world. This spontaneous awareness of oneself in this world is the only door to the various fields of science. In this spontaneous and lived encounter with reality, we already understand the latter in a prereflective manner: all sorts of ideas and representations already give us an empirical interpretation of reality and of our life in this world. Moreover, we always get back to a world which is already filled with human values, already humanized (or dehumanized): a *human* or cultural world. Neither is the realm of science independent of this primitive historical data. And thus our immediate expe-

[2] Cf. K. Rahner, "Wissenschaft als 'Konfession'?" in *Schriften zur Theologie*, 3 (Einsiedeln: Benziger, 1954), pp. 455–472.

rience of the world will always influence our explanation of the world, the human awareness of the world in which we live. It can be said that our awareness of the world, without which no science can exist, is a vision of the world, because human existence is always an existence that is trying to understand itself. The mere fact (which is also an intelligibility) of living as a man in a world, is to live within a certain vision of reality. However confused it may be, prereflective experience is already a form of understanding. This is why the stimulus of research in this world is an existential imperative: "We must *strive to understand* the world, because it is impossible for us to live in it otherwise."[3]

The main existential problem—how man can survive in the material world of nature—is the origin of the search for exact knowledge of the *Umwelt:* the natural sciences and technology. But then there are also the deeper problems: Why do we live? What is the meaning of reality and, within reality, what is the meaning of human existence? Man cannot overlook the problem of his contingency in an equally contingent world, even if he were to dismiss the question as absurd.

The prereflective, self-understanding existence of man in the world—that is, the prescientific *Weltanschauung,* the conscious existence in the world—is of a threefold nature: a physical vision of the world, a metaphysical vision of the world and finally an ethical image of man. And these three elements are constantly interacting.

Philosophy, a positive investigation of the same type as the sciences of nature and of the mind, is therefore a prescientific presupposition. Prereflective human experience is always— however confused it may be—a self-understanding experience and thus a *Weltanschauung.* This experience is the immediate source and the presupposition of all science, and also the horizon and the background against which all our specific reflective thoughts are outlined, whatever their nature. It is only when a particular aspect (social interrelationships, for example)

[3] J. H. Walgrave, "Verantwoording en uitbouw van een katholiek-personalist-ische gemeenschapsleer," in *Welvaart, welzijn en geluk,* 1 (Hilversum, 1960), pp. 12–13.

arouses a strongly concentrated emphasis in this prereflective experience—and this subject to socio-economic circumstances —that a new specialized science will see the light (sociology, in this case). It is precisely because the prescientific experience has ontological, ethical, and anthropological implications that our systematic study of a given aspect of this experience will give rise to a formalization which is, however, still outlined against a wider background that is methodically neglected by the new specialized sciences. In spite of its abstract character, the formalized aspect of these sciences implies (in the whole of man's understanding of the world) a reference to an initial totality and in fact to the primitive metaphysical principle.

Because of this formalization, a science (as a human science) is not yet completed when it obtains results and even reaches a synthesis within the frame of its own formalization. Such a synthesis will always be tentative, open to revision, awaiting new eventualities. In spite of the value of its own intelligibility and of the pattern of practical meaning which it reveals for human life by growing clear from within as a partial entity, it finally gains by reintegrating into the initial whole from which it derived its formalization.

TO CLARIFY THE TOTALITY

Because the content of prereflective experience gave rise to many formalized sciences, the interdisciplinary approach will obviously come to play a role in this reintegration. But one does not reach a fully reflective insight into this initial totality by means of a mere dialog between representatives of the various positive sciences, each laying claim to the monopoly of "scientificalness" or by reconstructing this totality by combining the partial aspects brought to light by formalization. Philosophy, on the other hand, is the science whose sole object is prereflective spontaneous consciousness; its aim is precisely to clarify the totality as such. This is why it begins with a phenomenological inventory of the facts it wishes to clarify in their intelligibility. In so doing it must not overlook the results of the investigations of the exact sciences, because formalization does not prevent these results from revealing an authentic aspect of the initial principle. But philosophy will have to set this formalization between parentheses for a while, by transposition, if it wishes to be enlightened by scientific perspectives.

The initial prereflective experience, therefore, calls on the one hand—by virtue of its confused insight into the totality—for the advent of the various positive sciences (specializations); and on the other, by virtue of its original totality, for an interdisciplinary approach and philosophical consideration.

It can be said (we are still setting theology aside) that the idea and the ideal of the university as *universitas scientiarum* arose from this very situation. It did not, therefore, begin as a gathering together for utilitarian reasons (to share the same buildings, for instance) of various independent sciences in a university complex. It is rather the result of an intrinsic requirement of the very intelligibility of reality and of human existence: the connection of each partial reality with the totality, and the human meaning of each science in its very "objectification." Each science, as a human science, needs to be in contact with the other sciences, and they all need the light of philosophy.

Philosophy and the idea of man (we do not yet consider the central import of religion) are therefore the uniting factor in a *universitas scientiarum*. Where they are no longer the structural principle of the university structure, the university as a *universitas* becomes meaningless and at the same time denies its vocation and its special mission. From a totally human point of view, the university is then a headless and limbless body. It is no longer but a heterogeneous city of scholars, not an orderly *polis* of wise men from which mankind can expect an irreplaceable contribution to the humanization of the world. And because the university is failing in this manner, the fate of the world in moments of crisis is surrendered to other hands.

It is true that the university is neither a parliament, nor a sort of United Nations or UNESCO. It is not a universal government, or an organization devoted to helping developing countries. It does not bring security to the world. But on the other hand, neither does it merely provide "training," in order to "manufacture" lawyers, doctors, social workers, congressmen, politicians, etc. The universities are the *brains* of the world; they raise prereflective human experience to the level of reflective thought. It is true that reflective thought and the scientific scheme are but one factor in helping mankind progress toward true humanity, because sciences and philosophy have human meaning and value only in relation to other value levels of human life. But the scientific function of the university as a *universitas scientiarum* (and thus not merely as a conglomeration of various sciences), has its own unalienable role in which it cannot fail without in some way injuring mankind. As a *universitas scientiarum*, it starts from the prescientific *Weltanschauung* characteristic of the consciousness of being-in-the-world, and emerges with a critically justified *Weltanschauung*. In view of its scientific role and of its academic freedom, which is restricted by truth alone, the university, in its whole being, leads to a *Weltanschauung* without which we cannot truly live as men in this world. Our time has discovered that in the name of science itself we must consider out-of-date the reaction against a relationship between *university* and *Weltanschauung*, even though such a relationship often occured in the past in a nonscientific and hence nonuniversity fashion (for believers as well as for non-believers). Besides, such a reaction is but fiction, for the rejection of all *Weltanschauung* cannot be justified by positive science itself and is therefore a new extra-scientific choice. By this very fact, it therefore implies (if only negatively) an actual *Weltanschauung*.

In view of what we have been saying, the idea of a "Catholic university" is already less likely to cause surprise a priori. We cannot, however, overlook the very real problem arising here. We can certainly begin by clearing away all forms of prejudice, the least of which is not that of a contradiction between academic freedom and acceptance of dogma,[4] as though freedom and obedience were not compatible, or as though freedom and whims were identical.

---

[4] Cf. N. Luyten, "Idee und Aufgabe einer katholischen Universität," in *Universität und moderne Welt*, pp. 593–609. Cf. also *Theology and the University: An Ecumenical Investigation*, ed. J. Coulson (Baltimore: Helicon Press, 1964).

It is precisely the *eros* of a consciousness which sees itself obligated to and bound by truth alone, which is the unique claim to nobility of the university. It is from this enslavement that it draws its academic freedom, even with respect to political powers. (One might wonder if and to what extent the state's interference with university education—however useful it may be in view of its financial contributions and of their fair distribution among the various universities within the country—does not violate this academic freedom and is thus in actual fact a disservice to the country. In the *universitas doctorum et studentium* of the Middle Ages, independence from all nonuniversity influence was a *sine qua non* condition). Faith is by definition the submission to divine truth: a submission which occurs in complete surrender, but nonetheless receives its full ethical meaning from prior justification.[5] Science and faith, in spite of their completely different nature, are closely related in this conscious enslavement to truth alone.

Moreover, faith shares with science the conviction that the world of human experience is the *only* means of reaching any truth. For outside of human experience, there is no other source of knowledge. How could we hear a revelation from God which would fall beyond the realm of our experience? How could it be a revelation to man? It is not possible to know about realities which we do not experience in some way. Because of this sensible basis to all human knowledge, the world is our only means of access to an explicit and actual knowledge of all other eventual realms of the real; that is, of total reality. In this sense we really know only this material world and hence all that is connected—and inasmuch as it is connected—with this material world. First of all, we know "I" and "Thou" precisely as being-in-the-world; then God as the Creator of this world or eventually as manifesting himself in this world by means of grace. This is why, in the Christian view, God's revelation occurs in human history itself, which is thus transformed into the history of salvation. And thus the conscious experience of the being-in-the-world forms the basis and the matrix of

[5] Cf. E. Schillebeeckx, *Personale Begegnung mit Gott* (Mainz, 1964), especially pp. 38–51.

science as well as of faith. In certain scientific circles, truth is confined to what can be immediately verified, or this "world" is considered not only as the unique means of access to all other reality but indeed, as the exclusive horizon of all human knowledge.[6] This is an unverifiable and extra-scientific postulate which amounts to a prescientific interpretation of the world. Disregarding the fact that such a *Weltanschauung* is open to criticism, we claim that any scientific scheme which competely denies any role to faith or a religious *Weltanschauung* in the university community, can be ascribed not to science, but to another *Weltanschauung*.

GOD'S SCIENCE ITSELF A REVELATION

Why should the belief in the transcendence of being be out of place in the university, whereas its negation would be acceptable, though they are both of an extra-scientific nature (since they are both beyond the positivity of science)? This belief in the absolute receptivity of the human mind to the whole of reality seems to us precisely the justification of a *universitas scientiarum,* as well as the precondition to all science. This is why we earlier assigned a central position to philosophy in the university. This view has indeed been endorsed recently by the Dutch law on higher education which raised philosophy to the status of an independent faculty with the meaningful name of "central interfaculty."

Religious faith, and mainly Christianity, claims that man, in his absolute receptivity, is always confronted with the absolute person of God who, through his personal-being, can manifest himself freely and thus reveal man to himself, and that he has indeed done just this. We can even say that this revelation from God is necessary (God's manner of being for us): for either God speaks, or he says nothing. In view of the transcendental openness of the human mind, God's silence, his nonrevelation, is itself a revelation for man; God's eventual silence also says something to the absolute receptivity of the human mind,[7] and

---

[6] M. Merleau-Ponty, "La métaphysique dans l'homme," in *Sens et Non-sens* (Paris, 1948), pp. 165–195.

[7] See in particular, K. Rahner, *Hörer des Wortes* (Munich, 1963), p. 117.

for this reason tells us something about the ultimate sense—or perhaps the non-sense—of human life. This is why, by virtue of the transcendental openness of his mind; that is, on a *human* basis and not owing to a mysterious, unique and irrational source of knowledge—man must allow a priori for a possible word of God. But if God should actually speak, this message of salvation is, in view of the transcendental openness of the human mind, the supreme fulfillment—a transcendental fulfill-ment it is true, but nonetheless an *inner* one—of our "man-being," through which man is simultaneously revealed to himself. Faith therefore opens up a very special perspective on human life: man fully realizing himself only through salvation, which God offers to him by a supremely gratuitous grace.

Only then does man fully realize that without grace—over which he has no control—he is no longer so self-sufficient, and that his most vital human problems (more especially his ulti-mate destiny), are questions which even the *universitas scienti-arum* would have to leave essentially unanswered. The ultimate substance of the man-being would thus be seriously threatened. The *universitas scientiarum,* with its interdisciplinary approach and philosophy must therefore comprise a faculty of theology, by virtue of the very ideas of totality and humanity which gov-ern the university. The idea of humanity intimately connects religion with the scientific goals of the university. This view can claim at least as good a scientific justification as that which sees no place for faith in the university. In other words, though it is admissible to reject all religions and hence Christianity, this does not mean that the integration of faith into the univer-sity structure represents a serious threat, if not the destruction, to the idea of a university.

And there is more. We have spoken of "lived and ingenious experience" as presupposed to any scientific discipline. If it is true, as claimed by religion, that man, through the transcenden-tal openness of his mind, is always confronted with the God of grace, this implies that revelation is present in all lived experi-ence, as an acceptance or a refusal, if only implicit or "anony-mous." Therefore, the concrete attitude of receptivity which man adopts in life and by which he admits the fundamental mystery of this life, is already an authentic faith, the primitive form of a still "covert" religious faith. Religion is the true form of a way of life which views with respect and fear the mystery of the objective reality in which we are living and chooses to abide by its laws. Faith, therefore, comes to man at that level of transcendental openness which is also the precondition to all science. This is why, in its existence as in its practice, faith is essentially beyond the reach of all science. Just as science cannot give me faith, it cannot either (at least per se) take it away from me. If science is thus, in one form or another, the critical explicitation of the "lived experience" in which I encounter the world of things and of other men, it will then turn to all scientific disciplines—including this scientific explicitation which we call theology—for information on this inexpressible reality. This shows, in view of the *praesuppositum* of all science, that theology, as the study of faith and of intraworldly reality in the light of this faith, can claim a central and fully justified position in the *universitas scientiarum*. In the believer's view it is theology together with philosophy, that deserves the name of "central interfaculty," because its goal is to penetrate—by means of scientific reflective thought within the frame of faith—to the ultimate foundation of all reality and humanity. On the other hand, theology is anxious to cohabitate with the other faculties.

The situation of a school devoted entirely to theology is usually precarious and unfavorable to theology. For it is in the very essence of theology, in order to be practised as it should be, to be integrated into a university, into the *universitas scientiarum* where mutual growth is structurally possible. This is precisely what is lacking in such a school of theology, for whatever scientific investigation brings to light is of importance for the understanding of revelation. And the profane sciences in turn need to be enlightened on the ultimate meaning of reality. If the theologian is not aware of the evolution of the other science, he is bound to miss the point in his Christian interpretation of secularity and of the unprecedented dimensions human life is assuming today.

So far we have only underlined the scientific necessity of a faculty of theology in a university, as well as the necessity of a university for the best possible practice of theology. We have not yet specified whether it should be a faculty of *Catholic* theology, nor defined the meaning and the purpose of a Catholic university. It is indeed very easy to conceive of a secular university when a faculty of Catholic theology would exist with a faculty of Evangelist or of Buddhist theology, for instance, or even with an interdenominational faculty. There would be great advantages to such a situation in our pluralistic world dedicated to dialog. Any argument in favor of a Catholic or a Reformed university cannot be an exclusive argument in favor of a unique possibility; i.e., it must remain a possibility among others. But this concrete possibility offers—together with the threat of "monolithism" which is contrary to the academic spirit—certain special advantages if it does not cut itself away from other universities with a different *Weltanschauung*. We will now try to show these advantages.

What is the function of the Catholic university today? In trying to define it, we do not exclude the fact that in the past the foundation of a Catholic university might have been inspired by other reasons which might indeed still be affecting us today. It is an historical fact that as a result of the quarrel between science and faith, the universities set themselves up as strongholds of antireligiousness. On the other hand, the churches themselves shared the responsibility for the abyss separating science and faith. Anticlericalism was to prevail in many a university and some Catholic universities were to promote "concordism," sometimes even to the point of absurdity. History also shows that the Catholic universities which were founded since the last century were created (among other things) to prove that believers can also be devoted to science without being guided by prejudice (though it was hardly noticeable then how late it was). But many other reasons came into play, such as those which gave rise during that same period, to all sorts of Catholic or Evangelical societies created to ensure a sterilized environment for Christian students and to preserve them from the dangers of the state university. Let each period have its own practical truth and its own ethical imperatives.

We now wish to determine the role of the Catholic university in our time.

THE TOTAL HORIZON

We must first show that this means something more than the mere presence of a faculty of Catholic theology in a non-Catholic university. What the idea of unity and universalism is to a university characterized by scientific pluralism, will be —for a Catholic university—the Catholicity of its vision of the world. The latter presupposes the philosophical predication of the transcendental openness of the human mind as an inevitable *praeambulum fidei*. This outlook leaves its mark on the whole Catholic university, which means that every teacher or student—even though he may not necessarily be Catholic— knows that it is structurally the inspiration of this university organism in its totality, and therefore does not concern only the faculty of theology. Let us hasten to say that this does not mean that the nontheological sciences are restricted in any way, as though the idea of Catholic biology or Catholic astronomy made sense. Catholicity demands that each branch of science follow its own methods impartially, with regard for truth alone in its own field of formation. And *here*, any sort of constraint— whether from the other sciences, from philosophy, from faith or from the churches—must be condemned. On the other hand, we have already seen that each field of formalized truth is outlined against a total horizon which each branch of positive science systematically sets aside, but in such a way that the portion of truth they contain is always dependent on this initial totality. It is at the level of this totality that the Catholic vision of the world plays an essential role. It is not in the various sciences as such, but at the level of the idea of totality, from which the idea of a *universitas scientiarum* is derived and on which is based its justification as a *university* (if we do not wish to reduce it to a conglomeration of scientific studies), that the Catholic vision has an essential function.

In a Catholic university the sciences are not Catholic sciences; it is the *universitas scientiarum,* as such, which is Catholic. This implies that in a Catholic university the concern for integrating scientific knowledge into religious thought should not be the duty of philosophers and theologians alone. It is a scientific task in which all members of the community must share; a task which justifies the existence of a Catholic university only inasmuch as it is performed and considered equally important as the study of science itself. Though philosophers and theologians have a preeminent and irreplaceable role in the investigation of the totality (because, unlike the other sciences, theology deals with totality itself), the Catholic university would not be worthy of the name if the other faculties relegated all philosophico-theological preoccupations with totality to the philosophers and theologians alone. This could be done equally well in a faculty of theology in a non-Catholic university and the idea of a Catholic university then becomes superfluous.

It seems then that a minimal amount of preparation in philosophy and theology for those teachers who are not philosophers or theologians would be a sine qua non condition for a Catholic university, as a university, to justify its predicate of "Catholic." Collaboration between scientific and theological thought is necessary to reach a total vision combining faith and the scientific view of the world. The theologian who is not himself a physicist cannot achieve this alone or even through teamwork within the faculty of theology alone. Even if certain fundamental facts are communicated to him by the faculty of sciences, this is very valuable but not sufficient. The physicist, on the other hand, may be neither a philosopher nor a theologian, but he is nonetheless a man. And since the human mind is a mind in search of a meaning and oriented toward totality, he will—as a man—meditate spontaneously on the meaning of scientific truth in terms of the whole of reality and of human experience. The biologist for example cannot, as such, make any pronouncements concerning man; he is qualified only to make a biological judgement of man. He is leaving his own field of competence and becomes a philosopher—and usually a poor philosopher, if he is not familiar with philosophical methods—when, seeing for example that removing part of the brain has the "consequence" of destroying all sense of ethics and of religion, he concludes that the religious sense is but an epiphenomenon or a function of a given nervous center. But because the question of totality is characteristic of man, we always run the risk of making a noncritical change of planes, so that statements which are not scientific but are rather dependent on a philosophical *Weltanschauung* are taken to be the results of purely scientific investigation. In the same way, a believer can integrate his faith and his scientific knowledge in a noncritical manner, violating the integrity both of his science and of his faith.

IMPEDING THE DEEPER MEANING

The spontaneous inclination inherent to the transcendental openness of the human mind to form an opinion of the totality, must be systematically and ascetically curbed in the study of the various branches of science by virtue of the scientific requirements of each branch. But on the other hand—and precisely at the level of the university—all its rights must be restored in a scientific and reflective statute. In a Catholic university, this implies the integration of philosophico-theological scientific thought by the whole academic body, each one in his own perspective. It is only when the whole university sees to it that each faculty—beyond the scientific viewpoint (and the freedom) of its own discipline—makes its own contribution to a critically justified unifying vision of total reality and the meaning of human existence in the light of Catholic faith, that the Catholic university will be truly worthy of its name in our times.

The absence of all religious vision will in no way hinder or restrain the development of science, nor is the purity of its scientific goal violated in any way. But from the viewpoint of its human role and of the integration of scientific knowledge into a total vision, it will nonetheless be impeded in its deep human meaning—if only in that it wants, in its isolation, to set up its own total (and thus philosophical) views as exclusive and definitive affirmations. This would seriously affect the elucidation of the ultimate meaning of human life, which can only be granted by God as a grace. Without this word we cannot but consider as total, a task which is most certainly authentic but still only partial, and thus form an incomplete picture of our concrete human being. This could lead to the depersonalization of the whole of mankind.

On the other hand, God's decisive teaching on human life—both in words and in actions—does not make human research pointless: revelation gives this research its true perspective. The God of creation and of salvation, in whom the believer sets his trust, is not an immediate criterion of truth for man, but the supreme guarantor of the nonabsurdity of our quest for truth. "God is no ready-made solution, but exigence to find one, as well as the guarantee that it is not finally absurd to search for a meaning and try to achieve something."[8]

His Catholic vision of the world, set in practice first of all by action inspired by faith and then throwing light on the ultimate meaning of his human existence—including its scientific dimensions—in this world, does not hinder the Catholic teacher in his impartial search for truth. Its ultimate foundation (which the member of a university, as such, should not try to avoid, no matter his specialization), is rather a liberating perspective leading to the ultimate truth which is finally revealed to us by grace. In the Catholic *universitas scientiarum* Catholic thought and scientific knowledge are scientifically integrated. As a scientific integration into a unifying vision (which must always be revised), this integration is the special task of a *universitas doctorum et studentium in* the organization of a *universitas scientiarum*. This is why Catholic intellectuals, in the name of their faith, demand their own Catholic universities. But because Catholic faith is in fact but a religious faith in the midst of religious plurality and in a world whose vision is becoming every day more secular, the Catholic university cannot justify its claim to be a university unless it remains in constant dialog with the other universities with different orientations. This means that the purely academic task

---

[8] Cf. J. Lacroix, *Le sens de l'atheisme moderne* (Tournai-Paris, 1958), pp. 58–64.

of the Catholic university teacher or of the Catholic university student (considered individually), does not per se need the Catholic university to be fully realized.

It is, however, the role of the Catholic university to be—in its own special way—in the eyes of the forum of mankind and of its sister universities, a *signum levantum:* the visible sign of a well-ordered collective caritas which demonstrates that on the level of science a Catholic *universitas scientiarum* can also make a contribution to the betterment of mankind in its earthly and eschatological aspirations.

The Difference

LORENZO ROY

Today, a university may be called Catholic either because of the people who are there, because of its juridical status, or because of its teaching and its research.

In speaking of the people who are there, according to the mediaeval expression *universitas magistorum et scholarium,* it may be said that a university is Catholic because its professors and students are all or in great majority Catholic, as an environment may be called Catholic because of the attitudes of those who live in it. Although this concept deserves to be retained, it should be noted, however, that while a Catholic university may be a center of religious life—which is very desirable—this is not the essential. Any university, even when it is called "Catholic," is above all a center of intellectual life and should, in the first instance, be defined in intellectual rather than religious terms.

A university may also be recognized as Catholic by virtue of its juridical status, because it has been established under canon law, and because it is attached to the Congregation for Catholic Education (until 1968, called the Congregation for Seminaries and Universities). But in this perspective, two qualifying remarks are necessary. First, let us point out that only the disciplines of theology, canon law, and philosophy are attached to this congregation at present. How then, and in virtue of what, would we attach to the Congregation for Seminaries and Universities, the teaching of mathematics or geophysics, a department of civil law, medicine, science or literature? Secondly, it is important to make a distinction between the juridical status of an institution and the life which animates it. Such distinction applies to the Catholic university which may be attached to the Church only by virtue of its juridical status, and be Catholic only juridically if—in the organization of its teaching and the pursuit of its research—it is not different from other universities.

Thus we are led to consider as preferable to the two preceding descriptions a third definition of the Catholic university: the *universitas scientiarum*. We will thus attempt to study the Catholic university in its teaching and its research, and above all in the concept of the world and of man which follows from its intellectual life. For the Catholic university is first of all a university.

In its research and through its teaching, the Catholic university—just as any other university—should be a place where human intelligence is perfected in one or another field of knowledge, and where the different sciences are coordinated in a unified concept of man and the universe. In addition, it aims to be Catholic, tending toward a total concept of man and the universe in the light of faith in the Word of God. Of course, neither the Catholic university nor the faith may be imposed on society, and a society cannot be forced to accept the former, not any more than an individual can be forced to accept the latter.

This is why it would be well to establish two main steps among others, in our consideration of this subject. First, we should agree to consider the Catholic university as a positive value. Then we should try to see if this value is practical in given circumstances. In other words, we should make a distinction between the idea and the realization of the idea, between the idea of the Catholic university and the Catholic university as it exists today.

The Catholic university is first of all a university. Therefore it should include the various fields of study that are normally found in a university. And in each of these fields, it should guarantee an instruction and research whose conditions are comparable to those found in any other university. In its teaching of physics or its research in nuclear physics, the Catholic university should realize the necessity of establishing conditions equivalent to those found in the "neutral" universities. Otherwise, it will be concluded that the natural sciences (or at least some of them) are neglected when they are included in the program of the Catholic university.

As a university, the Catholic university should first of all show beyond any doubt that each of the disciplines which make up its curriculum—except for those concerning theology—is definable in a natural order. In fact, each science has its own object and its own method. Moreover, scientific findings are valid only insofar as they account for reality. On this point, Pius XII was so explicit that his words are appropriate here:

> *The ideology of a research worker and of a scientist is not in itself a proof of the truth and value of what he has found and explained. The Pythagorean theorem or the observations of Hippocrates which are recognized as exact, the discoveries of Pasteur, the laws of Mendel, do not owe the truth of their content to the moral and religious ideas of their authors. They are not pagan because Pasteur and Mendel were Christians. These scientific observations are true because, and in the measure in which, they correspond to objective reality.*[1]

Scientific findings have their own value; they should be neither retained nor left aside merely because their author agrees or disagrees with the Church. They most certainly do not owe their worth to the religious attitude of the university from which they come. When these things are not clearly discerned, both the natural disciplines and Catholicism may be misrepresented, and both intelligence and revelation may be disfigured.

There is, therefore, no reason to believe that certain disciplines will be more perfect because they are in the framework of a Catholic university. Of this Catholic environment, chemistry or linguistics, civil engineering, or public law should make no demands for their respective fields. Each of these disciplines must develop according to its own method. According to this

[1] Pius XII, September 14, 1952. Cf. *Documentation catholique*, 1952, col. 1227.

method, nothing of what is relevant to the specific purpose of such discipline should be expected from the Catholicism of the university of which it is a part. What, then, characterizes the Catholic university?

In the expression *Catholic university,* the word *Catholic* qualifies not the parts, but the whole; not each of the disciplines which compose the university program, but the university itself. A Catholic history, geometry, or physics does not exist. The sciences develop according to their respective methods within the frontiers of a natural order. They owe their progress to the vitality and acuity of the intellect. Therefore, to say that each science can be Catholic would tend to favor the interference of supernatural faith in the scientific process, and thus the alienation of the latter. However, the university itself can be called Catholic to the extent that it is a meeting ground for scientific findings and revelation; that is, a place where the laws controlling the relationships between nature and grace are applied to the intellectual life.

And what does this mean? That the university is not simply a juxtaposition of disciplines which are foreign to one another, but that the meeting of these disciplines, and interdisciplinary research, are normally the subject of a constant preoccupation. And in this meeting, as well as in this research, the Catholic university is first of all characterized by the theology which is inscribed in its curriculum.

The Catholic university is thus the meeting ground for theology and the other sciences. Consequently, it is a place where a concept of man and the universe is brought into agreement with the word of God; a place where such a wisdom is developed that seeks to show the hierarchy of values according to man's highest principles. Such a meeting is desirable because it includes advantages for both theology and the other sciences.

Theology can be classified as a science, because faith respects the intellect with its natural curiosity and questioning. Thus, the intellect, when receiving the word of God, does not renounce its inherent qualities. On the contrary, the divine word is better received and better rooted in the intellect when the latter is better equipped with reasons and arguments. It is therefore necessary that theology remain in contact and dialogue with the other sciences, especially with those which are the closest to it: biblical exegesis with linguistics, church history with secular history, canon law with civil law, moral theology with psychology and sociology, and dogmatic theology with philosophy.

Isolated from the other sciences, theology can become immobilized in the consideration of certain problems which have become outdated, and even neglect the questions which are of greatest importance to contemporary man. The teaching of Vatican II is explicit on this point: "In fact, the most recent research and discoveries of the sciences, as well as those of history and of philosophy, raise new questions which imply consequences for life itself, and demand new research on the part of theologians themselves."[2]

Each science offers a certain vision of the universe. This vision is partial; it shows only certain aspects of man and of things, aspects which become more and more limited as science refines its tools of research. Thus, a global view of the universe requires that the different fields complement one another. With the help of theology, such a vision is enlarged beyond the natural order and tends towards a perfect universality. Moreover, the complementarity of the sciences and the contribution of theology to this complementarity help to direct the intellectual life and the sciences, to lead this life towards an integral vision of the world, towards a unity of knowledge and peace of mind.

The theologians are primarily responsible for the meeting between theology and the other sciences, and it is wise to consider the seriousness of this responsibility. If theology is not present at the meeting between the other sciences which make up the curriculum of the university, other voices than its own will make themselves heard. Then, the reception of the word of God will be more difficult, and the intellect will eventually tend to reject it.[3]

---

[2] *Gaudium et spes* (Montreal: Fides Editions, 1966), p. 237.

[3] See J. H. Walgrave, O.P., " John Henry Newman and the Problem of the Catholic University," in *Recherche et Culture*, ed. N. A. Luyten (Friburg: Editions Universitaires, 1965), pp. 152–153.

This meeting between theology and the other sciences raises difficulties, especially in our times. At first sight, these difficulties come from a difference in semantics. But on closer scrutiny, they are seen to spring from the differences between two types of reasoning, two modes of intellectual elaborations whose initial data come from distinct sources. On this subject, Arthur Eddington has the following comments:

> *As a conscious being I am involved in a story. The perceiving part of my mind tells me a story of a world around me. The story tells of familiar objects. It tells of colours, sounds, scents belonging to these objects; of boundless space in which they have their existence, and of an ever-rolling stream of time bringing change and incident. . . .*
>
> *As a scientist I have become mistrustful of this story. In many instances it has become clear that things are not what they seem to be. According to the story teller I have now in front of me a substantial desk; but I have learned from physics that the desk is not at all the continuous substance that it is supposed to be in the story. It is a host of tiny electric charges darting hither and thither with inconceiveable velocity. Instead of being solid substance my desk is more like a swarm of gnats.*
>
> *At one time there was no very profound difference between the two versions. The scientist accepted the familiar story in its main outline; only he corrected a few facts here and there, and elaborated a few details. But latterly the familiar story and the scientific story have diverged more and more widely—until it has become hard to recognise that they have anything in common.*[4]

Underlying these considerations is the difference between common experience and scientific experiments. These are two very distinct sources of data of which the one provides the background for a philosophical concept while the other gives rise to a scientific theory. Thence comes the difficulty of a

[4] Arthur Eddington, *New Pathways in Science* (New York: Macmillan Co., 1935). Quote taken from paperback edition (Ann Arbor, Michigan: University of Michigan Press, Ann Arbor Paperbacks, 1959), pp. 1–2.

meeting between theology and the physical and mathematical sciences. On the one hand, the latter—being properly characterized by the application of mathematics to the study of natural phenomena—utilize the data of scientific experiments. On the other hand, theology—in the investigation of the contents of revelation—draws from the data of common experience; from this it draws ideas like those of fatherhood, love, good, etc., ideas which are foreign to scientific experimentation and irrelevant to mathematical application. Thus, it is not strange that the language of theology and that of the physical and mathematical sciences are not the same, and that a meeting between them is difficult for both.

There are two postulates for this difficult meeting between theology and the other sciences, and this meeting will be neither easy nor fruitful without two prerequisite conditions: the education of the intellect and the presence of philosophy.

It has been pointed out that students arriving at the university are almost completely unaware of the distinction between the different modes of knowledge. I am not able to state positively whether this affirmation is true or false. But if it is true, it follows that these students are incapable of judging the right way of approaching a problem. Thus they will wait indifferently for an orator's convincing and irrefutable demonstration, or a geometrician's moving and persuasive argument. In short, their intellect has not been educated. Of course, someone who seeks certainty in matters that cannot carry more than mere opinion shows a lack of intellectual education. This is likewise true for someone who does not seek certainty in matters which require it.

There is no education without good manners, which can be defined as "a way of acting or behaving in life and in the world." Thus, an educated man is capable of several ways of acting or being, according to the circumstances. He does not behave with a child as he does with an adult, with a poor person as with a rich one, with a robber as with an honest man. He behaves differently in mourning and in good fortune.

Similarly, there is such a thing as an intellectual education. And this education should attempt to initiate the intelligence not only to a single way of thinking, but to the different manners appropriate to the different fields of learning.

At the end of this education, it is expected that the cultivated man should possess a general knowledge in each field, the sum of what he had to learn in order to be initiated into the different methods of the arts and the sciences. He will probably not be able to judge the validity of such or such a hypothesis, the truth or falsity of such or such a conclusion belonging to a particular field. In order to do this, he must specialize in one. However, we can expect that he should be able to judge the merit of a process from which a conclusion is drawn. He should know that a moral rule is not justified in the same way as a geometric theorem. He should not confuse the respective processes of the historian and of the playwright when they treat the same characters. It is thus a question of teaching him to distinguish between the different modes of learning and between the method which conforms to the subject treated in an exposé and that which does not, so that in each matter he is prepared to require the appropriate degree of certitude.

This intellectual education, very quickly sketched here, guarantees the receptivity of the intellect. In fact, an intellect which is marked too soon by the habitual and exclusive use of only one method will become easily closed to everything to which the same method does not apply. Indeed, nothing is more contrary to the normal life of the intellect, which is open to all beings and naturally curious to know everything. On the other hand, an intellect which has been initiated to the different methods of investigation, even though it is specialized in only one of these methods, remains receptive towards everything that it can understand and which deserves to be acquired. Thus conceived, intellectual education seems one necessary postulate for the meeting between theology and the sciences.

But this meeting also presupposes the presence of philosophy, understood as a wisdom which is open to the acquisitions of each of the sciences, and leading to a reflection on the universe in its entirety and on the destiny of man.

As a part of the curriculum of the Catholic university, philosophy is situated between theology and the other sciences. It is so necessary for the theologian that without it he could not continue his investigation of the body of revelation. And the scientist—who devotes himself to the application of a particular method—must expand his reflective efforts beyond the application of this method, in a philosophy which sees things in a wider text; in a wisdom which is developed, thanks to the effort of successive generations. Otherwise, many things will escape his notice, and the dialogue with the theologian will not be possible for him.

In short, there is no Catholic university without a faculty of theology which is alive and interested in meeting with the other sciences whose ensemble defines the university. There is no Catholic university if—as a primary condition for this meeting—there is not a philosophy towards which the specialists of each science are aiming.

But what will this philosophy be? That of Aristotle, or that of Kant? Or a completely different one?

Just as in the case of any other science, philosophy is defined within the frontiers of the natural order. It is defined, as such, exclusively by the effort of the intellect, and the history of philosophy shows clearly that there are several philosophies incompatible with one another. From this arises the problem of finding a philosophy whose elements are compatible with the data of revelation.

It does not follow, however, that a faculty of philosophy should limit itself to the teachings of Aristotle and St. Thomas Aquinas. The open-mindedness of this faculty is more necessary today than ever before. In addition to the philosophy accepted by the Church, it should include the thinking of all the great philosophers who left their mark on their times. Moreover, within the framework of a Catholic university, it should also lead towards a philosophy which is in agreement with the word of God.

Such is the principal characteristic of the Catholic university. It is the meeting place for a dialogue between theology and the other sciences, a dialogue directed towards an integral vision of man and the universe, a place where this meeting is prepared for by the education of the intellect and the presence of philosophy.

However, between an idea and the concrete realization of the idea, there are many complex circumstances to inventory and analyze. As noble as it may be, the idea is not sufficient to justify the organization and the maintenance of an institution in a given environment at a given period of its evolution. This explains why many questions are raised about the existence of the Catholic university in different countries today. In order that they be treated as they deserve, these questions require us to consider them as concretely as possible.

Finally, when it is desired by the society in whose service it will further its work, the Catholic university can rival in excellence any other university. And it can be, in addition, a place where persons who are engaged in higher education and research can bear witness to God's admirable respect for man's intellect.

Ways and Means to Its Mission

LUCIEN VACHON

There are at least two ways of treating this topic. Given a hypothetically ideal Catholic university with a correspondingly ideal mission, we could try to discover the best means possible of accomplishing this ideal mission. This method is undoubtedly useful, and may even be thought necessary whenever the feasibility of a Catholic university is either questioned or denied. A second and more practical method attempts to furnish answers to the following questions: Does this or that type of Catholic university—or this or that actually existing Catholic university—possess the means of accomplishing its ideal mission? Can they ever come to possess such means? Needless to say, this second method is necessary for several reasons.

First of all, it is obviously not sufficient to demonstrate the validity of the idea of a Catholic university in order to arrive at conclusions regarding either its feasibility or its opportuneness in a concrete situation. Simply to point this out is embarrassing though perhaps not entirely useless.

It is possible then that what we call the "mission" of a Catholic university is not a simple and indivisible reality. I do not, for instance, believe that all Catholic universities either can be, or even should be, "laboratories of the Church," perfectly abreast of all that is going on in the world. This kind of achievement necessitates a wealth and depth of resources obviously denied to many a Catholic university. However, must a diminished achievement bring about the disappearance of those

Catholic universities which lack the requisite wealth and depth of resources? To affirm this would be premature.

Thirdly, it is not certain that only one type of Catholic university exists. Indeed, when examining attentively the idea of a Catholic university, we uncover a number of traits which such a university possesses. And in trying to explain this profusion of traits, we are led to discuss the origin of Catholic universities, their motivations, their differing juridical status, the concept of denominational institutions including relations with the state and with Rome, and other circumstances peculiar to each university.

In accordance with the second and more practical method which I have outlined above, I should now like to offer some observations which I think will help us to adopt a realistic attitude to the problems confronting Catholic universities today. Obviously, this more practical approach to the topic necessitates detailed knowledge of the situation of Catholic universities throughout the world. But since I am conversant only with the problems confronting the French-Catholic universities in the Province of Quebec, my discussion will bear upon them.

The only three French universities in Quebec have been Catholic since their inception, and all three have ecclesiastical charters. This rather peculiar situation is accounted for by the fact that at the time the universities were created, Quebec's population was overwhelmingly Catholic. One must remember, too, that in Quebec a large number of private educational institutions (*e.g.,* classical colleges, teacher training colleges for girls, nurseries, etc.), are officially denominational—indeed Catholic for the most part. This situation suggests certain comments.

The French universities in Quebec were created by the Church because this was the normal thing for the Church to do at that time.[1] And these universities have been subsidized

---

[1] It is also the case, for instance, with the Middle Ages.

"The university naturally plays a rôle in the eschatological unity of the medieval period. . . . Having to undergo the general discipline of Roman Christianity, the medieval world bears witness to the unity of a same inspiration in each of its aspects. The Church, by reason of its omnipresence in the western world, takes under its aegis all the citizens and

to a considerable extent by the state. State aid was not given to them so that they might counter a growing indifference to religion among the public or so that they might repulse an invading ideology—as was, for instance, the case with many European[2] and American[3] universities established during the nineteenth century. This fact probably prevents French universities in Quebec from acquiring a "ghetto" spirit or giving much prominence to apologetical or self-justifying preoccupations.

Moreover, they have not had to compete with other universities and therefore have not profited from competition. Without having directly maneuvered to obtain it, Catholic universities in Quebec have actual control over the university education dispensed to the French population. This highly criticized control compels them to provide for all the wants of the population where advanced education is concerned, and so to assume the character of public institutions.

So where Quebec is concerned, it is unthinkable that the Catholic universities wholly adopt a project such as that formulated by Pierre Haubtmann, the rector of the Catholic Institute of Paris, to give priority to those areas of study which are more closely related to the mission of the Church. One must also bear in mind that professors and students in Quebec are not necessarily attracted to the Catholic universities because they are Catholic; they have nowhere else to go. In fact, many people in Quebec are demanding public or state universities, rather than private or denominational ones.

---

peoples, all human powers and functions, through the use of an immense apparatus of theological concepts and liturgical rhythms. . . . Since authority exerted at a distance is less dangerous than authority (episcopal) stationed nearby, the schools united in a single community will request recognition and protection from the Holy See. . . . At the outset, the university is far more dependent upon ecclesiastical authority than upon civil; since all of her personnel are clerics, she comes to seem like the Church exercising her teaching function" (G. Gusford,, *The University under Scrutiny*, [Paris: Payot, 1964], pp. 15–26, *passim*).

2 Jacques Leclercq, "Catholic University," *De Maand*, May 1964.

3 E. J. Power, *A History of Catholic Higher Education in the United States* (Milwaukee: Bruce, 1958).

Though they are private institutions, our universities are becoming increasingly public in character, as they are almost completely subsidized by the state. Eventually, this extensive financial assistance will inevitably result in the state's assuming some control over the universities' policies. At any rate it will compel them to adopt standardization measures to insure the best quality of teaching possible and service to the entire population.

Finally, our Catholic universities must now take into consideration the fact that the population of Quebec is no longer homogeneous where religion is concerned, and therefore the universities have to accept professors and students who either belong to other denominations or are simply unbelievers.

Have universities in Quebec been truly Catholic? I do not say *perfectly,* but *truly* Catholic? In a certain sense they have been, of course. They have maintained an orthodoxy of doctrine. There has been the presence of numerous priests on the campus. There has been religious teaching in the faculties, though this is now discontinued. There have been a number of manifestations of Catholic culture. In general, there has been a preoccupation on the part of a good number of the university authorities to preserve a Christian climate at the universities. These universities can be called Catholic in the sense, too, that they have never believed—let alone taught—that to science belongs the definitive pronouncements regarding the real world, man's place in it, and the meaning of life. These universities have also affirmed their Catholic character by teaching that there is no essential conflict between faith and reason or between the Christian and secularist cultures.

Have they been Catholic according to the true significance of the term? Have they been efficient witnesses of the unity and plenitude of the truth? Have they shown how the most disparate truths in nature can be integrated into a vision of totality, thus bearing witness to the existence of a divine wisdom? Have they brought together in harmonious combination the philosophic and the scientific reason, Christian and secularist modes of thought? Have they been the source of a Christian philosophy founded upon an authentic dialogue between theologians and scientists, technicians and artists? Have they shown the feasibility of synthesizing human knowledge along Christian lines?

Have they been the terrain for a network of values in which all intellectual endeavour may fruitfully be carried out? Have they been a bridge between man and science? An arena for the clash between the great currents of ideas? The incarnation of Christ in that social and cultural entity which is called a university?

Truly Catholic universities bear witness to the Church's respect for, and interest in, science and culture; they are laboratories or study centers where the Christian ideal is explored in depth. Moreover, such universities must show that the Church is always keenly aware of the evolution of society, and they set the patterns of Christian thought before the world at large. If such are the lineaments of the truly Catholic university, then there can be no doubt: the universities in Quebec have not been Catholic in this sense.

In proof of this, I should like to point out that the faculties of theology in the Quebec universities exert no real influence, whereas we are all agreed that a faculty of theology is the chief element in a Catholic university. Nor would I be unjust in pointing out the lack of a genuine dialogue between the different disciplines, principally between philosophy and the sciences.

One possible explanation for this could be the fact that the university authorities have probably never "wanted" a Catholic university with all that that implies, or else they have come to the conclusion that a genuinely Catholic university is not a viable institution.

And this brings us to the second question: Is it actually within the means of our Catholic universities to remain such? Before attempting to answer this question, it might be useful to set down the most discussed aspects of the problem.

It is affirmed that any Catholic university is a Christian institution which must be regarded as a tool utilized by the Church for impressing its dictates upon the temporal life. Such an institution is analogous to those created by civil society, and is—like them—a product of our civilizing tendencies.[4] Now, if it is true to say that the Church has accomplished its mission in the field of higher education by means of the Christian institutions commonly designated as Catholic universities, there seems now to be taking place a shift in the Church's educational role. The Church should now be "animating from within all the activities of education,"[5] espousing "a new type of relationship with temporal society, not juridical in character but spiritual, by inspiration rather than by establishment,"[6] by being a living witness to the truth rather than the owner of so much university property. To prove that this is indeed the Church's new role in education, prophetical biblical literature, deliberations of recent councils of the Church, and contemporary theological essays are used.[7] In brief, the Church (according to this view) should give up possession of the concrete educational establishment in order to affirm "the Christian presence in the school for everyman."

Generally, the reply to this line of reasoning is that the Church has a duty to preserve its visible, tangible links with society by maintaining educational institutions (such activity being essentially within its scope). Or that the Catholic university is essential to the Church's role of making the impact of Christ felt upon the social and cultural entity which is called a university. Or that the concrete difficulties inherent in this immense task result precisely from the fact that these institu-

---

[4] The reference is to the distinction made by P. A. Liégé, "The Conspiracy against Christian Institutions," *Parole et Mission*, no. 15 (October 15, 1961), pp. 495–506. This was emphasized once again by P. Angers, "Tasks of the Church in the Field of Education," *Prospectives* I, 4 (September 1965), 27. Attention is therefore drawn to the distinction between the "ecclesial" institution (sacramentality, episcopate . . .), the "ecclesiastical institution" (diocese, parish, religious orders, faculties of theology . . .) and the "Christian institutions" (the state, the press, the school, the Christian labour union).

[5] Angers, "Tasks of the Church in the Field of Education," p. 29.

[6] A. De Bovis, "The Church and Temporal Society," *Nouvelle Revue Theologique* (1957), p. 237.

[7] Particularly: K. Rahner, *L'Eglise a-t-elle encore sa chance?* (Paris: Cerf, 1952); K. Rahner, *Mission and Grace*, I (Tours: Mame, 1962); Y. Congar, essays collected in *Sacerdoce et Laicat* (Paris: Cerf, 1962); and J. Grand'Maison, *Crise de prophétism* (Montreal: Action Catholique Canadienne, 1965).

tions are not authentically Christian. In fact, deformations of the Christian ideal (such as clericalism) are not uncommon; the personality and teachings of Christ himself often suffer distortions; a "Catholic ghetto" is born, the attempt to exert influence upon the temporal plane is grossly confused with the actual possession of such influence, etc.[8]

It is further stated that a Catholic university has real difficulty in achieving the rank of a genuine university while holding fast to its Catholic character. This assertion rests upon the belief that science is nondenominational; that is to say, that a Catholic physics or a Protestant biology are incompatible with a true scientific spirit. It is alleged that the universality of science—together with its objectivity—promotes a unity of endeavor, and not conflict; the advancement of science would thus be furthered altogether independently of religion. Thus, a university that is professedly Catholic is involved in many absurdities, and never manages to achieve that universality of purpose which is the hallmark of the true university. Hence the confusions and the equivocations that are born from the attempt to conceive a "Catholic university."

Moreover, adherence to the Catholic religion implies the acceptance of a number of dogmas or truths which, though founded upon absolute truth, are not amenable in principle to scientific control, thus emphasizing the incompatibility of such terms as "university" and "Catholic." Alexander Wittenberg has been able to set forth clearly this whole line of reasoning.[9]

---

[8] Cf. H. Holstein, "The Christian School, Institution of the Church," *Revue trimestrielle de l'union des Religieuses enseignantes,* no. 3 (1965–66); and H. Larrain Acuña, "Catholic Universities: Encouraging and Alarming Developments," *Message,* March–April, 1964, quoted by the *Informations catholiques internationales,* July 15, 1964, pp. 29–30.

[9] *On the other hand, religious observances of any kind have no business whatsoever in the official and ceremonial life of the university. This principle is a direct consequence of the basic commitment of the university. The university is dedicated to the pursuit of truth, wherever this may lead. . . . The function of the university, I said, is to maintain that commitment vigorously alive; the university is the organ that serves that function. In other words, the university really is the affirmation of that commitment and its translation into practical reality. Dedicated to every aspect of the search for truth, and to everyone of its yet unspecified future*

Furthermore, a university's Catholic affiliations constitute a genuine impediment to its becoming a first-rate institution, since in theology and philosophy it severs itself from the significant research that is being conducted in non-Catholic institutions of higher learning. It fails, therefore, to take into account the religious fragmentation characteristic of the milieu in which it operates, giving as a result inadequate preparation to its young citizens about to be brought into contact with a de facto diaspora.[10] It is reluctant, too, to collaborate fully with the other national (or provincial) bodies to ameliorate the functioning of the civil and social machinery of the nation or the province. Further, it limits the area of fruitful intellectual cooperation with non-Catholics, thus inhibiting to some extent the emergence of a needful critical spirit peculiar to the adult person (who should normally arrive at the expression of genuinely personal views). Such a university, paradoxically, is conspicuously less creative than its non-Catholic counterpart, even though it has less to suffer from the profusion of subjects to be taught.[11]

Finally, the liberty of action in a Catholic university is imperilled in a number of ways. First, by Catholic public opinion, naturally conservative and conformist, and enamoured of the uniformity of belief supposedly insisted upon by "the Church" —a public opinion which deliberates technical matters with

---

implications, the university does not identify itself with any of them. The university is thus the very model of a free society. . . . In the last analysis, it is clear that this kind of commitment cannot coexist on a par with a religious commitment. It must either claim precedence over the latter, or submit to its pre-eminence. A religious faith is exclusive by its nature. A university that would be exclusive is not a university. There cannot be a monastery serving two different gods at once. There cannot be a university dedicated to the service of only one god. There is an inherent conflict between the absolute commitment to one particular truth that is held revealed by God, and the university's open commitment, which is a commitment, not to a truth, but to a search for truth wherever the search may lead (Alexander Wittenberg, in *Religion and the University* [Toronto: University of Toronto Press, 1964], pp. 115, 125–126).

[10] Cf. K. Rahner, *Mission and Grace*, II (Tours: Mame, 1963), p. 229.

[11] D. Callahan, "The Catholic University: The American Experience," in *Theology and the University*, ed. John Coulson (Baltimore: Helicon Press, 1964), p. 73.

which it is not the least bit conversant and which should be left to the university personnel. Secondly, by the episcopate upon which the university depends and which it would be unwise to offend. Third, by those people who contribute financially to the upkeep of the university: "If it (the Catholic university) accepts to be poor, it must content itself with possessing inferior faculties, such as are incapable of accomplishing significant research; on the other hand, if it is to be a genuine research institution competing with other universities, then it runs the risk of impairing its liberty of action by placing itself under the tutelage either of the wealthy or of the state."[12] And other such arguments might be produced.[13]

The usual answer to these objections is that, first of all, the terms "catholicity" and "universality" are identical in meaning. Hence, it is always possible to discern behind the "spirit of universality" a *Weltanschauung*, or a point of view, such as that all human knowledge is "perspective," i.e., an apprehension of the truth from a definite point of view. Without such "perspectives," no scientific activity, or no thinking of any significance can be carried out—which is precisely the reproach from which Catholics are shielded because in their search after the truth they adopt a Catholic point of view.

Secondly, to distinguish the Catholic (who adheres to a ready-made body of truths), from the ideal university researcher (who is in constant quest after the truth), is to misapprehend the nature of "Catholic truths." As is the case with all other kinds of truth, these are in fact successive approximations to a central truth whose full apprehension is denied to human intelligences. (By "successive approximations" I mean truth such as lies within the ken of human beings, and which we feel to be constantly and intrinsically adumbrating the truth.) Moreover,

---

[12] *Informations catholiques internationales*, July 15, 1964, p. 29.

The wealthy class, writes Mgr Leclercq, benefits from social abuses and does not wish to eradicate them. It would withdraw its support if the social doctrine of the Church were taught. Since, however, it is inconceivable that this doctrine be not taught in a Catholic university, the subterfuge most frequently adopted is to teach this doctrine in so abstract a manner that no students retain any impression of its importance in life.

[13] Cf., for instance, D. Callahan, pp. 75–76.

the Catholic as such does not think himself alienated from a "free society" as St. Paul so beautifully explained in his letter to the Romans.

Furthermore, why should it be impossible for science and religion to coexist? Better still, why should there be conflict between science and theology, in view of the fact that both are justly autonomous within their own spheres?[14] That is to say, they "belong to two different existential dimensions, and thus deal with truths and values of an altogether different nature."[15] "It is up to us," says Dondeyne, "whether these two modes of apprehending the real world can be reconciled."[16] Reference here can also be made to the writings of Cardinal Newman upon this topic.[17]

Again, it is really a contradiction to assume that a Catholic university is not a feasible or even an appropriate institution of higher learning in our contemporary world. With the existence of a pluralistic society, or of a "contemporary ecumenical climate" hospitable to a number of different conceptions of the world, there can obviously be no genuine dialogue between the Catholic and secularist viewpoints if each is not given the fullest opportunity to express itself. It would be truer to say that secularism today is more individualistic than agnostic.[18] What I mean is that the proponents of a secularist attitude maintain a respect for persons groping after the truth even

[14] "Accordingly, the problem is better stated here in THEOLOGICAL rather than in RELIGIOUS terms. The reason for this is that theology consists of knowledge to which the dignity of science has been imparted—knowledge which is at once rooted in the revealed data and rationally developed, logically and systematically articulated" (Jacques Maritain, *Towards a Philosophy of Education* [Paris: A. Fayard, 1959], p. 184).

[15] Cf. A. Dondeyne, *Faith Listens to the World* (Paris: Editions universitaires, 1964), p. 210; cf. all of chapter 7.

[16] *Ibid.*, pp. 225–226.

[17] See *The Idea of a University* (Garden City, New York: Doubleday-Image, 1959), especially chapters 1, 2, and 9.

[18] "Absolute freedom before the truth" which is qualified as an "intolerant tolerance which draws upon a perpetual suspicion of all truth": the assimilation of metaphysical and theological learning to learning of a scientific character. Cf. Jacques Croteau, "The Catholic University in a Secularist Society" (text of a *lectio brevis* delivered at the University of Ottawa, October 1, 1963), p. 3.

while being antagonistic toward *revealed* truth, and a sacred respect, too, for truth itself. (Though no doubt is cast upon the nature of the intelligence, it is held that truth can only be received as truth.) Jacques Croteau has said well: "The Catholic university claims the right to exist, and professes to be even an opportune institution, on the basis of contemporary secularism's respect for the individual's point of view. And the Catholic university respects the right of other universities to exist."[19] However, for the defenders of Catholic universities the crux of the matter rests upon two considerations.

Though biology and physics are obviously not intrinsically Christian or Catholic, culture is not neutral. Moreover, culture falls short of being completely human if it does not take into account God as He is—as He manifests Himself in our redeemed world.

It is undeniable that the progressive disintegration of the different disciplines (scientific-philosophical-theological) has resulted in the emergence of "pseudo-physics and pseudo-biologies which it is a mistake to regard as exact sciences, since their findings rest upon fallacious philosophical and theological grounds."[20] In other words, one of the principal defects of our university culture is that such culture, "as a result of its incapacity to tackle directly matters of religion, confusedly embraces a theology of whose true nature she remains ignorant.[21] As the same authority explains:

> Science, in the course of its advance, is inevitably led to make use, in the formulation of its theories, of concepts metaphysical in character, such as space, time, objectivity, etc. Now science wishes to give precise definitions of these concepts by subjecting them to its own peculiar modes of investigation. Science, as a result, without being aware of it, often lapses into metaphysical reasoning—and this is surely not the least dangerous way of conducting such reasoning.[22]

[19] *Ibid.*
[20] P. H. Larrain Acuña, *Informations catholiques internationales*, July 15, 1964, p. 30.
[21] *Ibid.*
[22] *Ibid.*

It must also be admitted that culture is not neutral, indeed it cannot be so. Though culture necessarily rests upon a sub-stratum of acquired knowledge, its primary manifestation is as "knowledge which imparts judgment."[23] In other words, culture demonstrates itself by knowledge, which permits the person owning it to grasp the right relation in which a single truth or body of truths stands to a plurality, or to a praxis and an ontological investigation of the absolute.[24] A culture which refuses to be committed, or spurns wisdom, or leads nowhere—a "neutral" culture—does not deserve the name culture.[25]

It follows that the university, which is a haven for the higher culture at the same time that it dispenses a professional education, cannot be neutral.[26] Believers, moreover, are of the opinion that a complete human culture can only be Christian. "No education is complete if it does not provide for the intellectual, moral, religious and spiritual formation of the student. . . . The university assumes a direct responsibility for the moral, religious and spiritual formation of its students. It should further be pointed out that the spiritual development of its students constitutes the essential aim of a university as such (that is to say, a university conceived along the lines of Jesuit thinking)."[27] Solutions other than those envisaged in the structure of a Catholic university provide no adequate answer to the question asked; their inadequacy is reflected in the fact that they do not transform the nature and the value of the institution itself.[28] It is nonetheless affirmed that the problem is one

[23] J. T. Delos, "The Problem of Catholic Universities," *La Vie intellectuelle,* 62, 1939, 252–271. Article reprinted in Msgr. L. A. Vachon, *Communauté universitaire* (Quebec: Presses de l'Université Laval, 1963), pp. 86–119.

[24] On the multidimensional structure of human truth, cf. Dondeyne, *Faith Listens to the World,* pp. 79–84.

[25] Delos, "The Problems of Catholic Universities."

[26] *Ibid.* "The future eminence of those young men and women who are later to form the elite is plainly discernible between the years of 18 and 25. . . . And the period at which the personality is definitely formed comes later in life if the youth or maiden is destined to play an eminent role in society" (p. 80).

[27] In *Christus,* no. 43, pp. 404–410.

[28] For instance, instead of a Catholic university, collaboration in the achievement of a university's aims by concentrating upon the study of the sacred sciences; the presence of Catholics in a non-Catholic university; Catholic action; complementary and peripheral circles, etc.

of institution.[29] The writings of Etienne Gilson will often be mentioned in the debate over the priority of aims in the university.[30] The Church has a civilizing mission: her duty is to Christianize culture and to disseminate it in this form. In the domain of higher learning, this aim cannot be achieved in universities that are not professedly Catholic.

Finally, emphasis will be put upon the irreplaceable "human climate" (the human implanting, context, conditioning) which scientific research requires if it is to be efficacious. A Catholic university is as articulate as the neutral one in emphasizing the importance of this climate. Therefore, it ought not be criticized for this.[31]

This aspect of the matter is increasingly associated with the following consideration: Catholic universities have never been so necessary *as they are today.* The different disciplines are becoming increasingly autonomous and drawn in upon themselves. There is now a task of "salvation" to be accomplished here: a task of synthesis, integration, a vision of totality, such as only the Catholic universities can furnish, since they command the utmost heights of the pyramid—alpha and omega.

The peculiar mission of a Catholic university today consists in striving after the unity of truth, after "the integration of disparate truths into a vision of totality."[32] This has been, of course, the mission of a Catholic university all along; but its accomplishment is more urgent today than ever it has been before. Our times are marked by the emergence of a pluralistic society which has lost its rational faith in the truth and is undergoing a severe crisis, epistemological in character. In so grave a situation, the unifying labors of the faculties of theology and philosophy are not equal to the task confronting them. As it goes about fulfilling its concrete responsibilities, each of these faculties should be constantly preoccupied with integra-

[29] Delos, "The Problem of Catholic Universities."

[30] E. Gilson, *Towards a Catholic Order* (Paris: Desclée de Brouwer, 1934).

[31] N. A. Luyten, "Why Establish a Catholic University?" *Research and Culture: Tasks of a Catholic University* (Fribourg, Switzerland: Editions universitaires, 1965).

[32] Croteau, "The Catholic University in a Secularist Society," p. 6.

tion, with promoting totality; constantly striving to advance and to impart science in the light of ontological considerations on the one hand, and in the light of the faith on the other— preventing both these domains from impinging destructively upon each other.[33]

When the question is asked whether a Catholic university as such retards the development of a nation, the defenders of this kind of university reply that a nation has, in effect, need of such an institution to climb the highest peaks of achievement. In fact, it is alleged that this kind of university "saves" a pluralistic society from the evil effects of its latent agnosticism, from such effects, too, as result from the fragmentation of the disciplines. Moreover, to those who claim that a neutral university poses fewer administrative problems than a Catholic one, Catholic apologists reply that the burdens of administration ought not to be lightened when this entails the sacrifice of an essential element in the formation of students.

Finally, on the one hand certain investigations into this matter seem to lead to the conclusion that Catholic universities do not in fact lack autonomy despite their relationship to the Catholic hierarchy.[34] On the other hand, the sociological investigation conducted in the United States by Andrew Greeley and his co-workers seems to underscore the fact that there is no basis for thinking that (1) Catholic schools are academically inferior to the others; (2) a Catholic education alienates those who are subjected to it from other American citizens. Greeley goes on to say, moreover, that despite legitimate criticism leveled at Catholic schools from different quarters, these schools (together with the Catholic universities), are extremely popular.[35]

Everyone agrees with the following observation: The Church as such needs the university. The university is a place where

[33] *Ibid.* Cf. T. M. Hesburgh, "Notre Dame Reorganization," *Christian Education,* March 1, 1967, p. 7.

[34] René Thery, "The Autonomy of Catholic Universities," report presented at the 7th General Assembly of the F.I.U.C., Tokyo, August 28, 1965.

[35] A. Greeley, "Father Greeley on the Greeley-Rossi Report," *Christian Education,* February 5, 1967, p. 1ff.

the Church can at least partially accomplish its task of cogita-
tion. Moreover, in a university, the Church can transmit its
theological tradition in a philosophical guise to a certain elite.
Catholic universities are study centers for the Church,[36] which
is as much as saying that faculties of theology play an indispensable role in the life of the Church; such faculties as are
particularly open, competent, ecumenical, and established upon
secular campuses.[37]

On the other hand, writes Msgr. A. Descamps, "Is it necessary to establish entire universities for this purpose? Do such
universities, moreover, have to be justified on the ground that
they provide the best assurance for the proper development of
dogma? Such a conclusion does not necessarily follow, but it is
doubtless true to say that the symbiosis of the theological and
secular faculties conduces to the advance of theology, to say
the least."[38]

Jacques Leclercq asks "whether the old conception of a
Catholic university should not be modified, and universities
conceived according to the old pattern be split into two." He
explains:

> Grouped around the faculty of theology would be such
> faculties as have a religious orientation—the faculties of
> philosophy, religious psychology, religious sociology, etc.
> This aggregation of faculties would be called the "Catho-
> lic university," or institute, or any other name. Meanwhile,
> the aggregation of the secular disciplines would constitute
> another university which would not be called Catholic,
> and which would be directed by professional men. Such a

[36] For example: Jacques Drezo, "The University in Contemporary Society and
the Future of Louvain," *Revue Nouvelle* (Belgique), June 15, 1965; Msgr. A.
Descamps, "The Purpose of Catholic University Teaching," *Lovaniensia* (Louvain), September 1965; and A. Greeley, "The Possibility of a Catholic University,"
report presented at the annual assembly of the Catholic Commission for Intellectual and Cultural Affairs, Chicago, May 7, 1966.

[37] For example: Leonard Swidler, "Catholic Colleges: A Modest Proposal,"
Commonweal, January 29, 1965, pp. 559–562.

[38] Descamps, "The Purpose of Catholic University Teaching."

university, established by Catholics—though not officially
Catholic—would be favorably disposed toward religion. . . .[39]

More radical thinkers believe that the purpose of a "Catholic
university" does not consist in providing the kind of teaching
which imparts technical mastery of a science. This purpose
should rather be to set up the means whereby the Church
shall remain abreast of the best developments of contemporary
thought. A university established along these lines would be
equivalent to a "rostrum for those thinkers who are able to
assist the missionary purposes of the Church.[40]

Finally, Jacques Drezo declares it essential for certain Catholic universities to undertake the special mission of "playing *for*
the Church and for Christendom at large the role of a permanent conscience in the evolution of the world, representing all
the while *for an evolving world* the very conscience of Christian thought."[41] Though it be true that all Christians are committed to the continuation of the work of redemption in the
unity of their spiritual and temporal engagement ("at the
center of worldly activity"), the need still remains for a small
group of overtly Christian university professionals to form, as
Drezo puts it,

> *a living hinge between the world of today and that of to-*
> *morrow; to these people would devolve, more particularly,*
> *the task of carrying this unity forward, and of seeing to it*
> *that redemption operate at the very heart of the world's*
> *evolution; thus they would be throwing light upon the*
> *essential lineaments of the future society and avoiding*
> *fruitless study of its more evanescent manifestations. Cer-*
> *tain Catholic universities, therefore, have consciously to*
> *assume such a role by grouping together the required num-*
> *ber of talented people in a more systematic and far-sighted*

[39] Leclercq, "Catholic University."

[40] G. Lemaire-Dallaporta, F. Ferry, and P. Longchamps, "The Reform of the
Catholic University," *Esprit*, March 1966, pp. 388–412.

[41] Drezo, *op. cit.*

manner than is possible presently to the learned Catholics
dispersed in far-flung neutral institutions.[42]

In *The Secular City,* Harvey Cox devotes a chapter to the subject: "The Church and the Secular University."[43] This chapter is one of the three illustrations furnished by Cox in his attempt to think out theologically the implications of contemporary "urbanization" and "secularization." After demonstrating that this contemporary secularization is far from clashing with the biblical account (more particularly, the mystery of the Creation, Exodus and the Sinaitic alliance), he goes on to sketch the main features of the "secular city": the more palpable characteristics of its society (such as its love of anonymity and its extreme mobility); its cultural aspect (reflected in its pragmatic outlook and secularist bias); and the role of the Church in the new city.

With respect to the relations between the Church and the universities, Cox throws light upon new facts of the situation today: the nonreligious character of the modern humanism (analysed by Dietrich Bonhoeffer); the gradual disappearance of a traditional theocracy in the university community; the democratization of access to the university; the difficulty which the churches have experienced in the course of their missionary activity in abandoning sociological tenets reminiscent of matriarchal, agrarian and prescientific epochs, etc. Cox emphasizes the significance of these last facts by dwelling upon the successive attempts of the Church to make its presence felt in the university community: establishment of its own colleges and universities; working through nearby residential congregations; transplanting onto the university campus a denominational church.

After having identified the Church as being a reality which, though not invisible, cannot however be "empirically detected and located by a bulletin board or a sociological survey," Cox goes on to say that "the Church is an object of faith, not of sight . . . a church is not a building, a budget, a program, an

[42] *Ibid.*
[43] Harvey Cox, *The Secular City* (New York: Macmillan Co., 1966), chapter 10.

organization. It is a people in motion, an 'eventful movement' in which barriers are being struck down and a radically new community beyond the divisiveness of inherited labels and stereotypes is emerging. . . ."[44]

Thereafter Cox describes the triple mission of this *laos thēou*, people of God, at the university: (1) a sacerdotal mission: "restrained reconciliation"; (2) a prophetic mission: "candid criticism"; (3) an ascetic mission: "creative disaffiliation."[45] The Church, as agent of the reconciliation brought by Christ, bears the responsibility of making its influence felt at all the critical conjunctures in the life of the university.

In view of the fact that the gospel does not constitute an ideology similar in outline to others, the reconciliation which the Church will bring about cannot be termed a conversion, but rather a liberation of persons such as permits them to live together *in spite of* ideological, theological, and political differences—"as men with men."

Insofar as it is an establishment devoted to intellectual pursuits, the university has a mission of critical importance to fulfill in the evolution of society. Similarly, the chosen people of God, by virtue of their prophetic mission, are entitled to criticize both the university and the churches. This criticism, however, should not be adolescent, negative, or demanding, but should bear the imprint of positive and committed spirits— "creative criticism," in a word. Furthermore, this criticism should stimulate the university to accomplish its aim. "We must," says Cox, "challenge the university to be the university."[46] In addition, those Christians attached to a university community constitute the intellectual elite of the Church. In consequence, they must be regarded as a kind of lay theologian whose duty it is to offer "the critical support and correction of the community of faith."[47]

Because the universities are generally burdened today with extensive plant facilities which constitute, in reality, formid-

---

[44] *Ibid.*, pp. 225–226.
[45] *Ibid.*, p. 227.
[46] *Ibid.*, p. 228.
[47] *Ibid.*, p. 229.

able obstacles (such as isolation and conservatism) to the successful prosecution of their proper aim, the people of God has sometimes to disentangle itself from them so that the Church might remain what it is.

Cox concludes the chapter by insisting upon the fact that the organizational church, in contradistinction to the "church of faith," must remain outside the "main lines of the Reformation tradition in theology and ecclesiology."[48] I am of the opinion that Harvey Cox's observations upon the relationship between Church and university deserve serious examination on the part of all Catholic thinkers interested in these matters.

But in view of all that has been said, two conclusions can be drawn. First, it is quite clear that the Church requires the assistance of the human reason as much for the scientific investigation of the revealed data as for the transmission—in a scientific form—of its tradition of faith. To play such a role adequately, the Church has need—amongst other institutions—of faculties of theology and research centers which would bring together researchers in all the disciplines and of all faiths. Needless to say, the local churches would do well to display a real interest in these centers, by having them propose solutions, for instance, to the problems encountered by the churches in the discharge of their functions. Evidently, such research centers need not be identical with the numerous Catholic universities already known to us, though it must be understood that a Catholic university can achieve the rank of a first-rate research center.

Secondly there is no denying that the Church has a role to play at the university. She has to maintain a visible presence in the world because she has the "sacrament of salvation" within her keep; the task of redemption, reconciliation, and sanctification which is carried out within the university community is exclusively hers to accomplish. Further, not only has she to exert influence upon the university personnel, but she also has to make the impact of her teaching felt upon the policies and research of the university as a whole.

48 *Ibid.*, p. 235.

Though it be true that the Church can exert substantial influence upon the university community without either owning or administering universities herself, it is nonetheless incontestable that a university which is professedly Catholic affords the Church a better means of making its presence felt in the field of higher learning, and of ensuring, too, that her teaching will preserve at once its consistency and continuity.

Reflections on Newman's *Idea*

GEORGE N. SHUSTER*

One hundred and fifteen years ago, John Henry Newman published a volume entitled *Discourses on University Education,* which consisted of public addresses given on the occasion of his becoming rector of the newly created Catholic University of Ireland. This he followed, five years later, with another publication, entitled *Lectures and Essays on University Subjects.* The two were edited and what was then called "refined," and were published in 1873 as *The Idea of a University.*

Since that time so much has been written about education that offhand one might ask: Who would so much as dream of reading even the major part of it? Why then does this book still crop up wherever there is serious discussion of the university? Every reader is likely to have his own reasons, and I shall take the liberty of giving my own.

First, the major principles which the author seeks to expound are those which higher education must always consider; otherwise there would be no adequate reason why it should exist. Second, there are so many things in the book that the

* I regret that in the quite personal paper which follows virtually no effort is made to consider the character of university education in countries other than the United States. Such an effort would have involved extraordinary difficulties. On the one hand, documents such as the Franks Report on Oxford would have had to be considered with the requisite care, and on the other hand it would have been necessary to go deeply into the current discussion of German university reform. The result could only have been the torso of a volume. Land O'Lakes would not have been the right place to read that kind of book, even if I had been able to write it.

reader knows that everytime he looks at it again he can always find something new, something he did not really notice before. And third, it is written with more sophistication than one expects of a treatise on education. There are very few authors of whom that can be said—Whitehead certainly, Spranger and Scheler probably, Hutchins and Maritain maybe.

I have elsewhere summarized the major themes or principles which *The Idea of a University* presents and shall therefore quote myself:

> *Newman held that a university could not profess to be the exponent of universal knowledge unless it had a Faculty of Theology; that the purpose of "liberal education," the primary business of the university, is neither to inculcate virtue nor to prepare for a vocation, but rather to train the mind; that the values served by such mental training are not absolute but are none the less good in themselves; and that the inculcation of a philosophic temper is of great service to society.*[1]

We shall now try to define what Newman meant by these terms. As is well known, he did not suggest that religion in its essence is ecclesiology or even Christianity, though of course he does not neglect these. He took the universal concern of all great religions with the reality, attributes, and power of God to constitute the essence of theology. This he believed to be "concise and persistent in its intellectual structure."

Newman concludes his discourse on the "Bearing of Theology on Other Knowledge" by saying:

> *. . . if this science, even as human reason may attain to it, has such claims on the regard, and enters so variously into the objects, of the professor of universal knowledge, how can any Catholic imagine that it is possible for him to cultivate philosophy and science with due attention to their ultimate end, which is truth, supposing that system of revealed facts and principles, which constitutes the Catholic*

---

[1] John Henry Cardinal Newman, *The Idea of a University* (Garden City, N.Y.: Doubleday-Image, 1959), p. 30. Introduction by George N. Shuster.

faith, which goes so far beyond nature, and which he knows to be most true, be omitted from among the subjects of his teaching?[2]

The converse, he said, is also true. Human nature has an ingrained urge to speculate, to imagine, create and establish individuality. But if a man proceeds to indulge this urge without bearing in mind that God remains always the core of the drama of life, he will end up on the one hand by making his art or his knowledge no longer a servant to revealed truth, but an autonomous god serving his purpose.

For god of some kind, *summum bonum* of some kind, he must have. Men who draw the boundary line of their autonomous science or art so rigidly that God is left outside "teach what in its place is true, though when out of its place, perverted or carried to excess, is not true. And as every man has not the capacity of separating truth from falsehood, they persuade the world of what is false by urging upon it what is true."

In short, Newman argues that if theology be absent from the university, other sciences will usurp its throne. "The human mind cannot," he says, "keep from speculating and systematizing; and if theology is not allowed to occupy its own territory an adjacent science, nay sciences which are quite foreign to theology, will take posession of it." In other words, the *Wesensschau* of the human intelligence will then look at the landscape, its hills and valleys, without taking into account the sun.

We come now to the most famous of Newman's assertions about education. First, it serves liberal learning by creating a place, a university, in which all the branches of knowledge are professed and cultivated. No man can, to be sure, pursue them all. But their presence instills a "philosophic temper" in the student. "He profits by an intellectual tradition, which is independent of particular teachers, which guides him in his choice of subjects, and duly interprets for him those which he chooses. He apprehends the great outlines of knowledge, the principles on which it rests, the scale of its parts, its lights and its shades,

[2] *Ibid.*, pp. 102–103.

the great points and its little, as he otherwise cannot apprehend them. Hence it is that his education is called 'liberal'."

But the argument that this liberal education produces neither virtue nor skill in utilitarian pursuits cannot be controverted. Men are sometimes more virtuous when they leave the university than they were when they entered, but often they are not. We should therefore cheerfully admit that the university exists only for its own sake, which is to be committed to "liberal" studies and to the inculcation of the philosophic temper. In order to progress in virtue, the student must seek out another rigorous discipline, which will make him unselfish in the presence of "those giants, the passion and the pride of man."

This is heady enough doctrine, but Newman's thought is still more subtle on the subject of the values—real though not absolute—of liberal education. Justice certainly cannot be done to it by excerpting this or that part of the argument, but we can point out that education—as Newman thinks of it—is very hard work, and that perhaps its major service to virtue is a special kind of discipline. He says:

> *I say, then, if we would improve the intellect, first of all we must ascend; we cannot gain real knowledge on a level; we must generalize, we must reduce to method, we must have a grasp of principles and group and shape our acquisitions by means of them. It matters not if our field of operations be wide or limited; in every case, to command it is to mount above it.*[3]

He is very critical of every kind of higher education which is false to this injunction. One must not get lost in the pursuit of associations of ideas through overtaxing the memory. We must not call "stuffing birds or playing stringed instruments" education. For "education is a high word; preparation for knowledge, and it is the imparting of knowledge in proportion to that preparation. We require intellectual eyes to know withal, as bodily eyes for sight. We need both objects and organs intellectual; we cannot gain them without setting about it; we cannot gain them in our sleep or haphazard."

[3] *Ibid.,* pp. 160–161.

Third, this education which produces the "philosophic temper" can be of benefit to civil and ecclesiastical society. I shall
not undertake to examine the argument as a whole, but shall
content myself with quoting in full the famous passage on
education and the Church:

> . . . *we see at once a momentous benefit which the phi-*
> *losopher is likely to confer on pastors of the Church. It is*
> *obvious that the first step which they have to effect in the*
> *conversion of man and the renovation of his nature is his*
> *rescue from that fearful subjection to sense which is his*
> *ordinary state. To be able to break through the meshes*
> *of that thraldom and to disentangle and disengage its ten*
> *thousand holds upon the heart, is to bring it, I must almost*
> *say, halfway to Heaven. Here, even divine grace, to speak*
> *of things according to their appearances, is ordinarily baf-*
> *fled and retires, without expedient or resource, before this*
> *giant fascination. Religion seems too high and unearthly*
> *to be able to exert a continued influence upon us: its effort*
> *to rouse the soul, and the soul's effort to co-operate, are too*
> *violent to last. It is like holding out the arm at full length,*
> *or supporting some great weight, which we manage to do*
> *for a time, but soon are exhausted and succumb. Nothing*
> *can act beyond its own nature; when we are called to*
> *what is supernatural, though those extraordinary aids from*
> *Heaven are given us, with which obedience becomes pos-*
> *sible, yet even with them it is of transcendent difficulty.*
> *We are drawn down to earth every moment with the ease*
> *and certainty of a natural gravitation, and it is only by*
> *sudden impulses, and, as it were, forcible plunges that we*
> *attempt to mount upwards.*
>
> *Religion indeed enlightens, terrifies, subdues; it gives*
> *faith, it inflicts remorse, it inspires resolutions, it draws*
> *tears, it inflames devotion, but only for the occasion. I re-*
> *peat, it imparts an inward power which ought to effect*
> *more than this; I am not forgetting either the real suffi-*
> *ciency of its aids, nor the responsibility of those in whom*
> *they fail. I am not discussing theological questions at all,*
> *I am looking at phenomena as they lie before me, and I say*

*that, as a matter of fact, the sinful spirit repents, and pro-
tests it will never sin again, and for a while is protected
by disgust and abhorrence from the malice of its foe. But
that foe knows too well that such reasons of repentance are
wont to have their end: he patiently waits, till nature faints
with the effort of resistance, and lies passive and hopeless
under the next access of temptation. What we need then
is so expedient an instrument, which at least will obstruct
and stave off the approach of our spiritual enemy, and
which is sufficiently congenial and level with our nature
to maintain as firm a hold on us as the inducement of sen-
sual gratification. It will be our wisdom to employ nature
against itself.*

*Thus sorrow, sickness and care are providential antago-
nists to our inward disorders; they come upon us as the
years pass on, and generally produce their natural effects
on us, in proportion as we are subjected to their influence.
These, however, are God's instruments, not ours; we need
a similar remedy, which we can make our own, the object
of some legitimate faculty, or the aim of some natural affection, which is capable of resting on the mind, and taking up its familiar lodging with it, and engrossing it, and
which thus becomes a match for the beastly power of sensuality, and a sort of homeopathic remedy for the disease.
Here then I think is the important aid which intellectual
cultivation furnishes to us in rescuing the victims of passion and self-will. It does not supply religious motives; it
is not the cause or proper antecedent of anything supernatural; it is not meritorious of heavenly aid or reward;
but it does a work, at least* materially *good (as theologians
speak), whatever be its real and formal character. It expels
the excitements of sense by the introduction of those of
the intellect.*

*This then is the prima-facie advantage of the pursuit of
knowledge; it is the drawing of the mind off from things
which will harm it to subjects which are worthy a rational
being; and, though it does not raise it above nature, nor
has any tendency to make us pleasing to our Maker, yet is*

it nothing to substitute what is in itself harmless for what is, to say the least, inexpressibly dangerous? Is it a little thing to exchange a circle of ideas which are certainly sinful, for others which are certainly not so? You will say, perhaps, in the words of the Apostle, "Knowledge puffeth up;" and doubtless this mental cultivation, even when it is successful for the purpose for which I am applying it, may be from the first nothing more than the substitution of pride for sensuality. I grant it. . . .[4]

There is much else in the book, but here I shall isolate only a recurrent theme which is "academic freedom," though the term is nowhere used in it. Of course Newman is not using it in some of the pragmatic senses currently emphasized by the academic fraternity. That is, he does not lay down the conditions under which employment may be terminated, or discuss the requirements for promotion. But his stance in all such matters is that traditionally adopted at Oxford—which university he was of course seeking to transfer to Dublin—with the difference that a Catholic faculty of theology would occupy much the same place in it as did the Oxford Movement in the great school of learning which it served.

Nevertheless Newman's concept of liberty of learning within the framework of a Catholic institution is illustrated on almost every page of *The Idea of a University*. To be sure, as I shall try to emphasize later on, his implicit definitions of Catholic theology are more precise in outline than they probably can be for us of the present.

And so, with a sincere tribute to his farsighted and imaginative treatment of the liberty which the pursuit of learning no doubt requires, I shall begin my discussion of what may no longer be helpful in Newman's book with some consideration of the role of theological studies in a free-wheeling Catholic university of our day.

I shall start with an account of a brief conversation I had with a Notre Dame student while walking across the campus. He was writing a senior essay in theology. The subject was a compari-

[4] *Ibid.,* pp. 197–199.

son between the journals of Kierkegaard and the autobiography of Dag Hammerskjöld. This seems a fairly typical concern.

As a consequence of the vast improvement which has taken place in Catholic secondary schools and colleges, as well as of the impact of the literature produced by scholars in secular universities, literate young Catholic men and women were quite ready to accept the heady conclusions of the Vatican II, while many of their elders (including the clergy) often lived—still live —in a state of shock. It would be a mistake, indeed, to assume that they do not wish to be good Catholics and fervent Christians—though they often make what seems to me an untenable distinction between the two. But they are persuaded that they are much farther along the road to meaningful theological insight than are the clergy and even the hierarchy; and until these are presumed to have caught up with the procession, there will be a feeling of tension which can too easily be interpreted in terms of disrespect. And it may well be that this tension will have serious consequences, not indeed in terms of what might too easily be defined as orthodoxy, but in terms of the reverent courtesy which the teaching authority should elicit.

No young Catholic scholar of our time would, I believe, find it interesting to comment on this or that proposition of Garrigou-Lagrange. But the best of them will be persuaded that it is exceedingly worthwhile to contemplate Catholic and Christian responses to the great Hegelian revolution which swept over the universities of the Western world—responses, that is, which are contemporary and not traditional. The Catholic avant-garde is everywhere Augustinian in the sense that it contemplates a quite personal concern with the erosion of three centuries of thinking, which was on the one hand idealistic and on the other perenially philosophical of outlook.

Nor would they agree with Newman that intellectual pursuits have no "tendency to make us pleasing to our Maker." They have been too strongly influenced by more modern thinkers—Teilhard de Chardin and Gabriel Marcel, for example— to make that kind of cleavage between the pursuit of knowledge and the pursuit of virtue. Yet if they do not do so, one of the basic assumptions of Newman is challenged; namely, that the purpose of the university is purely intellectual. I would myself tentatively state the matter in this way: Christian *formation* is not the business of a Christian university, but Christian *experience* is.

There is something else to be thought of when one considers the future role of theology in the university, and that is the distinction between inductive and deductive reasoning (which Newman adumbrates but does not wrestle with), simply because it springs from a later order of historic time than his. Theology remains in large part, of course, a science based on deduction. But one of the major commonplaces in contemporary university reality is the sponsorship of inductive reasoning as the avenue to truth. The first question characteristically asked is, then, "What does theology mean to me?" This must not be taken to indicate a falsely assumed autonomy of the personality. It can, as a matter of fact, be a very humble, again a very Augustinian question. But it is radically different from saying that theology posits a vade mecum of propositions and regulations one must accept because *extra Ecclesiam nulla salus*. That battle cry of a Church facing a world changed by the Reformation cannot be effective on the present scene.

I would say, then, that the role of theology in a Catholic university of our day must probably be this: it must be more "pervasive" than has normally been assumed. The humanities, for instance, (which Newman wisely called literature) are allies of theology because they contain the experience of the race, the vicarious sharing which helps greatly to make the "natural man" see what theology means. But on the other hand, theology also must be experience—above all, the experience of mankind with God, with Christ Jesus, with the Church. Personally I think that this will mean a far greater emphasis on the great saints in our treatment of the subject, and a diminished concern with Denzinger. To take a modest saint as an example, I believe that if we could have five replicas of the Curé d'Ars in this country and we could keep them away from the mass media and prevent their being written up in *Time,* we would have no reason to worry about apostasy.

We go on to consider the difference between a university's

general "shape"—to borrow a sociological term—in Newman's thought and one of our day. His was small enough, and in the best sense aristocratic enough, to make viable the concept of a universally applicable intellectual insight. Today that is no longer possible. The university is a congeries of specializations. Whether it should be this is another question, and certainly there are many who not only worry about it but try to do something about it (such as Columbia University's seminars for faculty members). We should agree, I think, with Newman in holding that a Catholic university should foster a gamut of basic disciplines. If the natural sciences and the social sciences were not taught, students might well think they were not deemed important, or that indeed the university was afraid of them. Of course one must be careful not to unduly enlarge the gamut of specialization. We all know that once we set one of them up in business it is likely to go on forever, in accordance with Parkinson's law.

For us, the concept of specialization is at any rate supreme in our thinking about the university's business. Newman's "philosophic temper" must therefore come primarily—though of course not exclusively—through absorption in a specialization. And perhaps this is one of the basic reasons why a Catholic university ought to exist. It can round out the order of perceived being revealed through a specialization—biology, for example —with another order which is especially human because it is rooted in the whole of humanity's beneficent experience with the divine.

In other words, I would equate Newman's "philosophic temper" with ontological awareness. The Catholic university (and here I am quoting something written elsewhere)[5] is the consequence of a congruence. That is, it is the coming together of men who serve the cause of learning with rigor and courtesy because they have accepted the Pascalian wager that God *is* and *exists*. Together they determine, though their own theological and philosophical experience may be quite disparate, the overall character of the institution. They are the keystones of the

[5] George N. Shuster, *Catholic Education in a Changing World* (New York: Holt, Rinehart and Winston, 1967), *passim.*

university arch. Newman's book says practically nothing about the faculty, though it does prove that he himself would have been an excellent member of any Catholic university faculty. He does state that if a university were headed the wrong way— that is, if it became a kind of cafeteria serving driblets of this or that—the only hope for the dialogue which must precede the acquisition of the philosophic temper would rest with the student body itself. And that is a sobering enough thought.

As yet, no acceptable theory of what a Catholic university faculty should be exists. No attempt to outline one will be undertaken here, no doubt to your great relief.

I will conclude with a reference to what has long seemed to me a special weakness in Newman's book. This is a relegation to the university limbo of the aesthetic experience. He assumed (doubtless again because of the time in which he lived and of his special intellectual preoccupations), that the whole world of the arts was somewhere beyond the pale. The arts were properly servants to some other endeavor, for example, the Church. But they seemed to him obstreperous servants always putting on airs. He did not much care for Pugin's obsession with the restoration of Gothic art; in this he was, of course, right. But that seems an insufficient excuse.

Still—and I think that the younger generation would often agree with me here—one cannot well expect religion to humanize rigorous intellectualism (and in his own inimitable way he explained how difficult that is), unless one concedes to the arts a comparable role, though at a lower level, of course, in the order of being. I am not, may the Lord forbid, recommending art for art's sake or eulogizing the painter as a priest. But the fact remains that the music of Bach is the first coda in which Catholic and Lutheran experience came together in harmonious union. It was the first great page in the ecumenical movement. And I submit that it is not any easier to read that page aright than it is to wrestle with Whately's logic.

But all this comment does not detract in the least from the abiding greatness of *The Idea of a University*. A great many have marveled at it, and I hope that you do, too. Perhaps we need to consider it often and carefully because of the basic difference of orientation between it and our own. The American university in our day is primarily public-service oriented. This is perhaps the result of two separate strains of educational thought which have developed during the past: one, the concept of the land grant college, which was primarily concerned with the development of technological teaching and research; and the other, that of the liaison between the university and the public domain, deemed desirable because it led out of the irovy tower into contemporaneousness.

In these, our departure from the model of the Humboldtian university found its rationale. For that university was by definition autonomous—"ivory tower." We adopted much of the German program for organized and specialized research and tried to copy the *Lehrfreiheit* and *Lernfreiheit* of the universities which sponsored that program—concepts of freedom which are applicable to research but hardly to teaching in the "liberal" sense. Newman's university seems to me Humboldtian in so far as it would isolate the university from vocational and moralistic services. But again it is not; for its commitment to the presence of theology makes it always conscious—though perhaps uneasily—of the necessary limitations of the pursuit of knowledge for its own sake. It is therefore clear that *The Idea of a University* sponsors a dialectic between intellectual pursuits and theological commitment which, it is true, is not resolved. We have not resolved it either, so that the book before us is not in every sense an end but in some senses a beginning.

A GLOSS

I shall add a gloss on two statements.

The first is quoted from the address on "Duties of the Church Towards Knowledge." Newman says ". . . physical science is in a certain sense atheistic because it is not theology."

The second is taken from "Christianity and Letters" in which Newman says: "The medieval sciences, great as is their dignity and utility, were never intended to supersede that more real and proper cultivation of the mind which is effected by the study of the liberal arts."

Newman spends a great deal of time commending the natural sciences for all that they have added (and in his mind no doubt would go on adding), to human knowledge and welfare. But he also takes cognizance of a phenomenon which was to concern him ever more deeply; namely, that the panorama which the sciences reveal to the imagination can be so rich and in a sense so seductive that the Jewish-Christian-Catholic religion, which is summarized in a single volume written long ago, will come to seem very simple, static, and moralistic. He says that in the view of the scientist, theology thus conceived lies wholly beyond the realm of experimentation. The scientists are shocked by the Catholic assumption that "God's mind is greater than theirs." But if they can "take the sacred text as a large collection of phenomena," as Protestantism does, they can arrive at religious convictions which "approve themselves" to their own judgment.

The statement is profound and the stress on the element of the imagination is one which we ought to take seriously. But he tends to reduce the documentation of theology to so sparse a doctrinal outline that it is difficult to see how he could expect that it would in turn greatly influence the imagination. He takes refuge in the fact that it had always had influence, at least over a period of time and in many societies. Perhaps for us the basic problem for the time in which we live—having seen so much of evil and repression—is that although the imagination is kindled by a need for religion, it finds the documentation which Newman adduces lacking in inspiration. For Dostoevski it was the discovery of the person of Christ which was the deciding factor, and this made the Grand Inquisitor (whom of course Newman does not commend) abhorrent. Simone Weil longed for God because He was perfection, which could be nowhere else. To what extent can we use our time, without in any way minimizing the sovereign significance of the basic structure of theological belief?

I believe that one way out of the situation lies in a consideration of what the scientist himself feels is the result of the "atheism" of his discipline. This feeling was certainly present in Einstein and Oppenheimer, Spinoza-oriented though they were. Oddly enough, Wittgenstein may have much to say here.

The second statement may seem to reflect the prejudices of a first-rate Oxford classical scholar and teacher (the piece about "Elementary Studies" is one of the most intriguing in the book). But there is more support for it in contemporary American educational reflection in the United States than one might assume, provided of course one is not thinking of the liberal arts in terms of the study of the classical languages.

One source of support for the argument is that the natural sciences, apart from their descriptive role, have become so difficult as disciplines that many find them inhumanly restrictive. The number of students who survive in a good college of science is small. Nor is it very inspiring to go through the ordinary academic routine in chemistry or physics.

Another and weightier reason is that social-ethical problems weigh so heavily on the contemporary mind. Reviewing Hazel E. Barnes' *An Existentialist Ethic in America,* Father Quentin Lauer, S.J., says: "One need not agree with all Miss Barnes' conclusions to feel the impact of her challenge to rethink traditional ethical ideals." A critic could of course legitimately say that what is happening on many campuses is "re-feeling" rather than "rethinking." But it is even so impossible to ignore the fact that the debate about "traditional ethical ideals" is the core of the discussion.

If this is so, only a liberal arts course of study can provide the depth dimension which the situation requires. Newman's definition of literature as the recorded experience of our race is accordingly as pertinent as ever. It is only this which can make clear what the "traditional ideals" have been, and how persistently they have been subjected to reexamination. But no doubt his insistence on rigorous intellectual discipline is also pertinent. A mere quantitative approach to the study of what we call the humanities results only in indigestion. But we have as yet found no satisfactory way of circumventing that approach. Some argue for a new insistence on foreign (or ancient) language study. Others would foster dialectic. At any rate Newman's concern must be ours, too.

In an Ecumenical Age

THOMAS E. AMBROGI

The widespread awakening of ecumenical sensitivities is one of the signs of the times which poses serious questions concerning the nature and role of the contemporary Catholic university. A mandate to ecumenism has been issued by Vatican II. As it begins to be implemented in all its fullness throughout the Church, the face of Catholic higher education will undergo some rather startling transformations.

To attempt to describe all the specific areas in which an ecumenical reappraisal is due would require far more space than that afforded by this paper. We should like to limit our perspectives to the distinct area of academic theology, for the department of theology would seem to be the central terrain on which the task of renewal must be worked out. What is done there by way of new orientations will have profound effects on the ecumenical horizon of other departments and on the total life of the university as a whole. For the sake of a more precise focus of discussion, therefore, we shall limit our reflections to the future of theology within the Catholic university in an ecumenical age.

The nature and role of the department of theology in the Catholic university will be influenced to an ever greater degree by two major phenomena within the contemporary scene of religious education in this country. The first phenomenon is the extraordinary proliferation of departments of religion in secular universities, both public and private, within the past decade. The second is the crisis of identity which this development has generated in the professional theological school. We shall therefore describe briefly the situation in these two areas, and then proceed to certain observations about the distinctive role of theology in the Catholic university of the future.

Religion in the American university has had a very checkered career. Both public and private institutions of higher education have reflected rather accurately all the major movements of American religious history. Yale was founded in 1701 for the purpose of promoting Christian piety. In the century which followed, distinctions between public and private control were made and the wall of separation between church and state was gradually assembled, so that when the first nonsectarian university under public auspices was founded, the University of Virginia in 1822, Thomas Jefferson felt compelled to exclude all theology from its curriculum. With the contemporary reinstatement of full-fledged departments of religion in public and private universities it would seem that we are entering into a new era, one which will more accurately reflect in higher education the maturing lines of American religious pluralism.

The increasing interest in the study of religion in American universities is a fact of enormous importance which has not yet been adequately researched and documented. Some unpublished figures, however, have been gathered by Milton McLean of Ohio State University, and were reported by Robert Michaelsen at the consultation held by the Department of Higher Education of the National Council of Churches on January 26–27, 1967. McLean found that six state and four private universities had enrollments of over 1,000 students in religion courses during 1965–66. Altogether, there were more than 13,000 enrollments in religion courses in nine state universities, and 10,000 enrollments in eleven private universities. A single course at the University of Iowa has been enrolling a thousand students a year, and there were more than 3,000 overall enrollments in religion courses at that Big Ten school. Departments or some other type of curricular program in religion have been started in recent years at such state institutions as Indiana, Illinois, Tennessee, West Virginia, Alabama, Western Michigan, Penn

State, Florida State and the University of California at Santa Barbara. The same kind of growth can be seen on many private campuses around the country. Robert McAfee Brown's course on "Theology and Contemporary Literature" enrolls students by the hundreds each year at Stanford. Religion courses attract increasing numbers at such schools as Brown, Columbia, Dartmouth, Oberlin, Yale, Princeton and the University of Pennsylvania.

These courses are not merely serving the general interest and curiosities of the undergraduate. The specialized undergraduate major is also beginning to appear, and the number of graduate programs is increasing every year. Private institutions such as Columbia, Pennsylvania and Princeton enroll significant numbers of graduate students, and at least two state universities, Iowa and Temple, are now offering a Ph.D. program in religion.

It is extremely difficult to analyze just what the present generation of students is seeking in this renewed interest in religious studies. For our purposes here, however, it is sufficient to observe that, for perhaps the first time in history, the study of religion is being widely accepted by the American university community as an academically respectable discipline, even capable of generating real intellectual enthusiasm. Full departments of religion are being established in a wide range of universities where no formal curricular provision for the study of religion could have been found a decade ago. This fact cannot help having a profound effect on the shape and mission of theology in the American Catholic university.

Before turning directly to the Catholic theological scene, it will be helpful to describe some of the tensions which have arisen in the secular university because of the establishment of academic departments of religion. The most serious of these tensions, and the one which interests us most in our considerations here, is the identity crisis which is occurring within the divinity school as a result of the acceptance of religion within the college and graduate school structure.

Religious studies (or theology in the broadest sense of the term) has been primarily the domain of the seminary in this country. It has belonged almost exclusively within the area of the professional training for the ministry. To a limited degree, this theological training of the clergy has been carried on in divinity schools attached to private universities, such as at Harvard, Yale or Chicago; but for the most part it has been done in small denominational seminaries unrelated to university structures. Theology was generally the private preserve of the clergy, and the university was more than willing to let it remain so. What was done "over there" in the seminary, or even in the professional school of divinity within the university, was somehow tolerated by the university as necessary for the professional formation of the clergyman. But it could never be allowed the full status of a legitimate academic enterprise, on an equal footing with the intellectual endeavor of the rest of the university community.

Now that the doors of the university have been opened to the study of religion, it is becoming increasingly difficult to clearly differentiate what is being done in the university departments from what is done in the professional schools of theology. A good case in point is that of Yale University. Prior to 1963, the study of religion at Yale was concentrated almost exclusively in the professional rather than the academic area. The Divinity School offered the professional B.D., S.T.M., and M.A.R. degrees. No Th.D. was offered. Yale Divinity School was, as it is now, a full professional school of the university like the schools of law and medicine, with its own dean, budget, faculty and power to call professors. Interdenominational in its church affiliations, its aims and objectives were—as they continue to be —the theological and pastoral formation of Christian ministers.

At the same time, a department of religion did exist in Yale College, responsible for undergraduate instruction in religion. Its course offerings included a broad range of subject matter rather loosely connected with the phenomenon of "religion." No parallel department existed in the Graduate School, although there was a nondepartmental faculty of religion drawn from the Divinity School, the undergraduate department of religion, the departments of Near Eastern languages, history, philosophy, and other related fields. Graduate courses offered by this faculty were acceptable in the degree programs of other departments, but a Ph.D. in religion was not offered.

In 1963, the department of religious studies was established in Yale College and Graduate School. The department exists parallel to the departments of history, English, etc., within the Division of Humanities in the Arts and Sciences faculty. It is responsible for teaching and research in religious studies both in Yale College and in the Graduate School. Besides its undergraduate courses, it offers a Ph.D. with five general areas of concentration: history of religions, biblical studies, history of Christianity, Christian ethics, and theological studies (historical, systematic, philosophical). At the present time, the department has seventeen members, of which nine are joint appointments with the Divinity School.

In terms of program content, it is somewhat difficult to distinguish many of the offerings in the graduate department of religious studies from those in the divinity school. It is true, the latter is a professional school, primarily oriented toward the training of ministers, while the former aims at training scholars specializing in any of its four areas of concentration. But outside of pastoral field work and certain emphases on practical questions of the ministry, much of the curriculum in the divinity school runs rather parallel to that in the graduate department, at least as one reads the catalogue description of courses. The difficulty of sharp identification is further pointed up by the fact that about half of the university department faculty also teaches in the divinity school. Is this simply a duplication of programs, or is there an essential difference between the kind of religious study which goes on in the professional school and in the graduate school?

This search for a definition of role in the area of religious studies is being pursued in many other institutions besides Yale. And in certain corners it has led to lengthy discussions about the future of the professional school in theological education. Given the history of American higher education, a new department of religious studies which is fully integrated into the graduate faculty of arts and sciences automatically enjoys more academic prestige from the beginning of its existence than that which has traditionally been accorded the professional school of divinity, whether related or unrelated to a university. In most cases the new department would also have access to greater budgetary resources than either the divinity school or the independent seminary has usually been able to muster. This implies, of course, an enormous advantage for the university department in the acquisition of first-rate faculty personnel.

In this regard, what is happening at Temple is to many observers a very significant straw in the wind. A few years ago, Temple University became structurally affiliated with the state school system of the Commonwealth of Pennsylvania. Up until that time its department of religion had a staff of two or three members, and religion was one of the most insignificant areas of university life. The addition of very considerable funds from the state, however, has permitted the department of religion to launch out upon a highly ambitious new program. Present plans call for a department of twenty-five professors, adequately representing all major faith traditions, including Roman Catholicism. The public financial resources now at Temple's disposition make it a formidable competitor for the limited pool of first-class theological scholars, and its ability to hire professors away from smaller seminaries and divinity schools—Catholic and non-Catholic alike—is already being felt. Likewise, the exciting new ecumenical program which it has been able to mount will quite clearly become a challenge to existing theological programs in other institutions.

The prospect of this kind of growth on a broader scale has led some to question whether the traditional divinity school or denominational seminary can possibly survive under such pressure. Is the trend such that the center of theological activity will gravitate away from the professional school and into the academic departments of the secular university? And if so, what does this imply for the future of theology as such in this country?

We would maintain that the professional school of theology will indeed remain an integral structure in American theological education. In fact, we would maintain that it simply must continue to exist, regardless of how rapidly the secular university departments develop in the future. And the reason for our contention is that the professional school is the only place within the secular university where creative systematic theology can flourish as a major commitment and discipline.

One of the few distinguishing elements of the university department of religion, as opposed to the professional school is that the former demands no commitment of faith in the religion which is taught there. Religion is treated as an objective historical and cultural phenomenon, to be taught and judged on precisely the same basis as other courses in the humanities and the social sciences. The primary emphasis in the academic department is therefore on such disciplines as comparative religion, history of religions, philosophy or anthropology of religion, historical-critical biblical studies. Ethics is generally taught far more in a historical setting than as a normative science. There is sometimes room for a limited amount of systematic theology, it is true, but this can never become the primary orientation or commitment of the department, and hence will never assume proportions of any significance in the total endeavor of the department. The university is still far too suspicious of dogmatic presuppositions to permit it to accept with equanimity the legitimacy of genuine systematic theology as an academic discipline in itself.

The professional school, on the other hand, is by definition a school of Christian theology. Its orientation toward service of the church demands of both faculty and students a Christian faith-commitment which determines essentially the type of theologizing experience which it fosters. The school of divinity may be either denominational, interdenominational, or nondenominational, but its theological research is carried on within the explicit context of the Christian revelation, and this fact is the distinguishing mark of its commitment to the theological enterprise. It is, therefore, only within this academic framework that the continuing work of creative systematic theology can be carried on, only here that "confessional" theology—in the best sense of that term—can be seriously and scientifically pursued in a university context.

Much of what has traditionally passed for systematic theology in divinity schools and seminaries, both Catholic and non-Catholic, has too often been merely confessionalistic evangelism, and not legitimate intellectual inquiry at all. "Denzinger theology" has had its counterpart in the narrowly confessional traditions of all the divided Christian churches, and it is precisely this which has tended to isolate the church-related school of theology from the world of free intellectual discourse which is the university community. There is reason to hope, however, that contemporary theology is becoming ever more sensitive to its need for academic respectability. The university's current interest in religion is certainly helping to encourage this, and broadening ecumenical perspectives are forcing a serious reappraisal of theological method within many of the Christian churches. What would seem to be needed is not the abandonment of theology to the secular university departments of religion, but rather a renewed professional theological school which will be truly ecumenical in its horizon and academically competent in its method. Only then can the future of American systematics be safeguarded and the professional school retain its legitimate place in theological education.

This brief description of the contemporary situation of religious studies in the secular university leads us to certain conclusions about the future direction of Catholic universities, and in particular about the role of theological scholarship there. In an ecumenical age, any consideration of the role of theology in the Catholic university must be essentially related to developments in theological education beyond the realm of the specifically Catholic. The contemporary religious and educational scene, therefore, can and ought to offer the Catholic university valuable insights in its continuing quest for a distinct identity. Let us first consider briefly the nature of theology as it has been traditionally found in the Catholic college and university, and then attempt to sketch certain outlines of its mission for the future.

It could seem, first of all, that an undergraduate department of "Catholic" theology, as it has existed in the Catholic liberal arts college in this country, is something of an educational anomaly. The unbiased outside educator might well be excused if he wonders whether, in principle, a professedly limited confessional theology can be the stuff of a legitimate academic discipline. In fact, a good case could be made for the academic illegitimacy of much of what the Catholic college has called theology. Our present undergraduate theology departments have evolved out of religion courses which earlier generations felt were necessary for the safeguarding and deepening of the faith of the Catholic students they were educating. Graduate courses, or even undergraduate majors, were never a consideration for lay students. Academic theology, in so far as it was done, was done in pontifical faculties, the exclusive preserve of ecclesiastics. All professors in our religion or theology departments were not only Catholic, but clerics. The college curriculum was therefore an adapted version of the tractate curriculum which these priests had experienced in seminary, with all the limitations thereof. Our method was primarily evangelical or catechetical, and our purpose was essentially to hand on the "tradition"—every last word of it—so that we might produce adult Catholics well-informed about their faith. Without underestimating certain positive values which might have been realized in such an indoctrinating system, it does not seem too severe to say that it was not academically respectable theology which was being done, and that, generally speaking, no one seemed to care that it was not.

But the experience of Vatican II has spurred a remarkable renewal in Catholic theological scholarship. It is in the Roman Catholic world that much of the most penetrating and exciting theology is being done today. The death-of-God theologian, Thomas J. J. Altizer, recently acknowledged this fact in a colloquium at Catholic University on "The Problem of God in Contemporary Thought." "In the United States, at least," Altizer asserted, "and perhaps in the world at large, Catholic theology is passing through a revolutionary transformation, and one which has no real counterpart in either past or present forms of Protestant theology". This vital renewal is evident to anyone who attempts to keep even barely abreast of the most significant theological literature as it appears. In its methodology, in the depth of its scholarship, in the relevance of the problems it is asking, Catholic scholarship is assuming a significance which it has rarely enjoyed in the past. This new impetus is certainly being felt in the theology which is being taught in most Catholic seminaries. It is also being felt in Catholic colleges and universities, where graduate departments of theology are finally beginning to appear and the scholarly quality of undergraduate offerings seems generally to be improving.

To us, this total situation appears to be placing the Catholic university in this country in a position of extraordinary challenge and promise. For the first time in our history, the conditions of possibility exist whereby theology can be genuinely integrated into the academic center of the Catholic university enterprise. As we indicated in the first part of this paper, the current tension between professional and academic religious studies within the secular university grows out of a basic historic presupposition in American higher education that systematic theology, precisely because it demands a faith-commitment of its practitioners, cannot be accepted as an equal partner in the scholarly dialogue of the university community. We would submit that the disproving of this thesis is the most distinctive and challenging mission of the Catholic university of the future. The discipline of Catholic theology will continue to deepen the foundations of intellectual prestige which it is now slowly establishing. The traditional acceptance of theology within the institutional framework of the Catholic university means that there are no a priori barriers to its exercising a position of academic influence there. What is now required is that contemporary Catholic theological insight be allowed to take possession of the academic structures of the Catholic university, both graduate and undergraduate.

The mission of Catholic higher education at this moment in its history is to demonstrate to the American university community that "confessional" systematic theology can indeed be a respectable academic enterprise. In order to do this, however, we shall have to move decisively out of the enclosed horizon of the exclusively Catholic tradition and incorporate the ecumenical vision of the total Christian revelation into the very substance of our theologizing activity. We shall have to accept on a broad scale the conviction of Vatican II that all theology is by definition ecumenical theology. The theologizing community within the Catholic university will be deeply rooted in the Catholic tradition, but its works will have to be far more than sophisticated catechesis in that tradition. Its task will be scholarly inquiry into all the profound depths and nuances of the Christian revelation in its meaning for modern man, and this in conscious and sustained dialogue with all the theological traditions of the divided Christian churches. It will have to demonstrate that the more Catholic theology becomes ecumenically catholic, the more authentically Christian it becomes.

The practical implications for implementing this ideal are many and varied, undoubtedly too complex to be described in detail at this point. We shall have to discover many of them in the very process of launching out upon the commitment. Our theology departments will have to be broadened to include professors of various Christian denominations, as well as theologians representing non-Christian traditions. A similar breadth of vision will have to be exercised in the recruitment of scholars in the various disciplines which are related to theology. Depending upon circumstances, a positive effort may be required to attract other than Catholic students, in order to create a sufficiently ecumenical variety of religious backgrounds within the student body. And all of this will have to be done not in token gestures, but in a substantial and permanent institutional commitment. The dialogic nature of genuine ecumenical theology will require living voices in scholarly confrontation all across the pluralistic university community.

Many educators are noting with increasing alarm that Catholic universities seem to be rushing to conform almost completely to the ideal of the excellent secular university, instead of working through the painful analytic process of articulating a goal and a style which would make them unique. As the trend toward greater secularization of the Catholic university continues, the inclination may grow strong to abandon our departments of Catholic theology in favor of more fashionable departments of religion along the secular pattern, where less and less systematic theology would be done and more and more of the so-called "objective" study of religion. Such a capitulation would be to miss a privileged moment in the history of Catholic higher education. The ideal of the great Catholic university of the future is not simply to approach ever more closely the "Harvard image." A major element in the distinct identity of the Catholic institution should be its commitment to the integration of creative systematic theology into the academic structure of the university. The realization of this precise function is both possible and highly desirable. It could have far-reaching effects, both on the future of theological scholarship and on the role of theology in the academic world at large.

The International Dimension

JOHN E. WALSH, C.S.C.

That the vast majority of universities in America and elsewhere throughout the world are rapidly becoming much more international in outlook, in spirit, in courses and programs offered, in geographical areas studied, and in international exchange of faculty and students is—of course—commonplace. Even now there is probably no university of consequence in the world that does not have nationals of other countries among its faculty members and its students.

In the United States, for example, the International Education Act of 1966 highlighted the maturing of public concern for international education. Robert Hutchins has recently pointed out that "nothing is more certain than that the Americans of the future must be citizens of the world and that the great universities of the future must be world universities."[1] Both the nature of the times and the nature of the university itself demand that this should be the case.

If it is true that international education has always been a proper and necessary concern of every great university and that it is even more true today, is there anything special or distinguishing to be said about the international dimension of the Catholic university as Catholic? In other words, is the Catholic university any more international, or international in a differ-

---

[1] Robert M. Hutchins, "The University and the Multiversity," *The New Republic* 156 (April 1, 1967), pp. 15–16.

ent way than other kinds of universities might be? Does the
Catholic university have certain opportunities and responsibilities in international education that other universities do not
have? It is the purpose of this paper to explore these basic
questions and to propose some tentative answers.

A discussion of the international dimension of the Catholic
university must begin, of course, with a brief consideration of
what is meant by the term, "Catholic university." For the purposes of this paper, the overly simplified operational statement
that a Catholic university is a university which identifies itself
as, or considers itself to be, Catholic will suffice. (This kind of
statement will not be surprising if one considers that after all
these years, the best definition of a nation still is "a body of
people who feel they are a nation.") Of course it is a distinct
possibility that a university might consider itself a Catholic
university and not be one, in keeping with any commonly
agreed on description of what a Catholic university ought to
be. Clearly the Catholic character of a university has much
more to do with the goals, aspirations, spirit, and the leitmotiv
of the university than with the juridical control of the university. Importantly, too, in the context of this paper, it is quite
possible that an understanding of the international dimension
of the Catholic university will contribute in no small way to
what might be a better philosophical understanding of what
the Catholic university is in itself.

Since, then, a Catholic university is one in which the members of the university (i.e., the students, faculty, alumni, and
administration) consider themselves either part of, or in basic
sympathy with, the Catholic Church and its educational mission, an earlier or further question would have to be asked.
What does it mean to be a Catholic? Presumably the Catholic
is one who fully and freely accepts and affirms the essential
teachings of the Catholic Church, not necessarily as finished
formulae but certainly as wellsprings of life and sources of
grace. Among these essential teachings, of course, are the doctrines of the corporate unity in Christ of all mankind, the dignity and indestructibility of the human spirit redeemed by

Christ, the primacy of love and charity in man's relationships with his fellow men, and the transcendence of God as the source and end of all creation. The Christian God is clearly not a nationalistic God. The individual Catholic, the Catholic Church and *a fortiori*, the Catholic universities are not limited in their concerns by nationalistic, territorial, or even cultural boundaries.

Nowhere is the universality of the church's concern—i.e., its supra-nationalistic purpose and outlook—more beautifully expressed than in the opening paragraphs of the document of Vatican II entitled, Pastoral Constitution on the Church in the Modern World. For example:

> *Therefore the Council focuses its attention on the world of man, the whole human family along with the sum of those realities in the midst of which that family lives. It gazes upon the theatre of man's history, and carries the marks of his energies, his tragedies, and his triumphs; that world which the Christian sees as created and sustained by its Maker's love, fallen indeed into the bondage of sin, yet emancipated now by Christ.*

Consider, too:

> *The Council brings to mankind light kindled from the gospel, and puts at its disposal those saving resources which the Church herself, under the guidance of the Holy Spirit, receives from her Founder. For the human person deserves to be preserved; human society deserves to be renewed. Hence the pivotal point of our total presentation will be man himself, whole and entire, body and soul, heart and conscience, mind and will.*

> *It (the Council) offers to mankind the honest assistance of the church in fostering that brotherhood of all men which corresponds to this destiny of theirs. Inspired by no earthly ambition, the Church seeks but a solitary goal: to carry forward the work of Christ Himself under the lead of the befriending Spirit. And Christ entered this world to*

give witness to the truth, to rescue and not to sit in judg-
ment, to serve and not to be served.[2]

That international education is of great concern to the
Church is obvious. But what exactly is it, and what does it
seek to accomplish? (*Intercultural education* would be a much
more appropriate term than *international education* but the
latter has wider general acceptance in both scholarly and popular circles.) There are many kinds and degrees of international
education and, of course, both informal and systematic efforts
in international education are not new by any means. Broadly
stated, education is that process by which knowledge, skills, and
attitudes are discovered and transmitted. International education is simply the process by which these things are done across,
between, or among different nations and cultures.

But whatever its form or level, the heart of the problem
of international education is the differences and similarities
among cultures in the basic ways of viewing man, life, the
world, society, and God. There is, for example, very little problem or difficulty when physicists or mathematicians of one
country or culture assist in the education of physicists or
mathematicians in another culture. Physics and mathematics
are clearly recognized as international or non-national. There
could well be the prior cultural problem of whether the host
country wants the assistance of physicists and mathematicians
and what importance it puts on this assistance, but once that is
decided, the physicists and mathematicians can communicate
fairly easily with one another. Similarly, for example, there is
little problem in UNESCO's International Program in Fundamental Education. Such is not the case, however, when the content of education involves ideas about, or attitudes toward,
theology, philosophy, the humanities, or even the social sciences—all disciplines which lead to or entail a strong value
commitment or judgment.

[2] Pastoral Constitution on the Church in the Modern World, *The Documents
of Vatican II,* ed. Walter M. Abbott, S.J. (New York: The America Press, 1966),
pp. 200–201.

Chancellor Samuel B. Gould of the State University of New York, has pointed out that, "International education, in spite of its growth, still has many weaknesses and temptations to overcome".[3] There is good evidence that the main weakness and the main temptation in international or intercultural education is that, in the absence of a comprehensive theory of international education which attempts to delineate its immediate and long range objectives, many of those persons most involved in it do not regard it as subject to the same principles which apply to all education. If international education is to be worthy of the name education and not simply a collecting of interesting facts for comparative purposes, it must be open to the kinds of methodological precision, analysis, generalization, criticism, and evaluation that prevails in all other types of education. International education ought not to be the same thing as international consciousness or awareness, although these elements would be the beginning stages of it.

International education in the twentieth century, on the other hand, should not be regarded as a separate discipline in and for itself. Rather the international or intercultural dimension or perspective is an integral and essential part of every discipline. Of course there are degrees of depth and generality in any discipline, and no man can be expected to know everything about each and every discipline. For example, the Chinese economist has a very limited and inaccurate view of economics if he has confined his studies to the Chinese economics system and has not seen this system as part of a worldwide study of economics. Similarly, the western theologian who has never concerned himself with the theological systems of the East can hardly be said to have explored his discipline; i.e., the study of God in its international or intercultural dimension. In the same way, the study of the law which does not include the study of the legal principles that govern the relationships between and among nations cannot be said to be adequate in an age in which nations are so close and accessible.

---

[3] Chancellor Samuel B. Gould, address at the twenty-second National Conference on Higher Education, sponsored by the Association for Higher Education, Chicago, March 7, 1967.

The most common strategy for strengthening international education in both research and instruction in the United States is the development of interdisciplinary "area studies" programs in our colleges and universities. These have been of immense value in gathering data and furthering understanding. Ordinarily, the college or university selects one or more geographical areas or regions on which it can concentrate its intellectual power and its financial resources. Frequently, too, these programs offer work at the undergraduate level as well as at the graduate and advanced research level.

Sir Eric Ashby summarizes much of the thinking behind area studies programs and many other forms of international education when he writes, "To have some knowledge of the culture of one quite different race will be regarded as an integral part of a liberal education, on the ground that every highly educated citizen in a nation with great international responsibilities must have an accurate awareness of one pattern of living apart from his own."[4]

Against this necessarily sketchy background, what is to be said specifically of the Catholic university and its role in international education, or what might be called its international dimension?

It is the thesis of this paper that the Catholic university is in a unique position to help carry international education to its fullest strength and significance at each of the three levels at which international education must function. The first of these is the level of simple international awareness. The second is the understanding of the concept and nature of culture. The third, and most difficult of all, is the level of evaluation and judgment.

Frequently the purposes of international education are stated, as Sir Eric Ashby wrote in the foregoing quotation, as the developing of an "accurate awareness" of a pattern of living apart from one's own. In other contexts this same idea is stated as the search for a greater understanding and appreciation of other

[4] Sir Eric Ashby, *Burglars Under the Bed: Personal Reflections on Government and Higher Education in America* (Aspen Institute for Humanistic Studies, "Man in 1980"), paper no. 2, p. 14.

peoples as part of man's unending quest for knowledge about whatever falls within his experience. Sometimes international education is said to be the basis of world peace and prosperity and the instrument of international cooperation and world trade. Such statements of the objectives and purposes of international education (and others that might be added to them) are good in themselves, but they are in fact first level purposes. To be integral and genuine, international education must come to pass far beyond international awareness, no matter how accurate. At this level it is still possible for some Americans—for example, even those who have a fairly extensive awareness of various world cultures—to naively classify most foreigners as "underdeveloped Americans." Such an attitude is reminiscent of that of the minor theologian in the Middle Ages who pointed to God's wise husbandry in letting the rain fall on the fertile valleys and plains rather than on the desert where it would be wasted.

The Catholic university, by reason of its very Catholicity, is concerned with man and with the human condition everywhere. At its best it knows no national boundaries, although it has a profound respect for local customs and traditions as expressing man's individuality and personality. Man is a citizen of the world but he is also a citizen of the primary groups on whom he most immediately depends and with whom he most closely associates. As such, the Catholic university enters the forum of international or intercultural education not without loyalties, but with openness and without fear; and with a set of supranationalistic values, judgments and standards which it offers to peoples of all cultures and which it uses in assessing other ideas and values. Neither the Catholic university nor the individual Catholic scholar starts from the assumption that all cultural patterns are equally good, worthwhile, enriching, or humanly fulfilling. The point is that only because the Catholic university has a system of thought and belief to which it adheres can it take its legitimate place in all international and intercultural discussions. It offers a starting point from which fruitful international education and intercultural dialogue can begin. It represents, as one way of stating it, a theology and a theory of man and culture which is open to all to examine and evaluate. It does not ask anyone who does not want to do so or have reason to do so to accept its basic teachings. But at the same time it does not hesitate to present its credentials and to advance its evidence.

In 1934, Rabindranath Tagore wrote, "In India what is needed more than anything else, is the broad mind which, only because it is conscious of its vigorous individuality, is not afraid of accepting truth from all sources."[5] He continues:

> *I have come to feel that the mind which has been ma-*
> *tured in the atmosphere of a profound knowledge of its*
> *own country, and of the perfect thoughts that have been*
> *produced in that land, is ready to accept and assimilate the*
> *cultures that come from foreign countries. He who has no*
> *wealth of his own can only beg, and those who are com-*
> *pelled to follow the profession of beggary at the gate of the*
> *intellectually rich may gain occasional scraps of mental*
> *food, but they are sure to lose the strength of their intel-*
> *lectual character and their minds are doomed to become*
> *timid in thought and creative endeavor.*[6]

It may seem somewhat strange to draw on the thought of an Indian philosopher, poet, and mystic in an attempt to clarify the role of the Catholic university in international education. Yet in speaking of and for India, Tagore has touched excellently on a fundamental and essential point of all deeper level international or intercultural education. The Catholic university has a distinctive role in international education precisely because it is conscious of its own vigorous individuality and because it is not afraid of accepting truth from all sources. Precisely because the Catholic university has been matured in the atmosphere of a profound knowledge of its own ideas and values, is it ready to consider, accept, and assimilate ideas and values that come from other cultures. It is precisely because the

---

[5] Rabindranath Tagore, *International Education: A Documentary History*, ed. David G. Scanlon (Columbia University, N. Y.: Bureau of Publications, Teachers College, 1960), p. 113.

[6] *Ibid.*, p. 114.

Catholic university is intellectually rich that it need not be timid in thought and creative endeavor. In short, if there is any one field in which the Catholic university should assume a natural leadership it is in the field of international education.

The objection has often been advanced that the Catholic university represents a closed system of thought and that in intercultural discussion or international education it presents final uncompromising answers rather than open hypotheses. In one sense this is true. As long as it remains a Catholic university it cannot abdicate its commitment to the essential teachings of the Catholic Church. If it did so, it would obviously cease to be a Catholic university. But a Catholic university is a community of individual scholars and students, each contributing to the pursuit of the purposes and ideals of the university and each examining and testing for himself the faith which he holds and his reasons for doing so. Each scholar and student comes to the Catholic university out of his own convictions and free choices. If, in following his primary intellectual responsibility to pursue the truth as he sees it, from whatever source, he arrives at conclusions unacceptable to the Catholic Church and the Catholic university, he has no choice but to follow his conscience. His human dignity and his intellectual integrity require him to do so. This point is made abundantly clear in the document of Vatican II entitled, Declaration on Religious Freedom:

> *Truth, however, is to be sought after in a manner proper to the dignity of a human person and his social nature. The inquiry is to be free, carried on with the aid of teaching or instruction, communication and dialogue. In the course of these, men explain to one another the truth they have discovered, or think they have discovered, in order thus to assist one another in the quest for truth. Moreover, as the truth is discovered, it is by personal assent that men are to adhere to it.*

> *On his part, man perceives and acknowledges the imperatives of the divine law through the mediation of conscience. In all his activity a man is bound to follow his con-*

science faithfully, in order that he may come to God, for whom he was created. It follows that he is not to be forced to act in a manner contrary to his conscience. Nor, on the other hand, is he to be restrained from acting in accordance with his conscience, especially in matters religious.[7]

The Catholic university, in the service of genuine international education as well as in the service of the Church itself, is in a most advantageous position to do precisely what Brock Chisholm, a distinguished psychiatrist and former director-general of the World Health Organization says must be done; namely, "to reexamine all of the attitudes of our ancestors and to select from those things which we, on our own authority in these present circumstances, with our knowledge, recognize as still valid in this new kind of world."[8]

With remarkable clarity, Vatican II has shown the Church's willingness "to reexamine all of the attitudes of our ancestors" and to enter into dialogue with all religions and all peoples on all the subjects of the most profound importance to all men. The Catholic Church and the Catholic university are willing to accept the truth from whatever source and to attempt to see all things in their true perspectives and relationships to one another.

The second level at which international education necessarily functions, and to which the Catholic university can make a distinctive contribution, is the level of understanding the concept and the dynamics of culture. Though it is important to know *what* other persons and other cultures think (first level), it is even more crucial to come to an understanding of *why* they think as they do. The Catholic university, by reason of its openness and its broadness—because it comes to the intellectual community not as a beggar (to use Tagore's word), but with a position and a tradition—is most free to explore the "whys" of the various world cultures.

---

[7] Declaration on Religious Freedom, *The Documents of Vatican II,* ed. Walter M. Abbott, S.J. (New York: The America Press, 1966), pp. 680–681.

[8] Dr. Brock Chisholm, quoted by Senator J. William Fulbright in "The University and American Foreign Policy," *Vista* II, 5 (March–April, 1967), 4.

This is not the place to discuss in detail the nature of culture or the many different ways in which that word is defined and interpreted. In this context it must be understood that the word "culture" is taken in its broadest sense and that the concept of culture is the key idea in much of modern sociology and most of modern anthropology. The fact is that there are at present many different ways of organizing life, of thinking, and of perceiving and conceiving the basic assumptions about all of the important things in life; i.e., religion, the family, the state, the economic system, and even of man and the meaning of man himself. To be illuminating in itself and productive of new hypotheses any good theory of international education would have to draw heavily on the insights and principles already known to the students of culture. One simple example will suffice at this point. The anthropologists tell us that in Japan emotion or feeling is ranked very high. On the other hand, logic, as it is known and understood in the West, is not highly valued by the Japanese. It is important for international education not only that one be aware of the fact that emotion or feeling in Japan is highly valued; one must try to discover *why* it is highly valued and why, conversely, logic is not highly valued. It is this kind of question which the study of culture attempts to answer. There are Catholic colleges and universities located in many—though of course not all—of the major culture centers of the world. These are an important network of information and possible insight. But much more to the point at the present time is the concern of certain Catholic scholars for "cracking the culture code" as a way of further illuminating the essential unity of mankind. One recalls particularly the work of Teilhard de Chardin.

Since E. B. Taylor first offered his definition of culture in print in 1871, there have been, of course, literally thousands of volumes written on various aspects of this subject. The best attempt at a comprehensive theory of culture, however, with which I am familiar is that of Edward T. Hall in his book *The Silent Language.*[9] Hall bases most of his thinking on the prem-

---

[9] Edward T. Hall, *The Silent Language* (Garden City, New York: Doubleday, 1959).

ise that "there is no such thing as *experience* in the abstract, as a mode separate and distinct from culture." He goes on to say, "culture is neither derived from experience nor held up to the mirror of experience. Moreover, it cannot be tested against some mystical thing thought of as experience. *Experience is something man projects upon the outside world as he gains it in its culturally determined form.*[10]

In outlining his theory of culture, Hall states that "culture is communication" and he describes the Primary Message Systems of communication. Only the first of these—namely, interaction—involves language. The others—namely, association, subsistence, bisexuality, territoriality, temporality, learning, play, defense, and exploitation or use of materials—are all nonlinguistic aspects of culture; or, as Hall calls it, "the communication process." Further, in attempting to understand a given culture, one must first consider the sets, the isolates, and the patterns proper to that culture.

One of Hall's many important insights, and perhaps the most important one for any theory of international or intercultural education, is that "people reared in different cultures *learn to learn* differently."[11] The implication, of course, is that the learning process itself and the substance or content of learning cannot in fact be separated. Though there is still much to be learned about the learning process, it is already clear that what is learned depends at least in part on how people learn to learn. The university, including the Catholic university which is serious about international education and its responsibility in this area, cannot ignore the fact that learning to think "internationally" or "interculturally" is in itself a learned process. The student or scholar in a Catholic university (at least in theory if not always in practice), perceives the international dimension of education almost from the beginning by sharing in a culture system which is worldwide and Catholic by nature.

The third level, and the most important and difficult step in international education is the evaluation or judgment level. Up to the present, international education, as it relates to the

[10] *Ibid.*, pp. 143–144.
[11] *Ibid.*, p. 71.

most serious and basic questions, has been regarded mostly as a kind of comparative study. The idea seems to be to explore, to point out similarities and differences in cultures, to search for hypotheses and unifying concepts, to exchange ideas, but never to evaluate. Rarely, if ever, is it asked whether one cultural pattern is better than another, and if so how and why. Each culture has its own way of viewing and doing things, and whatever that way may be, it has the sanction of having worked at least in a particular culture. International education, seriously pursued, has more often led to cultural relativism than to cultural imperialism. Because it is the most difficult level of international education, it is also the level at which the sharpest thinking and the greatest scholarship still remains to be done.

Yet, in the final analysis, international education will never be complete without evaluative criteria which preserve the beauty and vitality of cultural diversity but which at the same time help to make clear that not all cultural principles are equally valid. The essence of all education is to develop the ability to make deeper and wiser judgments, and until it supplies some bases for judgment, international education will remain unable to produce anything like a "broad mind," a "universal conscience," or a "culture of man."

The Catholic university has perhaps greater opportunities and responsibilities in international education than other universities, especially in the almost overwhelming task of attempting to develop evaluative criteria. As Catholic, the Catholic university is interested in man everywhere; it is not, or should not be in concept, as culture bound as other universities almost inevitably are. As university, it hopes to help find the answers to those questions which are most fundamental and most meaningful—as well as most difficult—to men in every culture and all cultures. Because it has a consciousness of its own vigorous individuality, it is able to be open and inquiring, able to seek and accept truth from all sources.

International education would be a necessary and noble pursuit as part of man's knowledge of himself and the world in which he lives, even if there were no threat of global war. The international dimension of the Catholic university would be clear and certain in principle even though its development might not be so manifest. But the continual threat of war makes international education in its highest and best forms crucially necessary. Aldous Huxley has written: "There may be arguments about the best way of raising wheat in a cold climate or of reforesting a denuded mountain. But such arguments never lead to organized slaughter. Organized slaughter is the result of arguments about such questions as the following: Which is the best nation? the best religion? the best political theory? the best form of government? Why are other people so stupid and wicked? Why can't they see how good and intelligent we are?"[12]

The fact that asking some of the foregoing questions may have in the past led to organized slaughter does not mean that they should not be asked. Hopefully ways can be worked out to prevent the organized slaughter, but there is no possible way of avoiding the questions. Such questions, phrased differently, are basic to international education. The Catholic university, internationally committed and oriented by its very nature, should be a leading force in helping to answer them.

[12] Aldous Huxley, quoted by Senator J. William Fulbright in *Vista* II, 5 (March–April, 1967), 9.

The Governance

NEIL G. McCLUSKEY, S.J.

From the earliest beginnings of the university, there have been three discernible patterns of government: student-oriented as at Bologna, faculty-oriented as at the Sorbonne, and administration-oriented as at any of the pioneer American universities. A complicating factor relative to American institutions is that without exception the earliest foundations were under church sponsorship and clerical control. The reason is obvious: the churches supported the institutions. Little money was forthcoming from Congress or the state legislatures. The era of princely private benefactions did not dawn until huge personal fortunes became relatively common. Storr notes that "between the Revolutionary and Civil Wars, Harvard received less than a quarter of a million dollars in large gifts, exclusive of funds raised by subscription, although its alumni and friends must have included many of the richest college men in the country.[1]

The Puritans had founded Harvard College in 1636, modeled on Emmanuel College of Cambridge with the mottoes *Christo et Ecclesiae* and *In Christi Gloriam*. The Anglicans undertook William and Mary in 1693 and by the dawn of the American Revolution seven other colleges were organized under religious sponsorship: Yale, Princeton, Washington and Lee, Columbia, Brown, Rutgers and Dartmouth. An eighth, Pennsylvania, was the only one without direct church affilia-

[1] Richard J. Storr, *The Beginnings of Graduate Education in America* (Chicago: University of Chicago Press, 1953), p. 4.

tion. Ordained or licensed clergymen filled the chief administration offices and did much of the teaching. Even into the
twentieth century, clergymen held the presidency of such
institutions as Princeton and Brown.

In fact, American society early became used to the idea that
the support and management of higher education were a prime
responsibility of church people who used the colleges to prepare the clergy. Colleges were numerous, many built on the
most precarious financial foundation. Taking the Catholic
collegiate foundations alone, only one out of four founded
before 1850 survives today, about one in three founded between
1850 and 1899 are still doing business, and a bare 36 percent
of those opened between 1900 and 1955 are yet with us.[2]

The instinctive reaction of some people to the thought of
transferring title of ownership to the laity, or even sharing
responsibility for ownership with them, is that proponents of
these ideas are betraying the order's patrimony and surrender-
ing to secular forces. Alongside the fear and insecurity is a
legitimate concern, for it is true that the control of property
is a basic protection for educational commitment. It would be
absurd to set in motion a train of circumstances that would
empty our institutions of the very reason for their existence.
One can look in any direction today and see great institutions
that began with a firm religious commitment—Harvard, Yale,
Columbia, Southern California, Chicago, Amherst—and have
lost all but symbolic vestiges of their Christian origin. Those
who push these examples, however, lack confidence in the kind
of machinery that could be established and the kind of trustees that could be assembled to guarantee a perpetuity of the
original commitment by the founding group.[3]

---

[2] Edward J. Powers, *A History of Catholic Higher Education in the United
States* (Milwaukee: Bruce Publishing Co., 1958), p. 47.

[3] Notre Dame and St. Louis both have made provision for reasonable insur-
ance against an abrupt reversal of basic commitment to the Christian and Catholic tradition embodied in each place, respectively for 125 and 150 years. At
Notre Dame, two-thirds of the "fellows of the university" (of the twelve fellows,
one-half are Holy Cross priests) must approve changes in the bylaws. At St. Louis,
a two-thirds vote of the trustees is required for a substantive change in the bylaw
or disposal of major property. Indeed, this is a common arrangement. For

It seems incomprehensible that a group of lay trustees would make the superhuman effort to finance and operate a university indistinguishable from its neighboring state-supported or richly-endowed private rivals. Moreover, given a clear definition of the nature and objectives of the institution in its new charter, it should not be difficult to select as members of the board persons who are known to be in complete sympathy with the broad objectives that have guided the institution from its inception. If no such laymen can be found among its alumni, friends and benefactors—that is, men and women, lay and cleric, who are as deeply committed to the goals of the institution as the founding religious group—then our Catholic colleges and universities have indeed failed.

In what may well have been the most important innovation in the history of Catholic higher education, during the first months of 1967 three religious orders that run institutions of higher learning—St. Louis, Notre Dame, and Webster—announced plans to surrender immediately the exclusive ownership and their control over policy. While the Society of Jesus, the Congregation of the Holy Cross, and the Sisters of Loretto, respectively, remain the sponsoring group, legal ownership and final authority over administration and policy have become invested in boards of trustees whose majority is lay. At the same time a score of other Catholic-managed institutions began to invite "outsiders" to serve on their legal governing boards.

Nor was money the primary reason, even though there are Catholic educators who still labor under the illusion that the principal problems besetting Catholic higher education are financial. Granted, these problems are enormous and pressing, but they are not the critical problems. A blank check on the state treasury or the federal reserve would not solve problems like the dominance of religious orders, reliance on Old-World tradition, amateurish administration, shortsighted financial policies, confusion between the pastoral and academic areas,

---

example, at Emory 70 percent of the board members must belong to the Methodist Church; at American, 60 percent; at Southern Methodist, 50 percent. Until relatively recent years Chicago and Southern California reserved places on the board for members of the church.

insulation from the main stream of contemporary thought, and lack of definition of purpose. Almost all of these are problems that flow from nonrecognition of the character of the work of contemporary higher education.

A university is something that belongs to the natural order, and its operational principles and the virtues of its community are not those of the religious house and its community. The university community functions in a collegiate manner as it discharges its responsibility for the discovery, transmission and application of truth. Apprentices are admitted to the community to learn from masters and doctors. Competence, experience, and seniority are the coin of the university community. Senior professors and scholars earn the right to enter into the appropriate level of policy-making both directly and through representatives. The Catholic university or college can by no means escape the natural law governing the operation of the academic community. In the university community, religious paternalism is out of place.

Vatican II's Decree on the Apostolate of the Laity insists that all the elements making up the temporal order "possess their own intrinsic value," and that this value "has been implanted in them by God, whether they are considered in themselves or as part of the whole temporal order."[4] Moreover, even though God has united all things, both natural and supernatural in Christ Jesus, this "not only does not deprive the temporal order of its independence, its proper goals, laws, resources, and significance for human welfare, but rather perfects the temporal order in its own intrinsic strength and excellence and raises it to the level of man's total vocation upon earth."[5]

Moreover, the document argues: "The laity must take on the renewal of the temporal order as their own special obligation. Led by the light of the gospel and the mind of the church, and motivated by Christian love, let them act directly and definitely in the temporal sphere. As citizens they must cooperate

---

[4] Decree on the Apostolate of the Laity, *The Documents of Vatican II*, ed. Walter M. Abbott, S.J. (New York: The American Press, 1966), p. 497.
[5] *Ibid.*

with other citizens, using their own particular skills and acting on their own responsibility."[6]

Three important conclusions emerge from these words: (1) the temporal order (including the academic world) enjoys its own God-given autonomy; (2) the presence in time of the historical Christ or of the ecclesiastical Christ does not reduce the independence of things in the temporal sphere (including the academic community); (3) the layman has a special obligation and competence for action in the temporal sphere (including the academic area).

People today expect to find at least the same standards of excellence in Catholic schools that they demand of the best private and state institutions. And the present system of government is simply not improving Catholic institutions rapidly enough. It is questionable whether, even with increased financial resources, it ever can do so. If Christian humanism is worth supporting, lay men and women must assume at least equal, and eventually dominant, responsibility for Catholic higher education. Indeed, many thoughtful observers feel that such broader support is contingent upon the orders' abdicating *exclusive* control over their institutions. We are no longer living in the collegiate world of the forties or fifties or even sixties. Today's college has its own style and character.

Perhaps the most relevant change today is in the composition of student body, faculty, and administration. Imperceptibly, but inexorably, a shift has taken place away from the primary and immediate emphasis in the Catholic collegiate institution. Few, if any Catholic institutions, would not claim to be at least partially selective in admission of students; few, if any of them, can make provision for large numbers of applicants who are unable to pay their own way. In brief, the desire of the student of 1970 for a distinctive Catholic education is largely conditioned by his academic achievement and potential as well as his ability to pay for it. These schools no longer cater to the "poor but good" boy. Catholic higher education is no longer formally and immediately apostolic.

[6] *Ibid.*, p. 498.

As these institutions expanded in size and complexity, they recruited more and more lay teachers and increasingly opened up administrative posts to them. Among lay faculties of Catholic colleges and universities everywhere, there has developed a growing interest in a larger role in everything that affects the institution's operation. Here then is the clash.

The old monastic and religious-order forms of government are, in the nature of things, authoritarian. Dioceses and monasteries and religious houses, despite the development of the concept of collegiality in the church, are still essentially structured by "line" authority. In other words, authority is given to an appointed or elected superior, who then exercises his office as God's representative. His subjects freely submit their will to his as part of their dedication as religious. Obedience, humility, and docility are Christian virtues and many religious in their following of Christ attempt to practice them. But the monarchical structure of the monastery and the ascetical attitudes of the monk obviously cannot be extrapolated bodily from the cloister to the campus. To try is to introduce serious disorder into both.

In the past it was not unusual for religious subjects to be shuffled from their posts without prior discussion or notice, and while such a practice might have had some justification as part and parcel of a venerable ascetical tradition, in the contemporary college and university—for that matter, any kind of school—it is self-defeating. It is arguable, moreover, that the essentially familial quality of religious obedience has been overlooked and underdeveloped. Tenure for religious and priests may not be necessary to protect their income but it is vital to protect their status as teachers and researchers. Arbitrary or unilateral removal upsets the fundamental working conditions of the scholar. Granted that as part of religious commitment, a person has the right through a promise of obedience to place himself under the direction of a superior or bishop, this action cannot totally obliterate the natural freedoms of the academic world. If it must, then priests and religious literally have no business there. Some modified style of tenure for these people must be elaborated which will balance their religious commitment with their academic status, and some realistic recompense commensurate with their professional status must be found.

When we look at the scene today, the obvious question arises: Did the original religious constitutions envisage the modern, largely lay-staffed American Catholic university or university college? Is it not something of an anachronism in 1970 that one man or woman, the superior-president, should function as a corporation sole, with almost no institutionalized checks and balances; that practically absolute power—legislative, executive, judicial—should be concentrated in a single office? Is it not a further anachronism that the chief advisers to the superior-president remain the *religious* house consultors? These are the men or women with whom the president is usually required by the constitutions to discuss the major business of the religious house and, in the absence of any other group, of the university.

This anomalous situation is largely traceable to the failure to appreciate the difference between higher education in the United States and in Europe. The most obvious major difference is an essential one. American Catholic colleges and universities as institutions of higher learning receive their charter not from the Holy See, or their order, or the Roman Congregation of Seminaries and Universities, but by the act of the particular state in which they are located. Moreover, the continuance of the charter, to say nothing of extensions or modifications, depends upon the act of the particular state. Accordingly, American priests and religious engaged in college education are "stewards of the public trust."

It follows that the first duty of the college is to serve the community according to its needs and its moral demands. This is the sense of "community" or "society," as interpreted in Vatican II's Constitution on the Church in the Modern World and the Declaration on Religious Freedom. Awareness of this public responsibility does not detract from concomitant service to the church, but at the same time it broadens the service and removes it completely from any narrowly parochial or sectarian understanding. In other words, the Catholic college or university must exist to serve the whole American community in following out the reasonable norms and practices that the American experience in education has evolved. Service and influence, not ownership and control, are the overriding concepts. It is ironical that so many of the religious teaching groups whose founders sought only to serve and to bring Christian influence to bear on society through their pioneer educational ventures are today helplessly bogged down in proprietorship of real estate.

The priests and religious engaged in higher education rightfully look upon their institutions as a powerful witness to Christ, the inspiration and goal of Christian humanism. In varying degrees all those who join in the educational work must recognize this commitment. A professor whose personal philosophy of education is in basic disagreement with that of the institution would feel—and be—out of place. At the same time, if the institution fails to articulate its distinctive commitment, it risks its own integrity. It is inconceivable that a religiously founded and oriented institution would attract scholars and teachers by de-emphasizing or camouflaging its distinctive *raison d'être*. On the other hand, if the institution is not aware that it possesses a distinctive reason for being, the sooner it either passes out of existence or under other control, the better.

A school of thought among some Catholic administrators is to feverishly try to project a lay image. In other words, these religious and clerics think that excellence and achievement are measured by the number of lay deans or vice presidents which can be displayed in the roster of government.

There is another opinion that would allow every other kind of sponsorship of higher education except church or religious groups. But this is a crude form of discrimination. A religious congregation or a diocese has as much right to be in the field of education as any other group. In fact, if they had not been historically, many of the greatest institutions of the world would never have seen the light of day. It is necessary, moreover, to distinguish *control* from *sponsorship*. Jacqueline Grennan has stated that "the very nature of higher education is opposed to juridical control by the churches," and she is right.

But sponsorship or inspiration is a college of another color.

The financial foundations of Catholic higher education are not solid. For the less affluent and less prestigious schools, the situation in many places is moving from grim to desperate. Without massive assistance from both federal and state government, without enormously increased support from foundations, industry, and other private sources, many deserving institutions will have to sacrifice quality in order to survive, while many borderline or mediocre ones will most probably not survive. The competition for support prompted Cardinal Cushing's ominous prediction: "The future of higher education is on the state university campus because the charity dollar can no longer compete with the tax dollar."

A ray of sunshine in the darkening sky is that government is beginning to accept the position that it best serves the public interest by helping to maintain a strong system of nonpublic higher education. In turn, acceptance of this principle blurs the distinction between public and private education. Public institutions receive massive support from private sources—foundations, business, industry, friends, and alumni. For their part, some private universities are coming to be heavily subsidized by the state; for example, one-half of the operating budget for Columbia and Harvard comes from the federal government.

Private higher education sees that it has little choice but to turn to the state and federal governments for financial help. After going through literal bankruptcy, the University of Pittsburgh became a "state-related" institution of the Commonwealth of Pennsylvania, which means that over half of its operating budget now comes from the state. Temple University in Philadelphia has assumed the same relationship to the Commonwealth. By the terms of the "Bundy" law, collegiate level institutions in New York are able to qualify for direct grants by the state for each student enrolled. The size of the grant is determined by the degree level: for a student pursuing a bachelor's or master's degree the sum is $400, and for the doctor's degree it is $2,400. A growing number of states have established college scholarships given on a basis of ability and/or need to be used at any accredited institution within that state. Among these states are California, New York, Illinois, Washington, and Michigan.

In an historic about-face, the Association of American Universities in June, 1968, issued a joint appeal to the federal government to assume a greater share of the cost of higher education. The appeal by this prestigious 42-member organization combined the interests of both public and private education. They were in agreement that while present federal programs for specific purposes like research and residence halls are vital, there is a desperate need for operational subsidy on a regular and continuing basis for private education. They also stated that some national norms will have to be developed for distribution of federal largesse which would combine the quantity of service to the community and the quality of the education dispensed. What will all this mean for Catholic higher education?

Over the past twenty years Catholic institutions of higher learning have been able to grow, largely through participation in federal programs which provided loans and grants for housing and educational facilities. During 1967, for example, Catholic institutions received $125 million in grants and contracts, exclusive of repayable loans. It would be disastrous if they could no longer qualify for these governments grants and loans as well as for research and equipment funds, fellowships, and scholarships, just as other institutions do. In June of 1967, however, the Maryland Court of Appeals ruled that three state grants to church-affiliated colleges were invalid. The attorney general of Maryland then appealed the decision to the U.S. Supreme Court. The Court did not see fit to accept jurisdiction and allowed the lower court decision to stand. The eligibility of any sectarian institution for federal grants has already been challenged on grounds of violating the First Amendment, and the U.S. Supreme Court is about to address itself to this issue.

Would a restructuring of ownership and control obviate this problem? Some years back, when Loyola University was competing for the New Orleans' CBS television outlet, the question of foreign ownership came up. The U.S. Court of Appeals (District of Columbia circuit) upheld Loyola's claim that it was a "domestic" (i.e., American) corporation chartered by the State of Louisiana, despite the fact that final control was then thought to be vested in the Holy See in Rome. The U.S. Supreme Court declined review. Had jurisdiction been accepted, however, and a contrary decision handed down, all Catholic institutions would probably have been barred from federal programs. If the same question arises again, the federal courts will doubtless demand complete local autonomy—i.e., separate incorporation of the institution from the sponsoring religious order—as one of several conditions for participating in federal programs.

The question of public support from the states is more complicated, by reason of the restrictions written into most individual state constitutions. In the fall of 1968 Fordham released a study by Walter Gellhorn and R. Kent Greenawalt of the Columbia University Law School which addressed itself to the question: "What must Fordham do to achieve legal parity with other private independent universities in New York State?" The study was commissioned by Fordham to determine what modifications in its structure and mode of operation might be necessary to become eligible for financial assistance from the state. The so-called Blaine Amendment bars public moneys to any school under denominational control. Several recommendations dealt with the governance with a view of establishing the clear independence of Fordham from church control. These were followed out and in the spring of 1970 Fordham qualified for state assistance under the terms of the Bundy law.

It helps clarify the basic question to ask who actually own the buildings, property, and other assets which make up Georgetown, or Santa Clara or St. Catherine's. Technically, ownership is vested in a self-perpetuating board of trustees, comprising three or five or seven or whatever number of members of the religious order, appointed by the provincial superior. "Ownership" here, however, is used only by analogy. The ownership of a university or college does, of course, in several ways resemble ownership of income-producing property, but in at least two crucial aspects it does not.

The men and women associated in the work of higher education are not simply employees with an exclusively salary relationship to the trustees of the university. The young, highly professional lay teacher resents the "master-servant" idea of his relationship to the university. Any talk of a lay-religious "partnership" in higher education makes little sense until the assets of the college are completely separated from those of the religious community. A number of Catholic institutions have taken, or are taking, this step. If there is any lingering ambiguity on the point, it should be dispelled by the McGrath study, *The Canonical and Civil Law Status of Catholic Institution in the United States*. One key paragraph states:

> *Charitable and educational institutions chartered as corporations under American law are not* owned *by the sponsoring body. The legal title to the real and personal property is vested in the corporation. It is the corporation that cares for the sick or grants academic degrees. It is the corporation that buys and sells and borrows money. If anyone* owns *the assets of the charitable or educational institution, it is the general public. Failure to appreciate this fact has led to the mistaken idea that the property of the institution is the property of the sponsoring body.*[7]

The ownership of a college or university is not proprietary, but rather a trust with accountability to the various publics the institution serves and with responsibility for attaining the objectives for which it was chartered. By contrast with the misunderstanding in the Catholic sphere, no one regards the civic leaders making up the Harvard board of overseers or the board of trustees of the University of California as "owners" of these institutions in any literal sense. They are considered as public servants holding a public trust. The college or university, no matter the sponsorship, is a creature of the natural order and hence is governed by the laws and principals of the natural academic order. It is chartered by the state as a civil corporation for a public purpose, and as such enjoys certain privileges and immunities, such as, tax exemption, eminent domain, draft

[7] John J. McGrath, *Catholic Institutions in the United States* (Washington, D.C.: Catholic University of America Press, 1968), p. 33.

deferment of students, and judicial exception. Administrators and trustees of a Catholic college or university are also then stewards of the public trust.

The Church has need of the Catholic university of tomorrow, and the greatest service the colleges and universities can offer the Church is to be true to their own inner finality. One writer has called them the Church's "open door into democracy and the democratic process." In singling out the principle reason why this is true, he offers matter for careful pondering:

> *Up to now Catholic colleges and universities are the only structure within the Church which has successfully declericalized functions—in other words, the only place where by intent and pattern, laity and clergy have learned to work together. There are excuses for the length of time it has taken to accomplish this, and I am careful not to claim that they work perfectly together. Their mixing is a new and heady blend—and one which excites and frightens us. But there is among many of us the beginning at least of a unity of function to match an already established unity of purpose.*[8]

Perhaps the college and university world will serve as a pattern for a new Christian society of God's people.

---

[8] Timothy S. Healy, S.J., "The Emerging Role for Catholic Higher Education," *Fordham* I, 8 (April–May, 1967), 18.

The University and Christian Formation

WILLIAM J. RICHARDSON, S.J.

Assuming that we agree on what a university is, we are asking, I take it, about one function of the specifically Catholic university. But may we assume that we agree on what *that* is? Obviously we have no choice but to do so, if we are to proceed any further with the question—yet there is at present no clear consensus on what this ought to mean. To assume one particular conception of the Catholic university, then (in order to reflect further on an individual function of it), risks seeming to presumptuously adjudicate a highly controversial matter or, at the very least, to beg the question. On the other hand, it is a simple dialectical necessity, so let us make the assumption in cold blood and be done with it. As a starting point, the present writer assumes the conception of a Catholic university discussed in a following chapter. "Pay Any Price? Break Any Mold?" Anyone who rejects the argument articulated there will not find these pages any more palatable.[1]

The question becomes, then, the following: Given the conception of the Catholic university as that institution through which the Church becomes present to the academic world and the academic world present to (and operative in) the Church,

---

[1] This paper was conceived in desolation and born in pain. It can pretend to be no more than a beginning. In substance it is the writer's own work, but he wishes to acknowledge with great gratitude the criticism and suggestions of Rev. Francis Canavan, S.J. and Rev. Robert O'Connell, S.J. Their help was invaluable. Given the nature of it, there is no way to indicate their specific contributions other than by this general announcement of debt.

how is such an institution to go about "forming the Christian"?
"Forming the Christian"! Can we assume that we agree on
what *this* means? Taken at the letter, the phrase would of
course seem to imply that the Christian was an amorphous
mass to be "shaped" somehow by the university mold (that
famous mold!) in such fashion that the result could be called
"Christian." In that case, the resulting "Christianity" would be
as superficial and extrinsic as the process itself, giving form
only to a man of clay—passive, cold and lifeless. No one would
seriously propose this as the ideal of Christian education (even
if it has often been the caricature). Christianity is, before all
else, a life—not just a "way of life" (i.e., a special moral code),
but a new kind of living by which we are united with Christ
so profoundly that we, too, have a right to call God "Father."
To be a Christian, then, means to live the life of divine son-
ship—life accepted through faith and ratified through baptism.
To "form" such a Christian can only mean to allow this life to
unfold, to let Christ himself be "formed" in men.[2]

How the Catholic university can help make it possible for
Christ to be formed in its students is of course a rather complex
affair. To begin with, the student himself is a rather complex
affair.[3] Beyond that, the precise nature of this formation in
Christ is a theological problem of the first order that we cannot
attempt to explore here. In the simplest terms, however, we
can say that the faith by which the Christian responds to the
Someone who, through revelation, invites him to special intimacy, is a total response, involving the whole man. Involving
the whole man, faith comports first of all the acquiescence of
man's *intelligence* to the mystery of God-become-Man-in-
history. What the full scope of this mystery might imply we
have tried to suggest elsewhere. It is important here only to
remark that for human intelligence to address itself to the task
of articulating this mystery in meaningful manner is not only
to perform in its own way a liturgy of action (an act of wor-

[2] Gal. 4:19.

[3] Complexity will be compounded as we go along, so let us make at least one
gesture toward simplicity by assuming that some of the Catholic university's
students will be nonbelievers—baptized or unbaptized.

ship) but also—on the level, at least of intelligence—to become "formed" in Christ. In other words, if the task of the Catholic university is to bear witness to the Church's respect for human intelligence and creativity, then its first responsibility in helping to make possible the "formation" of Christ in its students is precisely a profound and manifest commitment to the values that are proper to intelligence and creativity; i.e., to the excellence that academia regards as proper to itself.

Its first responsibility! But is it the only one? For the whole man is more than his intelligence—he is incarnate freedom. That Christ be formed in him, his acceptance of Christ's gift (*charis*) must be a free response. And this free response may well involve to some extent a way of life, i.e., certain moral commitments. But what is the responsibility of the Catholic university here? Does the achievement of its task require a concern for the student's use of his freedom, for his religious and moral life? Or is this an invasion of his privacy? If the university does not concern itself with the student's use of freedom but restricts its attention to the purely academic, can it really claim to facilitate the forming of Christ in him—or, for that matter, to educate the whole man? And yet if it does, can it express this concern without attempting to train him and impose a moral code from the outside, i.e., to coerce his freedom, which is, in effect, to deny it? We come here to the heart of the issue: How ought the Catholic university as an institution (i.e., as a juridical structure headed by its chief administrative officers) conceive its relationship to the freedom of its students in the nonacademic (and here we restrict this to the religious and moral) dimensions of university life?

The classic answer that comes easily to such a question is that the university stands *in loco parentis* to the student and has the right to address that freedom in religious and moral matters with an authority analogous to that of his parents. If one accepted this facile answer, the issue would then turn around the question as to what right the parents have in these matters with regard to late adolescents (we assume here the normal age of eighteen years and over), and how best to exercise these rights in contemporary society. Here the answers would be less facile! But ought we accept the classic answer in the first place? Does the university really stand *in loco parentis* to its students? This larger question brings into focus all the major issues involved in this delicate matter, so let us approach it from three different points of view: 1. The juridical problem. 2. The theological problem. 3. The practical problem.

THE JURIDICAL PROBLEM

What in fact *is* the warrant for maintaining that the university stands *in loco parentis* to its students? Is there any basis in law? The point has been denied, and indeed, in so astutely prepared a document as the recent (May, 1967) "Report of the Advisory Committee on Human Conduct" at Brown University:

> *We know of no legal code that imposes such an obligation on the university, and the* in loco parentis *phrase is commonly cited in a disparaging fashion by those who criticize existing student conduct rules and who fear an excessive paternalism on the University's part. In our view, the concept of* in loco parentis—*if indeed it can be dignified by calling it a concept—is essentially irrelevant to the problems confronting Brown University. . . . The University, while undoubtedly an* alma mater *to many of its sons and daughters in a certain nostalgic sense, is not equipped to serve as a surrogate parent for its students. Most Brown and Pembroke students are fortunate in having parents, and parental control is properly their—not Brown University's—responsibility.*[4]

But the matter is not as easily disposed of as that. There is some warrant, if not in statutory law at least in American judicial practice, for claiming that the university has the right, if not the obligation, to act *in loco parentis.*[5]

---

[4] *Community and Partnership: Student Conduct at Brown University,* Report of the Advisory Committee on Student Conduct (May, 1967), p. 11. See *New York Times,* May 14, 1967, E p. 9. The Committee based its report on a questionnaire sent to its students, faculty, and alumni, as well as to deans and student government officers at thirty-seven other institutions.

[5] See *American Jurisprudence* 39, no. 61.

The classic case is that of *Gott v. Berea College* (1913), where the court on appeal, in a suit brought by an entrepreneur whose restaurant had been declared off limits by the college authorities, observed:

> *College authorities stand* in loco parentis *concerning the physical and moral welfare, and mental training of the pupils, and we are unable to see why to that end they may not make any rule or regulation for the government or betterment of their pupils* that a parent could for the same purpose. *Whether the rules or regulations are wise, or their aims worthy, is a matter left solely to the discretion* of the authorities, or parents as the case may be, *and in the exercise of that discretion the courts are not disposed to interfere, unless the rules and aims are unlawful, or against public policy. . . .*[6]

As precedent, the court cited *People v. Wheaton College* (1866), where the court upheld the college's right to expel a student for joining a secret society (and a temperance society

[6] Gott v. Berea College, 156 Ky. 376 (1913), p. 379. Writer's emphasis. The court continues (p. 381), ". . . For the purposes of this case the school, its officers and students are a legal entity, as much so as any family, and like [sic] a father may direct his children, those in charge of boarding schools are well within their rights and powers when they direct their students what to eat and where they may get it; where they may go and what forms of amusement are forbidden. . . ."

> *"A discretionary power has been given [to the trustees and faculty] to regulate the discipline of their college in such a manner as they deem proper, and so long as their rules violate neither divine nor human law, we have no more authority to interfere than we have to control the domestic discipline of a father in his family. . . . When it is said that a person has a legal right to do certain things, all that the phrase means is that the law does not forbid these things to be done. It does not mean that the law guarantees the right to do them all times and under all possible circumstances. A person in his capacity as a citizen may have the right to do many things which a student at Wheaton College cannot do without incurring the penalty of the law. A person as a citizen has a legal right to marry or to walk the street at midnight or to board at a public hotel, yet it would seem absurd to say that a college cannot forbid its students to do any of these things. So a citizen as such can attend church on Sunday or not as he may think proper, but it would hardly be contended that a college would not have the right to make attendance upon religious services as a condition of remaining within its walls"* (Writer's italics, p. 382).

at that!)[7] After 1913, it is *Gott v. Berea College* that is cited as precedent. Thus, for example, in *John B. Stetson University v. Hunt* (1924) the court conceded to the university by reason of surrogate parenthood, the right to discipline a student for "hazing the normals, ringing cow bells and parading in the halls of the dormitories at forbidden hours, cutting lights and other such events."[8]

In the same tenor, we find the decision of the *Tanton v. McKenney* case (1922).[9] Michigan State Normal College was conceded the right to refuse the readmission of an eighteen-year-old girl to the spring semester (because "she smoked cigarettes on the public streets of Ypsilanti, rode around the streets in an automobile seated on the lap of a young man," and was guilty of "other acts of indiscretion"—not the least of which was airing her subsequent disenchantment in the public press), for "in the school, as in the family there exists on the part of the pupils the obligation of obedience to lawful commands. . . ."[10]

These, as far as we have been able to determine, are the judicial precedents for the *in loco parentis* theory of the university's authority. What emerges from these texts is not simply that the university has a right to discipline its students, but that this right is grounded in the structure of the university conceived as a family, in which authority is essentially parental. No one would maintain, of course, that these decisions are to be interpreted as a legal prescription in positive terms of what the relationship between university and student ought to be. At most they indicate the court's judgment as to the limits of a state's right to interfere in the administration of an educational institution. In this sense their function is purely negative. Nonetheless, they offer valuable testimony to the cultural milieu in which they were formulated. Notice that the most recent case cited dates from 1924.

The precedent cited in *Gott v. Berea College*—most explicit judicial statement of the *in loco parentis* theory—is the *People v. Wheaton* decision of 1866, a date that marks the high water-

[7] People v. Wheaton College, 40 Ill. 186 (1866).

[8] John B. Stetson University v. Hunt, 88 Fla. 510 (1924).

[9] Tanton v. McKenney, 226 Mich. 245 (1924).

[10] *Ibid.*, p. 249, citing 24 R.C.L., p. 646.

mark of nineteenth century academic paternalism. What this paternalism was rooted in would be the task of a social historian to explain. No doubt the strong religious influence—often enough Calvinist in tenor—in the leading private colleges of the East played a significant role. This tradition demanded orthodoxy in doctrine and conformity in practice. As Noah Porter, president of Yale put it, "To hold the student to minute fidelity in little things is an enforcement of one of the most significant maxims of the gospel."[11] Besides this, the psychological theories of the time may have been influential, specifically a rather naïve "faculty" theory that conceives of man's intellect and will as instruments of the soul that could be trained for life in much the same way that a soldier's skills may be trained for war. The chief fruit of an educational process based on such a psychology would be the mental and moral *discipline* of the man.[12]

Whatever the reasons for academic paternalism, its effects were clear: a concerted effort on the part of academic authority to control the student's private life by disciplinary means. In 1865, for example, Harvard's rules for the deportment of undergraduates came to an eight-page list of detailed injunctions. Columbia was able to buttress compulsory chapel attendance with two full pages of itemized prescriptions. Yale for a while demanded from the students a loyalty oath to the administration and one president of Princeton (F. L. Patton, 1889) declared (with a candor that might even have disarmed Stokely Carmichael), that students had no civil rights whatsoever.[13]

If such were the social and academic context out of which the 1866 decision came, it is perfectly understandable why the court would maintain that it had no more right to interfere in the college's discretionary use of disciplinary authority than in "domestic discipline of a father in his family." The *Gott v. Berea* decision (1913), which cites the 1866 decision as prece-

---

[11] N. Porter, "Inaugural Address," *Addresses at the Inauguration of Professor Noah Porter* (New York, 1871), p. 50, cited by D. Callahan, "Student Freedom," *Academic Freedom and the Catholic University* (Notre Dame, Indiana: Fides, 1967), p. 126.

[12] See Callahan, *ibid.*, p. 126.

[13] F. L. Patton, *Religion in College* (Princeton, 1888), pp. 12–13, cited *ibid.*, p. 125.

dent, is equally paternalistic in tone.[14] And in *Tanton v. Mc-Kenney*, eighteen-year-old Alice was not only an infant in the eyes of the court (though her smoking habits and "other acts of indiscretion" suggest to the nonlegal mind a rather precocious infancy), but the court's argument for justifying the college's disciplinary action against her was based upon the analogy with the authority of the local school boards that supervise *grammar school* education!

But that was 1924. Since then, Freud's influence has had its effect, and psychology generally has agreed that an earlier conception of paternal authority was far too simplistic. We have, for example, a far more subtle awareness of the meaning of adolescent rebellion as a search for self-possession. Even if we were going to defend parental authority as the paradigm university authority in our day, we would have to be far more nuanced than the texts we have considered. But we are not going to defend it. Nor do the courts allude to it further. What they do cite gives us a completely different conception of the student-university relationship.

The significant case in our own day is that of *Carr v. St. John's University* (1962).[15] Howard Carr and Greta Schmidt, both seniors at St. John's, were married in the presence of two witnesses who were also St. John's students, before a city clerk of the city of New York. All parties were Roman Catholics, hence their action a clear violation of canon law.[16] After a hearing before a faculty-student committee on student integrity, all four students were dismissed from the university.[17]

---

[14] For example, the court maintained that Berea College did not exceed its discretionary power in forbidding access to an off-campus restaurant because (among other things) " . . . one of the chief dreads of college authorities is the outbreak of an epidemic, against which they should take the utmost precaution. These precautions, however, may wholly fail if students carelessly or indiscriminately visit or patronize public or unsanitary eating houses." (156 Ky pp. 380–381).

[15] Carr v. St. John's University, 231 N.Y.S. 2d 403, 410 (1962).

[16] Can. 1094. See Bouscaren and Ellis, *Canon Law: a Text and Commentary*, 3rd rev. ed. (Milwaukee: Bruce Publishing Company, 1957), p. 562.

[17] The students were informed orally of their dismissal on April 12, 1962, and that evening the couple were remarried in a Roman Catholic ceremony. Written notice of their dismissal did not arrive until April 18.

In justifying its action, the university cited the 1961–62 bulletin of the University College as follows: "In conformity with the ideals of Christian education and conduct, the university reserves the right to dismiss a student at any time on whatever grounds the university judges advisable. Each student by his admission to the university recognizes this right. . . ."[18] The trial court did not question the university's right to take disciplinary action against students for an alleged violation of regulations. What the court objected to was the vagueness of the phrase "in conformity with the ideals of Christian education and conduct," since this could be interpreted in various ways by students of various backgrounds and thus did not establish a norm of conduct "standard in application."[19] It ordered reinstatement. The appellate court, however—on the grounds that to the Catholic students and authorities of the university the word "Christian" meant quite clearly "Roman Catholic"—reversed the lower court (3-2),[20] and the reversal was affirmed later by the New York Court of Appeals.[21]

What is significant for our purposes is not the court's affirmation of the university's right to impose certain standards of moral conduct on its students, even though the violation of these standards is not contrary to civil law nor regarded by society in general as immoral. What is interesting is what the court understands here to be the basis of this right. The court makes no allusion (nor does the university in presenting its case) to the *in loco parentis* privilege. The court sees the right as based upon a *contract*—not between the university and the parent but between the university and the student.[22]

---

[18] Cited 231 N.Y.S. 2d 403, p. 407.

[19] *Ibid.,* p. 410.

[20] *Ibid.,* p. 414.

[21] 148 N.Y.L.J., No. 111, p. 15, col. 1.

[22] 231 N.Y.S. 2d 403, pp. 407–409. To be sure, the court remarks (p. 409), that " . . . parents placing their children in these universities often desire that they shall be brought under such [moral and religious] influences . . . , but this is not the basis of the university's right." The court goes on to say: " . . . Shall a court say that such rules and regulations may not be imposed upon students merely because one or more of them may object to obeying them? It would appear that the appropriate solution is that those [students] who do not wish to conform may seek their schooling elsewhere." In other words, the students may simply dissolve the contract.

Now the authority of a parent—even a surrogate parent—over his child is not based upon contract. Apparently the authority is.[23] In a contractual relationship of this kind there is implied an obligation on the university's part to permit the student, once admitted, to work towards and receive his degree[24] and an obligation on the student's part to avoid such "misconduct as would be subversive to the discipline of the college or school, or as would show him to be morally unfit. . . ."[25] The term "morally unfit" has been taken to have a scope that extends beyond the purely academic, i.e., specifically "student" activity of student life.[26] Hence it has the very broad meaning that describes any conduct that may interfere with or injure the university, or lessen its proper control over its student body, or impair its influence for good upon its students and the community.[27]

The evaluation of the "moral unfitness" of a student—and therefore the judgment as to whether he has broken his contract falls within the discretionary powers of the university. Thus in *Anthony v. Syracuse University*,[28] for example, the regulation of a private university reserving the power to dismiss a student

[23] 1 Williston, *Contracts*, 3rd ed. (1957) no. 90 D, p. 317. See, for example, Anthony v. Syracuse University, 224 App. Div. 487, 231, N.Y. Supp. 435 (4th Dep't, 1928). Here and in the analysis of the contractual relationship that follows the writer has drawn heavily from the material collated in "Case Notes," *Fordham Law Review* 31 (1962), 215–231.

[24] People ex rel. Cecil v. Bellevue Hosp. Medical College, 60 Hun 107, 14 N.Y. Supp. 490 (1st Dep't), aff' d men., 128 N.Y. 621, 28 N.E. 253 (1891).

[25] Goldstein v. New York Univ., 76 App. Div. 80, 83, 78 N.Y. Supp. 739, 740 (1st Dep't 1902).

[26] "The implied stipulation for good conduct, variable in its meaning and incapable of precise definition as that term must always be, is not . . . to receive the restricted construction that the student's conduct may be the subject of control only insofar as it relates to his actions in his capacity and status of student." (Samson v. Trustees of Columbia Univ., 101 Misc. 146, at 150, in *Fordham Law Review* 31 [1962], 218).

[27] Just how broadly this has been interpreted we see from the 1958 decision of a Florida court that upheld the right of the University of Miami to preclude a student from continuing his studies towards a teaching career because of the undesirable effect his fanatical atheist ideas *might* have on his future pupils (100 So. 2d 442 Fla. [1958]).

[28] Anthony v. Syracuse University, 224 App. Div. 487, 321 N.Y. Supp. 435 (4th Dep't 1928).

for any reason without disclosing the reason was upheld. The court stressed the contractual freedom of both parties, and the student's consent to such a regulation by registration.[29] Of course, the universities may not be arbitrary or capricious in their action;[30] but in general, the courts have been reluctant to decide against them in such matters.[31] Whatever the reason for such an attitude, this much is clear: the courts so far concede that the discriminatory powers of the university in deciding whether a student has broken his contract are relatively broad. Be that as it may, what is important for us is that the paradigm of university authority is not the parent in a family but the party to a contract.

But the contractual conception of the student-university relationship is not without its difficulties, and, indeed, severe ones. Many would maintain that the language alone is contractual, and that—in effect—a university's authority is based on nothing more than its status before the law.[32] Historically, the authority to discipline students was not created, it would seem, by an agreement between the parties but apparently arose from

[29] *Id.,* at 490–491, 231 N.Y. Supp. at 439. As we all know, it is common practice—as in the case of St. John's—for a university bulletin to include sweeping "reservation" clauses by which the student, in registering, concedes *ipso facto* to the university the right to force him to withdraw for any reason deemed sufficient.

[30] Anthony v. Syracuse Univ., 224 App. Div. 487, 231 N.Y. Supp. 435 (4th Dep't 1928); People ex rel. Cecil v. Bellevue Hosp. Medical College 60 Hun 107, 14 N.Y. Supp. 490 (1st Dep't) aff'd men, 128 N.Y. 621, 28 N.E. 253 (1891).

[31] One reason apparently is the simple recognition of the fact that the universities are better qualified to judge a student's fitness than the courts. (Woods v. Simpson, 146 Md. 547, 126 Atl. 882 [1924]; Edde v. Columbia Univ., 8 Misc. 2d 795, 168 N.Y. S. 2d 643 [Sup. Cit. 1957], aff'd mem., 6 App. Div. 2d 780, 175 N.Y.S. 2d 556 [1st Dep't 1958]). Another pragmatic factor may be the courts' salutary fear that if they were to consider cases seeking reversal of school disciplinary determinations they would be inundated with this type of litigation. (See, for example, Pugsley v. Sellmeyer, 158 Ark. 247, 250 S.W. 538 [1923]). On both of these reasons, see T.N. Davis, "The Court and the College," *America,* June 23, 1962, pp. 422–424.

[32] Such is the thesis of a Case Note, "Expulsion of College Students," *New York University Law Review* 37 (1962), 1164–1170. For much of the factual data on the problem of the status-theory of student-university relationships we rely on data collated in this article.

the need of the university to maintain itself.[33] The medieval universities of Oxford and Cambridge, as communities[34] with powers of self-regulation, exercised their own jurisdiction over criminal as well as civil matters:[35]

> *It is not very probable that so great a body as the university could have existed so long, without having some power within itself of controlling and checking those evils which, without correction, would be subversive to all discipline in the university. Discipline is the soul of such a body; and if persons egregiously offended against that order and discipline so necessary to be preserved in the university, the latter must have had a power to correct such offenses. . . .*[36]

In other words, the power to regulate or discipline was inherent to the university and arose simply from its status, i.e., its essential structure before the law.

One argument for the status-theory over the contract-theory of a university's disciplinary authority is the fact that the courts so far as we have already seen, have generally conceded to the university, one of the contracting parties, the right to declare the contract broken by the other contracting party (the student), in virtue of its broad discretionary powers, without recourse to a third party such as the court.[37] There would seem to be here a basic inequality in the contractual relationship.

[33] See The King v. Chancellor of the University of Cambridge, 6 T.R. 89, 101 Eng. Rep. 451 (K.B. 1794).

[34] See Le Seignoir Norths Case, Noo. K.B. 361, 72 Eng. Rep. 630 (1688).

[35] See The King v. Chancellor, Masters & Scholars of the University of Cambridge, Bentley's case, 2 Raym, Ld. 1334, 92 Eng. Per. 370 (K.B. 1723); 9 Halsbury's Laws of England 519, 549-51 (3rd ed. 1954).

[36] The King v. Chancellor of the University of Cambridge, 6 T.R. 89, 106, 101 Eng. Rep. 451, 460 (K.B. 1794). Cited according to "Expulsion of College Students," (See note 34), p. 1166.

[37] The cases already cited confirm this sufficiently for our purpose. Other instances are cited in "Expulsion of College Students" (See note 34), p. 1166. On the other hand, there have been instances where the court indicated that a university has no power to decide on its own for the purpose of expelling a student and rescinding its contract, whether or not the student was in breach. See, for example, Goldstein v. New York Univ., 38 Misc. 93, 77 N.Y. Supp. 80 (Sup. Ct.), rev'd on other grounds, 76 App. Div. 80, 78 N.Y. Supp. 739 (1st Dep't 1902).

Another inequality appears in the relative lack of freedom of one of the contracting parties, i.e., the student.[38] He would seem to be not really free to disagree with anything the college proposed. Nor is he free to insist that the regulations that prevailed when he first entered into the relationship are binding on the university as well and therefore may not be changed during his four-year sojourn there. Such a procedure would hamstring any change or growth in the university.

It would seem, then, that the more adequate way of conceiving the university-student relationship in the light of the legal documents available to us so far, is in terms of the essential structure (status) of the university community itself rather than in terms of a "contract" between two obviously unequal parties. In any case, the *in loco parentis* theory seems dead. *R.I.P.*! The status theory itself deserves further reflection, but before we turn to it one might do well to insist that the issue is far from closed. With the college degree becoming more and more a staple in American life, some have maintained that the harm threatened a student by expulsion or other disciplinary action may be far greater than that resulting from the prison sentence given a professional criminal, inasmuch as he is not only defamed but probably forever barred from attaining his professional goals.[39] Under these circumstances, it would be naïve to assume that the American Civil Liberties Union will not apply more and more pressure to increase judicial scrutiny of the university's use of its discretionary power in the disciplining of students.

No matter what may be the direction of subsequent court decisions, however, we have—in the conceptions already deline-

[38] "Whether the relationship in question is contract or status, should be decided by examining the actual freedom exercised by the parties entering such relationship. If the freedom of one or both parties is only nominal, the relationship should be treated as a status irrespective of the fact that it was entered into under the guise of contractual forms." (Endrey, Contract and Status, 29 Austl. L.J. 333, 337 [1955], cited in "Expulsion of College Students," [see note 34], p. 1168).

[39] See Seavey, "Dismissal of Students: 'Due Process,'" *Harvard Law Review*, LXX (1957), 1406–1407. See also Hacker, "The Boy Who Doesn't Go to College," The *New York Times Magazine*, June 24, 1962, p. 11.

ated—a valid starting point for reflecting on the nature of the university's disciplinary authority. Of the three conceptions mentioned, the status-theory seems to be the most satisfying. For one thing, it is the most organic. The university is conceived as a community with its own life and those prerogatives that arise from the demands, i.e., the "laws" of life. To speak of the student-university relationship as a "contract" seems no more than a legalistic way of saying that in entering the university the student agrees to permit this community life to be itself, and the university agrees to permit the student to share this life in order to let the student thereby be (in the most profound sense) *him*self. What is decisive, then, is the nature of the community life as such. And one would think that what might account for the appeal of the *in loco parentis* tradition (socio-historical considerations apart), is the fact that in a simplistic way the family is the most obvious paradigm for a community living that has its own organic structure.

An organic structure, the university community lives and grows with the larger community that creates it and which it serves.[40] No wonder, then, that the standards of conduct for university life should be deeply influenced by contemporary social and cultural patterns. The fact that such things as the use of cosmetics,[41] membership in fraternities,[42] and even marriage,[43] were once grounds for dismissal but now are accepted mores on most campuses, does not argue to the arbitrariness— still less to the sheer relativism—of disciplinary authority, but only to its intrinsic historicity.

But what precisely is the nature of the university commu-

[40] We have here in mind the fact that every university, as a legally constituted corporation, is "created" by the legislature, with only those rights and powers conferred upon it by the state.

[41] Pugsley v. Sellmeyer, 158 Ark. 247, 250 S.W. 538 (1923).

[42] Coggins v. Board of Educ., 223 N.C. 763, 28 S.E. 2d 527 (1944); People ex rel. Pratt v. Wheaton College, 40 Ill. 186 (1866); cf. Satan Fraternity v. Board of Pub. Instruction, 156 Fla. 222, 22 So 2d 892 (1945).

[43] Hall v. Mt. Ida School for Girls, 258 Mass. 464, 155 N.E. 418 (1927); State ex rel. Thompson v. Marion County Bd. of Educ., 202 Tenn. 29, 302 S.W. 2d 57 (1957); cf. Kissick V. Garland Independent School Dist., 330 S.W. 2d 708 (Tex. Ct. Civ. App. 1959).

nity? The problem has never been posed more acutely than in our own time, for the emergence of the New (or Radical) Left among student activists has cast a glaring light upon the entire structure of university life. What exactly is their complaint? And what do they propose as a remedy?

Perhaps we should begin by recalling how the New Left conceives the structure of society at large:

> *To the left is, of course, the Radical Left itself. In the conventional center the student sees the modern liberal. At the right is "the system." "The system" encompasses any social, political or religious organization which is large, affluent, organized, technical, and above all, highly impersonalized. Grouped together, therefore, on the right are such unlikely bedfellows as big government, big business, laissez-faire capitalism, Communism, and organized religion. In the liberal camp the student places persons (usually over thirty) and groups that think radical (who say they want to change "the system") but who somehow have a stake in "the system" and so cannot really be trusted. At the radical left are those who are willing to risk all (or who have nothing to risk) for the social changes that are necessary to dethrone "the system."*[44]

On the university level, the system is found in its present juridical structure—a system that imposes an education the students find irrelevant and impersonal.[45] What do they pro-

[44] P. H. Ratterman, S.J., "The Vision of Christ and Christian Freedom: Student Problems on the Catholic Campus," *Jesuit Educational Quarterly* 30 (1967), 12.

[45] For example, a recent summary report on "Students, Stress, and the College Experience" tells us that three themes kept recurring in the sessions: students wanted "an educational experience more relevant to the modern world; more authentic and personalized relationships between students and faculty; and the revision of the campus community from a nest of adversaries into a viable group of collaborators. (E.J. Shoben, Jr. in his summary of the National Conference on Student Stress, sponsored by the United States National Student Association under grants from the National Institute of Mental Health and the Danforth Foundation, and held in Warrenton, Virginia, November 11–14, 1965). *Students, Stress, and the College Experience* was published by the USNSA in May, 1966. Cited here according to R. Hassenger, "Freedom and the Quality of Student Life," *Academic Freedom and the Catholic University*, ed. E. Manier and J. Houck (Notre Dame: Fides, 1967), p. 159.

pose instead? A radical restructuring of university life in a way that would offer some secure base for student rights and freedoms. Hence they speak of making the three traditional sectors of university life—students, faculty, and administration—completely autonomous, each with the ultimate right of free decision with respect to its own particular functions in the university society (with some working agreement to adjudicate the inevitable conflicts).[46] Let us call this the three-sector theory of university structure. The result would be a university society that would be completely egalitarian, where every citizen would be entitled to one vote.[47] As for disciplinary regulations, none would be imposed that were not ratified by the students themselves. Hence, administrative authority as such extends only to academic affairs. Beyond that, students have all the rights of private citizens and any attempt on the university's part to regulate moral behavior is simply an invasion of privacy.[48]

To be sure, the Radical Left does not have many representatives on the Catholic campus but who will deny the influence of its ideas there? We must take account of this conception of campus life, then, if we are to ground the university's right to concern itself with student behavior and, in the Catholic university, with his formation in Christ.

First of all, in positive terms how ought we ourselves conceive the organic structure of university life? We take at full seriousness the notion of a "community of scholars in search of truth." The heart of the community is, of course, the faculty—the senior scholars. The students, too, are an integral part of the community, as junior scholars—some more scholarly than others, no doubt, but scholars all! Their work is essentially one of collaboration. But the scholars taken by themselves are a plurality—they do not become a unity, still less a community, without some unifying principle that organizes the whole. It is the task of the administration through its organizational function to serve as this unifying principle. I say to *serve* as

[46] See Ratterman, p. 14.

[47] See R. Heynes, "Extremes of action are polarizing our campuses," *College and University Business* (January, 1967), p. 46.

[48] *Ibid.,* p. 17.

this unifying principle. Its chief role then is one of service through unification, and this service is the basis of the administration's authority.

Now, can such a community be completely egalitarian? It would seem not. For a community of scholars in search of truth shares a common life that is itself structured both by the exigencies of scholarship and the nature of truth. Scholarship as such has its techniques, its norms, and its discipline, and as in any craft it is the skill itself which differentiates those that possess it from those that do not. Truth as such has its own secrets, and it is the secrets themselves that differentiate between those that are familiar with them and those that are not. Disparage as one may the teacher-student relationship, as suggesting too much the superiority of one and the inferiority of the other, still one cannot eliminate the difference between those who know and those who don't. Consequently, the life these collaborating scholars share (unified as it is by the organizational function of the administration) is also differentiated—not by some extrinsic authoritarian structure or legalistic tradition, but by the laws of life itself.

It is the law of life that demands the preservation of life, and the ancient experience of university life says that its self-preservation demands the right to enforce discipline. For ". . . discipline is the soul of such a body; and if persons egregiously offended against that order and discipline so necessary to be preserved in the university, the latter must have had a power to correct such offenses. . . ." Does it follow that this disciplinary power extends only to what pertains to the academic level of campus life (such as cheating, library violations, etc.) but not to the level of the students' personal lives (such as drink, drugs, and sex)? Certainly the Radical Left would say "yes," but many a sober "liberal" would join them here.[49] But is this not to restrict the educational aim to the level of the intelli-

---

[49] Disciplinary power is ancillary to educational aims, they would say, and it is exercised validly only in relation to this aim. Such, at least, is the position of the anonymous author of the Case Note, "Expulsion of College Students" (note 34). In the Carr-St. John case, for example, this author maintains that according to the contract-theory the Appellate Court's reversal was justified, but that according to the status-theory, where the case situation would have been judged for itself, the trial court's order of reinstatement should have been upheld.

gence alone and disregard what the Radical Left wants most to vindicate, i.e., the value of the student as a *person?* It is the person of the student that lives in a community of persons, so it would seem that the community has the right, at least (no matter how it may choose to exercise it), to be concerned with the behavior of students as persons, in their personal life—in relation with other persons in the community. Thus, the Brown report on student conduct, though contemptuous of the *in loco parentis* theory, remarks:

> *It is nonetheless clear to us that Brown University as a university community, cannot function without some minimal rules intended to keep order, to maintain, as much as possible, a way of student life that is physically and psychologically healthy, and to preserve satisfactory relations with the larger civil community of which the university is a part. . . .*[50]

What all this adds up to is that the status of the university, i.e., its own organic nature, offers a valid foundation for the university's elemental right to enforce discipline among its students, even (so it seems) in nonacademic matters. Nothing has been said about the scope of this right or the best manner of exercising it. Here the matter is more delicate. For both scope and exercise of such a right are conditioned by the historicity of the university community itself. In this respect, the New Left may, in its own peculiar way, be one of the signs of the times.

The spirit of the New Left, for all its excesses, is actually the transposition onto the university level of the spirit of the times, marked as they are by the search for human freedom. In its most superficial form, this freedom is conceived to be the exercise of civil liberties. Now, civil liberties connote to contemporary Americans a different kind of freedom than is suggested by the human rights of which the founders of the Republic spoke. For them, the fundamental rights of man were understood as natural to him, i.e., grounded in his nature, ratified by natural law, guaranteeing him personal autonomy. Let us call

---

[50] *Community and Partnership*, p. 9.

this the freedom of "independence." With the broadening experience of democratization in the nineteenth century, however, it became more common to conceive of man's rights as created and guaranteed by the Constitution, so that his rights became liberties that were identified with his status as a citizen—human rights became "civil liberties." And the surest testimony to them was the fact that a man could by his vote participate in the government that guaranteed his rights. Civil liberties culminated, then, in the right of political self-determination. Call this the "freedom of participation."[51]

But the twentieth century has given man a new experience of what human rights are (and thereby a new notion of freedom). They are rights of an economic and social character which permit a fuller human life. They find their best articulation in the Universal Declaration of Human Rights of the United Nations (1948) and include the right to work, to rest and leisure, to education, to an adequate standard of living, to social security, etc. In other words, they are the rights that enable a man to achieve personal fulfillment and may be called the freedom to create—to create, most of all, himself.[52]

When contemporary man seeks his freedom, then the word connotes for him (if only unconsciously) all three nuances: freedom to be autonomous, freedom to participate in government, freedom to achieve self-fulfillment. Today's student enjoys this experience of what freedom means. If he seeks the same kind of freedom on the level of his university education, this is not because he is an anarchist at heart but only that he is a child of his time. If one had to reproach him, it would not be because he takes his freedom too seriously but that he does not take it seriously enough. For the evolution of man towards the unfolding of his freedom in the exercise of civil liberties has moved further than the students seem to realize. They have not gone far enough with the movement of history:

The work of prehistory, archaeology and anthropology has shown man always to have lived in some kind of commu-

---

[51] See C.J. Friederich, "Rights, Liberties, Freedoms: a Reappraisal," *The American Political Science Review*, 57 (1963), 841–854.

[52] *Ibid.*, p. 843.

nity, and the free man is therefore not seen as the isolated man, the Robinson Crusoe, but as the man who lives in effective interdependence with his fellow men. Freedom means to be free to share and the sphere of independence is not primary, but a corollary of participation in the community and of contribution to it through one's creativity.

This profound shift in outlook and emphasis is even beginning to affect the conception of freedom for peoples and politics; while independence still dominates the oratory, every emergent nation seeks fulfillment in the voluntary and active participation in, and contribution to, mankind, even as imperfectly organized as it is in the United Nations.[53]

The movement of history, then, is toward freedom through *interdependence.* The most telling critique of the three-sector theory of university structure is that in refusing any concessions to inter*dependence* it fails to respect the law of man's evolving freedom—the theory's only possible source of validity.

The principle of interdependence that characterizes the common quest for freedom in our time finds its expression on the university level through the organic structure of the community itself. It makes demands of all the sectors of university life. It demands respect from the students for the laws of community living that give the administration the right to enforce discipline even in nonacademic matters. But it demands, too, that the administration (and faculty) respect the right of students to achieve their personal independence by sharing in the processes that determine the canons of discipline. The students are part of the community of which the administration is the unifying principle. Moreover, they should be able to do this creatively, and that means to so share in the deliberative process that they are able to experience how and why the regulations that are imposed upon them are a means to their own self-fulfillment.

A principle such as this could have major consequences on the academic level, of course, but we are considering only the

---

[53] *Ibid.*, p. 850.

address to the student's freedom in nonacademic matters. It is striking that the most sophisticated and most recent approach to the problem (the Brown report) should express the same approach to the problem that our more reflective method has yielded:

> *On the matter of making and enforcing social policies and student conduct rules, we believe that the university's common interests can best be identified and pursued through a partnership process. More specifically, it is our conviction that the students' role should be very substantial. First, social and student conduct policies and procedures impinge directly and almost exclusively upon the students; their impact, moreover, is doubly significant at a primarily residential university such as Brown. Second, we believe that students are more likely to act maturely and responsibly within a social system which they help to create and to enforce.*[54]

With this much of the Brown report the Catholic educator could live, perhaps, in peace. The rub appears, however, when the report considers how the university community relates to contemporary moral standards. If contemporary culture is extremely permissive with regard to the major problem areas (drugs, drink, sex), "a university has neither the power nor the sanctions to reverse these behavioral patterns." At best, it is "a continuous forum where the consequences of certain kinds of behavior are evaluated in the light of student interests and problems."[55] In other words, a university can have no moral commitments of its own.

Here we are at the heart of things. Is it possible for a community of scholars that *does* have moral commitments—i.e., a commitment to the Christian faith with consequences in the moral order—to accept students (who have been saturated in such a culture) as junior partners in determining the behavioral norms that the students will follow? The dilemma is clear. If one retains the old paternalistic manner of the past,

[54] *Community and Partnership*, p. 8.
[55] *Ibid.*, pp. 13–14.

does one not repudiate the movement of history and renounce any claim to being part of the mainstream of American education? Yet if one efficaciously accepts the principle of interdependence in our present cultural framework, is there not a real risk of abandoning one's Christian heritage?

It will be the purpose of the next section to show that to radically renounce paternalism is not to renounce the Christian heritage, and that to accept the principle of interdependence with discretion is the only way to salvage this heritage in our time.

THEOLOGICAL

Let us begin by admitting candidly that the courts have clearly recognized the right of church-affiliated institutions to impose standards of behavior on their students congruous with their own specific educational purposes, i.e., with the kind of institutions that they are. In the *Carr v. St. John's* case, for example, the court cited the New York State Education Law, section 313:

> *It is a fundamental American right for members of various religious faiths to establish and maintain educational institutions exclusively or primarily for students of their own religious faiths or to effectuate the religious principles in furtherance of which they are maintained. . . .*[56]

Leagally there seems to be no obstacle to a Catholic university's pursuing its authoritarian ways, if it insists.

But the issue is much larger than that. The question is, ought it do so? Given the legal right, does the Catholic university have a theological right to impose moral standards on students in authoritarian fashion? Certainly the Church itself recognizes the contemporary search for human freedom as a legitimate quest for fulfillment. It is one of the signs of the times that must be scrutinized and interpreted in the light of the gospel:[57]

---

[56] 231 N.Y. Supp. 2d 408.

[57] Pastoral Constitution on the Church in the Modern World, *The Documents of Vatican II*, ed. Walter A. Abbott, S.J., (New York: The America Press, 1966), pp. 201–202.

The People of God believe that it is led by the Spirit of the Lord, who fills the earth. Motivated by this faith, it labors to decipher authentic signs of God's presence and purposes in the happenings, needs, and desires in which this People has a part along with other men of our age. . . .[58]

Are we not, after all, going through a "new stage,"[59] "a new age in human history"?[60] And is this age not characterized by the fact that "modern man is on the road to a more thorough development of his own personality, and to a growing discovery and vindication of his own rights . . ."?[61] Surely in our present historical perspective we are not to see the movement, for all its excesses, as a degeneration, for "historical studies make a signal contribution to bringing men to see things in their changeable and evolutionary aspects. . . ."[62] Rather, ". . . we are witnesses of the birth of a new humanism, one in which man is defined first of all by his responsibility. . . ."[63] Certainly "God's Spirit, who with a marvelous providence directs the unfolding of time and renews the face of the earth, is not absent from this development. The ferment of the gospel, too, has aroused and continues to arouse in man's heart the irresistible requirements of his dignity."[64]

If such is the vision of the Church as a whole, how much more does it belong to the university, by which the academic world becomes present to (and operative in) the Church, to bring its competence to bear in the task of general discernment—and of implementing the consequences of what is discerned? In other words, should not the Catholic university be the first to discern—and, indeed, with effect—the authentically human (and therefore Christian) dimension of the present quest for student rights? And, reciprocally, if the Church has recently experienced a fresh awareness of the dignity of human

[58] *Ibid.*, p. 209.
[59] *Ibid.*, p. 202.
[60] *Ibid.*, p. 260.
[61] *Ibid.*, p. 240.
[62] *Ibid.*, p. 260.
[63] *Ibid.*, p. 261.
[64] *Ibid.*, p. 226.

freedom, ought not the university testify to this experience before the academic world? Ought it not bear witness, by the way it treats its students, to the fact that:

> God has willed that man be left in "the hand of his own counsel" (Eccl. 15.14) so that he can seek his Creator spontaneously. . . . Hence man's dignity demands that he act according to a knowing and free choice. Such a choice is personally motivated and prompted from within. It does not result from merely external pressure.[65]

In other words, if it is the role of the university to bear witness to the Church's respect for human intelligence and creativity, ought it not also bear witness to the Church's respect for the human conscience? If so, then it must radically renounce paternalism and authoritarianism in any form. But this is negative. What does this mean positively? Positively, we can begin with the thesis already proposed: that the university's role is to achieve a reciprocal presence between Church and academia. In effect, this means that it is an institutional witness. Maybe we might say simply that the university testifies to the Church's respect for the human conscience to the extent that it bears witness to its own witness.

In one sense, we might say that it is in the role of witness that a university is most profoundly Christian, for Jesus Christ himself came into the world for the purpose of giving witness to the truth,[66] and the apostles were commissioned to be first of all witnesses to what they had seen and heard.[67] But the witness par excellence for our purposes, is the most articulate of the apostles, Paul. We are familiar with the ancient story:

> "I am Jesus, and you are persecuting me. But get up and stand on your feet, for I have appeared to you for this reason: to appoint you as a servant and as witness of this vision. . . . I shall deliver you from the people and from

[65] *Ibid.*, p. 214.

[66] John 18:37. Cf. John 3:11, 32.

[67] Acts 1:8. The primary function of the apostles is to bear witness, not only to the resurrection (Luke 24:48; Acts 2:32; 3:15; 4:33; 5:32; 13:31; 22:15) but also to the whole of the public life (Luke 1:21; John 15:27; Acts 1:22; 10:39 ff).

the pagans, to whom I am sending you to open their eyes, so that they may turn from darkness to light, from the dominion of Satan to God, and receive, through faith in me, forgiveness of their sins and a share in the inheritance of the sanctified."

After that, King Agrippa, I could not disobey the heavenly vision. On the contrary, I started preaching. . . .[68]

Notice here that the Lord's commission to Paul was to serve him as a witness, that his testimony was to open the eyes of the gentiles that they of their own accord might turn from darkness to light, that the testimony took the form of preaching, and that preaching, understood as bearing witness, was his response to the Lord's invitation, i.e., the form of his own life of faith.

How Paul lived his vocation as witness we shall see shortly, but for the moment let us pause over the word *witness*. It suggests a double communion: a communion between the witness and the truth, or person, to which/whom he testifies; a communion (to be established) between the truth/person and the tribunal, or persons, before whom the witness testifies. This double communion is suggested by the formulae *being* witness and *bearing* witness.

What is it to *be* witness to a truth or—as we shall consider it here for the case of Paul—to a person? It is not merely to observe this person from a psychological distance but to be committed to him, identified with him in such a way that to deny him would be to deny oneself. "Whether to fact or to truth [or a person] . . . the witness consists in the commitment of a person to [what] he attests."[69]

It will follow, then, that the quality of the witness will be measured by the intimacy of the union between the witness and the one to whom he testifies, the extent to which they become one. So it happens that Christ's appeal to Paul to become his witness was first and foremost an invitation to profound union

---

[68] Acts 26:15–20. Unless otherwise noted, translations are taken from The Jerusalem Bible (Garden City, New York: Doubleday, 1966).

[69] J.L. MacKenzie, S.J., ed., "Witness," *Dictionary of the Bible* (Milwaukee: Bruce, 1965), pp. 933–935.

with Himself. Hence, too, the acceptance of Christ's invitation to be a witness was primarily a free response of love, i.e., of faith.

The role of witness, however, implies not only *being* witness but *bearing* witness. This implies the establishment of the second communion, i.e., between the person to whom one testifies and the person or persons who receive testimony. Notice the mediational character of the witness's function. As a witness the person cannot be satisfied with only personal union with the one to whom he is committed; the witness must share this person with other persons. In helping others gain access to the person to whom he testifies, he shares with them the communion that he himself enjoys, thereby growing more deeply in it himself.

Perhaps we could describe this function of mediation best as one of "translucence." The witness is to convey to other men the luminosity of the light, not by reflection without absorption, as the moon reflects the sun, but by a luminous interiority, as a window pane transmits light. If the metaphor is acceptable, the function of the witness as witness is to achieve translucence.

But the metaphor may *not* be acceptable, if only because persons usually suffer when they are likened to things. When we say that the witness is translucent, we imply a certain self-effacement in him—but we must not think of this as a self-negation. The commitment of one person to another person in being the latter's witness is precisely *as* commitment (self-donation) a fulfillment of himself in all his unique individuality. In other words, he finds himself in losing himself. The individuality of the witness gives a specific character to his testimony. This is what differentiates one witness from another, making Paul's witness different from John's—though both bear witness to the same Jesus.

There is another aspect of self-effacement, implicit in the metaphor of translucence, that must not be misunderstood. Translucence is a form of mediation, to be sure, but when the witness supplies this function, does he not seem to lose any significance in and for himself, once the second communion is established? No—we must not think of it that way. The witness in his individuality encounters his hearers in their individuality. There arises a personal relation between them—communion of another (third) kind. It is through *this* communion that the hearers gain access to the Lord and enter into communion with Him. Note, however, that they gain access to the Lord through Paul *as* Paul; and the Lord comes to them in Paul *as* Paul. In other words, one function that the witness performs is to testify that communion with the Lord does not destroy the individuality of the person, but fulfills it. When all is said and done, Paul's witness, in effect, is an invitation to those with whom he has entered into a human communion to share with him his communion in the Lord, so they, too, may find in Him the fullness that Paul has found. That is why when Paul turns to exhortation he finds it so natural to appeal to the brethren to *imitate* him. To imitate Paul is to freely accept the gift (*charis*) of the Lord so that He may be in them *as* them. In this way they are formed in Christ.[70]

It cannot be our purpose here, of course, to analyze in detail how Paul went about bearing witness to Christ. Let it suffice to say that in bearing witness he never ceased to be witness—"I live now not with my own life but with the life of Christ who lives in me."[71] More important for us is that his bearing witness took the form of the entire apostolic endeavor to share with men "the Good News of God's grace."[72] Moreover, the Good News was not simply a message about Christ but the power of God made available to men through Paul's ambassadorship.

It was God who reconciled us to himself through Christ and gave us the work of handing on the reconciliation. In

[70] In this section the writer is especially indebted to the criticism of Robert O'Connell, S.J. He suggests the possibility of conceiving the witness not as translucence but as "symbolic embodiment." He writes in a personal communication: "The 'symbolic embodiment' must always be seen and reverenced in and for itself, but that reverence for it must be reverence for a *symbolic* embodiment, i.e., go beyond the embodiment to the 'world of values' symbolically embodied, without *short-circuiting* the embodiment; (i.e., to get to the world of values as though the embodiment were a transparency) and without, on the other hand, stopping short at the embodiment as though it were not symbolic embodiment (i.e., of a world of values transcending the embodiment)."

[71] Gal. 2:20.

[72] Acts 20:24.

other words, God . . . has entrusted to us the news that men
are reconciled. So we are ambassadors for Christ; it is as
though God were appealing through us, and the appeal
that we made in Christ's name is: be reconciled with God.[73]

To be sure, the word of God is powerful,[74] and Paul is its
legitimate ambassador; but no effort is made to compel its
acceptance. All that Christ does through Paul is to appeal for
human response.

For the truth to which Paul is witness solicits response—like
the Jesus of the gospels—but does not compel it. To be sure,
there are moral consequences for those who have become God's
adoptive sons and Paul doesn't hesitate to spell them out. But
the tone is always one of exhortation. He begs the faithful to
accept himself as witness—to imitate him. "Brothers, all I ask
is that you should copy me as I copied you."[75] It is by following
a model that one learns best how to live as a son of God. "Take
as your models everybody who is already doing this and study
them as you used to study us."[76] And in counseling Titus as
to how to deal with the unruliness of youth, he insists on the
importance of example as a means of instruction:

In the same way, you have got to persuade the younger
men to be moderate and in everything you do make your-
self an example to them of working for good: when you
are teaching, be an example to them in your sincerity and
earnestness and in keeping all that you say so wholesome
that no one can make objections to them.[77]

But imitation for Paul is not merely a means of instruction.
It is also a criterion of success. Through this success the communion spreads among still others and the community grows
slowly towards the fullness of Christ:

We know brothers, that God loves you and that you have

[73] 2 Cor. 5: 18-20.
[74] 1 Cor. 1:18; Rom. 1:16.
[75] Gal. 4:12.
[76] Phil. 3:17.
[77] Tit. 2:6.

been chosen, because when we brought the Good News to you, it came to you not only as words, but as power and as the Holy Spirit and as utter conviction. And you observed the sort of life we lived *when we were with you, which was for your instruction, and you were led to become* imitators *of us, and of the Lord. . . . This has made you the great example to all believers in Macedonia and Achaia since it was from you that the word of the Lord started to spread— not only throughout Macedonia and Achaia, for the news of your faith in God has spread everywhere. We do not need to tell other people about it: other people tell us [about it]. . . .*[78]

Finally, it is through this appeal for imitation by the faithful alone that Paul exercises the prerogatives of his very legitimate parenthood:

My dearest children. . . . You may have thousands of guardians in Christ, but no more than one father, and it was I *who* begot you *in Christ Jesus by preaching the Good News.* That is why I beg you to copy me, *and why I have sent you to Timothy, my dear faithful son in the Lord: he will remind you of the way that I live in Christ, as I teach it everywhere in all the churches.*[79]

Here, then, is paternity without paternalism.

What follows from all this? It follows that the principal means available to the Catholic institutions to help its students to be formed in Christ is its mediation between them and Him—its function of translucence. This comports both being witness and bearing witness to Him. The first way for it to be witness to Him is its uncompromising commitment to truth, where truth, once more, is not some*thing* but Some*one:* a Person—the God-become-man-in-history.

What this implies in terms of the university's horizontal orientation toward academic excellence we have already tried to describe. What it means in terms of a vertical orientation

---

[78] 1 Th. 1:4–7.
[79] 1 Cor. 4:15–17, (writer's italics). Cf., 1 Th. 2:11; 2 Cor. 14, 17.

toward union with Christ in the Church we have also suggested: a liturgy of action (i.e., academic endeavor conceived
as itself an act of worship), and a liturgy of sacrament (i.e.,
the public address to God by the community, in community-
fashion). It might be worth insisting that this public gesture
toward God flows from a certain kind of community that at
the same time it helps to sustain. What specifies the kind of
community is the vertical orientation itself. But what does
orientation of a community mean? How does it come about? At
this point, we move into a philosophical area that might be
better left to philosophers. Let us content ourselves with the
obvious: the orientation of a community such as we have in
mind will somehow involve the self direction of a significant
number of its members toward an ideal they find commonly
acceptable, in such fashion that there will be not simply a common activity but a certain style of life that they share, hence
a mood or atmosphere characteristic of the community as such.
It is in this sense that we can speak of the spirit of a university
community—intangible, indefinable but quite real.

Now the style of living that characterizes a university's vertical union with Christ, experienced as synthesis of God and man
(truth as revealed and truth as discovered) comports more
than a commitment to explore this polyvalent truth concep-
tually according to the professional standards of academia. It
comports doing the truth as well.[80] Nor is this a uniquely
Christian insight. Was it not the experience of Plato as well?
In any case, this type of effective commitment to truth is
implied one would think, in the deepest meaning of wisdom.

Now wisdom thus understood, i.e., as a style of living that
implies doing the truth as well as knowing it, is an essential
element in the formation of the Christian. Yet it can neither
be taught in the classroom nor tested in exams. In this sense it
is profoundly nonacademic. But by the same token, it cannot
be inculcated by the dean of men. To do the truth is to do it
freely. One must accept Truth-as-Person of one's own accord
after one has gained access to Him (often enough through the

---

[80] John 3:27; 1 John 3:29 ff.

mediation of personal witness). If one learns anything in this regard from the mediator, it is principally by way of imitation. In other words, one comes to share the fellowship of human communion with the witness and through this subtle pedagogy learns from him the secret of finding one's life by losing it.

We would be inclined to argue, then, that whatever is to be said for disciplinary regulations, they contribute little to the student's formation in Christ and conceivably could contribute to his de-formation. The students of today will grow in Christ only to the extent that they encounter authentic Christian witness. This they should find first of all on the institutional level where the community of scholars really is what it claims to be—a group of persons totally committed to the search for truth, with all the intellectual integrity and academic freedom that this implies. They should find it, too, on the institutional level where the liturgy of action crystallizes in a liturgy of sacrament that is genuinely meaningful for them, both as a community gesture and as an address to God. But they should find it most profoundly and most intimately in the men and women with whom they live.

This last phrase is deliberately vague. We all know as a matter of fact that the most decisive influence in the formation of students is the students themselves. Was it not Cardinal Newman who claimed that if he had to choose between the education in the classroom and that of the dormitories, he would choose the latter? And did not Stephen Leacock affirm that if he were to found a university, he would establish first smoking rooms, then a library, then dining halls, then a faculty —in that order? Just why this is the case, is the task of a social psychologist to explain. One reason might be that, generally speaking, nothing can touch a person so profoundly as another human person. The reason why the classroom may have less to do with the educational process than the dormitory is that the former is where the mind meets mind, but the latter is the place of personal encounter. Ideally, then, one should find among the students themselves authentic Christian witness. But this is not a constant on which we can count. The faculty, however, is such a constant—and they are the senior scholars. It would seem then, that the most eloquent testimony to the Christian vision of God-Man-in-history is the witness of the faculty (and administration), not simply in the classroom but on the level of personal encounter.

What such a faculty witness on the level of personal encounter might involve is a question that must be reserved for some other occasion.[81] Let it suffice to say for the moment that if this theory is defensible, we would have some way of approaching the difference that ought to exist between institutions that are all Catholic by commitment but run by various religious communities or by diocesan priests. The difference would not be found in the respective curricula, nor even (at least directly) in the traditions of the several institutions, but rather in the characteriology of the group itself, insofar as each group will have its own proper way of rendering its witness to Christ.

There are three pieces of evidence that one might point to as confirming the thesis that has been developed, namely that the power role of the Catholic university in the formation of the Christian lies not in its disciplinary regulations but in its Christian witness. The first is the testimony of several Notre Dame students with regard to the pastoral gap they had experienced on campus. Their testimony is valuable because it articulates an attitude that characterizes, as far as we know, almost every Catholic campus.

Senior history major: *Theology here doesn't rise above the level of an intellectual game. I think about Christianity*

---

[81] The dimensions of the problem are suggested by the following notation from Robert O'Connell, S.J., with regard to this argument: "I think a theological reflection on all this would do justice to what is meant (without doing justice, *bêtement*, to each atomic expression) in terms of the (a) density of each individual personal witness, enhanced by (b) the union with the Personal-Truth involved, so that (c) the individual witness becomes himself more fully in the vis-à-vis with this Personal-Truth, which is a constant dynamic growth in free, gratuitous interpersonal love, such that (d) the instinct develops for the same kind of relationship with others to whom witness is being borne: the same dynamic growth in free, gratuitous interpersonal love is seen as valid and needed in his relation with the hearers of his witness, the witnesses of his life of bearing-and-being-as-one. What is saved is all the appeal to freedom you want; what may be required is a kind of personal respect on the part of the hearers for the witness and the idiosyncratic conditions of his personal witness, which may make some kind of discipline not only a practical but a theological necessity."

but who can I turn to to witness to me how to live it? Certain priests can teach me to lose my childhood faith but there is very limited witness to the life that you live after you pass through this stage.

Junior philosophy major: *Witness is paramount. Theology classes and theological talk don't help. There has to be witness. The priest has to be Christian manifestly. He has to have willingness to give of himself. Of the chaplains in the halls how many do the students even feel approachable? The priest would have to go out to the students. Intellectual life seems non-essential to Christian life. The only one I know who ties the two together well is Father* _____.

Senior English major: *The academic discipline is the best place for the priest to be. . . . A priest in an academic discipline is setting an example I'd like to follow because I'd like to do something like that.*[82]

In a word, these students seem most of all to want authentic witness.

Another testimony is an observation of A. M. Greeley, who in the confidential discussion draft of his *Academic Growth in Catholic Colleges,* discusses student attitudes and remarks:

Some of them will leave the Church, but the vast majority of them will not. But almost all of the creative, concerned, committed minority seem to come out of the Catholic colleges with a great deal of suspicion and contempt not only for the religious orders that run the college, but also for the whole institutionalized Church. The words "hypocrite" and "phony" seem to be on the lips of most of the student leaders that were interviewed in the course of our study.[83]

Here again, it would seem that what the students found wanting was genuine Christian witness.

[82] R. Hassenger, G. Ranch, "Problem Areas: The Student," *The Shape of Catholic Higher Education,* ed. R. Hassenger (Chicago: University Press, 1967), pp. 217–221.

[83] From A.M. Greeley, *Academic Growth in Catholic Colleges,* Confidential Discussion Draft, p. 31.

Finally, we have a document that is extremely relevant at the present time, partly because it represents quite clearly the beginning of a trend, partly because the attitude behind it is extremely suggestive. The bylaws of St. Louis University declare that "the University will be publicly identified as a Catholic University and as a Jesuit University," and that "the University will be motivated by the moral, spiritual and religious inspiration and values of the Judaeo-Christian tradition." Fair enough; but when the Jesuit community began to negotiate its separate incorporation it became necessary to spell out what would be the relationship between the community and the university. Hence, the whole question of "Jesuit presence" was at stake. In the introduction to a brochure entitled *Foundation Statements and Articles Relevant to the Jesuit Residence at St. Louis University,* we have some indication of what it is to mean. The statement says:

> *When speaking of Jesuits assigned to St. Louis University and the Provincial's relationship to the Jesuits, nothing more is intended than would pertain to a Missouri Province Jesuit changed to the faculty of e.g., Harvard.*[84]

Is it fair to infer that the role of the Society of Jesus at St. Louis University is to be henceforth what it would be if it were affiliated with Harvard, i.e., one of individual and collective witness? The impression that this is the case is confirmed when the question of Jesuit orientation, sponsorship, and support of the university is discussed. All of these are guaranteed by supplying the president, hopefully some major administrative officers, some faculty, ten professors for the divinity school, a university chaplain, and by maintaining the college church.[85] Nothing about discipline! When all is said and done, the influence of the Society of Jesus will be maintained essentially by the *witness* of its members.

This may all be very well, but there are certain practical problems.

---

[84] *Foundation Statements and Articles Relevant to the Jesuit Residence at St. Louis University.* Pro manuscripto.
[85] *Ibid.*

THE PRACTICAL PROBLEM

Let us review our reflections thus far:

1. In the formation of the Christian, the university must address itself to the freedom of the student but has the right to impose certain standards of behavior.

2. This right is not based on the fact that it is a surrogate parent to the student nor that it is an equal party to a contract with the student. It is based on its own status as a community of scholars, which—as an organic unity—has an indigenous structure of its own that imposes on the entire community (students included) a pattern of living that derives from the law of life itself.

3. A Catholic university is a special kind of community of scholars. It is differentiated from other such communities because it has a vertical orientation toward Christ in the Church; it is witness to Him and bears witness to Him, not only seeking the truth but in doing it. It bears this witness first of all to its own students both collectively (as an institution), and individually through its members—and, in a special way, through its faculty. It is the type of witness and not the paternalism of the discipline to be found in the Catholic university that ought to differentiate it from other university communities.

More precisely, what do we recommend? It seems to follow from our argument that in a community of scholars, which is an association of collaborators—differentiated among themselves, to be sure, by seniority, learning, and experience, but nonetheless, co-workers and interdependent—there should be a certain partnership in the determination of the standards of behavior and also in implementing them. I say a certain partnership. I mean that students should have a place on the board which determines (and implements) the norms of student conduct. I would even think that they should be given a deliberative vote in the matter, though by no means a dominant one (according to the one-person one-vote theory). Unless we are willing to go this far, I suspect we do not take the principle of interdependence seriously enough.

The principle of interdependence does not say egalitarianism; still less does it say life without structure. On the contrary, it says that the structures of life follow the laws of life, in this case the laws of community living. In formulating regulations for student behavior the legislating body would follow, we presume, the basic principles of good lawmaking in moral matters, principles that themselves are formulated as a result of a long experience of community living.[86] We need not discuss them in detail here, but it would be well to recall that good jurisprudence seeks an equilibrium between two operative principles that could easily oppose one another. The first would be that "to change the law on a subject of public morality is all too often taken by a part of the population as a modification of morality itself."[87] The second is, law ". . . reflects the community's moral conscience. For this reason, laws that impose moral standards on personal conduct ought to enjoy the support of a consensus."[88] In any case, what are at stake in both cases are the moral values of the community that are prior to law.

Specifically, what are the laws of life that arise from the demands of university living? In some measure they have been embodied in certain standards of behavior that have become traditional on university campuses. But what must be made clear to the students is that they are not part of contemporary university life because they are traditional, but that they have become traditional because they are demanded by the laws of a university life itself. Extremists apart (but they are relatively few), what the students object to is the sheer formalism of imposed standards whose only apparent warrant is the authoritarianism with which they are imposed. What they want to do is see the reasons for the standards and see them for themselves. How does one determine the laws of life that are indigenous to a community of scholars? The Brown report offers a good example of sound collective wisdom and we would like to offer it as a tentative working formula.

[86] A bibliography here could be extensive. For a fine brief treatment, however, see F. Canavan, S.J., "Law and Morals in Pluralistic Society," *Catholic Mind* (April, 1966), pp. 49–65.

[87] *Ibid.*, p. 53.

[88] *Ibid.*, p. 52.

In general terms, the Brown report makes clear that the university is not indifferent to the moral dimension of student life but that it sees its concern as best expressed through positive efforts of education and counselling rather than through the negative measures of disciplinary rules.[89] In terms of the Catholic campus, the instructional aspect of moral formation would take place in the normal way through courses in theology, philosophy (ethics), liturgical homilies, etc.; and in particular areas (such as sex) through specialized courses. As for the counseling aspect of the problem, one would think that this is one area in which the Catholic campus should excel. It would be naïve to assume, of course, that an abundance of priests and religious are generally speaking not equipped to be competent counselors to college students. Moreover, counselors are not enough. There must be psychiatrists, too. What the ratio should be between psychiatrists and students is for others to decide.

How the Brown report deals with individual issues (drugs, drink, sex, etc.) may best be examined in detail at leisure. As some indication, however, of how the principle of interdependence (when interpreted with discretion) does not lead to lawlessness, we might examine the advisory committee's attitude toward sexual intercourse on campus:

> *The university assumes that its residential units will not be used for sexual intercourse. The principal reason for this policy is concern for the quality of the collective life in its residential units. Abuse of the university's position may result in disciplinary action. However, in specific disciplinary cases that may arise, the university's primary concern should be for the emotional and physical well-being of the individuals.*[90]

In a supplementary explanation of its position, the committee adds:

> *Although the primary emphasis must be on counseling and education, this does not mean that it is inappropriate for*

---

[89] *Community and Partnership,* p. 9.
[90] *Ibid.,* p. 26.

Brown University to state an explicit policy as to sexual behavior by students within its residential units. To do otherwise is to leave students with the belief that the University . . . condones and indeed facilitates sexual permissiveness. Brown University cannot regulate the sexual behavior of its students off campus, but it can insist on the observance of certain rules of behavior on campus consonant with standards that it thinks proper.[91]

In citing this passage, we do not wish to argue that the Catholic university should make the statement its own. All we wish to say is that this particular student-faculty committee does take some stand on the matter. The principle of interdependence, properly understood, does not mean complete capitulation to the passions of youth. In this issue, there are other arguments—not mentioned by the Brown committee—why any university has a right to take a strong stand against sexual intercourse on campus.[92] One could add to these the right of other students not to be pressured into an unwanted type of intramural competition; the right of those in doubt (as to moral values in general and sex in particular), to form their consciences at their own pace without living in an atmosphere that forces decisions before their time; the right of the university, like any landlord's, to refuse to have its premises turned into a brothel; and finally, the right of the university to avoid misrepresenting itself by giving the impression that it really doesn't care. At any rate, these considerations could be made intelligible to the students, too, so that they could see that regulations are not prescribed merely in the name of authority, nor to impose a private morality. They are intended to let the entire community (with all its differentiation) be more completely itself.

Let us conclude by dealing with one objection that might be raised. Do we not, after all, attribute to the student a matu-

[91] *Ibid.*

[92] See, for example, "Sex," in G.B. Blaine, Jr., M.D., *Youth and the Hazards of Affluence* (New York: Harper and Row, 1966), pp. 43–64. W. Dalrymple, M.D., "A Doctor Speaks of College Students and Sex," in *University* (Princeton University Magazine), 1966.

rity (therefore responsibility) that exceeds the fact? And is not this responsibility the price that he ought to pay for his freedom of participation? The objection is substantive. Neither we nor the advisory committee at Brown wish to deny that adolescence is a legitimate concept.[93]

Still less do we wish to deny the built-in drag toward evil in man. These are all contributing factors to the problem, but the fundamental question is: What is maturity? How does one achieve it? Different men mature at different paces and different levels of the same man have a different tempo. Nonetheless, there is a cut off point in a young man's development, highly conditioned by the culture in which he lives, where the imposition of behavior patterns *de facto* cease to be educative and the only educative way to influence his development is through an appeal to intelligence and freedom. Is there not reason to argue that in contemporary society the cut off point has already been passed by the time he reaches college age? Explain it in whatever way you will, the fact is that youngsters who have been raised in the electronic age have, by the time they reach college, been thoroughly exposed to all the sordid amenities of life in the global village. Certainly they are sharper and better informed than their fathers were at their age. By the age of eighteen they have been exposed to all of the vicarious thrills that television can supply; they are old enough to drink in public (in New York), old enough to drive a car, old enough to die in Viet Nam and now, perhaps, old enough to vote. With this experience and these privileges, who is to say that they are not ready for the adult world? In any case, here they come ready or not! The formation of their freedom, one would think, comes about by letting it be itself, letting it find its own intrinsic limits and thereby discern its own structure. For freedom is structured and the proper functioning of this structure is dictated by the laws of life.[94]

We must trust the laws of life. They direct the unfolding

---

[93] *Community and Partnership*, p. 9.

[94] This is the principal point we took J.G. Milhaven, S.J. to be making in his controversial article, "Be Like Me! Be Free," *America* (April 22, 1967), pp. 584–586.

conscience of our students and determine the structure of their freedom. They operate in the deepest center of man, where the Spirit has taken up his abode:

> *Conscience is the most secret core and sanctuary of a man. There he is alone with God, whose voice echoes in his depths. In a wonderful manner conscience reveals that law which is fulfilled by love of God and neighbor. In fidelity to conscience, Christians are joined with the rest of men in the search for truth, and for the genuine solution to the numerous problems which arise in the life of individuals and from social relationships. . . .*[95]

We must trust the laws of life. Through them the Spirit "with a marvelous providence directs the unfolding of time." In their own mysterious way they move the universe slowly toward the fullness of God-become-Man-in-history. To recognize these laws and learn to correspond with them is not to renounce our heritage but to vindicate it and live the Christian witness in our time.

[95] *The Documents of Vatican II*, pp. 213–214.

Development Problems in America: 1968-1975

PAUL C. REINERT, S.J.

What are the development problems facing American Catholic higher education in the period between 1968 and 1975? The answer may be found by analyzing the resources for current operations, the resources for capital expenditures, the financial crisis facing private universities, and the alternatives for financial stability.

A comprehensive source of facts on current operations is the United States Office of Education Report of 1963–1964, based on a financial study of eighty-eight public and fifty-eight private American universities.

TABLE I

CURRENT FUND INCOME OF UNIVERSITIES—1963–64

	Public	Private	St. Louis University
Tuition and Fees	10.2%	25.6%	35.7%
Federal Government	24.5%	33.6%	15.1%
State Government	36.6%	2.3%	. . . . .
Local Government	1.5%	.5%	. . . . .
Private Gifts	2.9%	8.8%	7.2%

As table 1 indicates, tuition and fees for public universities amounted to only 10.2 percent of the total current fund, while at private schools nationally the comparable amount was 25.6

percent. At Saint Louis University, we show a figure of 35.7 percent. It is apparent that a virtually insignificant amount comes from state and local governments, with 2.3 percent from state government and only .5 percent from local government. Thus, we can only conclude that private universities—and in particular, Saint Louis University—will have to depend on tuition and fees as their prime source of current income.

Private gifts amounted to a very important source of current fund income, yet this figure in 1963 and 1964 was merely 8.8 percent for private schools nationally, and a bit less than that (7.2 percent) at Saint Louis University.

Among the significant factors affecting tuition as a source of income, there is the increased local competition, particularly in urban centers, resulting in many cases from the growth of junior and community colleges and the effect of the branches of the state universities. Enrollment trends also greatly affect tuition income. Most of the recent data indicates that approximately two-thirds of today's students are in public institutions, but in the next ten years this alarming statistic will expand to about 80 percent.

Because of the need of private universities to increase tuition fees, private higher education is in danger of being priced out of the market. Socioeconomic factors also affect tuition as a source of income because of the growing danger that private institutions may find themselves catering to the upper-income strata of our society.

Several factors inhibit consideration of the federal government as a major source of income. For one thing, support from the federal government aims primarily at research, and this support of research generally tends to concentrate on a small percentage of the larger more prestigious institutions. Moreover, such government grants do not cover overhead or hidden costs connected with the operation and administration of research.

Government grants seem to entice institutions to go beyond or outside of their general objectives and potential. Often the attractiveness of grants for public purposes changes the institutional purposes so that grants can be acquired. This factor is closely related to the fact that the federal government in this way tends to exercise indirect control over the institution through restrictions and requirements. Institutions also must realize that if they become highly dependent on substantial amounts of government support, they can create excessive dependence on federal aid as a single source of support, thus weakening their overall financial potential.

In considering the state government as a source of current income we must recognize the fact that centralized state planning for public institutions frequently ignores the place and contribution of private institutions. There are a few exceptions, notably the states of New York, Maryland, Illinois and Wisconsin. State legislatures have been unwilling to support programs that would be of direct or indirect assistance to private institutions, particularly in the areas of scholarships, tuition grants, and building loans. This may be changing.

Gifts from private sources contribute significantly to current income. However, studies by the Council for Financial Aid to Education point out that while support of higher education by business corporations has steadily increased, the total is not in proportion to the needs of the institutions. Moreover, although most of the major national corporations have sophisticated programs of aid to colleges and universities, the base of giving has not been sufficiently spread among what might be called "second-echelon" but nonetheless profitable corporations.

TABLE II

PRELIMINARY FINDINGS FROM THE CFAE SURVEY "VOLUNTARY SUPPORT OF EDUCATION, 1965–1966"

	Grand Total of Support	Alumni	Corporations & Business
Major Private Universities (55)	$444,201.052	$95,792,300	$55,767,398
% Change, 1964–1966	− 7.8%	− 4.2%	+11.4%
State Universities and Colleges (170)	232,219,482	45,875,654	58,911,023
% Change, 1964–1966	+19.9%	+49.7%	+21.6%
Associated Colleges of the Midwest (9)	15,738,663	2,800,409	2,132,504
% Change, 1964–1966	− 5.5%	−49.4%	− 8.1%
Great Lakes College Association (11)	22,998,163	6,269,175	3,029,704
% Change, 1964–1966	+ 5.6%	−15.9%	− 1.1%
The Ivy League	157,873,407	53,229,137	15,180,753
% Change, 1964–1966	−27.8%	−22.2%	+ 4.7%

The CFAE reports of 1962–63 and 1964–65 indicate that alumni giving has been increasing, but—again—not in proportion to the needs or in relationship to other sources of support. CFAE reports that "among all groups which support education, alumni increased their gifts nearly 12.4 percent between the biennial CFAE surveys of 1962–1963 and 1964–1965—the smallest gain registered by any source except religious denominations." Even more alarming is the fact, as Table 2 shows, alumni gifts to private institutions are falling.

Gifts from foundations to higher education have been on the increase, but these, too, have been highly categorized and have tended to supplement rather than support the hard core of university operational expenditures. Some foundations, noticeably the Ford Foundation, are moving away from—rather than toward—direct institutional support.

Special gifts as a major source of income, either directly from individuals or through deferred methods such as trusts, constitute one of the most promising sources of support, but inevitably tend to be restricted. Finally, few private institutions have been able to build up substantial endowments, with the result that endowment income plays a decreasingly significant role in the support of annual operations.

Resources for capital expenditures come from private sources and from the federal government, in the form of grants and loans. The Higher Education Facilities Act is a prime example of federal government grants. This act provides grants up to one-third of construction costs. However, our experience indicates that many private institutions are having difficulty in securing the other two-thirds. In the area of federal loans, the HEFA loan program for student residences and other income-producing facilities has been of tremendous assistance, but due to huge governmental commitments tied to the Viet Nam war, loans for these purposes are extremely difficult to secure.

Foundations serve as resources for capital expenditures; but in general, they refuse to provide funds for capital expenditures, and those that do are rare. The potential of individuals as resources for capital expenditures is heightened by the attractiveness of memorials in brick and stone. These constitute a much greater appeal to individual donors than gifts toward operational expenditures. However, such gifts rarely cover more than construction costs and place the university in the difficult position of securing additional funds for the increased operational budget which every new building creates.

It is obvious after considering sources of current income and resources for capital expenditures that the private university is currently faced with certain financial crises. In the last five years most private universities have allocated too large a portion of their unrestricted income to capital expenditures. Several factors influenced this situation, among them the demands of rapid enrollment increases, replacement of obsolete facilities and the necessity of correcting the defects of deferred maintenance. The result has been serious, if not tragic. Current funds have been exhausted, excessive borrowing either from internal funds or elsewhere has been approved, and operational budgets have been squeezed to a point where serious academic deficiencies have resulted.

Rapid physical expansion without adequate projection of concomitant demands in terms of personnel, maintenance, utilities costs, etc., has created an additional squeeze on the operational budget. As a result of this physical expansion, most private institutions are operating with a substantial gap between their operational income and expenditures. The normal sources of support are totally inadequate to meet the demands of the current situation. Tuition is already dangerously high; endowment capital and income is low; support from foundations, corporations, alumni, and friends is—at best—leveling off. And governmental aid continues to be specialized and categorical. At the same time, costs—especially in the competitive, essential area of faculty salaries—are increasing at a rapid pace. To a greater or lesser degree, private institutions have not found the answer to the critical problem of the basic and sustained funding of their general operations.

In speculating toward steps for financial stability in the future, it would seem that three proposals would be in order. Private higher education must learn to explore all possible resources, must decide on the uniqueness of its contribution, and must clarify its public policy regarding the desirability of a diversified pattern of higher education.

It appears that federal support will have to move in the direction of general institutional support, as recommended by the American Council on Education, the Association of American Colleges, and the Association of State Colleges and Universities and Land-Grant Colleges. Along with general institutional support could come tax credits and credits for tuition or gifts.

Tuition income will have to be increased; but with an accompanying enlargement of available student aid, particularly in the form of grants and loans. Corporate support will have to increase substantially, particularly by spreading the base to many more local and national businesses. And giving by individuals—especially alumni—must be increased, particularly through the various methods of deferred giving which are encouraged by the federal government.

Well-established, continuing departments of development will be necessary, not solely for occasional capital funds campaigns, but as an integrated factor in securing annual operational income. One of the major criticisms which emerged from the Danforth Study of the 817 private church-related colleges in the United States is the fact that few of these institutions have development departments whose personnel are accepted, respected, assisted, and professionally integrated into the rest of the institution.

Private higher education must define the unique contribution which it is capable of making in the United States, and on the basis of recognized objectives and limitations it must determine the level of educational endeavor which it can afford to offer. When private higher education considers its unique contribution, avenues will be opened for many consolidations and mergers. Institutions will be forced to follow guidelines based on what is most beneficial to themselves and the communities they serve.

Private higher education, with the exception of a limited number of the most prestigious institutions, will not be able to continue its significant contribution to American higher education unless there is a clarification of public policy regarding the desirability and need for a diversified system of higher education. The clarification of public policy would affect different segments of private higher education in different ways, but its implications for the large, complex, private, church-related university may be stated as follows.

The evolving relationship of the federal government to these institutions must include the following concepts:

1. Since these institutions have consistently made a substantial contribution to the undergraduate, graduate, and professional educational resources of this country and will continue to do so, all federal programs relating to higher education should be equally and proportionally available to these private universities as well as to their public counterparts.

2. In accordance with the general principle that private institutions can respond to national needs at least as quickly and creatively as public institutions, the federal government's efforts to establish and increase outstanding national centers of excellence should be as specifically directed to private as to public institutions which possess the necessary potential for such development.

3. Since the federal government is committed to the policy of increasing the number of universities over and above the relatively small group of institutions now carrying on distinctive research work, this commitment should be exercised for the development of a proportionate number of private universities, not now in the "top ten," as well as for additional state universities.

4. The church-related institutions number over 800 out of the 1,420 private colleges and universities in the country. If these institutions are to continue to make a significant contribution to the total American educational effort, the federal government will have to take whatever means are necessary to place these institutions in the public eye in a position of equality and legal acceptance as bona fide education institutions. While it is unfortunately true that

there are church colleges and universities in the United
States that have been and may still be guilty of regulations
and practices which violate the commonly accepted norms
of academic freedom for their faculty and student-body,
the general assumption that a religiously-oriented agency
cannot conduct an educational institution without vitiat-
ing its essential academic character is a misconception.
Violations of academic freedom, obsolete policy-making
relationships between trustees and administrators, and inadequate internal arrangements for faculty participation
in decision-making, as well as any other deviations from
good academic policy and practice should be censured in
church colleges by accrediting agencies just as they are for
other institutions.

On the other hand, several decades of experience on the
part of some church-related institutions demonstrate that
the student in such a college or university can and often
does receive as objective and solid an intellectual training
as he might have in a different type of institution. This
fact should not now be cast aside in favor of the position
taken in the 1967 decision in the Maryland Court of
Appeals. In this case, the assumption would seem to be
that, regardless of the quality of the educational process
for which it may be responsible, a certain degree of
"church-relatedness" automatically denies a college's position in the academic community. If this norm is nationally
accepted, over 800 of the country's colleges and universities will thereby be reduced to the status of "second-class
citizen."

5. Federal programs in higher education should, on the one
   hand, require church institutions as well as others to conform to the generally recognized criteria for protecting
   and promoting a sound educational process. But such programs should consciously avoid requirements for participation that would force or even encourage church institutions to lose their unique characteristics and to become
   more or less identical with other types of colleges and
   universities.

The evolving relationship of the state government to the large, complex, private, church-related university must include the following concepts:

1. The existence of one or more strong or potentially strong private church-related universities within a state should be recognized and acknowledged as a valuable segment of the state's educational resources.

2. State commissions on higher education and state departments of education should make certain that the contribution of private church-related universities be incorporated in the state's educational planning, not merely as an appendage or supplement but as an integral part.

3. The educational policies of the state should give concrete evidence of the esteem in which its private church-related universities are held, by promoting programs of substantial assistance to these institutions and to the students who wish to attend them. Among these programs would be the state scholarships now available in nearly half the states; incentive or cost-of-education grants such as are now available in New York and Wisconsin and, wherever possible, capital assistance for facilities at private universities.

4. The leadership of such states as New York should be followed in other states in securing changes in the state laws so as to create an equitable situation in which church-related universities are given opportunities to participate in state educational programs.

5. As many state colleges and universities seek to initiate or expand their programs in philosophy and religion, state authorities and policy-making bodies should call on the unique resources in these fields to be found in church-related universities.

Intensive and immediate consideration must be given all of these factors if the American Catholic university is to enter the last quarter of this century with any hope of continuing its significant contributions to American higher education.

A Tradition of Autonomy?

JOHN TRACY ELLIS

Persuaded that irreligion and immorality in a youth, por-
tend the most fatal evils to subsequent periods of life, and
threaten even to disturb the peace, and corrupt the man-
ners of society at large; the directors of this Institution
openly profess that they have nothing so much at heart as
to implant virtue and destroy in their pupils the seeds of
vice— Happy in the attainment of this sublime object, they
would consider their success in this alone, as an ample
reward for their incessant endeavours.[1]

Such was the way in which Georgetown College, the first
Catholic institution of higher learning in the United States,
conceived its principal objective in a prospectus dated January 1, 1798. That document offers a striking contrast to the

[1] Archives of Georgetown University, #62-9, *College of Georgetown, (Potomack)*
in the State of Maryland, United States of America [printed prospectus], p. 1.
In a similar prospectus twenty-two years later, *Georgetown College, District of*
Columbia, 1820, under the name of the president, Enoch Fenwick, S.J., there was
a paragraph which read:

> *As the members of the College profess the Catholic religion, the exercises*
> *of religious worship are Catholic; but members of every other religious*
> *Denomination are received; of whom it is only required, that they respect-*
> *fully assist at the public duties of Religion with their companions. Were*
> *not this enforced, no proper order, such as should be found in large liter-*
> *ary institutions, could exist in the College* (p. 1).

The writer wishes to express his thanks to Lawrence C. Chamberlain of the
Riggs Memorial Library at Georgetown University for kindly offering to secure
xerox copies of a number of pages from early catalogues of the institution.

spirit now pervading American Catholic institutions, suffused as they are by the broadened concept of human freedom and personal responsibility that informed Vatican Council II, as well as by the radical changes that have overtaken the thinking of American youth and the general society of which they form a part. Catholic circles have seen the change manifested in a hundred different ways as, for example, at Saint Mary's College, Winona, where a young instructor in classics—a former Catholic—married a Catholic girl from the neighboring College of Saint Teresa before a justice of the peace. The instructor was ultimately dismissed; thus do pastoral judgments in the Catholic community at times impinge on academic matters.[2]

Georgetown's statement of purpose at the end of the eighteenth century was in no sense peculiar to that time. Practically all the colleges then existing had owed their origin to a religiously affiliated group, and in a discussion of these institutions in 1740 one of the most learned and respected Protestant divines of colonial America, Jonathan Edwards, had stated:

> *they should be. . . . fountains of piety and holiness. There is a great deal of pains taken to teach the scholars human learning; there ought to be as much, and more care, thoroughly to educate them in religion, and lead them to true and eminent holiness. . . .*

[2] *Providence Journal*, May 22, 1967, p. 6. The instructor was ultimately dropped from the faculty and the case was investigated by the American Association of University Professors. The report of the committee's findings was published under the title, "Academic Freedom and Tenure: Saint Mary's College (Minnesota)," *AAUP Bulletin* 54 (March, 1968), pp. 37–42. John P. McCall and his colleagues found much to recommend at the college, but the committee concluded:
> *That Mr. Caldwell, once his marriage became a public issue, had served to frighten the governing authorities and the academic community into agreeing on his dismissal points to something else: the extent to which Saint Mary's College has failed to distinguish between its roles as an intellectual and a religious institution. This failure occasioned deep divisions within the academic community and permitted one man to suffer as a teacher partially as a result of his misgivings as a believer. Under present circumstances there is no assurance that the same thing could not happen again, and this is especially unfortunate because there is much about Saint Mary's College, its openness and liveliness, which suggests that it could enjoy a promising and attractive future* (p. 42).

And I cannot see why it is not on all accounts fit and convenient, for the governors and instructors of the colleges, particularly, singly and frequently to converse with the students, about the state of their souls.[3]

True, by reason of the Enlightenment and the advance of science, the late eighteenth century had witnessed considerable secularization of learning and a freer and more open style of operation in these early colleges. Yet higher education in the new republic still continued to be dominated largely by its religious commitment, and this fact was accentuated when the early nineteenth century revivals that stirred American Protestantism caused the conservatives to retrieve much of the ground they had lost in the academic community. Thus it was the religious conservatives who strongly influenced the thinking of many of the founders of new colleges, while at the same time they were able to hold the line in most of the older institutions. The Unitarian triumph at Harvard in 1804–1806 was, after all, the exception rather than the rule in the American academic world.[4]

Given the status of Catholics as a disdained minority in the strongly Protestant atmosphere then prevalent throughout the United States—to say nothing of the open and organized hostility toward their Church that developed in the 1840's and 1850's among groups like the Nativists and the Know-Nothings—it was to be expected that the Catholics would reflect these environmental influences in their educational system. When Canon Josef Salzbacher of Saint Stephen's Cathedral, Vienna, arrived in this country in April, 1842, his observant gaze took in more than the conditions among the German-speaking Catholic immigrants whom he had come to study. Of the Catholic colleges of the period he said:

---

[3] "Thoughts on the Revival of Religion in New England, 1740," *The Works of President Edwards* (reprint of the Worcester ed., New York: Leavitt & Allen, 1885), III, 414.

[4] For a general treatment of the eighteenth century and the period up to the Civil War in regard to academic freedom and kindred topics, see Richard Hofstadter and Walter P. Metzger, *The Development of Academic Freedom in the United States* (New York: Columbia University Press, 1955), pp. 152–274.

*Since many Catholic youth want to obtain a higher educa-
tion to become physicians, attorneys, or priests, it has long
been the ambition of the bishops to erect such higher institutions of learning and to supervise them in order that
these young men, who otherwise would attend the public
state schools, might not go astray. . . .*[5]

While there was obviously nothing wrong in this point of view,
the lack of more than a hint of any intellectual motivation was
not without significance. The attitude of the hierarchy became
fixed in this pattern, and even today—a century and a quarter
after the Austrian canon's visit—it is doubtful if more than a
small minority of the more than 280 bishops of the United
States would view higher education in a radically different
manner from that of their predecessors of 1842.

Nor were matters essentially otherwise among the religious
orders and congregations who were responsible for the majority
of the eighty-four colleges opened under Catholic auspices
between Georgetown's first classes in 1791 and the outbreak of
the Civil War.[6] It was in the same year that Salzbacher visited
this country (1842) that the University of Notre Dame had its
beginnings with Father Edward Sorin, C.S.C., and his confrères
of the Congregation of Holy Cross. At the close of Notre
Dame's first quarter century the prospectus expressed satisfaction with the system of education that had been adopted and
gradually developed. There was no precise or detailed statement
of aims in 1867, beyond that of saying that "the same energy
and reliance in God" that had brought about striking changes
in Notre Dame's physical appearance since 1842

*have been busy in increasing and perfecting the means of
rendering the youth of Notre Dame thorough students,*

[5] John Tracy Ellis, ed., "Canon Salzbacher's Observations on American Catholic
Colleges for Men, 1842," *Documents of American Catholic History*, 3rd rev. ed.
(Chicago: Henry Regnery Co., 1967), I, 261.

[6] Philip Gleason, "American Catholic Higher Education: A Historical Perspective," *The Shape of Catholic Higher Education*, ed. Robert Hassenger (Chicago:
University of Chicago Press, 1967), p. 17.

while in the Institution, and good citizens hereafter in the various walks of life.[7]

But no doubt was left about the spirit of paternal guidance that governed the lives of the students whose morals and general deportment were "assiduously watched over" in what was described as the institution's "retired position" from the distractions of city life. Under the heading, "Regulations of the University," there were listed twenty-five rules that indicated the closest supervision from the students' required attendance at religious worship, the careful avoidance of "every expression in the least injurious to Religion, their Professors, Prefects or fellow-Students," the banning of tobacco and intoxicating liquors, to the final regulation which stated:

No book, periodical or newspaper shall be introduced into the College, without being previously examined and approved by the Director of Studies. Objectionable books found in the possession of Students, will be withheld from them until their departure from the University.[8]

Numerous examples of the same paternalism, the same protective note in regard to students' religious faith, and the same lack of emphasis on intellectual pursuits and the ideals of scholarship, could be cited from other Catholic institutions for the half century after these statements were published in Notre Dame's catalogue of 1867.[9]

---

[7] *Twenty-Fourth Annual Catalogue of the Officers and Students of the University of Notre Dame, Indiana, for the Academic Year 1867–68* (Notre Dame: Ave Maria Steam Power Press Print, 1868), p. 7.

[8] *Ibid.*, p. 17.

[9] Two examples from Jesuit institutions in the South in the early years of the present century will illustrate the point. At Spring Hill College, Mobile, the administration acknowledged in 1901 their responsibility to show at all times what was termed "a paternal solicitude" for the students and to keep "a careful and active watch over their conduct." While Spring Hill was a Catholic institution, those of other denominations were received as students, "provided that, for the sake of order and uniformity, they are willing to conform to the exterior exercise of worship" (*Catalogue of Spring Hill College (St. Joseph's) Near Mobile, 1901–1902* [Mobile, 1902], pp. 7–8). At Loyola University in New Orleans a decade later the system of education was said not to share "the illusion of those who seem to imagine that education, understood as an enriching and stimulating of the

Up to that time Catholics were in this regard still members of a numerous company in American higher education, although the number was steadily diminishing. The years after the Civil War, however, were to bring about a kind of revolution in higher learning in the United States with the spread of Darwin's theories, the advance of the natural sciences, and the growth of the methods of critical scholarship, a revolution in which the Catholics remained almost entirely uninvolved until the closing years of the century. Speaking of the radical changes of the postwar period, one historian of American higher education has said:

> *The new era, which was about to dawn, would pass the old-time college by or perhaps convert it into a precious preserve of gentility or into a defiant outpost of denominationalism. In any case, it would never be the same again.*[10]

Nor would the burgeoning university which came into its own only after the Civil War, ever be the same again. To the critical observer of the educational scene in the generation between Appomattox and the 1890's, Catholic institutions—insofar as he adverted to them at all—probably seemed to be far more "defiant outposts of denominationalism" than vibrant and relevant centers of learning that had a contribution to make to the nation's intellectual life. To the Catholic administrator and faculty member, on the other hand, the only course

---

intellectual faculties, has a morally elevating influence in human life." True, education energized and refined the imagination, taste, understanding, and powers of observation, but the Jesuit system held that "knowledge and intellectual development of themselves have no moral efficacy." The principal faculties to be developed were moral, and it was morality that must be the "underlying base, the vital force supporting and animating the whole organic structure of education." It was the belief of the administration at Loyola that morality "must be the atmosphere the student breathes; it must suffuse with its light all that he reads, illumining what is noble and exposing what is base, giving to the true and false their relative light and shade" (*Loyola University, New Orleans, La., 1911–1912: Announcements, 1912–13* [New Orleans, 1912], p. 10). The writer wishes to express his thanks to his friend and former student at Brown University, Joseph A. Tetlow, S.J., for the material from Spring Hill and Loyola.

[10] Frederick Rudolph, *The American College and University* (New York: Alfred A. Knopf, 1962), p. 241.

to pursue amid the rising tide of secularization then engulfing the college world seemed to be to heed the warnings of the Church against what an instruction from the Holy See in November, 1875, called "evils of the gravest kind" that would be likely to ensue from attendance of American Catholic students at other than Catholic schools.[11] The dangers to the religious faith of Catholic youth were indeed real, even as they were to prove real for some in the Church's own institutions. That fact, plus the hostility of so many Americans toward the Catholic Church, helped to solidify the ghetto mentality which, in turn, gave birth among Catholics to the concept—and to the charge—of "godless schools," a charge that was not limited to schools on the elementary and secondary levels.

In another respect the Civil War marked something of a dividing line in American higher education. Up to that time the differences in religious motivation and the policies that it inspired between the Catholic and the non-Catholic colleges had not been too stark, in the sense that the latter had also been characterized by paternalism and a vigorous religious commitment that brooked no differences. And needless to say, where paternalism and a pervading authoritarian spirit prevailed, one found little of what is today termed academic freedom, for the protective tendency extended to faculty as well as to students. In the prewar period the concept of academic freedom, as we understand it, had received no marked emphasis or distinct formulation, and when it began gradually to emerge it was precisely those colleges and universities with the deepest religious commitment that found it the least acceptable. As Hofstadter has remarked:

> *In fact academic freedom first appeared in the guise of religious liberty for professors . . . . So long as most colleges had a denomination affiliation, it was all but impossible for any educator to assert with success his right to*

---

[11] John Tracy Ellis, ed., "Instruction of the Congregation de Propaganda Fide Concerning Catholic Children Attending American Public Schools, November 24, 1875," *Documents of American Catholic History*, 3rd rev. ed. (Chicago: Henry Regnery Co., 1967), II, 261.

be judged on his competence alone without regard to his religious opinions; but he might manage to persuade many men that it would be expedient *not to stand too firmly on doctrinal grounds.*[12]

To institutions commited to the basic Protestant principle of individual interpretation—for its implications could not indefinitely be held in check—the accommodation and adjustment necessitated by Darwinism and the ramifications that accompanied it were much easier than for Catholic institutions. The latter were answerable to an authoritarian Church, as they were in most cases answerable as well to an authoritarian president and administration. In the generation after 1865, dozens of faculty members in non-Catholic colleges, seminaries, and universities became central figures in a series of heresy trials on the score of their espousal of the theory of evolution. But allowing for silent struggles that may have taken place in Catholic circles on this and other academic issues of which the writer has no knowledge, not until 1889 did traces of the prolonged and bitter debate immortalized by the title of Andrew D. White's famous work, *A History of the Warfare of Science with Theology* (1896), come to the surface among the Catholics.

In this instance, opponents of evolution invoked the Church's traditional teaching by way of preventing the suggested appointment to the original faculty of the Catholic University of America of Saint George Jackson Mivart (1827–1900), English biologist and evolutionist, convert to Catholicism at seventeen, and professor at both Cardinal Manning's University College, Kensington, and the University of Louvain. Both the rector of the university, Bishop John J. Keane, and John Ireland, archbishop of Saint Paul, were eager to engage Mivart for the new institution scheduled to open in November, 1889. Opposition arose, however, from Michael A. Corrigan, archbishop of New York, who was quietly supported by Patrick J. Ryan, archbishop of Philadelphia. In the summer Keane informed Corrigan of the desires of Ireland, himself, and others concerning Mivart, and he maintained the English scientist would be admirably

[12] Hofstadter-Metzger, *Development of Academic Freedom,* p. 263.

fitted, as he said, "to give our Divinity students the scientific knowledge so necessary in our times." Moreover, Mivart would lend prestige to the new university by his name, for without some name of that kind, said Keane, the faculty

> *no matter how learned and eloquent in Latin, will count for very little in the estimation of the American public, whose expectations ought to count for something with us.*

Though aware of the suspicions about Mivart's orthodoxy, Keane believed that all reasons for anxiety had been removed by his recent publications.[13]

But the archbishop of New York remained unconvinced. In his opinion a risky appointment should not mar the start of the university's life; perhaps later on Mivart might be engaged. Meanwhile Ryan was showing himself even more cautious when he told Cardinal Gibbons, the university's chancellor, that John J. Williams, archbishop of Boston, had counseled that they first consult Cardinal Manning about Mivart, and Ryan then added:

> *The Pope's recent recommendation of his new book would not be sufficient in itself, and anything like a suspicion even of unsound philosophy in the new institution might prove a permanent injury to its character.*[14]

In the sequel, Mivart was set aside and the English-born Paulist, George M. Searle, a Harvard graduate of 1857, onetime instructor at the naval academy and assistant at the Harvard observtory, convert to Catholicism in 1862, was appointed to lecture on astronomy and physics.

While the misgivings of Corrigan and Ryan were borne out some years later by Mivart's excommunication for doctrinal

---

[13] Archives of the Archdiocese of New York, C-16, Keane to Corrigan, Cape May, New Jersey, August 2, 1889, in John Tracy Ellis, *The Formative Years of the Catholic University of America* (Washington: American Catholic Historical Association, 1946), pp. 354–355.

[14] Archives of the Archiocese of Baltimore, 86-M-3, Ryan to Gibbons, Philadelphia, September 9, 1889, *ibid.*, p. 355.

errancy,[15] it was unfortunate that the number of Catholic educators—such as Bishop Keane—who were conscious of the need to bring the Church's institutions of higher learning abreast of the age, was so limited in this critical period of American university development. For by the time the question of the Mivart appointment arose (1889) the prime forces that were to shape

[15] On Mivart, see Jacob W. Gruber, *A Conscience in Conflict: The Life of St. George Jackson Mivart* (New York: Columbia University Press, 1960). That Mivart erred in matters of doctrine, there would seem to be no doubt. When he wrote a letter to *The Times* of London accusing J. G. Snead-Cox, editor of *The Tablet*, of having misrepresented his position, the latter reprinted excerpts from five leading English non-Catholic publications, including *The Spectator* and the *Church Times*, to show that they, too, found it difficult to square Mivart's position with the teachings of the Catholic Church. Snead-Cox closed his reply to Mivart by saying:

> *He here commits himself to the proposition that men who deny the Gospel account of the Resurrection and the Virgin-birth of our Lord may still be regarded as 'good' and 'devout Catholics.' In other words, he asserts that belief in the Resurrection and the Incarnation is not essential to the faith of Catholics. If Dr. Mivart honestly thinks that, I venture to say that before many days are over he will find he is grievously mistaken* (The Tablet 63 [January 20, 1900], 105).

A few weeks later the lenten pastoral letters of several English bishops bore out Snead-Cox's prediction. That of Herbert Vaughan, Cardinal Archbishop of Westminster, "The Work of the Catholic Laity in England," contained a section under the heading, 'Catholic Newspapers' which doubtless made grim reading for more than the journalists. In secular concerns, it was said, the Catholic journals were perfectly free to take what position they pleased. But when it came to the Church, the pope, the Roman congregations and cardinals in curia, the bishops in their official capacity, etc., it was altogether different. "This," said Vaughan, "is holy ground," and he then continued:

> *The Church is governed by a Hierarchy, not by a House of Commons. Her constitution is divine, and not dependent like a political machine upon popular agitation and the seesaw of public opinion. Bishops have received a divine mandate to rule and govern their flock. They are teachers and judges in matters of faith, moral conduct, and ecclesiastical discipline. It is chiefly for them to determine the policy to be followed in defence or furtherance of Catholic claims. The appeal against them is not to the people, but to ecclesiastical tribunals and to the Sovereign Pontiff.*

> *The office and the honour of a Catholic journalist is religiously to follow the lead of the Church in matters that concern the Church; to strengthen her action upon the world; to defend the faith and Catholic interests with skill and courage; sentire cum ecclesia in all things. . . .*

> *But if a Catholic journal habitually fail in its mission, by weakening*

the future of the university in the United States were already in motion, advancing at a rapid pace. For example, the Morrill Act had passed Congress in July, 1862, out of which were to emerge the great state universities; the Eliot presidency at Harvard which inaugurated the elective system in education had begun in 1869; and in 1876 there had opened at Baltimore the Johns Hopkins University where Daniel Coit Gilman presided over the country's first exclusively graduate institution.

Meanwhile Americans in general were giving a wider and deeper acceptance to the German university system, and the increasing benefactions of the new multimillionaires enabled higher education to take a strong forward step in centers like the Stanfords' new university at Palo Alto (1885) and the revitalized University of Chicago, where John D. Rockefeller's millions helped to support new standards after 1892. It was these institutions that created the environment wherein academic freedom as we know it, began to strike roots: a concept that had won sufficient support by 1915 to warrant the founding of the American Association of University Professors. And it was the latter group, along with kindred learned societies,

---

respect for authority, by cooling the allegiance of Catholics, by sowing suspicions, doubts, discords, and scandals among the faithful, by opening its columns to the propagation of false and mischievous theories, by fostering a proud spirit of independence and of carping criticism in the sphere of religion, its circulation becomes noxious, like the spread of a plague or a pest (The Tablet 63 [March 3, 1900], 351).

William R. Brownlow, Bishop of Clifton, mentioned Mivart by name as guilty of denying the inspiration of the Scriptures, refusing to make a profession of faith demanded by Vaughan, and of stating that Leo XIII's encyclical, *Proventissimus Deus*, of November, 1893, made him conclude that Catholic doctrine and science "were fatally at variance." Brownlow then stated:

We commend this unfortunate man to your prayers, that he may have grace to renounce his errors before it is too late; and we exhort you to take warning, lest you fall into the same abyss of error. There is much light and dangerous talk abroad on these subjects. The spirit of the age exaggerates liberty into license, throws off those salutary safeguards by which the Church has marked out the way of salvation, and scoffs at the spiritual weapons of the Church 'which are mightly to God unto the pulling down of fortifications (of error), destroying the counsels (of the world-wise), and every high thing that exalteth itself against the knowledge of God, and bringing into captivity every understanding unto the obedience of Christ' (2 Cor. 10:4,5) (The Tablet 63 [March 3, 1900], 352–353).

that responded in 1925 to the call of the American Council on Education in drawing up for the teaching profession the first formal statement of principles on academic freedom and tenure.[16]

In all of this, however, Catholic institutions were conspicuous if in anything by their absence, excepting such rare instances as the Catholic University of America's admission as a charter member of the Association of American Universities in 1900. The result was that for the most part they stood on the periphery of the university movement in this country until well into the twentieth century. The point can be illustrated, perhaps, by inquiring how the Catholic colleges and universities conceived their aims and purposes in the year 1917, an arbitrary choice affording one the perspective of over a half-century. What change of emphasis and tone did the catalogues of a sampling of these colleges and universities reveal over what their predecessors had been saying throughout the nineteenth century? By this time, were their academic goals coming more strongly to the fore? Was there any adumbration in Catholic ranks of the dawning consciousness of the professional attitudes that had two years before been set forth at the birth of the AAUP?

It is not an easy thing to discover accurate answers to these questions. In order to make a judgment and to arrive at a satisfactory general impression, the historian has to have facts. Given that there was relatively little said about the purely academic aims of the Catholic colleges and universities in their annual catalogues, an expression of their educational goals had to be sought wherever it could be found; and that not infrequently was under the heading of "discipline" or "religious instruction." For example, at Georgetown University in 1917—to take the sample institutions in the order of their founding—religious instruction was considered "of the first importance in education," although non-Catholic students were exempt from the four years of courses required in that subject. "The discipline in force at Georgetown," it was frankly stated, "is

16 "Academic Freedom and Tenure: Statements of Principles," *American Association of University Professors Bulletin* 33 (Spring, 1947), 71–73.

paternal." Yet an elaboration of this point made it evident that the academic aim of the university was not altogether subordinated to that of religious instruction. The discipline, it was said

> *has in view the safeguarding of those hours of study so necessary to prepare for attendance at the various College exercises, which is required to produce that intellectual and moral training which it is Georgetown's aim to impart. . . .*[17]

At the University of Notre Dame, as at Georgetown, much was said about the institution's aims under the rubric of "discipline," and in 1917 there appeared a statement that had been carried for some years. It read in part as follows:

> *The University believes that an education which gives little attention to the development of the moral part of a youth's character is pernicious, and that it is impossible to bring about this development where students are granted absolute relaxation from all Faculty government while outside the class-room.*

A young man, it was thought, had to learn obedience to law by the actual practice of obedience, and "the quiet and concentration of mind" that were demanded for college work could obtain only where discipline was enforced. And as in previous years, Notre Dame was at pains to emphasize the advantage of its rural situation. "It is almost a sacrilege," it maintained

> *to cheapen and vulgarize a college by reducing it to the level of a mere classroom exercise and by stripping it of all that makes it distinctive and memorable in the experience of youth. Therefore, students of Notre Dame are expected to find their chief interest on the campus and in*

---

[17] *A Catalogue of the Officers and Students of Georgetown University* (Washington: University Press, 1917), p. 39. It is difficult to determine precisely what the writer had in mind when he entered the following statement into the catalogue for 1917: "Ever since its foundation Georgetown University has offered graduate students opportunities for advanced work and research in the various branches of the Arts and Sciences" (p. 44). It was added that a "systematic organization in this line" had been begun only in 1855–1856; but even then it would not approximate what is meant by graduate work today.

the companionship of college friends, rather than in the distractions of the city.[18]

In the case of the Catholic University of America (which from its opening in 1889 until 1905, operated as exclusively a graduate institution), the statement of purpose contained in the first article of its statutes could scarcely be improved upon. It declared:

> *The aim of the Catholic University of America is to search out truth scientifically, to safeguard it, and to apply it to the moulding and shaping of both private and public life.*[19]

The implementation of this lofty ideal at this institution, however, left much to be desired in later years, as we shall see. In the annual catalogues the immediate aims of the yearly instruction were, as in the case of Georgetown and Notre Dame, strongly moral in tone. In remarking in 1917 that the university used every effort "to develop character in its students," it maintained that the Catholic university's obligations to its students were in part fulfilled by the environment cultivated on its campus. In that connection it declared:

> *Daily association with a large body of Catholic teachers and fellow students is in itself a safeguard for their Catholic faith and principles, while the temptations and moral perils incident to student life are greatly diminished amid surroundings strictly Catholic.*[20]

[18] *Bulletin of the University of Notre Dame: General Catalogue, 1917–1918* (Notre Dame: University Press, April, 1918), p. 30. The religious emphasis was especially marked at Notre Dame during the years that John F. O'Hara, C.S.C., was prefect of religion. For example, in the *Religious Bulletin* which he inaugurated, it was stated in 1928: "It is the hope of this school that if it can cloister a boy for four years from the ways of the world and can give him a demonstration of the workability of its principles, it can send him out ready to pay tribute to Caesar without losing his soul" (Quoted in the senior essay of Raymond A. Foery, "Notre Dame: The Concept of a Catholic University," Department of History, University of Notre Dame, April, 1967, p. 23). The writer wishes to thank the Reverend James T. Burtchaell, C.S.C., for his kindness in furnishing a copy of this essay.

[19] *The Statutes of the Catholic University of America*, revised ed. (Washington: Catholic University of America, 1937), p. 11.

[20] *The Catholic University of America: Year Book, 1917–1918* (Washington: Catholic University of America, 1917), p. 193.

Meanwhile, Catholic higher education for women had been inaugurated in the United States by the College of Notre Dame of Maryland which conferred its first degrees in June, 1899, and at Trinity College in Washington which opened the following year. At the former, the *Annual Calendar* for 1917 noted—as had been true for some years previous to this date— the growing tendency for professional and technical education to overshadow cultural courses in men's institutions. This trend might be justified for men, but the college saw no similar reason for change in schools for women where, it was said, "culture in its broadest sense must remain the predominant aim." What the institution had in mind was in part conveyed in the following paragraph:

> *The inspiration and conservation of the noblest womanly character, the right direction of the distinctive possibilities of womanhood, the attainment of intellectual power, a guiding conservative philosophy, and a reverent and intelligent adherence to religious truth,—all these mark the unfolding and perfection of the woman destined for the subsequent elevation of society and the home, along the lines indicated by Divine Providence.*

In the problems facing the nation, Notre Dame envisioned the need for leadership from both men and women, a thing that could not be produced by wealth or aristocratic birth, but only "by forces of intelligence, by enlightened conscience, and by fearless expression creating higher and higher ideals of living." And at Notre Dame this would be achieved by holding to a curriculum that was predominantly cultural in content.[21]

---

[21] *Annual Calendar of Notre Dame of Maryland College for Women* (Baltimore: Notre Dame of Maryland, 1917), pp. 10–11. The college evolved from the boarding academy opened in 1863 by the School Sisters of Notre Dame. In 1896, the year permission was received to confer degrees, the catalogue made clear under 'Religious Instructions' that girls of all religious denominations were received, that "no undue influence" was exercised over nonCatholic students' views, but it was added: "For the maintenance of order, all pupils are required to be present at the brief religious exercises held every morning and evening, and at the public worship on Sunday" (*Thirty-Third Annual Catalogue of Notre Dame of Maryland* [Baltimore, 1896], p. 25). Sister Margaret Mary O'Connell, S.S.N.D., president of the college, and her secretary, Dorothy B. Hart, were kind enough to supply the materials from the Notre Dame catalogues.

As was true of the College of Notre Dame of Maryland, the statement of aims and purposes at Trinity College in 1917 was probably more clear-cut than in the men's institutions, and contained, perhaps, a less markedly moral and religious tone. At the same time it embodied an unmistakable identification as a Catholic college. The founders' purpose, it was said, was to provide for students

> *a liberal education that, while lacking none of the advantages offered to women by non-Catholic colleges of the first rank, would at the same time be permeated with Catholic principles and shaped in accordance with Catholic ends.*

In the implementation of this goal the Trinity girl was to keep before her a twofold objective. First, she was to aim to make herself a "true scholar"; that is, one endowed with "knowledge many sided as well as thorough, with a firm grasp of first principles, a just judgment, a well-trained power of reasoning," and a broad cultural appreciation. The expression of the second objective, that of the "true woman," was a happy blending of the religious and social aspects of a woman's life. It was stated that she should possess

> *a clear, reverent sense of her duty to God, herself, and her fellow-creatures, with every womanly gift and virtue well-developed, with a strong, self-reliant character, and with resourceful ability for highest womanly service, whatever be her destined sphere of life or her chosen field of labor.*[22]

While the emphasis on intellectual goals in American colleges and universities operating under Protestant auspices in the era of World War I was on the whole more pronounced than in Catholic institutions, in other respects the contrast was less striking. For example, at Princeton (1746), Oberlin (1833), and Vassar (1861)—to take a university for men, the nation's first coeducational college, and one of the earliest colleges for

---

[22] *Trinity College, Washington, D.C.: A Catholic Institution for the Higher Education of Women, 1917–1918* (Washington: Trinity College, 1917), pp. 17–18. The writer wishes to thank his friend and former student, Sister Joan Bland, S.N.D., formerly of Trinity College, for her assistance in securing the material from that institution.

women: all begun with an avowedly religious motivation—compulsory attendance at religious worship was still in vogue in 1917, even if attendance at Princeton's Marquand Chapel was limited to one Sunday in two, a requirement that might be satisfied by a student attending services at one of the churches in the town.[23] Moreover, descriptions of the religious life on these three campuses did not read in a radically different way from those in the Catholic colleges. Thus Oberlin sought to furnish an atmosphere in which parents on the lookout for "the completest education and the highest development in character" would gladly place their children.[24] And while Oberlin's Conservatory of Music did not find it practical to offer special religious training, yet it was the conservatory's stated aim "to throw around students such safeguards as are possible."[25] Both Oberlin and Vassar proclaimed their nondenominational character, but both also made special mention of the advantages to be derived from the courses offered in religion for students' moral life. The same was true at Princeton where the president, trustees, faculty, and national leaders of different religious denominations were said to be "united with the undergraduates . . . in supplying to the University a comprehensive religious program."[26]

But these resemblances to Catholic institutions were on a superficial plane, and as time went on they were becoming less and less distinct in the non-Catholic institutions' statement of aims. Generally speaking, the future in American higher education belonged not with those of deep commitment to traditional religious values but with the evolutionists, as more than a generation before influential university figures like Eliot, White of Cornell, and Gilman had predicted it would. Secularism and its principal handmaid, science, were capturing campus

[23] *Catalogue of Princeton University: 1917–1918* (Princeton: Princeton University, 1917), pp. 351–352.

[24] *Oberlin College: Bulletin of General Information* (Oberlin: Oberlin College, March 30, 1918), p. 32. See also *The Fifty-Third Annual Catalogue of Vassar College, Poughkeepsie, N. Y., 1917–1918* (Poughkeepsie: Vassar College Bulletin, 1917), p. 168; *Catalogue of Princeton University*, pp. 350–352.

[25] *Oberlin College: Bulletin*, p. 180.

[26] *Catalogue of Princeton University*, p. 350.

after campus, sometimes only at the end of a bitter struggle, and with their advent came a sharper and more critical attitude toward religion. In fact, nearly a half-century before the United States entered World War I the revolutionary changes that were to overtake higher education had been foreshadowed in such moves as that at Harvard where in 1869 the rating of students on the basis of moral character was dropped and their ranking based solely on academic grades.[27] Accompanying the new spirit was a corresponding change toward religious authority in general and that especially in its academic context. And as it steadily declined on the campus there was a parallel rise in emphasis on the individual teacher's and research worker's freedom of inquiry, along with the parallel growth in these circles of an eagerness and insistence upon hearing and disputing their findings in an open way.

With ideas of this kind constantly gaining ground it is not difficult to understand how the concept of academic freedom should gradually have taken hold and become a permanent feature of college and university life. One would have thought that Catholic institutions would have shown an awareness and response to these trends. But the circumstances that surrounded their origin and growth, and the philosophy that governed their administration, were sufficiently at variance with the ideas that had gained ascendancy in the country's leading universities, that like the clergy and laity who conducted and supported the Church's institutions, the latter existed in good measure apart from developments within the main stream of American higher education.

Only a knowledge of the background of these institutions will clarify this puzzling situation, for Teilhard de Chardin's dictum is as applicable to the Catholic colleges and universities of the United States as it is to any other work of man; namely, that "nothing is comprehensible except through its history."[28] For the most part they clung to the patterns of the past, a position that became all the more entrenched within the closed com-

[27] Rudolph, *American College and University*, p. 348.
[28] Teilhard de Chardin, *The Future of Man* (New York: Harper & Row, 1964), p. 12.

munities that were characteristic of American Catholic life up
to World War II. Years before, Newman with his extraordinary
perception had seen the dangers inherent in a static position
of this kind, but there would have been few Catholics in this
country then or later who would have embraced the vision
expressed in his notable work, *An Essay on the Development of
Christian Doctrine,* which appeared only a few weeks after his
conversion to Catholicism. There he had written, "in a higher
world it is otherwise, but here below to live is to change, and
to be perfect is to have changed often."[29]

Newman's mind certainly changed, and yet one of the gravely
inhibiting factors at work in the Catholic intellectual centers
of all countries was exemplified by the same Newman only a
year and two months after the publication of the book on doctrinal development. On this occasion he admitted to his friend,
John D. Dalgairns, that he was "terribly frightened" lest the
French translation of his university sermons should be brought
before the Congregation of the Index and condemned, as had
happened to the works of Antonio Rosmini and others. He
then continued:

> *It seems hard, since nations now converse by printing, not
> in the schools, that an English Catholic cannot investigate
> truth with one of France or Rome without having the
> Inquisition upon him. What I say is, "I am not maintain-*

---

[29] John Henry Newman, *An Essay on the Development of Christian Doctrine*
(New York: Doubleday and Co., Image Book, 1960), p. 63. In that connection
Philip Schaff, the Protestant church historian, countered Bossuet's argument that
the constant change and variation in Protestantism as compared to Catholicism's
fixity of doctrine proved the truth of the latter. Schaff declared that the argument
was plausible but not conclusive. "Truth in God," he said, "or objectivity considered, is unchangeable; but truth in man, or the apprehension of it, grows
and develops with men and with history. Change, if it be consistent, is not necessarily a mark of heresy, but may be a sign of life and growth, as the want of
change, on the other hand, is by no means always an indication of orthodoxy,
but still more frequently of stagnation (*The Creeds of Christendom,* 6th rev. ed.
[New York: Harper & Brothers, 1931], I, 87). One is reminded of a similar remark
in the contemporary idiom where Marshall McLuhan says, "Survival is not possible if one approaches his environment, the social drama, with a fixed unchangeable point of view—the witless repetitive response to the unperceived" (*The
Medium is the Massage* [New York: Bantam Books, 1967], p. 10).

ing what I say is all true, but I wish to assist in investigating *and bringing to light* great *principles necessary for the day—and the only way to bring these out is* freely *to investigate, with the inward habitual intention (which I trust I have) always to be submitting what I say to the judgment of the Church. . . ."*[30]

Unfortunately, the obscurantism that pervaded the Roman Curia and the Church's centers of learning deepened during the remaining thirty years of the pontificate of Pius IX,[31] and it was only partially and temporarily relieved by his successor, Leo XIII (1878–1903). The latter, indeed, was of another mind than Pius IX, and more than one scholar received from him the kind of encouragement given in 1892 to Monsignor Maurice d'Hulst, rector of the Catholic Institute of Paris, whom he told in audience:

> *There are some anxious and fretful spirits who press the Roman congregations to pronounce on questions that are still doubtful. I oppose this. I stop them because it is necessary not to hinder scholars from working. It is rather necessary to let them have the leeway to falter and even to err. Religious truth will only gain by it. The Church always arrives on time to put them back on the right road.*[32]

To be sure, there were not lacking high churchmen who shared Leo's view and who made sparing use of their authority by refraining from interference in the college and university world with censures and condemnations. Cardinal Gibbons was such a man, who in the midst of the controversy over pronouncing judgment on the Knights of Labor as a forbidden secret

[30] Newman to Dalgairns, Rome, January 12, 1847, in Wilfrid Ward, *The Life of John Henry Cardinal Newman* (New York: Longmans, Green and Co., 1912), I, 172–173.

[31] For the best treatment of that subject, see Roger Aubert, *Le Pontificat de Pie IX, 1846–1878* (Paris: Bloud & Gay, 1952), pp. 184–223. See also Canon Aubert's lengthy and perceptive essay, "Aspects Divers du Néo-Thomism sous le Pontificat de Léon XIII," *Aspetti della Cultura Cattolica nell' età di Leone XIII,* ed. Giuseppe Rossini (Roma: Edizioni Cinque Lune, 1961), pp. 133–227.

[32] Alfred Baudrillart, *Vie de Mgr D'Hulst,* deuxieme ed. (Paris: Ancienne Librairie Poussielgue, J. de Gigard, 1912), I, 456.

society enunciated a principle that would stand bishops in good stead in many circumstances. He said, "A masterly inactivity and a vigilant eye on their proceedings is perhaps the best thing to be done in the present junction."[33] But there were many highly placed ecclesiastics then and later who would not have subscribed to the formula of the "masterly inactivity and a vigilant eye," and as we shall see, there were two occasions when Gibbons himself abandoned it in cases that touched directly on academic freedom.

The fundamental difficulty that prevented a healthy growth of freedom in Catholic academic institutions had a twofold origin. First, there was the almost total failure of Catholics in higher education to clarify their own minds about the nature and true function of a college or university. As Philip Gleason has so well expressed it, it is scarcely exaggerating to say that Catholic higher education finds itself today facing its identity crisis "in a state of virtual amnesia," with little or no knowledge of its own history which, as he says, has led to the supremely ironic fact "that a Catholic academic community that is more and more disposed to accept a developmental view of reality has only the sketchiest notion of the pattern of its own development."[34]

As we have already seen, until recent years the purpose of these institutions was conceived principally as that of a citadel within which there took place a strengthening and defense of the students' religious faith; a place where, as Canon Salzbacher had observed as early as 1842, bishops thought young men would be prevented from going astray in the state institutions and, too, where they could prepare themselves to become "physicians, attorneys, or priests. . . ." The thought of learning for learning's sake was all but unmentioned, and beyond acquiring the requisites for future professional training, such a thing as developing young minds for leadership in the arts and sciences, or for policy-making posts in government and business,

[33] Gibbons to Elder, Baltimore, May 3, 1886, in John Tracy Ellis, *The Life of James Cardinal Gibbons, Archbishop of Baltimore, 1834–1921* (Milwaukee: Bruce Publishing Co., 1952), I, 494.

[34] Gleason, "American Catholic Higher Education," p. 53.

would have seemed even more remote, if they were thought of at all.

The result was that all through the nineteenth and well into the twentieth century few churchmen—for it was the clergy who were almost exclusively responsible for the Church's higher educational system—took education in a really serious manner. That fact was revealed in a variety of ways; for example, in the constant shifting of presidents and other academic officers of Catholic institutions to accommodate what were regarded as the more important pastoral needs. Thus while the average tenure through the nineteenth century of the presidents of Catholic institutions was slightly over four years, that of the presidents of the non-Catholic colleges was about fifteen years.[35]

Another manifestation of the same mentality governing the Catholic colleges, seminaries, and universities—and it is still painfully obvious in too many of these institutions—was the assignment of clerical professors to so many tasks that it rendered superior teaching impossible. Edward J. Hanna, at the time professor of dogmatic theology in Saint Bernard's Seminary, Rochester, was only reflecting a national phenomenon in Catholic circles when he complained in the autumn of 1904 to Patrick W. Riordan, archbishop of San Francisco, of the failure of Bishop Bernard J. McQuaid of Rochester to implement the legislation of Baltimore's Third Plenary Council. He added:

> *St. Andrew's Seminary, the most important institution in our diocese, is practically the tag end of the Cathedral, and the teachers have so much parish and other work to perform that there is no possibility of good college work.*[36]

Equally as detrimental (if not more so), to bringing the Catholic colleges and universities abreast of the progressive

[35] Edward J. Power, *A History of Catholic Higher Education in the United States* (Milwaukee: Bruce Publishing Co., 1958), pp. 154–155.

[36] Hanna to Riordan, Rochester, November 19, 1904, in James P. Gaffey, "The Life of Patrick W. Riordan, Second Archbishop of San Francisco, 1841–1914" (Ph.D. diss., Catholic University of America, 1963), p. 516. The writer wishes to thank his friend, Msgr. Gaffey, for this and other references that he has generously supplied in the past.

movements in higher education was the authoritarian temper that permeated the governing bodies of the Church, a spirit that was evident as well on all levels of the Catholic educational system. In other words, almost every aspect of the lives of Catholics—doctrinal, moral, educational, etc.—was determined on high. Deviations from the accepted pattern of belief and behavior were viewed at best as eccentricities, so completely and unquestioningly did the lower clergy and the laity accept the ruling of their major religious superiors.[37] This situation became acute when the Holy See felt doctrinal errors were circulating among the faithful, as was true in the days of the so-called heresy of Americanism; and more so, in the aftermath of Pius X's condemnation of Modernism in 1907. The point can be best explained by examining a number of individual cases where the issue of academic freedom was clearly at stake.

Not until the final decade of the nineteenth century did the excitement that had been disrupting the peace of non-Catholic academic circles for twenty or more years begin to be experienced in Catholic institutions. By the mid-1870's most scientists had been converted to the theory of evolution, but it was only in the 1890's that adherents were won in any number among Protestant churchmen. In the interval, repeated battles over evolution, higher criticism of the Bible, and the scientific method generally, were fought in institutions with strong Protestant traditions. It was especially notable in the seminaries, such as the feud over Crawford H. Toy at Southern Baptist Theological Seminary in 1879; the dismissal of the church historian, Egbert C. Smyth, from Andover Theological Academy

---

[37] While the advice given by Antonio Rosmini (founder of the Institute of Charity) to Luigi Gentili (superior of their English mission) was not exactly typical, it represented the attitude that was inculcated by many religious superiors long after Rosmini wrote. He said, "Wage war on the diabolical suggestion that superiors should not know everything, and that you can, on your own initiative, do greater good without being subject to them. On the contrary, take to heart and make your own the maxim that nothing is really good, except what my superiors approve; all that I do without their knowledge by applying a little cunning to keep it from them is bad (Rosmini to Gentili, n.p., July 3, 1840, in Claude Leetham, *Luigi Gentili: A Sower for the Second Spring* [London: Burns & Oates, 1965], p. 125).

in 1886; and the trial in 1891 of Charles A. Briggs at Union Theological Seminary, leading to his later resignation from the Presbyterian ministry. Nor did the colleges and universities of close religious affiliation escape these tensions as, for example, Vanderbilt University where in 1878 Alexander Winchell, one of the less advanced evolutionists of the period, was dismissed. At Yale the following year William Graham Sumner came under fire from the president for his use of Spencer's *Study of Sociology* as a textbook.

By 1890 the sharp divisions that for a decade or more had embittered the Catholic community of the United States—such as the nationality feuds, the differences between conservative and progressive bishops over the Knights of Labor, the Catholic University of America, the single tax movement of Henry George and Father Edward McGlynn's role in it, the controversy over parochial schools, and the so-called heresy of Americanism—had begun to move toward a climax. The initial advantage enjoyed by the prelates of progressive mind, the "Americanists" as they were called, was now slipping away. And the loss of favor of Francesco Satolli, first Apostolic Delegate to the United States and later Cardinal Prefect of the Congregation of Studies at Rome, was a signal of the change. Rome was hearing more and more critical voices raised against American tendencies in the Church, especially from French Catholic monarchists who resented having the Church of the United States held up as a model for their emulation by some of their liberal minded coreligionists. And when in 1895 Miecislaus Ledochowski, cardinal prefect of propaganda, received from Bishop McQuaid of Rochester a detailed indictment of the views and actions of John Ireland, archbishop of Saint Paul, and John J. Keane, rector of the Catholic University of America, two of the leading progressive bishops, it tended to confirm the unpleasant impression at the Holy See. *Inter alia* McQuaid told Ledochowski:

> *Of late years, a spirit of false liberalism is springing up in our body under such leaders as Monsignor Ireland and Monsignor Keane, that, if not checked in time will bring disaster on the Church. Many a time Catholic laymen have*

*remarked that the Catholic Church they once knew seems
to be passing away, so greatly shocked are they at what
they see passing around them.*[38]

Several months later the blows began to fall. Monsignor
Denis J. O'Connell (a close associate of Ireland, Keane, and
Cardinal Gibbons), who had been rector of the North American College in Rome for ten years, was peremptorily ordered
by Cardinal Ledochowski, acting in the name of Leo XIII, to
submit his resignation.[39] And these churchmen and their
friends and followers had scarcely begun to recover from this
reverse when in late September, 1896, Gibbons, chancellor of
the Catholic University of America, sent for Keane to come to
Baltimore where he handed him a letter from Leo XIII dismissing him from the rectorship. The expressed need for having
that office limited to a certain term of years, as had been true
of O'Connell's "ill health" the previous year, deceived no one
who possessed any sophistication in these matters. Nor was the
blow softened for Keane by the promise of an archbishopric.[40]
It was obvious that the so-called liberals in the American
Church had sustained a second resounding defeat, and in neither case was an opportunity offered for a hearing at which
O'Connell or Keane could learn the charges that had resulted
in their undoing. Neither man's administration had been free
of faults, but there would have been less lowering of morale
among those American Catholics engaged in higher education
had the service of the rectors of these two key institutions been
terminated with fairness and justice.

Neither Monsignor O'Connell nor Bishop Keane was a

[38] McQuaid to Ledochowski, Rochester, February, 1895, in Frederick J. Zwierlein, *The Life and Letters of Bishop McQuaid* (Rochester: Art Print Shop, 1927),
III, 224.

[39] On O'Connell's case, see Colman J. Barry, O.S.B., *The Catholic University
of America, 1903–1909. The Rectorship of Denis J. O'Connell* (Washington: The
Catholic University of America Press, 1950), pp. 17–21, and Robert F. McNamara,
The American College in Rome, 1855–1955 (Rochester: Christopher Press, 1956),
pp. 330–334; the latest study is the doctoral dissertation of Gerald P. Fogarty, S.J.,
"Denis J. O'Connell: Americanist Agent to the Vatican 1885–1903," Yale University, 1969.

[40] On Keane, see Patrick H. Ahern, *The Life of John J. Keane, Educator and
Archbishop, 1839–1918* (Milwaukee: Bruce Publishing Co., 1955), pp. 172–178.

scholar, although they were genuinely friendly and sympathetic to those who were. Among these friends was Father John A. Zahm, C.S.C. (1851–1921), who for forty years or even more was associated in one capacity or other with the academic advancement of the University of Notre Dame. During his scientific researches Zahm had become a convinced evolutionist, and in 1896 there appeared the volume, *Evolution and Dogma,* in which he sought to demonstrate the bearing of modern science on Catholic teaching. With the exception of a careless phrase here and there, the position taken by Zahm on the question of evolution has since been advanced by numerous Catholics without incurring any censure. In fact, the generally favorable reviews by two highly competent theologians which appeared soon after the book's publication in the thoroughly orthodox journals, the *American Ecclesiastical Review* and the *Dublin Review,* gave Zahm encouragement to believe it might escape condemnation. But the mounting tension in Catholic intellectual circles both here and in Europe at the time made any Catholic who entertained a friendly opinion concerning evolution suspect in the eyes of the conservatives. Thus in March, 1899, Archbishop Corrigan informed Bishop McQuaid that he had learned confidentially that

> *Dr. Zahm has been summoned to Rome, where he will be required to retract and repudiate the doctrines in his books; otherwise they will be condemned by the Holy Office.*[41]

As it turned out, Corrigan's Roman informant was for the most part correct, although Zahm had not been summoned to Rome.

The fact that Father Zahm had a reputation for being critical of such things as the backward state of Catholic higher education had not, of course, endeared him to the conservatives. Yet when he perceived weaknesses among Catholics, his open manner and love for the Church prompted him to say so, even if he was not always as open as he was with his brother,

---

[41] Corrigan to McQuaid, n.p., March 11, 1899, in Frederick J. Zwierlein, ed., *Letters of Archbishop Corrigan to Bishop McQuaid and Allied Documents* (Rochester: Art Print Shop, 1946), p. 201.

Albert, also a scientist. He wrote to him on one occasion regarding his Holy Cross confrères at Notre Dame:

> *With possibly one or two exceptions among the younger priests, not one at N. D., has the faintest conceptions of the wants of a university, and the demands of the age in which we live.*[42]

In the sequel the Congregation of the Index issued a decree in September, 1898, prohibiting the further circulation of *Evolution and Dogma* in any language, while granting its author the slender consolation of being heard out by his superior general with the chance to reprove his own work before the decree would be made public. Father Zahm accepted the decision of the Holy See without qualification, and thus ended a promising career in a field where Catholics were in desperate need of enlightened guidance. As one of his biographers stated, "Thereafter he published nothing more on science or on the relations of science and religion."[43]

This period of the Church's history was a singularly unpropitious one for men like Bishop Keane and Father Zahm. Although neither one of these men had the formal university training that is a commonplace today, both had made it their business to learn the nature and function of a university, so that they would have heartily agreed with Newman's definition which appeared in an essay he wrote for the *Catholic University Gazette* of Dublin in 1854. Asking the question, "What is a University?," Newman answered his own question in this way:

> *It is a place . . . in which the intellect may safely range and speculate, sure to find its equal in some antagonist activity, and its judge in the tribunal of truth. It is a place where inquiry is pushed forward, and discoveries verified and perfected, and rashness rendered innocuous, and error*

---

[42] Zahm to Albert Zahm, n.p., December 12, 1897, in Ralph E. Weber, *Notre Dame's John Zahm: American Catholic Apologist and Educator* (Notre Dame: University of Notre Dame Press, 1961), p. 105.

[43] Thomas F. O'Connor, "John A. Zahm, C.S.C.: Scientist and Americanist," *The Americas* 7 (April, 1951), 445.

exposed, by the collision of mind with mind, and knowledge with knowledge. . . .[44]

It is scarcely an exaggeration to say that most American Catholics would hardly have known what Newman was talking about, so unaccustomed were they to an experience of that kind in their institutions of higher learning. Consequently, the gulf that separated them from their contemporaries seemed to grow steadily wider as those who—to borrow a phrase from Teilhard de Chardin—were "diffident, timid, underdeveloped, or narrow in their religion," drew tighter the restrictions that bound the faithful and raised higher the barriers between them and the men of their time. Most of those who occupied the policy-making positions within the Church in the last years of the nineteenth and the early years of the present century would have been simply perplexed—if, indeed, they would not have been indignant—at Teilhard de Chardin when he reminded these fearful men

that Christ required for His body the full development of man, and that mankind, therefore, has a duty to the created world and to truth—namely, the ineluctable duty of research.[45]

To be sure, there were then (as there are in every age) many currents of thought that were openly and fiercely hostile to the *depositum fidei*. But it would never have occurred to most of the conservative churchmen that the Church stood only to gain from a frank encounter with these forces in an attempt to present the attractive features of her teaching after the manner suggested by Bishop Keane in relation to socialism. Early in 1896 he told W. J. Kerby, his future professor of sociology:

The study of the Socialist movement which you are able to make on the spot where it is most active, will, I trust,

[44] The essay was reprinted in *Historical Sketches* (London: Basil Montagu Pickering, 1872), p. 16.

[45] Quoted by Claude Cuénot from Teilhard de Chardin's work *Le Prêtre* (1918) in *Pierre Teilhard de Chardin: A Biographical Study* (London: Burns Oates, 1965), p. 40.

be very valuable to you. The principle underlying it is a true one; the lines in which men run in applying it are often sadly mistaken, but the principle is of such a character as naturally to arouse any man of mind and heart to enthusiasm. The proper policy for us is to grasp the principles clearly and strongly, to enter heartily into all that is right in it, to head off demagogues by surpassing them in true devotedness to the public welfare, and to captivate the multitude by showing them that we clearly understand their needs and the principles by which they should be met, and that we are at heart their best friends.[46]

Less than a year later, as we have seen, Keane was dismissed from the rectorship of the Catholic University of America. Keane's close friend, Archbishop Ireland, understood and approved the same kind of approach. When he preached the sermon at the mass commemorating Cardinal Gibbons' silver jubilee as a bishop in October, 1893, he entitled it, "The Church and the Age." Ireland frankly stated that the Church and the age were at war, a situation for which both were at fault. Enumerating the forces that had attacked and harassed the Church since the French Revolution and clearly indicting these movements for the evil he saw in them, Ireland yet maintained:

I am not afraid to say that, during the century whose sun is now setting, many leaders of thought in the Church have made the mistake of being too slow to understand the new age and too slow to extend to it the conciliatory hand of friendship. . . . They failed to grasp the age, to Christianize its aspirations, and to guide its forward march. The age passed beyond them. . . . The many saw but the vices of the age, which they readily anathematized; its good and noble tendencies they either ignored or denied.[47]

[46] Keane to Kerby, Washington, January 17, 1896, Archives of the Catholic University of America, Kerby Papers.

[47] John Ireland, *The Church and Modern Society: Lectures and Addresses* (Saint Paul: Pioneer Press, 1905), I, 108–111.

Ideas such as those expressed by Keane and Ireland would be thought altogether unexceptional today, but the mood of the Church in the 1890's was anything but receptive to them. On the contrary, in both France and Rome conservative churchmen found them especially unwelcome, and it needed little provocation to bring their hostility into the open. The occasion was provided by the French translation of the hasty and uncritical biography, *Life of Father Hecker,* founder of the Paulists, by his admiring subject, Walter Elliott, C.S.P. A quite extravagant introduction was furnished to the French edition by an ardent admirer of the Americans, the Abbé Félix Klein of the Catholic Institute of Paris, with the result that there was touched off a major crisis in Catholic theological circles over the alleged heresy of Americanism. So embittered did it become that Pope Leo XIII took the matter to himself, appointed a commission of cardinals to study the question, and finally issued in January, 1899, an apostolic letter, *Testem benevolentiae,* condemning the ideas which—the pontiff was fair enough to state—were said to be taught and circulated by some liberal-minded Catholics in the United States.[48]

Although Cardinal Gibbons, Archbishop Ireland, and others were prompt to say no such doctrinal errors existed among Catholics in this country, their opposite numbers in the conservative wing of the hierarchy declared they did. The episode served to make the atmosphere in the Church's institutions of learning still more cautious and tense with an unfortunate effect upon scholarship and research. Few had the courage of Bishop John Lancaster Spalding of Peoria who a year and two months after *Testem benevolentiae* delivered a memorable sermon in the Church of the Gesù at Rome in which he made a ringing defense of the free institutions of the English-speaking world. He entitled it "Education and the Future of Religion," and far from backing away from the touchy subject, Spalding championed freedom of thought. He declared:

[48] For the most detailed study of Americanism, see Thomas T. McAvoy, C.S.C., *The Great Crisis in American Catholic History,* 1895–1900 (Chicago: Henry Regnery Co., 1957).

To forbid men to think along whatever line, is to place oneself in opposition to the deepest and most invincible tendency of the civilized world. Were it possible to compel obedience from Catholics in matters of this kind, the result would be a hardening and sinking of our whole religious life. We should more and more drift away from the vital movements of the age, and find ourselves at last immured in a spiritual ghetto, where no man can breathe pure air, or be joyful or strong or free.[49]

Innocent as most students of this question have judged these Americans to have been of doctrinal errancy, what the so-called "Americanizers" did not realize was that there was slowly evolving in the minds of a number of Catholic intellectuals a set of ideas that were definitely at variance with the fundamental teachings of the Church. On both sides of the Atlantic there had been an admirable and sincere effort to have the Church adapt and accommodate herself to contemporary thought and action. But in the case of a few priests like Alfred Loisy (1857–1940) in France, George Tyrrell, S.J. (1861–1909) in England, Romolo Murri (1870–1944) in Italy, and the Americans, John R. Slattery, S.S.J. (1851–1926) and William L. Sullivan, C.S.P. (1872–1935), the accommodation went so far as to empty the Catholic creed of all substance. As George Santayana said of this movement known as Modernism:

It is the last of those concessions to the spirit of the world which half-believers and double-minded prophets have always been found making; but it is a mortal concession. It concedes everything; for it concedes that everything in Christianity, as Christians hold it, is an illusion.[50]

In this instance there was reason for concern, for Modernism was not a phantom such as Americanism. Pope Pius X and his secretary of state, Cardinal Raphael Merry del Val, struck hard; first through the syllabus of sixty-five condemned propositions

---

[49] J. L. Spalding, *Religion, Agnosticism and Education* (Chicago: A.C. McClurg & Co., 1902), p. 175.

[50] George Santayana, *Winds of Doctrine* (New York: Charles Scribner's Sons, 1913), pp. 56–57.

in the decree of the Holy Office—*Lamentabili,* of July, 1907—
and then through what may well have been the harshest encyclical of this century, *Pascendi dominici gregis,* dated the following September 8. No sincere Catholic concerned about the integrity of his faith would seriously question the condemnations
in view not only of the subversion of orthodox doctrine of
which certain college, seminary, and university professors
within the Church had been guilty; but, too, of the dishonest
tactics to which a few of the latter had resorted to conceal their
identity. The situation was grave and it called for grave means
to uproot it.

The manner of implementing these papal directives, however, was quite another thing. As it turned out, a veritable
witchhunt was launched in Catholic institutions of learning,
the evil effects of which endured long after the close of World
War I. The most odious aspects of the affair centered around
Monsignor Humberto Benigni (1862–1934), professor of
church history in the Urban College of Propaganda, who at
the call of Cardinal Merry del Val entered the Vatican secretariat of state in 1906. Benigni operated an elaborate spy system
the lines of which reached into practically every country of
western Europe with a chain of newspapers and journals
founded to serve the purposes of these so-called integralists. No
one was spared from their aggressive and insolent prying nor
from the deceit and dishonesty which they freely practiced to
accomplish their nefarious ends. As the present writer has stated
elsewhere:

> *The list of the victims was a long and distinguished one*
> *and included Cardinals François Richard and Léon Amette*
> *of Paris and Désiré Mércier of Malines; educational*
> *administrators like Paulin Ladeuze, Rector of the Catholic*
> *University of Louvain, Pierre Batiffol who was hounded*
> *out of the rectorship of the Catholic Institute of Tou-*
> *louse, and Henri-Marie Alfred Baudrillart, Rector of the*
> *Catholic Institute of Paris; celebrated scholars such as the*
> *Dominican friars, Marie-Joseph LaGrange and Antonin D.*
> *Sertillanges, and the Jesuits, Jules Lebreton and Ferdinand*
> *Prat, as well as widely known and revered laymen of the*

*stature of Georges Goyau, Léon Harmel, and Albert de
Mun. These and many others were savagely attacked as
modernists, liberals, or socialists, and their writings were
combed for passages that might lend themselves to suspicion of doctrinal errancy. Accusations were repeated again
and again in the face of the stoutest denials, and religious
authorities were inundated with both public denunciations
and anonymous delations in which the authors' words were
torn from their context and interpolated or edited in such
a way as to produce the desired effect.[51]*

What were the effects of this movement in the Church of the
United States? While the tentacles of Benigni's *Sodalitium
Pianum* (as his organization was called) did not reach out with
the same directness and persistence among Catholics in this
country that they had among the latter's European coreligionists, the Americans did not altogether escape. Suspicion was
aroused regarding the doctrinal soundness of eight or nine
priests. The *New York Review,* the most learned journal of
American Catholicism to date, was frightened out of existence
after three years of publication, creating an atmosphere of
uneasiness and fear in Catholic institutions of higher learning
that discouraged the little original and imaginative thinking
and writing then underway. Two of the priests in question,
John R. Slattery, S.S.J. (1851–1926), American-born provincial
of what up to 1893 was called the Society of Saint Joseph of
Mill Hill (forerunner of the present Josephite Fathers), and
William L. Sullivan, C.S.P. (1872–1936), Newman chaplain at
the University of Texas and pastor of Saint Austin's left the

---

[51] John Tracy Ellis, *A Commitment to Truth* [Wimmer Lecture XIX] (Latrobe,
Pennsylvania: Archabbey Press, 1966), pp. 41–42. The best general work on Modernism is Emile Poulat, *Histoire, dogma et critique dans la Crise Moderniste*
(Paris: Casterman, 1962). Among more recent studies on its unfortunate aftermath, see Louis Davallon [a pseudonym], " 'La Sapinère' ou brève histoire de
l'organisation intégriste," *Chronique Sociale de France,* 3 (May 15, 1955), 241–261;
Walter H. Peters, "Modernists and Integralists," *The Life of Benedict XV* (Milwaukee: Bruce Publishing Co., 1959), pp. 42–53; "Integrisme," *Catholicisme Hier,
Aujourd'hui, Demain,* ed. G. Jacquenct (Paris: Létouzey et Ané, 1962), V, cols.
1822–1834; Gerald J. O'Brien, S.J., "Anti-Modernism: The Integralist Campaign,"
Continuum 3 (Summer, 1965), 187–200.

Church, the former renouncing his priesthood in 1903, the latter departing in May, 1909. Both acknowledged that they had become convinced modernists.[52]

But it was otherwise concerning the orthodoxy of the majority of these suspected priests. There is neither need nor space to discuss each individual case in detail. A few words of explanation will suffice for most of them, with a fuller account of the difficulties of Henry A. Poels (1868–1949), Dutch-born associate professor of Old Testament in the Catholic University of America, and Edward J. Hanna (1860–1944), at the time professor of dogmatic theology in Saint Bernard's Seminary, Rochester.

It was the Scripture scholars who were the favorite target of the integralists, although the theologians and church historians were not overlooked. All but two or three of the priests who came under scrutiny were either members of the major seminary faculty of the archdiocese of New York, or were contributors or supporters of its scholarly quarterly, the *New York Review*. For example, James F. Driscoll, S.S. (1859–1938) and Francis E. Gigot, S.S. (1859–1920) were professors in the seminary and members of the *Review's* editorial staff, while men like Cornelius C. Clifford (1859–1938), Thomas J. Mulvey (1870–1952), and William L. Sullivan wrote for the journal. The New York picture was further complicated just at this time by the fact that Driscoll (then rector of Saint Joseph's), Gigot, and three other seminary professors withdrew from the Society of Saint Sulpice in January, 1906. There were a number of reasons that lay behind their action, including Gigot's resent-

---

[52] For Slattery, see his article, "The Workings of Modernism," *American Journal of Theology* 13 (October, 1909), 555–574; on Sullivan, *Letters to His Holiness Pope Pius X* (Chicago: Open Court Publishing Co. 1910); and the posthumous work, *Under Orders, The Autobiography of William Lawrence Sullivan* (New York: Richard R. Smith, 1944). A third American priest who left the Church at this time was Thomas J. Mulvey (1870–1952) of the Diocese of Brooklyn who was a contributor to the *New York Review*. Thumbnail sketches of all these men are contained in the master's thesis, "American Modernists," by Terence O'Donnell of Saint Joseph's Seminary, Dunwoodie, Yonkers, New York (1963). The writer wishes to thank his friend and former student, the Reverend Peter E. Hogan, S.S.J., archivist of the Society of Saint Joseph, for providing a copy of the O'Donnell essay.

ment of the strict censorship of manuscripts intended for publication by the Sulpician superiors, his belief that the society was not up to the standards required for training the clergy, and that "it was a notorious fact that inefficient teachers were too often left in charge of seminary courses."[53]

The troubled conditions in the archdiocese of New York were in part a reflection of the timorous and weak administration of its seventh ordinary, John M. Farley (1842–1918). A strong archbishop might well have intervened to allay suspicions, but it was Farley's first instinct to comply beyond the call of duty when, for example, the orthodoxy of the *New York Review* was questioned at Rome on the basis of such reports as that of Cardinal Diome de Falconio, O.F.M., the apostolic delegate. In commenting to Cardinal Gerolamo Gotti, prefect of propaganda, about the writings of Father Edward Hanna, Falconio remarked that the latter had written for the *New York Review* which, he added, "appears a little suspect of *Modernism*."[54] Scarcely more was needed than a remark of that kind from such a source to sound the death knell of a Catholic journal that specialized in biblical and theological questions. In any case, after three years of useful service to ecclesiastical scholarship, the *Review* was suddenly suspended with the issue of June, 1908. Nor did its founder and principal editor, James Driscoll, long survive at Saint Joseph's. While on a visit to Rome in July, 1909, the archbishop of New York cabled his vicar general to announce the appointment of John P. Chidwick, pastor of Saint Ambrose Church, as rector of the seminary, with Driscoll named as Chidwick's successor in the Manhattan pastorate.

Among the other editors and contributors to the controversial

---

[53] *To the Sulpicians of the Vicariate of the United States*, p. 70. This is a privately printed letter of Edward R. Dyer, S.S., Sulpician superior in the United States, dated Baltimore, April 18, 1906, dealing with the withdrawal from the Society of the five members at Saint Joseph's Seminary, New York. The writer is grateful to the late Lloyd P. McDonald, S.S., former Sulpician provincial, who kindly gave him a copy of this brochure (160 pages) from the archives of Saint Mary's Seminary, Roland Park, Baltimore.

[54] Falconio to Gotti, Washington, October 15, 1907, cited by Gaffey, "The Life of Patrick Riordan," p. 524.

journal, the French-born Francis Gigot (after leaving the Sulpicians) remained on at the New York seminary where he quietly continued to teach until his death in 1920. He published little after the demise of the *Review,* and when John A. Ryan—later to win fame as a moral theologian of social and economic problems—attempted around 1908 to tease him about dangers that confronted Scripture men because of the condemnation of Modernism, Gigot was not amused. He replied, "It is easy for you to joke about that matter but your time is coming; one of these days you will be censured for your economic doctrine."[55]

As for the other men connected at one time with the New York seminary or its *Review,* the French-born Sulpician, Joseph Bruneau (1866–1933), had taught both Scripture and dogmatic theology at Dunwoodie from its opening in September, 1896. He departed in January, 1906, when the other five Sulpicians, as we have seen, left the society and became priests of the archdiocese of New York. Bruneau had always been a serious student, and in his early years had studied under Loisy and Fulcrain Vigouroux, S.S. (1837–1915) at the Catholic Institute of Paris, and then under the eminent Semitic authority, Paul Haupt (1858–1926), at the Johns Hopkins University. After leaving New York he taught at both the Boston and Baltimore seminaries, and it was while he was at the latter that in March, 1910, Cardinal Merry del Val informed Archbishop Falconio, the apostolic delegate, that both the *Civiltà Cattolica* and the *Osservatore Romano* had recently severely criticized the errors contained in the French translation of Henry N. Oxenham's book, *The Catholic Doctrine of the Atonement.* This work had originally appeared in 1865 and had been translated into French by Father Bruneau from the English edition of 1908. Falconio was instructed to make the facts known to Cardinal Gibbons who, in turn, was directed to inquire into Bruneau's teaching and writing.

Within a few days after learning of Rome's uneasiness, Bruneau submitted to Gibbons a lengthy account of the circumstances surrounding his translation of the Oxenham book.

[55] John A. Ryan, *Social Doctrine in Action: A Personal History* (New York: Harper & Brothers, 1941), p. 116.

Bruneau explained that the latter was a convert who, perhaps, had laid too much stress on the Franciscan theory about the final motive of the Incarnation, but who had stated that he stood ready to eliminate at once anything that might be thought to lessen reverence for Christ or His atoning love. Bruneau now hastened to make Oxenham's words his own, to submit unreservedly to the judgment of the Holy See, and to express regret for any displeasure he may have caused the holy father. The episode was closed with Gibbons' letter forwarding the Bruneau statement to Merry del Val, with the comment that it had been very painful both to him and to the Sulpicians who since their arrival in Baltimore at the end of the eighteenth century had always been conspicuous "for piety, orthodoxy, and devotion to the Holy See."[56] Actually, Joseph Bruneau was entirely innocent of having harbored any unorthodox views.

Among the first contributors and most enthusiastic supporters of the *New York Review* had been Cornelius C. Clifford, a New York-born priest who for the twenty years preceding his withdrawal in 1899 had been a member of the Society of Jesus. While a Jesuit, Clifford had studied at Innsbruck and Louvain and spent time in England where he came to know well George Tyrrell, the later modernist, Baron Friedrich von Hügel (1852–1925), and others of their circle. Upon leaving the Jesuits, Clifford had a varied career, teaching a year at the College of Saint Thomas in Saint Paul, serving as editor of the *Providence Visitor* for two years, and in 1907 receiving an appointment to the faculty of Immaculate Conception Seminary located at that period at Seton Hall College, South Orange, New Jersey. Two years later he was removed from the seminary and given an obscure pastorate at Whippany, New Jersey, on the score that a decree of June, 1909, from the Congregation of Religious forbade former members of religious congregations to teach or to hold administrative posts in seminaries.

To Father Clifford and a number of his friends the removal from Immaculate Conception Seminary was due more to what some of those in authority regarded as his advanced views, his

56 Ellis, *Life of James Cardinal Gibbons,* II, 475–476. The Gibbons letter to Merry del Val, Baltimore, March 15, 1910, is summarized here.

friendship with a number of European modernists whose books he read and kept in his library, and to his failure to conform to the fixed patterns of thought and behavior that were believed to be a priest's obligation. Actually, no heretical views were ever formally charged against him, so that it would appear that another gifted and stimulating mind was sacrificed to the ultraconservative mood of the time. To Clifford, his own intellectual curiosity, his desire to be professionally informed for the sake of his students, and (in the case of several of the modernists) his sympathy for the man rather than a necessary agreement with his ideology, were reasons sufficient for his mode of action. He enjoyed a wide acquaintance in circles outside the Church, and he made a number of new friends after he began lecturing in scholastic philosophy at Columbia University in 1913. That there was widespread esteem for Cornelius Clifford among these people was evident on the occasion of his funeral at Morristown, New Jersey, in December, 1938, when Nicholas Murray Butler, president of Columbia, Dr. Alexis Carrel of the Rockefeller Institute, and other prominent figures were in attendance.

One of those who directly experienced the excessive zeal with which Modernism was at times combated was the Old Testament expert, Henry Poels, who had been added to the faculty of the Catholic University of America in 1904. Only an outline of this extremely complicated and prolonged case can be given here.[57] The difficulty arose from Poels' inability to assent to the Pontifical Biblical Commission's decision in June, 1906, to the effect that Moses must be regarded as having been the principal and inspired author of the Pentateuch—a position which, of course, has long since been abandoned by everyone save the most rigid fundamentalists. But coming as it did in the midst of the events leading up to the condemnation of the modernists, any hesitation in accepting a decision of this kind rendered a man immediately suspect. Matters were made more difficult by the university officials' determination that the institution's reputation must at all costs be saved from a second questioning

---

[57] On the Poels case, see Ellis, *Gibbons,* II, 170–182, and Barry, *Catholic University,* pp. 176–182.

of its orthodoxy, so soon after the excitement over Americanism with which Keane's dismissal as rector had been linked.

In the course of the nearly four years of negotiations between Washington, Baltimore, and Rome numerous people
were drawn in—from Pius X, Cardinal Merry del Val, and various Roman Scripture men on one side of the ocean, to Cardinal
Gibbons, chancellor of the university, its rectors, Denis O'Connell and Thomas J. Shahan, and leading members of the hierarchy in their capacity as members of the board of trustees. In
all of the exchanges from 1906 to the final action of the trustees dismissing Poels in April, 1910, there was never any doubt
expressed about his high priestly character. Yet in terms of the
procedures used in such cases in the best academic circles today,
Poels was not accorded a full and fair hearing, and there could
be little doubt that, aside from an understandable note of
chagrin here and there, his privately printed brochure of nearly
a hundred pages, *A Vindication of My Honor,* presented a plausible and cogent statement of his innocence. Poels was especially
hard on Gibbons who, he said, could not have failed to realize
that under the circumstances the cardinal's solution to the difficulty would have obliged him to disappear from the university
"with my honor under a cloud." Poels then continued:

> *But His Eminence seems to be afraid that the vindication*
> *of my honor might entail certain consequences which*
> *would be disagreeable to others, whose honor and welfare,*
> *to his mind, are of greater importance.*[58]

There could be no question about the determination of
Gibbons and Shahan, rector of the university, to prevent the
institution once again from coming under suspicion at Rome.
And in that sense Poels was correct, for in both the Poels and
Bruneau affairs the cardinal of Baltimore displayed a timidity
and fearfulness that were not in keeping with his customary
serene manner in dealing with the Roman Curia. The effect of
an action such as this on other members of the faculty of the
Catholic University of America, as well as on the faculties of

---

[58] Archives of the Archdiocese of Baltimore, 106-D. The Poels brochure was
printed in Washington in 1910.

Catholic seminaries, colleges, and universities throughout the country, need hardly be emphasized.

While the Poels case was under discussion a more famous episode in American Catholic history arose at Saint Bernard's Seminary in Rochester. By the spring of 1907 the archbishop of San Francisco, Patrick W. Riordan, had decided to ask the Holy See for a coadjutor with the right of succession, having begun to feel the need for assistance after twenty-three years of strenuous labor in that extensive jurisdiction. His choice was Father Edward Hanna, a priest of the diocese of Rochester who since the completion of his Roman training in 1887 had taught first at Saint Andrew's, the minor seminary, and then upon the opening of Saint Bernard's in 1893, had moved to the major seminary. On the latter faculty as professor of Scripture was Andrew J. Breen, also Roman-trained and three years Hanna's junior. As a recent study has said of Hanna and Breen, "their personalities differed widely, and one fine day they were going to collide."[59]

The "collision" was probably caused in part by the fact that Dr. Hanna was both socially engaging and highly competent academically. By the first quality he won many friends both within and without the Church, and by the second he came to have a growing reputation in scholarly circles. His publications included a lengthy essay, "The Human Knowledge of Christ," that appeared in three installments in the *New York Review* in 1905–1906; a brief survey called "Some Recent Books on Catholic Theology," that was carried in the January, 1906, issue of the *American Journal of Theology;* a learned review published by the Divinity School of the University of Chicago; and early in 1907, Volume I of the *Catholic Encyclopedia* contained his article on "Absolution." Hanna showed sympathy with the approach of the so-called "new apologetic" which sought to adapt the Church's teaching to the findings of current scholarship. But the new apologetic which had been developed among some European Catholic writers was condemned both in the

[59] Robert F. McNamara, "Archbishop Hanna, Rochesterian," *Rochester Review* 25 (April, 1953), 10.

Lamentabili decree of July, 1907, and the encyclical *Pascendi* of the following September.

In any case, it was not until November, 1907, that Archbishop Riordan learned that his request of the previous spring to secure Hanna as his coadjutor had encountered difficulty at the Congregation de Propaganda Fide because his candidate's orthodoxy had been called in question. Through some unknown source the matter was leaked to the secular press where it was given a fairly wide coverage, and it was through a medium of this kind that the identity of the accuser was ultimately narrowed down to a member of the faculty of Saint Bernard's Seminary. The forceful Bishop McQuaid lost no time in ferreting out the culprit who, it turned out, had been Breen—who promptly resigned and left Rochester after a public blast at the bishop.

Meanwhile Archbishop Riordan made a second attempt in the following year to secure his favorite candidate. Once again, however, Breen and Father Alexis Lépicier, O.S.M., professor of theology in the Urban College of Propaganda and a later cardinal in curia, submitted adverse reports. Lépicier had been deputed by Cardinal Gotti for this purpose, and in his report he stated that Hanna's writings unquestionably leaned toward Modernism, a damaging verdict that was supported by no better evidence than certain excerpts taken from the articles of Hanna, statements such as: "These formulae [dogmas of the Church] are ever inadequate, and will sometimes appear inaccurate if pressed too closely;" and another example: "There is a feeling that the old concept of doctrinal development was too narrow, too restricted; that a larger development must be admitted. . . ." In addition to Breen and Lépicier the former apostolic delegate to the United States, Cardinal Sebastiano Martinelli, O.S.A., had become what one historian has described as "the chief antagonist to Hanna's appointment."[60]

Under these circumstances it was not surprising that Father Giovanni Genocchi, intimate friend of Hanna and consultor

[60] Gaffey, "Life of Patrick Riordan," p. 550. The account of the Hanna case as given above is based on the McNamara article and more detailed treatment of the unpublished manuscript of Msgr. Gaffey.

to the Pontifical Biblical Commission, should have warned Riordan in the summer of 1908 that Cardinals Gotti and Merry del Val were "now 'absolutely' opposed to Dr. Hanna's nomination." By this time Riordan had become sufficiently discouraged to ask his friend, Archbishop Ireland, to furnish new suggestions for the coadjutorship, but not to include the name of any priest who had written anything because, as he said, "indications of Modernism will be found probably in the writings by his enemies." Disappointed in his hope for Hanna, the archbishop of San Francisco reluctantly agreed at the end of 1908 to accept as auxiliary bishop Denis O'Connell, rector of the Catholic University of America. Only upon the latter's appointment as bishop of Richmond in January, 1912, did he renew his plea for Hanna, and finally in October of that year the latter was appointed auxiliary—not coadjutor with the right of succession—for San Francisco. Five and a half years had elapsed since Riordan's original request, and during all that anxious time while men like Breen, Lépicier, and Martinelli were heard at Rome, Hanna himself had not been given the opportunity to appear there to answer his accusers.

By the time that Bishop Hanna reached San Francisco in the closing days of 1912 the storm stirred up by Monsignor Benigni and his *Sodalitium Pianum* had been felt in virtually every part of the Universal Church. So far, indeed, did the excesses of the integralists go that they did not leave untouched Monsignor Giacomo della Chiesa of the Vatican secretariat of state who in February, 1908, had been named archbishop of Bologna. Della Chiesa belonged to the party of Cardinal Mariano Rampolla, former secretary of state, and, therefore, was not in favor with the all-powerful Merry del Val; in the circumstances his appointment to Bologna was an illustration of the principle, *promoveatur ut amoveatur*. In May, 1914, della Chiesa was finally named a cardinal and in the conclave that followed the death of Pius X three months later he was elected to the papacy and took the name Benedict XV. In this improved climate of opinion the archbishop of Albi, Eudoxe-Irénée Mignot, wrote a memorable letter to the new secretary of state, Cardinal Domenico Ferrata, in which he summarized in dignified lan-

guage the incalculable damage done to the Church and to her
intellectuals by the events of the previous years. Mignot
acknowledged the dangers adherent in Modernism and the
necessity of stamping them out. But in deploring the extremes
to which some had gone, he reached the heart of the matter
when he wrote:

> *In this doctrinal reaction, have not some of the under-*
> *lings gone a good deal too far? Have they not sometimes*
> *given an impression of enmity to sincere and impartial*
> *research? There is no doubt of this. And in consequence*
> *there is a real wave of anger against authority among*
> *scholars and thinkers everywhere. The Church has lost*
> *some of the prestige which was hers under Leo XIII.*
> *Within the bosom of the Church, discouragement has*
> *seized upon intellectual and social workers. Denounced,*
> *spied upon, abused by the papers of the occult power;*
> *[Benigni's* Sodalitium Pianum] *held in suspicion by those*
> *deceived by false reports, the honesty of their intentions*
> *suspected—they found their work grown very difficult.*
> *Many a man withdrew once and for all from the lists who*
> *might have won many a victory for the Christian cause.*
>
> *This sense of unrest has made itself most unfortunately*
> *evident in many major seminaries, in religious houses of*
> *study and in university centers. Upon this, testimony is*
> *unanimous: our young men have lost the sacred passion for*
> *intellectual labor, and it is very difficult for their profes-*
> *sors to stimulate it. After the enthusiasm—the often fev-*
> *erish enthusiasm admittedly—for the study of apologetics,*
> *exegesis, positive theology, philosophy and sociology, the*
> *students are now satisfied with a dull flat study, and theol-*
> *ogy of the handbook sort. Natural laziness has something*
> *to do with this, but many certainly think it the best way to*
> *assure their future and further their personal ambition.*
> *The perpetuation of this state of things will mean an*
> *inferior clergy, more concerned with the externals of wor-*
> *ship than with the spiritual realities of interior religion—*
> *a clergy which will understand nothing of the intellectual*
> *and moral difficulties of the time, or of the movement of*

ideas, and the Church will be the loser. Such a clergy will stand motionless amidst a world on the march, a world whose light they ought to be. Neither their minds nor their hearts will be opened to those who are besieged by doubt, and so much in need of them.[61]

In the sequel Cardinal Ferrata died rather suddenly on October 10, 1914, and Mignot's letter in all likelihood was lost to view. But the point was taken up in the first encyclical of the new pontiff, *Ad beatissimi* (November 1, 1914) where Benedict XV acknowledged the dissension within the Catholic body and urged that every member of the faithful endeavor to act in such a way as to heal the wounds and to restore harmony. In that connection he warned:

Again let no private person, either by the publication of books or journals, or by delivering discourses, publicly assume the position of a master in the Church. . . . Concerning matters in which, since the Holy See has not pronounced judgment, saving faith and discipline, discussion may take place pro and contra, it is certainly lawful for everybody to say what he thinks and to uphold his opinion.[62]

It was a salutary rebuff to those who had set themselves up as guardians of the faith and judges of their fellow Catholics' orthodoxy. And if the most acute effects of the antimodernist movement described by Archbishop Mignot and rebuked by Benedict XV had not been felt in the seminaries, colleges, and universities of the American Church, it was in no small measure due to the fact that these institutions were the scene of relatively little original thinking and writing. We have noted certain exceptions at Saint Joseph's Seminary, New York; the

[61] Mignot to Ferrata, n.p., October, 1914, Nicolas Fontaine, *Saint Siège, Action française et Catholiques intégraux: Histoire critique avec documents* (Paris: Librairie Universitaire, J. Gamber, 1928), p. 133. It has been said that Fontaine was a pseudonym for M. Canet, an official of the Quay d'Orsay, who dealt with religious groups. Gerald J. O'Brien, S.J., "Anti-Modernism: The Integralist Campaign," *Continuum* 3 (Summer, 1965), 195.

[62] "First Encyclical of Benedict XV," *Catholic Mind* 12 (December 22, 1914), 745–746.

Catholic University of America; and Saint Bernard's Seminary, Rochester.

There were other disturbing episodes in Catholic academic circles, however, that had no direct connection with Modernism and the efforts to eradicate it. We have already spoken of the removal of Denis O'Connell from the rectorship of the North American College, Rome, in 1895, and Leo XIII's action in the following year which resulted in the dismissal of Keane from the Catholic University of America. In a similar move on a broader scale in May, 1911, it was announced by William H. O'Connell, archbishop of Boston, that the Sulpicians who had been in charge of Saint John's Seminary, Brighton, since it opened in September, 1884, were to be replaced the following fall by the diocesan clergy. O'Connell's action meant the breaking of a contract with the Society of Saint Sulpice, not because of any stated dissatisfaction with the teaching ability or spiritual direction of Saint John's professors, but because he wished complete control so that he might inaugurate the system followed at the North American College in Rome of which he had been rector. The archbishop of Boston was a close friend of Cardinal Merry del Val and a thorough disciple of the *Romanità,* a spirit that he was intent upon introducing at Brighton. The historians of the seminary acknowledged the Sulpicians' "righteous reluctance to retire under fire," as well as the local superior's "actual lack of authority to annul the contract spontaneously . . . ," and they concluded:

> *In the end, pronounced bitterness on the one side and a sense of unwarranted persecution on the other were left to be crystalized in parties, both in the diocese and the province, which made very difficult the task assumed by the diocesan priests, who took over direction of the Seminary.*[63]

It is needless to comment on what it means to the life of an academic institution that finds itself suddenly deprived of its head, to say nothing of virtually an entire faculty. One inescapable conclusion that emerges from these cases is that those

---

[63] John E. Sexton and Arthur J. Riley, *History of Saint John's Seminary, Brighton* (Boston: Roman Catholic Archbishop of Boston, 1945), p. 143.

who initiated and executed them had little comprehension or sympathy for the principal purpose that had brought these institutions into existence in the first place. Nor was this type of thing confined to a period when the Church here was still largely composed of an untutored body of immigrants or first-generation Americans, for whom one might offer the excuse of their ignorance of proper academic procedures. It has continued to occur in Catholic institutions of higher learning down even to the present times.

A case in point was the sudden removal of Bishop James H. Ryan, rector of the Catholic University of America, in August, 1935, when he was named ordinary of the diocese of Omaha. Ryan had taken office in 1928 and had given strong backing to Roy J. Deferrari in a badly needed reorganization that resulted in the creation of the Graduate School of Arts and Sciences with a corresponding college for undergraduates. Those who brought to the situation a firsthand knowledge and reasonable objectivity would not seriously dissent from Deferrari's judgment of Ryan when he said, "He was a great academic organizer, which resulted from a remarkable foresight, and this perhaps was his greatest contribution to the growth of the University."[64]

True, neither Bishop Ryan nor Dr. Deferrari possessed a conciliatory personality, and in consequence both made a number of enemies. But it was not the enemies within that accomplished Ryan's undoing; it was rather a powerful member of the board of trustees, John T. McNicholas, O.P., archbishop of Cincinnati, who objected to the rector's efforts to raise the university's standards to that of "a Catholic Harvard." McNicholas and his followers interpreted this goal as secularization in a doctrinal sense and felt that it constituted a serious threat to the university's character as a Catholic institution. The archbishop of Cincinnati succeeded in convincing the apostolic delegate to the United States of the danger, with the result that the latter had Ryan transferred to Omaha.

The facts as related above became generally known, and they

---

[64] Roy J. Deferrari, *Memoirs of the Catholic University of America, 1918–1960* (Boston: Saint Paul Editions, 1962), p. 410.

were confirmed for the writer who was at that time a member
of the university faculty, when in May, 1950, at Bern he visited
Archbishop Filippo Bernadini, apostolic nuncio to Switzerland,
who had been first dean of the university's School of Canon
Law.[65] Nor were such cases at all uncommon among the religious congregations of men and women that conducted institutions of higher education. There was more than one episode in
their ranks, such as the removal of Mother Mary Peter Carthy,
O.S.U., from the presidency of the College of New Rochelle
in June, 1961, due to the displeasure caused the late Cardinal
Spellman by certain remarks of the commencement speaker of
that year, Dr. John J. Meng, then president of Hunter College.

The 1960's witnessed more radical changes in Catholic higher
education in this country than any previous decade. In this
turbulent period two insistent and as yet unsolved problems
rivaled that of academic freedom among the Church's 305 colleges and universities with their 433,960 students as reported on
January 1, 1968. Since academic freedom is the central theme
of this essay other matters must not be permitted to distract us.
Yet to entirely ignore those problems would be to omit important factors that aggravated the situation and contributed not
only to the anxiety of administrators but also to the widespread
strain and tension that characterized Catholic circles in general
in the years following Vatican Council II. One was the fright-
ening rise in operating costs for private institutions of learning, a problem that haunted roughly two-thirds of the nation's
colleges and universities. The president of Yale University,
with an endowment of approximately $450 million, stated in
the spring of 1967 that Yale had never faced a more difficult
financial prospect, and there was no dissent when Kingman
Brewster added the comment that, "a serious strain on resources
for Yale is a crisis for other places."[66] Storm signals were clearly
visible in Catholic institutions, and the declared bankruptcy of
Loyola College of Montreal, and the grave financial condition
publicly acknowledged in April, 1968, by Fordham University

[65] Diary of John Tracy Ellis, April 22–June 27, 1950, pp. 56–59.
[66] "Universities: Anxiety Behind the Façade," *Time* 89 (June 23, 1967), 78.

and the Catholic University of America,[67] made all too real the judgment of Neil G. McCluskey, S.J., when he stated in the autumn of 1967, "the situation is moving from grim to desperate."[68]

The second problem was more closely related to that of academic freedom. The universal malaise that overtook traditional American moral values and social customs made itself felt among the Catholic college and university population as well as in that of their sister institutions. In noting the worldwide change of attitudes that was calling accepted values into question, the Pastoral Constitution on the Church in the Modern World, of Vatican Council II, promulgated in December, 1965, declared, "This is especially true of young people, who have grown impatient on more than one occasion, and indeed become rebels in their distress."[69] The depth and extent of youth's rebellion were to become startlingly evident in the years immediately following. That this all-pervading disillusionment of youth should in these circumstances have made inroads into Catholic schools should have occasioned no surprise. During its evolution many of their nearly 435,000 students, to say nothing of nearly three times that number of their coreligionists in secular colleges and universities, were brought to question the traditional answers furnished to them by the Church's spokesmen on matters relating to both doctrine and morals. Moreover, the avant-garde in their ranks went on to question essential truths of the Catholic creed such as the Trinity and the divinity of Christ as well as the infallibility of the pope, and the right of the Church's magisterium to speak authoritatively to them and for them on subjects like birth control and premarital sex relations. Should one have doubted the nature of Catholic youth's alienation on this score, he had only to listen to what

[67] *New York Times*, April 27, 1968, p. 22; *Washington Post*, April 17, 1968, p. B 1.

[68] "Financial Crisis in Catholic Colleges," *America* 117 (September 23, 1967), 304. See also Duncan Norton-Taylor, "Private Colleges: A Question of Survival," *Fortune* 76 (October, 1967), 152–154; 180; 185–186.

[69] Pastoral Constitution on the Church in the Modern World, *The Documents of Vatican II*, ed. Walter M. Abbott, S.J. (New York: The America Press, 1966), p. 205.

they were saying. Granted that what was said or written was not always representative of all American Catholic young people, samples such as *Commonweal's* symposium, "The Cool Generation and the Church," and the summary of student attitudes toward death that appeared a few months later,[70] contained enough that was typical to illustrate the intellectual revolution that had taken place among Catholic youth.

The acute financial difficulties forced curtailment of educational facilities which, in turn, aroused student protests, and the mounting spirit of student rebellion against the Church's teaching authority in her colleges and universities heightened the tension over issues directly bearing on academic freedom. It was an almost entirely new situation for the Catholic colleges and universities. The historians of academic freedom in the United States noted that the restrictive atmosphere of the old colleges and of the universities that had taken their rise after the Civil War, had been due chiefly to the "religious commitments and sectarian aspirations" of these institutions. For this reason, said Hofstadter and Metzger, religious leaders figured "in an exceptionally prominent way among the opponents of intellectual freedom"[71] down almost to the present century. Few —if any—Catholic names were found among these religious leaders, however, because of the almost universally docile acceptance in Catholic circles of not only the teachings of the Church, but too, of the authoritarian regimes that governed the Church's colleges. To question an article of belief or to challenge a ruling by a president or a dean in a Catholic institution would have been practically unthinkable.

Some years before Vatican Council II, however, a more critical spirit and a greater eagerness for the democratic process had begun to pervade the leading Catholic centers of learning. These factors made all the more acute the resentment the Catholic academic community felt in such episodes as the

---

[70] "The Cool Generation and the Church: A Symposium," *Commonweal* 87 (October 6, 1967), 11–23; John J. McMahon, "Catholic Students Look at Death," *Commonweal* 87 (January 26, 1968), 491–494. See also Donald McDonald, "Youth Loses Its Faith in America," *Saint Louis Review*, December 1, 1967, p. 16.

[71] Hofstadter-Metzger, *Development of Academic Freedom*, pp. xi-xii.

silencing for the better part of a decade of the best known theologian of the American Church, the late John Courtney Murray, S.J., who early in the 1950's was forbidden to write or to speak on the subject of his special competence—the theology of religious freedom. There was likewise the impounding by the superior general of the Congregation of Holy Cross of the volume, *The Catholic Church in World Affairs,* edited by Waldemar Gurian and M. A. Fitzsimons (University of Notre Dame Press, 1954), presumably because of the opening chapter, "On the Structure of the Church-State Problem," by the same Father Murray. Near the end of that decade, however, there came to the papacy the simple and direct man, Angelo Roncalli, who early in 1959 convoked the Church's twenty-first ecumenical council, and with Vatican Council II there was generated a liberating force throughout the Catholic world that was destined to change the course of the Church's history, and with it the history of all the institutions that operated under the Catholic name. With the new thinking inspired by the council, and with the accelerated movement for freedom of thought and action on most of the campuses of the United States, there ensued in Catholic circles a notable change in mood. It would have been altogether strange had such a change *not* taken place, for Catholics were as much the heirs of the American tradition as anyone else, and encouragement of this new mood was lent by the Pastoral Constitution on the Church in the Modern World promulgated in December, 1965. Speaking of the enhanced role of the educated laymen, it stated:

> *In order that such persons may fulfill their proper function, let it be recognized that all the faithful, clerical and lay, possess a lawful freedom of inquiry and of thought, and the freedom to express their minds humbly and courageously about those matters in which they enjoy competence.*[72]

One of the first places where the conflict between the proponents of a broader and mere genuine freedom for faculty and students and a highly conservative administration broke into the open was the Catholic University of America. In Feb-

[72] *Documents of Vatican II,* p. 270.

ruary, 1963, *The Tower,* the students' weekly newspaper, made
it known that the administration of the University had banned
four distinguished theologians as possible choices for a series
of student-sponsored lectures. The reason given was that since
these four men—Godfrey Diekmann, O.S.B., Hans Küng, John
Courtney Murray, S.J., and Gustave Weigel, S.J.—all represented the progressive school of thought, and since the institution belonged to the entire hierarchy of the United States,
the university should not show partiality to any single aspect
of theological thought, since, too, the ecumenical council
was still debating certain controverted issues on which the four
theologians were thought to hold a single point of view. In
banning the representatives of this point of view, an advantage
was implicitly given to the opposing side in a way that jeopardized the neutrality which the administration was desirous of
safeguarding—a fact that would seem to have been overlooked
by the rector of the university and his associates. In the sequel
the matter was not pressed by the students, but the widespread
publicity that attended the controversy made it something of
a *cause célèbre* both here and abroad, and three years later one
critic stated that this case "marked not only a new high point
in the intransigence of the conservatives but also a turning point
in the history of freedom in the Catholic Church in America."[73]

As the 1960's progressed there was a series of eruptions on
Catholic campuses over the freedom to which faculty and students felt entitled—either against the confining tendencies of
academic administrators, or against ecclesiastical authorities
who invoked their right to act as the voice of the Church's
magisterium. The most notorious case of the former was the
summary dismissal by the administration of Saint John's University, Jamaica, New York, in December, 1965, of thirty-three
professors—two terminations were later withdrawn—an action

---

[73] Leonard Swidler, "The Catholic Historian and Freedom," *American Bene-
dictine Review* 17 (June, 1966), 152. Another writer remarked about this case,
"Whatever happens at the Catholic University is therefore more than mere inci-
dent: it is often a reflection of crucial trends in American Catholicism" Jon
Victor [pseudonym], "Restraints on American Catholic Freedom," *Harper's Magazine* 227 (December, 1963), 33.

that was regarded as so reprehensible by the American Association of University Professors, that in passing censure on Saint John's in April, 1966, they stated:

> *Owing to the extraordinary seriousness of the violation of academic freedom and tenure by St. John's University, the Fifty-second Annual Meeting of the Association approved an action of Committee A which states that, although "we do not recommend imposing an absolute obligation upon our members to decline appointments, we do feel that in the case of St. John's University it would be inappropriate for our members to accept appointments at St. John's University."*[74]

Other institutions where less serious feuds arose over differences between administration and faculty were the College of Saint Thomas, Duquesne University, and the San Diego College for Women.

Nowhere was the issue of academic freedom vs. ecclesiastical authority more sharply joined than at the University of Dayton. There a dispute among certain members of the departments of philosophy and theology led to the charge of heresy against some of the professors. The controversy occasioned the appointment of a committee of investigation by the local ordinary, Karl J. Alter, archbishop of Cincinnati, as well as a later committee by the University's president, Raymond J. Roesch, S.M. After months of investigating the latter group's report of September, 1967, seemed to bring a quietus as far as the general public was aware. This committee maintained that the Church's teaching authority had only an "indirect" control over what was taught in a Catholic university. A university of this kind, they said, "cannot accept any direct relationship to the magisterium in academic matters," since, they contended, this was

---

[74] *AAUP Bulletin* 53 (December, 1967), 364. Unlike the AAUP, however, the Middle States Association of Colleges and Secondary Schools, the regional accrediting agency, did not drop Saint John's from the list of its accredited institutions (*New York Times,* May 4, 1968, p. 27). Two former members of the Saint John's faculty, Joseph Scimecca and Roland Damiano, gave their account of the controversy in *Crisis at St. John's: Strike and Revolution on the Catholic Campus* (New York: Random House, 1968).

confined to Catholic faculty members' status as individual
Catholics and did not relate to their role as university instructors. "To say otherwise," the committee concluded, "is to make
the university an organ of the official teaching Church."[75]

A constructive development from these controversies was the
serious discussion to which the entire issue of academic freedom in the Catholic framework ultimately led. A good sample
of this widespread concern in Catholic circles was the symposium held at the University of Notre Dame in April, 1966,
on the general theme, "Academic Freedom and the Catholic
University." The eight papers ranged over a broad spectrum of
topics that included the question of one's personal commitment, student freedom, the freedom of the priest-scholar, and
the knotty question of "The University and the Church." In
the mind of Philip Gleason who treated the subject from an
historical point of view, academic freedom was then "the most
crucial problem facing Catholic higher education." It was one
that Catholic universities should fearlessly approach since, he
said, it went to the very heart of the problem of faith and
knowledge

*at a time when their own theological, philosophical, peda-
gogical, and general intellectual positions are in greater
uncertainty than at any previous period in the history of
American Catholic higher education.*[76]

[75] *National Catholic Reporter,* October 4, 1967, p. 10. See also the twelve page
*Statement Relative to the Controversy Touching Academic Freedom and the
Church's Magisterium* dated April 10, 1967, and issued by Dayton's president. A
further controversy developed at the University of Dayton in the spring of 1968
when the student congress demanded that birth control information and material
be made available at the campus health center (*San Francisco Monitor,* April 4,
1968, p. 12).

[76] Philip Gleason, "Academic Freedom and the Crisis in Catholic Universities,"*Academic Freedom and the Catholic University,* ed. Edward Manier and
John W. Houck (Notre Dame: Fides Publishers, 1967), p. 53. The most recent
treatment of this and other phases of Catholic higher education is the lengthy
chapter of Christopher Jenks and David Riesman, "Catholics and Their Colleges,"
The Academic Revolution (New York: Doubleday & Co., 1968), pp. 334-405.
Jenks and Riesman do not give a very heartening picture of Catholic institutions,
especially on the graduate level. As Edward D. Eddy remarked in a review of
the book, the authors' conclusion was that the important question was not

John E. Walsh, C.S.C., maintained that it was a very serious mistake to speak of the Catholic university "as part of the teaching function of the Roman Catholic church or even its teaching apostolate." To Father Walsh the university was one of the manifestations—perhaps the highest formal, explicit, and systematic manifestation—of the Church *learning*."[77] In other words, the university was no part of what the theologians called the *Ecclesia docens,* and if that point should be universally accepted, much of the ground for dispute between the two would be eliminated. Speaking of the problems encountered by priest-scholars in relation to censorship of their writings, John L. McKenzie, S.J., stated that he would submit for consideration the thesis, "that the principle of censorship is basically irrational and immoral." The immorality of the action, according to Father McKenzie, lay in applying what he described as "crude power to resolve problems which of their nature demand close and methodical scholarly examination." The learned Scripture scholar then went on to say:

> *Censorship settles scholarly differences of opinion by a moral bludgeon. And censorship is totally unnecessary, because scholarship is equipped to do better what censorship pretends to do; and that is to protect the reading public from irresponsible publication.*[78]

These excerpts from the Notre Dame symposium of 1966 illustrate the candid and open criticism that Catholic scholars were currently applying to this delicate matter, and this was

---

whether a few Catholic universities could compete with Harvard and Berkeley, but whether Catholicism could provide an ideology or a personnel for the development of alternatives to Jenks and Riesman's Harvard-Berkeley model of excellence. "Obviously," said Eddy, "the authors do not think this to be possible over the long run." And after their more than seventy pages on Catholic higher education their verdict, he added, was "maybe so, but probably not" (*Saturday Review,* May 18, 1968, p. 87).

[77] Manier and Houck, eds., "The University and the Church," *Academic Freedom,* p. 109.

[78] John L. McKenzie, S.J., "The Freedom of the Priest-Scholar," *ibid.,* p. 173. See also the same author's trenchant comments in "Q.E.D.," *The Critic* 26 (August–September, 1967), 6–8, 79.

only one example of such.[79] It has been a problem for other religiously affiliated colleges and universities as well as for those of the Catholic church, and it became of sufficient concern to educators generally to warrant the American Association of University Professors in 1965 appointing a special committee on academic freedom in church-related institutions. Over a period of two years this committee worked out a statement which sought to elaborate on the AAUP's 1940 "Statement of Principles on Academic Freedom and Tenure" with the church-related college especially in mind. The committee made six general recommendations aimed to safeguard the individual professor's rights and at the same time to guarantee the institution's special character as one affiliated with a church and its creed.[80]

The year 1967 proved to be especially memorable in Catholic higher educational circles for the mounting emphasis on academic freedom. Saint John's and Dayton continued to draw attention, but the controversial issues that had involved these universities were quite overshadowed in April by the sudden and unexplained refusal by the Board of Trustees of the Catholic University of America to renew the contract of Father Charles E. Curran, assistant professor of moral theology. News of the board's action at its Chicago meeting set off a spontaneous reaction on the campus during which the faculty of the School of Theology unanimously reaffirmed their confidence in Father Curran, noted that no charges had been brought against their colleague, that he had been given no hearing, and stated, in the words of Walter J. Schmitz, S.S., the dean, that "the academic freedom and the security of every professor of this University is jeopardized." Under the circumstances, said Father Schmitz, "we cannot and will not function until Father Curran is reinstated."[81] He concluded by inviting the other schools of

---

[79] As a further example of the growing literature on this subject, see Robert Hassenger, ed., *The Shape of Catholic Higher Education* (Chicago: University of Chicago Press, 1967).

[80] "Report of the Special Committee on Academic Freedom in Church-Related Colleges and Universities," *AAUP Bulletin* 53 (December, 1967), 369–371.

[81] *The Tower*, April 25, 1967, p. 4. This publication is the students' weekly newspaper. In this connection one is reminded of the meeting of King Agrippa and the Roman Governor Festus at Caesarea, described in the Acts of the Apos-

the university to join the theologians' protest, an appeal that met with an immediate and overwhelming response from most of the other faculties, except that of the School of Education. Within a matter of almost hours the institution was brought to a standstill by a virtually total boycott of classes until such time as Father Curran would be restored to his post.

What made the action of the administration and the trustees all the more open to criticism was the fact that the faculty of the School of Theology had by a unanimous vote the previous November recommended Father Curran for promotion to the rank of associate professor, and the academic senate had unanimously approved this recommendation at its meeting on March 21, a meeting at which the top administrators in attendance had raised no objection. The reason for the punitive measure against Father Curran was never clearly stated, although it was rumored that it had arisen from his teaching on birth control, a rumor that was stoutly denied by the university's chancellor, Archbishop Patrick A. O'Boyle. In any case, the trustees' procedure at Chicago (to which Paul J. Hallinan, late archbishop of Atlanta, alone entered a negative vote), met with such instant, vigorous, and sustained opposition from both faculty and students that after a week of boycott the trustees capitulated completely and the chancellor announced that Father Curran had been reinstated and his promotion approved.

The boycott of classes during a week's time made academic history for the Catholic universities as well as for others—a fact that was indelibly impressed on the American public by the extraordinary publicity given to the case. Every academic institution has its hazards, and the Catholic University of America has been no exception. In both the Curran case and that of the banned theologians in 1963, informed persons realized that the progress of the university in these and other matters was hampered in no small measure by the prime weakness

---

tles. Festus acquainted Agrippa with the background to Saint Paul's arrest and imprisonment and stated that the high priests and elders of the Jews wanted to condemn Paul without so much as a trial. The governor then remarked:

> But I told them that Romans are not accustomed to give any man up before the accused has met his accusers face to face and has been given a chance to defend himself against the charges (Acts. 25:16).

from which the institution suffered and which lay at the bottom of many of its difficulties. That weakness arose from what might be described as "excessive ecclesiasticism" which periodically showed in various forms, especially in the use of the university as a stepping stone for careers in the Church and, secondly, in the interference from time to time in its academic affairs of high ecclesiastics whose knowledge and understanding of what a university was about, left much to be desired.

In contrast to such a lack of understanding, one of the most balanced presentations of the case for a Catholic university in today's world—quite at variance with the dictum of George Bernard Shaw that "a Catholic university is a contradiction in terms"—was that of Theodore M. Hesburgh, C.S.C., president of the University of Notre Dame. The occasion was the university's 125th anniversary, commemorated on December 9, 1967, when Father Hesburgh urbanely countered educators like Jacqueline Grennan, then president of Webster College; Rosemary Lauer of St. John's College, Annapolis; and other contemporary Catholics who subscribed more or less to the Shaw thesis. In doing so he was at pains to give due recognition to the special complexities of the problem, the while he made a stirring defense of freedom within the Catholic university. He then stated a principle which it were well that all churchmen connected in any way with a university would make their own. He said:

> *The university is not the kind of place that one can or should try to rule by authority external to the university. The best and only traditional authority in the university is intellectual competence: this is the coin of the realm.*[82]

[82] "The Vision of a Great Catholic University in the World Today," Documentary Service, Press Department, U.S. Catholic Conference, Dec. 14, 1967, p. 5. Another strong affirmation was made by Sister Margaret Claydon, S.N.D., president of Trinity College, for which see the *Washington Post*, Jan. 16, 1967. See also the Land O'Lakes Statement in the appendix. On the controversies at the Catholic University of America see *Dissent In and For the Church: Theologians and Humanae Vitae* by Charles E. Curran, Robert E. Hunt *et al.* (New York: Sheed & Ward, 1969) and *The Responsibility of Dissent: The Church and Academic Freedom* by John F. Hunt, Terrence R. Connelly *et al.* (New York: Sheed & Ward, 1969).

Less than two months before the Hesburgh address, the freedom of the Catholic university received eloquent expression from the Pacific Coast. The occasion arose when a highly vocal right wing element of the alumni of the University of Santa Clara sought to have cancelled the program of the university's newly founded Center for the Study of Contemporary Values because it included a Marxian theoretician and several controversial figures such as the then Protestant Episcopal Bishop, James A. Pike. "Antiseptically pure of ideas themselves," said Patrick A. Donohoe, S.J., Santa Clara's president at the time, "they cannot distinguish between dialogue and espousal." He went on to say that the Catholic university had to grow up, and he then added, "So do Catholic alumni and friends of the University. The formal work of the institution is not to prepare monks and nuns, but citizens of the world—and the world is made up of a vast spectrum of ideas ranging from Mao to Robert Welch."[83] Catholic educational circles had rarely if ever heard a stouter defense of academic freedom from a highly placed administrator than that of Father Donohoe.

Obviously, the complicated problems arising from academic freedom and its ramifications were not unique to the Catholic colleges and universities; tensions of one kind or another on this score plagued all institutions of learning, public or private, as they always will in any community of scholars and students, whether the institution that draws them together is affiliated with a particular church or not. The religiously oriented institution must sail between Scylla and Charybdis in these matters, but there is no intrinsic reason why it cannot complete a safe voyage without betraying either its religious heritage or its academic integrity. In that connection the formula of Pattillo and Mackenzie for what they termed the "free Christian college" (substitute "free Jewish college" as the case may be), would seem to merit consideration. Such a school, said these authors:

stands unapologetically for religion and liberal education, but it relies on example, persuasive presentation of ideas,

[83] *The Santa Clara,* October 20, 1967, p. 1.

and a climate of conviction, rather than on conformity, to accomplish its ends.[84]

Academic policy was conducted in an open and honest manner during the 1960's by a growing number of Catholic institutions like Saint Louis University—to cite but one example. In December 1966, that particular administration was not afraid to have students hear Roger Garaudy, a leading French Marxian theoretician, and this gave reason for believing that an era such as the Church's colleges and universities had not previously known, might well be at hand. One reason for optimism in this regard was the strong contrast of the 1960's with the widespread suppression of freedom of thought and expression that had characterized Catholic circles in the previous decade. At that time the tone had to some extent been set by the cautionary and warning words of Pope Pius XII's encyclical, *Humani generis,* of August 12, 1950. In the years that followed, prominent Catholic scholars both in Europe and in the new world—for example, the late John Courtney Murray, S.J.—had been frustrated and discouraged by repeated admonitions from ecclesiastical authorities, to the point where openness and freedom (which, as we have seen, had come to be a fairly general feature of Catholic university life in the late 1960's) were conspicuous by their absence. The former spirit was given striking expression in the American context on June 3, 1961, when Egidio Vagnozzi, at the time apostolic delegate to the United States, delivered a baccalaureate sermon at Marquette University. Alluding to the dangers facing Catholic intellectuals from what he described as "the modern, massive opposition of secularism and naturalism," he made clear that it was not the attitude of the secularist intellectuals and their errors that was on his mind. "I am concerned," said the delegate, "with the uneasiness and preoccupations of some Catholic intellectuals."[85]

[84] Manning M. Pattillo, Jr., and Donald M. Mackenzie, *Church-Sponsored Higher Education in the United States* (Washington: American Council on Education, 1966), p. 195.

[85] "Thoughts on the Catholic Intellectual," *Catholic Herald Citizen* (Milwaukee), June 17, 1961, p. 9, supplemented by a photostatic copy of the archbishop's sermon.

Apparently the archbishop had serious misgivings about the soundness of faith of some of the latter. In any case, one can readily understand the effect on the Catholic academic community of this country when the highest ranking representative of the Holy See in the United States was heard to say:

> *The complaint has been voiced more than once that in high ecclesiastical circles the intellectual is often under-estimated and also mistrusted. The question is whether we are confronted with true and genuine intellectuals, who are inspired by a sincere love of truth, humbly disposed to submit to God's Revelation and the authority of His Church, or whether we are confronted with intellectuals who believe, first of all, in the absolute supremacy and unlimited freedom of human reason, a reason which has shown itself so often fallacious and subject to error.*[86]

Less than a year and a half later, Vatican Council II opened at Rome, where a far different attitude toward intellectuals ultimately emerged both within and without the Church than that expressed by Archbishop Vagnozzi. The change was manifest on the closing day of the council, December 8, 1965, when one of the final addresses was directed to "men of thought and science." Its principal author was Cardinal Paul-Emile Léger, then archbishop of Montreal, who asked what the bishops' efforts had amounted to over the council's four years if it was not "a more attentive search for and deepening of the message of truth." For that reason, said the cardinal, "our paths could not fail to cross," and he then added:

> *Your road is ours; Your paths are never foreign to ours. We are the friends of your vocation as searchers, companions in your fatigues, admirers of your successes, and, if necessary, consolers in your discouragement and your failures.*[87]

---

[86] *Ibid.*

[87] "Closing Messages of the Council: To Men of Thought and Science," *The Documents of Vatican II,* ed. Walter M. Abbott, S.J. (New York: The America Press, 1966), p. 731.

This eloquent affirmation lent emphasis to the distance that official Catholic thinking had traveled in recent years, and it lent supporting evidence as well to the emergence of a new era for the Catholic institutions of higher learning. Only the future would tell what the ultimate reality would be, but there was reason to believe that it might not be as grim for these schools as one writer maintained when he said the idea of the Church conducting an institution identifiable as a Catholic university would "one day seem as anachronistic as the papal states. . . ."[88] This prediction may in time prove to have been a sound one, but since prophecy is not the historian's function, he can only state that the Catholic university and college had outlived a childhood and youth marked by their all too frequent subjection to the whims of local bishops or religious superiors. And now the best of these institutions—and it is only with "the best" that the future need concern itself—had come of age, and one of the most unmistakable signs of their adulthood was their forthright facing up to the intricacies of translating into reality their own freedom as centers of research and teaching within the American Catholic framework. If the reader feels that it has been on the whole a painfully negative account, the writer can only agree with him. But as an historian of the Church and her institutions he would remind the reader that one who attempts to record the past can never venture far beyond that of which history is made (namely, documents), and it has been documentary evidence that has governed most of what has been said here.

Yet the prospect is by no means entirely dark, and that for several reasons. First, in the "tradition of autonomy" of the Catholic university there have also been occasions when the freedom of faculties and students has found its last and best defender in an occupant of the throne of Saint Peter. For example, in 1225 when the professors of the University of Paris dared to make a great seal that enabled them, among other

---

[88] John Cogley, "The Future of an Illusion," *Commonweal* 86 (June 2, 1967), 310. See below page 291.

things, to borrow money, they brought down on their heads the wrath of the chancellor of the Cathedral of Notre Dame as well as the sharp displeasure of the papal legate, Romano, Cardinal of San Angelo. The masters and students did not hesitate to storm the latter's residence with such fury that the legate "was compelled to flee from Paris in hot haste."[89] And when three years later a series of student carnival pranks in the winter of 1228–1229 brought a pitched battle with the royal troops during which several were killed, the professors declared a boycott. The students joined in to a man, and in the sequel Pope Gregory IX not only recalled his haughty legate to Rome, but brought about a return of the masters and students to their classes when in April, 1231, he issued several papal bulls that forbade the interference in university affairs of the chancellor or the bishop of Paris and gave apostolic sanction to the faculty and students to suspend classes in case satisfaction for an outrage were refused after fifteen days' notice.[90]

It would probably never occur to anyone to think that a faculty-student boycott would ever have been legalized by a papal bull! Yet Gregory IX's action also forms a part, if remote, of the "tradition of autonomy" that is the subject of this essay. Closer to present realities, however, for those who administer, teach, and attend Catholic colleges and universities in this country, as well as for the Catholic students who are enrolled in secular institutions, the changing mentality in Catholic circles about academic freedom and all that this implies is a matter of paramount importance. The Catholic university is at present under siege, so to speak, from two powerful forces which cannot but transform the traditional Catholic attitude toward academic freedom in the years just ahead. One force is the enhanced position of that concept throughout the general academic community of the United States; the second is the extraordinary emphasis which the idea of personal freedom and the rights and dignity of each individual man received

[89] Nathan Schachner, *The Mediaeval Universities* (London: George Allen & Unwin, 1938), p. 66.

[90] Hastings Rashdall, *The Universities of Europe in the Middle Ages*, ed. F.M. Powicke and A.B. Emden (Oxford: Clarendon Press, 1936), I, 337–338.

during the sessions of Vatican Council II. In other words, the
historic pattern in which problems involving the freedom of
a professor or a student in Catholic institutions have been
solved in the past is shattered beyond recall, and it behooves all
who have any connection with these institutions—whether that
be direct or indirect—to quicken the pace of change in his own
thinking if he wishes to count for anything in tomorrow's
world of higher learning.

Two examples may be cited of how the pace is already quickening on the part of some to meet the demands of a new age.
One is the remarkable development among many Catholic college and university students since World War II. The writer
would like to think in that connection that the judgment of a
distinguished Harvard historian does not represent an altogether unique situation. In commenting on the Harvard graduate students in history with whom he had come in contact in
recent years, H. Stuart Hughes remarked that he found less
change in Protestantism on the Harvard campus than was true
of Judaism and Catholicism. He wondered if it might not be
due to the fact that Protestants had felt themselves less challenged than the Jews who experienced the shock of the Nazi
persecutions and the establishment of Israel which helped
awaken them to their inheritance. The Protestants likewise
never had the shock and awakening that came to the Catholics
with, as he said,

> *the pontificate of John, the Council, and what can only be
> called an intellectual renaissance among American Catho-
> lics. On this last point, one bit of evidence may epitomize
> the change. Before the war, Catholic graduate students in
> history at Harvard were few in number, mostly undistin-
> guished, and on the margin of intellectual exchange; the
> rest of us treated them with politeness, but it would not
> have occurred to us to discuss religious or philosophical
> matters with them (and perhaps they themselves would
> have been embarrassed to do so.) Today my Catholic
> graduate students are some of the very best I have, they
> are right in the center of student life, and they do not*

hesitate to discuss the most prickly topics frankly and cordially.[91]

Multiply Professor Hughes' experience a hundredfold across the land and one does not need to tax his imagination to understand what meaning the presence of these young Catholic scholars will have for academic freedom and all that it implies among their coreligionists.

A second encouraging aspect of the Catholic academic picture stems indirectly from Vatican Council II. Every informed Catholic is aware of the remarkable organization known as the Association of Chicago Priests which was founded in October, 1966. Informed Catholics will likewise recall the refusal in March, 1967, of the archbishop of Chicago to permit one of his priests, Father Peter O'Reilly, to join the faculty of Chicago's Illinois Teachers College, South. At a meeting of the A.C.P. in May, 1967, Father O'Reilly (who had been one of the faculty members summarily dismissed from Saint John's University in December, 1965) made a proposal that no priest involved in higher education should be removed from his post unless and until he had requested a transfer. After considering the proposal the A.C.P. ended by taking the sensible action of making what was described as the "serious problem of academic freedom" the subject of a special committee that would investigate and report its findings.[92]

This was in strong contrast to some of the cases involving academic freedom reviewed here; in brief, it was to treat the Catholic clergy's involvement in the delicate and sensitive area of academic freedom with the seriousness that it deserves.

It was an approach that would have pleased Cardinal Newman who would have seen in it the clergy acting in an open and responsible manner in what related to higher education. Some years after he left the rectorship of the Catholic University of Ireland, Newman was still ruminating about what he had experienced and witnessed of the Irish clergy's arbitrary and

---

[91] Hughes to John Whitney Evans, Paris, November 4, 1966. The writer wishes to thank Professor Hughes and Father Evans for permission to quote this letter.

[92] *Saint Louis Review*, May 12, 1967, p. 4.

uninformed ways in what pertained to university education.
He told a friend that he had come away with "the distressing
fear" that in that country "there was to be an antagonism as
time went on, between the hierarchy and the educated classes."
If the writer may risk a prophecy concerning kindred matters
in the American Church he would venture to say that one of
the most ominous clouds on the horizon for the Church of the
United States in 1970 is the danger of a major confrontation
between the bishops in their capacity as members of the magisterium and the professors as the guardians of academic freedom. The threat is real, especially at a time when the university
has entered upon an era of prestige and influence never before
known in American history.[93] It is to be hoped, therefore, that
those who are in a position to shape policy both in the hierarchy
and in the Catholic academic community will weigh Newman's
words when he told the same friend in regard to the university:

> *You will be doing the greatest possible benefit to the
> Catholic cause all over the world, if you succeed in making
> the University a middle station at which clergy and laity
> can meet, so as to learn to understand, and to yield to each
> other—and from which, as from a common ground they
> may act in union upon an age which is running headlong
> into infidelity.*[94]

[93] For a lively discussion on the new found prestige of the university in American life, see Richard Lichtman, "The University: Mask for Privilege," *The
Center Magazine* I (January, 1968), 2–10; and the five responses to Lichtman and
his own rejoinder pp. 10–17. For the most recent development in the sensitive area
of the relations between Catholic universities and the magisterium of the Church,
see Neil G. McCluskey, S.J., "Rome Replies (Act II)," *America*, 122 (March 28,
1970), 330–334.

[94] Newman to George Fottrell, n.p., December 10, 1873, in A. Dwight Culler,
The Imperial Intellect: A Study of Newman's Educational Ideal (New Haven:
Yale University Press, 1955), p. 262.

Pay Any Price? Break Any Mold?*

In the university magazine, *Fordham,* the then President Leo McLaughlin wrote: "Fordham will pay any price, break any mold, in order to achieve her function as a university."

The probing letter of an alumnus, asking if his alma mater were really prepared to "pay any price" or "break any mold" occasioned this response by Father Richardson in the form of the article which follows the letter. The alumnus, Michael Heffron, wrote:

> *Let us hope that the spirit of which he has written is, to use the words you quote of Fr. John Courtney Murray, the spirit of a university "permeated with an atmosphere of intellectual integrity—the integrity that ensures that man in a university setting examines honestly, without prejudice and without religious or any other bias."*
>
> *Pay any price?*
>
> *Break any mold?*
>
> *Without religious bias?*
>
> *I think that you have raised our hopes too high; it simply sounds too good.*
>
> *I suspect that what you mean in fact is that you will pay any price, etc. within limits—the limits being, to use Fr. Pedro Arrupe's word, those circumscribed by your "competence." The new superior general of the Society of Jesus*

* Originally printed in *America,* April 29, 1967 (The America Press). Copyright© 1967. Reprinted with permission.

is reported to have spoken about the limits of competence in these words:

"I am strictly opposed to any criticism of the Church. . . . It is intolerable that any defect of the Church, however real, should be broached publicly by individuals or groups, regardless of the good will they might have. . . . If the person who is critical is intelligent, he will be understanding and see that the best solution will be either to keep silent and wait . . . . or meekly bring the defects to the knowledge of the proper authority."

If indeed this be one of the limits of your competence, we must ask whether a university can commit itself, completely and without recourse to criticism, to a particular, controversial and all-encompassing interpretation of reality—such as is Catholicism—and remain at the same time ready to pay any price, free to break any mold, and without religious bias.

Can you define precisely, clearly, and unambiguously Fordham's commitment to Catholic doctrine, to religious faith, to intellectual integrity, and to academic freedom?

How are these elements related?

What is the priority of your commitment to each?

Will you, as fallible human beings, entertain the possibility that your judgment of the truth of Catholicism is an erroneous judgment?

Are you intellectually free and willing to change as your unbiased and sincere judgment might suggest?

Are you prepared to offer these as legitimate choices to your students?

Somehow—sadly—I think that your answer, if it is offered at all, will be that intellectual integrity and academic freedom are the handmaids of Catholic dogma and religious faith; that it is the purpose of the former to illuminate and justify the latter; that religious, ethical and philosophical problems are to be examined and judged only within the envelope of our commitment to Catholicism—but that the commitment itself is never to be judged,

only accepted; that one is free to be right but not to be
wrong—and the Church will tell you what is right.

What is it, to synthesize all these questions, that makes a
Catholic university Catholic, distinctively different from
non-Catholic universities?

Frankly, I am as curious to see whether you address the
issue as I am to see how you do.

WILLIAM J. RICHARDSON, S.J.:

We at Fordham are very grateful for the letter of Mr.
Michael Heffron that appears in the November issue of this
magazine—partly because the issues he raises are so meaningful
in themselves, partly because his manner of raising them is a
high compliment to our integrity by the very fact that it con-
tains so honest a challenge.

The fundamental issue is: What is this educational ideal
"that makes a Catholic university Catholic, distinctly different
from non-Catholic universities?"

It will be fairly easy for us to agree, I suspect, on what this
ideal is not. The ideal in our day is not that the university serve
as a bastion of Catholicism to protect its students from risks to
their faith should they venture outside its confines onto secular
campuses. This represents the ghetto mentality discreetly laid
to rest by Vatican II, long after the acceptability of religious
pluralism as a fact of American life made the defensiveness
of an earlier era no longer necessary.

Religious pluralism in America itself demands the maintenance of the Catholic institution at no matter what cost. This
is the spirit, I take it, of Fr. McLaughlin's promise that Fordham will "pay any price, break any mold, in order to achieve
her function as a university." For if a pluralistic society is to
grow in vigor, it is essential that the manifold value systems
that constitute its pluralism maintain their identity and that
each give a clear articulation of what it stands for. In the world
of academia, then, where institutions live together as so many
corporate persons, it is altogether fitting that there be institu-

tions among them that incorporate the values of Christianity in general and of Catholicism in particular. In a word, the role of a Catholic university today is to represent the Church in academia, i.e., to serve as that corporate person through which the Church becomes present to the community of academic institutions and they to it. This raises a double question: What is the nature of this "corporate person?" How are we to understand this "presence?"

By "corporate person" I mean a collection of individual persons conceived as a single whole, a union of minds and wills of many men that, however difficult it may be to analyze structurally, is none the less quite identifiable, with a personality and goals it can call its own. The country in which one claims citizenship would be a case in point. It is a good case, for it lets us see how loose this moral union can be. Its unity is often lived but not adverted to, admitting within it those who refuse to make their own its official image of itself (for example, not every Frenchman shared De Gaulle's vision of France). Perhaps this is because they seek the same concrete goals, though not in the same way or for the same reasons. In any case, the union that constitutes a corporate person does not necessarily imply perfect unanimity among its members.

"Presence" is a primitive notion rather to be mediated than explained. It suggests vitality, spontaneity, freshness, a process of steady emergence that is essentially dynamic in character. Note, however, that this dynamism has a double orientation, for we always speak about presence "of" and presence "to" (or "in"). In the case of the Catholic university, which serves as bearer of the Catholic tradition in academia, it supplies the presence "of" Christ in the Church—i.e., of the whole Christ and not simply of the Church as a humanly visible institution—"to" the academic community (and, of course, vice versa.)

Presence, then, suggests a single dynamism with a double polarity. One polarity is oriented, like a vertical axis, toward something transcendent, i.e., toward Christ (in the Church) and implies a profound union with Him; the other, like a horizontal axis, is oriented toward something immanent in the world, i.e., toward the men of academia, implying union with them. There is obviously a certain tension between these two axes of force; but this is hardly to be wondered at, for we arrive here at an ancient mystery: the correlation of transcendence beyond the world and immanence in it that characterizes the Church itself, insofar as it is the continuation in time of the Word made flesh.

Let us talk about the horizontal axis of this presence. How is it possible for an institution to embody the presence of the Catholic Church in the academic world without compromising either the integrity of its faith on the one hand, or the ideals of academic excellence on the other? One answer is that the God in whom Christians believe is a God become incarnate, who was born as a man among men, at a given moment of history. He who was *the image of the invisible God . . . in whom all things were created* thus became visible to men, so that thenceforth human eyes could discern in human values a new dimension according to which they would bear—beyond their obvious human importance—the visage of Jesus Christ. And truth itself—all truth that is discerned by human effort and bought with human pain—is somehow, for one who believes, the shining forth of Him who said: *I am . . . the truth.* The search for human truth that a Christian makes in union with other men does not compromise his union with the God-man but rather orchestrates it.

I must be more explicit here. In speaking of truth "discerned by human effort," I mean precisely that. The search for truth is the responsibility of all men, and discovery of it the prerogative of all, whether believers or not. As to method, the demands of scientific rigor are the same for everyone. As to content, the truth I particularly have in mind here is such as is discoverable in those disciplines that, because of their relevance to man as such, constitute the basic curriculum of any self-respecting university: truth about man's physical nature and the universe in which he finds himself (in the natural sciences); truth about man's social nature and its institutions (in the social sciences); truth about man's collective past that he still is-as-having-been (in the science of history); truth about the secrets of man's mind and heart as concretely lived out into language (in literature); truth about the ultimate meaning of man and the universe as discoverable through the powers of his own mind (in philosophy as it has unfolded through history).

In speaking of truth in this fashion, I have in mind, too, the truth explored in such a discipline as theology. This will have a special place in any Church-related institution, and though it is no less rigorous than the other disciplines, none the less it is by reason of its content (divine revelation) obviously of a different sort. In the Catholic university this will involve the opportunity to study the Incarnation itself with all that this involves in terms of complete salvation history. Here the student can come to understand all the more profoundly why it is that truth for its own sake, discerned in any way and by anyone, must engage the reverence of the Christian, not because he can make it serve some apologetic purpose, but simply because it is true. For anyone who really accepts the fact that God became man sees truth as more than just *something*—a human value, however noble in itself. For him it is essentially *someone* —someone, indeed, divine. And yet, human values are not valid because they are Christian, but Christian because they are valid.

A true Christian, then, loves the truth, the whole truth that has any relevance for man. Is there nothing specifically Christian at all about his approach to it? At most, it would be perhaps this: the desire—even if only unconscious—to see it whole. I am not sure that I know why. Perhaps the reason is an instinctive concern for the absolute value of the individual man (it was he for whom Christ died), together with the realization that the individual man may think of himself in segmented fashion, especially in the relatively abstract world of academia. But he must always *live* as a whole. Perhaps the reason is more profoundly that the search (and therefore, hope) for unity that is characteristic of every human mind becomes for the Christian (far more than for other men) a very concrete hope, to the extent that his optic is explicitly Christic.

By this I mean that the Christian, believing in the Incarnation, thinks of all human values as somehow finding, in addition to their separate individual importance, a complete synthesis with one another in the human nature of the Word, precisely because it is the humanity of the Word, e.g., because He is the *syn-thesis* of God and man. In this context we can see how in speaking of the educational ideal of the Catholic university, "catholic" (i.e., universal), and "Catholic" (i.e., believing in the Incarnation continued in the visible Church), fuse into a single concept that another generation spoke of more frequently than we do as "Christian humanism." Or, more simply still, "Christian wisdom."

Be that as it may, the ideal of a synthesis of truth presupposes that there be something to synthesize, and this must come from all the human sciences, each submitting to the exigencies of its own discipline. Such was the ideal of the Christian university in its very earliest form. Do you recall how one of its alumni, Gregory—later called the Wonderworker—speaks of his student years under the tutelage of Origen, its director? "Nothing was kept from us, nothing concealed or made inaccessible. We could learn about any theory, barbarian or Greek, mystical or moral . . . go into them all . . . and enjoy the good things of the mind. Everything true in the teaching of the ancients provided us with a wonderful store of material for thought of the most delightful kind . . . To our minds it was really . . . an image of paradise."

Briefly, then, the Catholic university, as embodying the presence of the Church (of the *incarnate* Word) in the academic world, is polarized along a horizontal axis toward the endorsement of every authentic human value, inasmuch as the Incarnation of the Word made everything authentically human a means of access to the divine. It would follow (would it not?) that any compromise of "intellectual integrity" or of "academic freedom" (if I understand Mr. Heffron correctly to mean that it is the function of the latter to safeguard the former), would be a compromise of its elemental Christianity, hence an infidelity to its religious commitment as such.

Before proceeding further in this direction, let me say a word about the other polarization of the Catholic university, i.e., the orientation of the corporate person along a vertical axis toward union with Christ, whose presence it embodies in academia. The matter here is delicate, of course, for it touches on the whole problem of religious atmosphere and, more poignantly, of religious practice.

To begin with, the horizontal polarity of the university as such is for the Christian a means of achieving vertical communion with the incarnate Word. I have in mind the example of St. Paul, whose total act of love toward Christ took the form of obeying the command to *serve and bear witness* to what he had seen, i.e., by making Christ's presence known among the Gentiles. But the demands of the apostolic work by which he bore witness to Christ, i.e., the total dedication of his energies to work with men, are a way in which he *worships* God in the spirit. In other words, Paul's relation to Christ as His witness before men was already such that to commit himself to communication with *men* was of its nature a liturgy of action that served as a gesture of worship to *God*, and a deeper means of union with the Lord whom he thus served.

But the liturgy of action is never separate from—in fact it is nourished by and finds it fullest meaning in—the prime analogue of all liturgy, the liturgy of sacrament. In this respect, if some of the venerable religious practices that once characterized the Catholic campus (such as required daily mass, annual retreat, etc.), have gradually diminished in recent years, much has been gained in terms of mature, personal commitment through the deepening experience of the liturgy of sacrament.

Just what the liturgical life at Fordham amounts to is too broad a theme for treatment here, but let me speak of one case in particular. It involves, to be sure, relatively few persons and only a single occasion, but it is important for what it implies. The students here have their own off-campus Coffee House, which they call, for no good reason at all, "The Compleat Works of Charles Dickens." Student-organized, student-supported, student-run, it grew out of the students' own felt need for a place where they and the faculty could come together informally to talk about anything at all, read their poetry to one another, write and perform their own plays, sing or dance or play what music they would—in short, engage in any sort of civilized social interchange or creative activity that seemed culturally worthwhile. On the last Saturday evening before Christmas, they arranged to celebrate the Eucharist—the liturgy of Advent—in the coffee house.

Three things should be made very clear about this event: (1) it was the result of student initiative (that "rebellious generation," as their critics call them); (2) it was undertaken with the knowledge and consent of episcopal authority; (3) a member of the teaching faculty was invited to celebrate the liturgy, even though there were priests available (graduate students) who are on the other side of the academic fence.

What was significant was not the fact that despite a minimum of publicity the coffee house was jammed to overflowing, nor that the group included members of the faculty (both Jesuit and lay, and among the latter both Catholic and non-Catholic), nor that a remarkably large number received Communion, nor that the entire community followed the ceremony with extreme reverence, nor that afterward many—including more than one who no longer attend mass at all—spoke about how deeply the ceremony had moved them.

None of this, I say, suggests the real significance of the event. What was significant was that it took place at all. For if you consider the official status of the celebrant, together with the meaning of the surroundings, there was a fusion of the academic and nonacademic, the speculative and the creative, into a single unity where the only common element was the specifically human value as such. It was this that went into the offertory. When the total human endeavor is gathered into unity with the sacrifice of Christ, it is then that He is most profoundly present in the Catholic university and the university in Him.

If you were to tell me that such a thing could happen on any secular campus, I would reply that it very well might. But the corporate person of a secular university as such, whatever the personal religious feelings of its members, would have to look on it with indifference because it is secular; whereas the corporate person of the Catholic university, whatever the religious —or liturgical—feelings of its individual members, has to look on it and say: "This is what we stand for." In any case, you may take this as indicative of what religious life on campus aims for at the present time: to incorporate the human into an affirmation of the divine through a liturgical union with the God-man that proceeds from the maturing responsibility of faculty and students together—responsibility personally assumed and freely fulfilled. I take it that, in the pluralism of values characteristic of contemporary American society, this type of value is worth preserving.

Such, then, is the way we conceive the function of the Catholic university: to serve as the corporate person in which is embodied the presence of Christ in the academic world, or (which is the same thing) to serve as witness to the Church's respect for human intelligence and creativity. It is no criticism of this conception to say that a group of individuals (e.g., numerous Catholic professors and students at New York University), or a formally constituted institute (e.g., the Leonine Commission at Yale), or even an entire faculty (e.g., the theology faculty in a German state university) can bear the type of witness we have described. No one will deny the value of such testimony. But the nub of the argument is this: in the present American world of academic institutions, it is fitting that the Catholic tradition have an *institutional* presence.

In such an institution, the tension between vertical and horizontal polarization (and it is a tension) must be maintained. To emphasize the vertical polarity at the expense of the horizontal is to compromise the academic in the name of the ecclesiastical. The trouble with this is not that the whole enterprise becomes insufficiently secular, but that it becomes—in the deepest meaning of the Incarnation—insufficiently Christian. Again, to compromise the vertical, religious orientation in the name of the horizontal, secular one is to forfeit any sense at all of religious affiliation; so that the university becomes—like so many prestigious institutions that we all know—Church-affiliated in origin, nonsectarian in fact.

Quite clearly, the Catholic university is anything but nonsectarian. Is it then "sectarian?" Not if this word suggests narrow-minded "religious bias." There is, after all, room within a corporate person of this kind for both students and faculty who do not share the Christian religious commitment, and who therefore do not make their own the ideal that the institution invisages for itself. It is not essential that they do so: union in the corporate person does not necessarily mean perfect unanimity among its members.

In fact, one would think that there *ought* to be non-Catholic and non-Christian members in the university family. One reason would be to testify to the Church's recognition that there are other ways to God than by the visible Church of Rome, even though a Catholic would believe that this is the preferred way, specifically indicated by God. Another reason would be the need in an ecumenical age for the university student to be seriously familiar with other religious orientations than his own, and it is clearly desirable that they be exposed to him by persons committed to them. Finally, there would be a value in having competent critical voices on any first-class faculty to serve as a challenge to, and therefore a visible guarantee of, the intellectual probity of any presentation of "Catholic doctrine."

What is important only is that these non-Catholic or non-Christian members of the family share the same concrete goals as the corporate person: love of the truth, and integrity in the pursuit of it. For the believer would look on such persons as in some way anonymously Christian. They are Christian because they are in fact united with Christ through communion in the truth, of which Christians believe He is the incarnation: yet they are anonymously so, for they refuse to call themselves by His name—either because they never really have known Him or, having known Him, they reject Him as being what the believer would claim He is not. Such persons as these a Christian is happy to make his collaborators in the common enterprise, leaving to Christ Himself—if He wills it—to reveal Himself *as* truth in His own way and time.

So much, then, for what we conceive to be the role of the Catholic university in our pluralistic society today. Yet to speak of the ideal of total dedication to truth, as we have done, does not yet touch the heart of Mr. Heffron's question. For the Catholic Church presumably has its own conception of what truth is, its own doctrine, its own "all-encompassing interpretation of reality" that is at best "controversial." How is it possible to be antecedently committed to a doctrine, hence to one side of a "controversy," and still claim to be able to investigate that controversy with intellectual integrity and without religious bias?

Let me begin with a parenthetical remark to the effect that this type of problem does not belong exclusively to the Catholic university. Granted that there can be a university without religious commitment, how is it possible for a university to be without *any* commitment? Even if the commitment be to the purest kind of secularism, this is an ideology in its own right, as Harvey Cox points out in *The Secular City*, functioning "very much like a religion." Commitment of any kind runs the risk of bias. And who of us has not met the self-proclaimed liberal who is fully as doctrinaire as any Roman seminarian? All this is said in passing, however, and does not pretend to answer the difficulty. Mr. Heffron asks:

> *Can you define precisely, clearly and unambiguously Fordham's commitment to Catholic doctrine, to religious faith, to intellectual integrity and to academic freedom? How are these elements related? What is the priority of the commitment to each?*

When Mr. Heffron speaks of Catholic doctrine, I understand him to mean "what the Church teaches." But what is it that the Church teaches? Does Mr. Heffron mean to suggest that it is simply an "all-encompassing interpretation of reality?" If so, then is there not a risk of identifying Catholic doctrine with some fixed theological formula or other that has become frozen in a given epoch of history? But what the Church teaches is much more than that—incomparably more than any frozen historical formula. The Church's magisterial task is to preserve in itself and communicate to men the revealing word of God— not some*thing* (e.g., an "interpretation of reality") but Some*one*.

Now, it is essential to the argument that we keep clearly in mind from the beginning three aspects of Catholic doctrine thus understood. (1) This Someone—the revealing Word—is a divine Word, and as such essentially beyond formulas. (2) The divine Word, in assuming flesh, entered into human history, and, indeed, in such fashion that it is with the phenomenon of man and through it that He slowly unfolds to His fullness (*pleroma*). As a result, all human efforts to give expression to this mystery are correlative to the evolutionary character of its unfolding, and the formulas that result cannot but be evolving formulas. (3) The Church, as the continuation of the incarnate Word in time, is itself engaged in this historical process, so that with the world and from the world it, too, gains a deepening understanding of the phenomenon of man. With this comes an expanding awareness, on the one hand, of the revealed Word (God-man) the Church conserves within it and, on the other, of itself precisely as announcing this Word through history.

So much, then, for our understanding of "what the Church teaches." In this context, it is important to distinguish clearly between the revealed word itself, thus understood, and the response that the Christian makes to it, i.e., his total acceptance of it simply because it is the word of God. It is this response, or acceptance, that we understand by "religious faith."

However difficult it may be (if, indeed, it is possible at all) to delineate in human, conceptual terms what the divine Word has revealed, the bare essentials can be formulated in terminology that has become familiar: the Son of God became man and died for us in order to share with us divine life. Now, it is perfectly obvious that for the thinking man (especially in our own day when God, the Revealer, is declared "dead") every word here is problematic. The problem begins with the question as to how we know this was revealed at all—for that matter, as to what revelation is and how it is related to the human (i.e., intellectual-cultural-historical) context in which it takes place. But thinking, however necessary for an intelligent faith, is as such *not* faith but rather the determination of, reflection upon, and articulation of, faith. In other words, theology is a completely human, highly fallible effort.

To be sure, certain theological controversies have been resolved in the course of time through formulas (like the Athanasian Creed) approved by the authority in the Church that fulfills a magisterial function in mediating the revealed

Word through the evolution of human history. As a result, what is enunciated by the formulas may be said without fear of error to be faithful to the initial revelation. A Christian accepts these formulas by faith as true, when taken in the sense in which they were intended, and this on the grounds that ultimately the authority for them is the revealed Word of God Himself. Such formulas in turn become grist for the theologian's mill, for they must first be understood according to "the sense in which they were intended," then perhaps reinterpreted in the light of human experience as it evolves, and even reformulated for the comprehension of another age—all of which is not faith but theology.

It is with the help of its theologians, then, that the Church in the course of history comes to comprehend and communicate the revealed Word it bears. To be sure, with the passage of time, the word "theology" has become more and more polyvalent. It can be used in a very general sense to designate a discipline that forms part of a university curriculum and can include within its compass anything that has to do with the science of religion in any form (e.g., history, psychology, sociology of religion). Again, it can refer more specifically to a whole set of cognate disciplines that examine areas relevant to different aspects of Christian religion and practice (e.g., exegesis, patrology, liturgical studies)—each with its own methodology, each supported in turn by other scientific disciplines (e.g., linguistics, archeology, comparative religion) whose collaboration is essential. More precisely still, it is often taken (and it is the way I intend it here) in the stricter sense of reflection upon the formulas with which faith has come to expression so as to comprehend better what the revealed word (to which faith responds) means, and thus be able to articulate the message of faith *meaningfully* for any given age. In this last sense, it is not a completely independent discipline but must rely upon other disciplines to supply it with the conceptual structures and significant language with which to perform its task.

In effect, both the structures themselves and the means of expressing them are correlative to the growth in human knowledge—in knowledge of man (and his universe) by man. For the revelation tells us more about man than about God—partly in the sense that the language by which it comes to expression in faith is always human language, partly in the sense that only so much is revealed to us about God (e.g., one—yet somehow three) as is necessary to indicate what has happened to man through the great redemptive act. And if man presumes to speculate about God on the basis of what He has revealed about Himself, even this must be done with human categories— applied "analogically," if you will, but human categories none the less.

Theology's manner of achieving its own function, then, changes with man's deepening knowledge of himself. For the medieval theologian, his chief ally for both structure and expression of thought was scholastic philosophy, which offered him, under the aegis of great Greek thinkers like Plato (through the early doctors, chiefly Augustine) and Aristotle, a fairly stable image of man in a fairly stable universe. For the theologian of today, however, that stability has gone. Man understands himself explicitly as part of the process of a cosmic evolution; the only thing stable is the evolutionary process itself.

In what concerns structure and expression of thought, the theologian may be unhappy with ancient scholastic categories, yet he finds no mode of contemporary philosophy sufficiently supple for his purpose. He turns to other human disciplines— to the natural sciences, social sciences, depth psychology, literature, etc.—to help him understand the contemporary human experience so that he can explain and communicate in terms of it. The task, of course, is gigantic, and although the theologian is no less aware of the dignity of that task than he ever was, he was never so conscious of his indigence, for man himself was never so conscious of his finitude.

In a more sanguine age, the theologian could regard his discipline as the queen of the sciences, and all other disciplines handmaids who would accept its formulations as a negative norm of the truth that they all separately sought. But ours is a less sanguine age. The theologian looks upon the human disciplines not as handmaids but as collaborators who help him to delineate evolving man's meaning to himself so that the theologian can come to grips with that meaning.

What, then, of theology as a "negative norm" of truth? Surely, what has been revealed in the incarnate Word, who called Himself "truth," can never really be at odds with truth discovered by an authentic exercise of human powers that the Word, in becoming flesh, somehow made His own. But the theologian is far less confident than before of the adequacy of the human expressions of revealed truth, far more aware than before of the historical (i.e., space-time-cultural) factors that influence them. The result is that today, when man conceives of himself as essentially part of a historical process, one of the greatest needs of the Catholic theologian is for a deeper understanding of his own historicity, i.e., for a clearly defined and usable method to rethink historically the classic human expressions of revealed truth without compromising orthodoxy on the one hand or historical contingency on the other. For dogmas, too—there is no doubt—evolve, and certain theological positions once thought immutable (the cases of usury, Church-State relations, Old Testament exegesis, etc., are already classical) have as a matter of fact changed. At any rate, the theologian of today would want to insist that the "negative norm" of truth is *not theology* such as we have been describing it here, but only the revealed Word of God Himself. Mr. Heffron further inquires:

> *Will you, as fallible human beings, entertain the possibility that your judgment of the truth of Catholicism is an erroneous judgment? Are you intellectually free and willing to change as your unbiased and sincere judgment might suggest? Are you prepared to offer these as legitimate choices to your students?*

What has all this to do with his objection? To the extent that what he calls the Church's "particular, controversial, all-encompassing interpretation of reality" is a *theological* interpretation, it is and remains the work of finite, terribly fallible human beings. To the extent that theology as such attempts to reflect upon and rearticulate meaningfully the human expres-

sions of divine revelation that are—because human—conditioned by the historical process of evolution, the theologian
must be "intellectually free and willing to change his interpretations as unbiased and sincere judgment might suggest" or fail
to be true to himself. To the extent that the student fails to
understand that theological interpretations are of their very
nature "legitimate choices," whose legitimacy is warranted by
their meaningfulness to man in terms of his own self-understanding in any given epoch of time, the students' faith can
be neither intelligent nor mature. And this means (for a university man) no faith at all. Mr. Heffron continues:

> *I think that your answer, if it is offered at all, will be that
> intellectual integrity and academic freedom are the hand-
> maidens of Catholic dogma and religious faith: . . . that
> religious, ethical, philosophical problems are to be exam-
> ined and judged only within the envelope of our commit-
> ment to Catholicism—but the commitment itself is never
> to be judged, only accepted.*

"Somehow—sadly" Mr. Heffron suggests what he expects us to
reply to his challenge. If it can be of any comfort to him, we
find his hypothesis as depressing as he does. By way of summation, let me try to formulate the matter differently.

In a free pluralistic society, Fordham's only commitment is to
the truth, however it is to be found, for it is truth that makes
men free. But truth is found in diverse ways. One way is
through the revealing Word of God Himself. To such truth,
Fordham is committed, hence to "Catholic doctrine" and "religious faith" inasmuch as (but only to this extent) these terms
designate the revealed word on the one hand and human response to it on the other. But truth can be discovered by human
powers in their own right. Fordham is committed, too, to such
truth as this—not on the condition that it fit within "the envelope of Catholicism," but simply because it is true. After all,
the envelope of Catholicism (if one insists on the metaphor)
is an always expandable thing, and it is precisely through the
discovery of human truth that it continues to expand.

Finally, Fordham is committed to the correlation of these
two modes of access to truth, i.e., to the theological enterprise

as such, whereby human intelligence, with the collaboration of the scientific disciplines, does the best it can in its finite way to delineate the truth that God has revealed and articulate it in terms that men find meaningful in the present epoch of human history. It is precisely this last aspect of Fordham's commitment that makes it profoundly aware that a commitment to the *enterprise* of theology is not a commitment to its *formulas,* but rather a commitment to constantly transcend these formulas (contingent, inadequate, fallible as they are) toward a deeper understanding and more relevant articulation of the mystery they express.

But what of the commitment to the commitment? Is it "never to be judged but only accepted?" Of course, it is to be judged! How else does it become mature? How else does the acceptance of childhood become genuine commitment for the full-grown man? To be sure, if this reexamination leads a man to honestly think his faith is unfounded (or runs counter to some other truth he feels "committed" in all intellectual honesty to accept), then all he can do is follow his conscience. But Fordham would maintain, I think, that it is precisely because the Christian believes the revealed word to be the synthesis of God and man (of truth as revealed to man and truth as discovered by him) that he reexamines his acceptance of the revealed Word without fear—confident that these two ways of experiencing truth can never really conflict. This *is* his faith.

The commitment, then, is clear—an unlimited commitment to polyvalent truth. But it becomes absolutely meaningless— and all of us at Fordham are deeply convinced of it—unless those who engage in this quest do so "without religious or any other bias" (i.e., with intellectual integrity), and with a tranquil sense of security that enables them to make the complete surrender to the proper demands of their discipline without fear of interference from anything outside it (i.e., academic freedom).

There is one more thing to say. I have spoken of theology as the reflection upon revelation and the meaningful articulation of it. This includes, of course, a reflection upon the Church itself and its function on the contemporary scene. To the extent that theology engages the collaboration of the secular disciplines in accomplishing its task, it integrates these disciplines into a common endeavor that might be called (to distinguish it from theology as a single discipline) the theologizing function of the university as a whole. It is in this common endeavor that the reciprocity of presence between Church and Academia is achieved.

Just as the federal government has learned to do, the Church must look to the university for help. For it is first of all here in the university—not first of all in Catholic newspapers, magazines and journals of opinion (still less in parish discussion groups)—that human intelligence, operating according to the highest standards of scientific excellence, offers its services to the Church.

It is in the university that all the data of the empirical sciences (physical, behavioral, social, etc.) are made accessible to everyone in the Church responsible for making decisions; it is in the university that the highest quality of informed counsel is available on social, economic, political, historical, liturgical and moral issues. It is in the university that theological reflection as such, scrutinizing the formulas of the faith in terms of the most recent findings of the secular sciences, helps the hierarchical Church to reflect upon its own function as mediator of the revealed word, and to achieve this function with respect for the demands of the most critical intellectual criteria available. It is precisely through such a theologizing function as this that the Catholic university becomes most completely itself; that place where not only the Church is present to the academic world but the academic world is present to—and operative in—the Church. This is its "competence." And no one has ever said this more explicitly than Fr. Pedro Arrupe, superior general of the Society of Jesus.

I obviously wish to come to grips here with Mr. Heffron's citation of Fr. Arrupe's remark that he is "strictly opposed to any criticism of the Church." The remarks were made in what seems to have been an informal, off-the-cuff interview with a reporter from the Spanish weekly *Ya,* shortly after his election as superior general.

Precisely what Fr. Arrupe had in mind (was it the "competence" of private individuals? of Catholic editorialists? of parish discussion groups?), I have no idea. I do know that, in terms of the "competence" of a true university, I find it as hard as Mr. Heffron does to reconcile this citation with the "intellectual integrity" and "academic freedom" that must characterize it.

Happily, however, this was not Fr. Arrupe's final word on the subject. Perceiving more clearly himself, apparently, the import of these remarks as reported in the United States when they were transposed onto the university level, he took special pains to zero in on the problem under the most solemn circumstances, when there could be no room for doubt about his attitude concerning the university's competence to exercise its critical function.

Addressing the formal closure of Fordham's 125th anniversary celebration on April 5, 1966, Fr. Arrupe declared his position: "The Catholic university represents a most appropriate organ of the Church's perennial function of self-study and reflection. The university must be free to analyze, therefore; and analyze not only false and ungrounded attacks upon the faith, but formulations, defenses and practical orientations which, in a phrase of St. Thomas used centuries ago, only bring the faith into derision. This critical function, she must exercise competently, responsibly—but frankly and honestly as well."

Does this "simply sound too good"? Let Mr. Heffron be assured that it is said without complacency. No one who has ever beaten his head against an intellectual problem that defies him has any illusions about how much "intellectual integrity" can cost. There are, besides, risks involved—serious personal risks in the type of research I have been suggesting. And I dare say that anyone who scoffs at such danger has never really faced it. Finally, man's critical intelligence, like a surgeon's scalpel, can cut deep and cause pain. Even if one could guarantee antecedently that the instrument would always be used with infallible discretion (and what university man will claim infallibility of any kind?), it would be naïve to think it can perform its task honestly without any misunderstanding or resentment.

As the postconciliar Church faces the "post-Christian" world, it needs a university more than ever to achieve the task of reciprocal presence.

The Future of an Illusion*

JOHN COGLEY

Recently, in a speech to the National Council of Catholic Men, Bishop John J. Wright (now Cardinal) distinguished between the Church *in* the future and the Church *of* the future. What the Church *in* the future will be like, Bishop Wright indicated, depends on how Catholics react to "the breakdown of classical culture," which he held is the source of the unsettled state of Catholics the world over.

The Bishop added that "this crisis will confront the unchanging faith with new opportunities, new labors, new structures." The Church *of* the future, then, will be the changeless mystery of the Second Vatican Council's Constitution on the Church. But the Church *in* the future may also be barely recognizable. Even we who are living in the wake of the Ecumenical Council may find the changes drastic.

This article is concerned with the Church *in* the future, particularly with one structure of the Church in the United States, the Catholic university.

Since the key words have already appeared, perhaps the best way to begin is to state the conclusion right off: I do not believe the Catholic university as such *has* any future.

In other words, the idea of the Church's conducting something identifiable as a "Catholic university," in the sense that Marquette, St. Louis, Fordham, Notre Dame, Georgetown and the Loyolas are today considered Catholic universities, will one

* Originally printed in *Commonweal*, June 2, 1967 (Commonweal Publishing Co.). Copyright © 1967. Reprinted with permission.

day seem as anachronistic as the papal states, the error-has-no-rights "Catholic State," or the Catholic penitentiary. These institutions had their last-ditch defenders before they expired. At least two of them, the papal temporal power and the confessional state, were once bolstered by elaborate theological theories. The few remaining confessional states, however, are now looked down upon elsewhere in the Church as embarrassing hangovers from the past.

To say that the American Catholic university as such has no future is bold. I would not have been so free about predicting it even a few years ago. But in the meantime it has become clear that what Bishop Wright described as "the breakdown of classical culture" is taking place faster than we thought it would.

How much Bishop Wright intended to include under the heading of "classical culture," I am not sure. In all probability it has something to do not only with ancient Greece and Rome but with the relationships between Church and state, Christianity and culture, and religion and society that have existed in one form or another since Christianity was established as the religion of the ancient empire.

As was dramatized in two recent films, *Becket* and *A Man for All Seasons,* these relationships have had their ups and downs. But as historians like Christopher Dawson have long been sadly telling us, and as others like Arnold Toynbee have coolly agreed: the age-old links are crumbling.

It is becoming clear that we are moving into a new situation —the situation Father Karl Rahner has described as "the Church in diaspora." The realization that this *is* the situation is the source of the intellectual and spiritual crisis confronting Christians the world over. We are being forced to recognize that, whether we like it or not, modernity has triumphed. Cardinal Wright, for example, is probably not happy about the breakdown of "classical culture," but apparently he is willing to accept it as a fact of contemporary life.

Though it was possible to see the "breakdown" coming, few of us were able to clock the speed with which the realization of it would reach the critical stage. If we failed to recognize it fully before the Second Vatican Council, it may have been because so many Catholic institutions had created a facade of relevance between their own cultural concerns and the rest of the world. The facade was so convincing, to Catholics if not to others, that we did not realize the secular revolution had gone as far as it had. At least we did not realize it had made such inroads within the Catholic community itself.

Not very many years ago, American Catholics spoke bravely of Renascences, Returns to Tradition, and Revivals. Catholic magazines and books appeared under such titles; such phrases expressed the spirit of literary movements, philosophical goals, and underlying educational motivations. I remember we once had a Catholic magazine desperately called *Integrity*. It began in the late 1940's, just around the same time I helped found one which was defiantly christened *Today*. It may be a sign of present health that a newer Catholic publication is called *Continuum*. The word "continuum" is defined in the desk dictionary as "something absolutely continuous and homogeneous of which no distinction of content can be affirmed except by reference to something else (as duration)." The movement toward secularity and modernity, seen in a certain way, may, then, represent not a rupture with the "classical culture" but a development—a continuum.

Speaking of the secular state, Jacques Maritain once wrote that "in proportion as the civil society, or body politic, has become more perfectly distinguished from the realm of the Church—a process which was in itself but a development of the Gospel distinction between the things that are Caesar's and the things that are God's—the civil society has become grounded on a common good and a common task which are of an earthly, temporal, or 'secular' character, and in which citizens belonging to diverse spiritual groups share equally." Perhaps, *mutatis mutandis*, something like that can also be said of the changing Catholic university.

THE HERITAGE OF ALL

Every university is concerned with higher learning. Today, the same higher learning is the heritage of all; it has become *mondialized*. I am convinced that, like the contemporary state, it too is now rooted in the secular, the rational, the scientific and a common pluralistic culture. The common culture of the world we live in is no longer grounded on revelation or ecclesiastical foundations, though it once may have been. Religion, specifically Christianity, is an important factor in the common culture but it is no longer a presiding principle. And we have no choice but to live by this learning if we hope to act in the real world of the here and now.

Long ago I accepted this fact. I recognized, for example, that I personally had become a very "secular" man. The realization caused a certain amount of spiritual uneasiness. For years, I frequently felt misplaced on Sunday morning. Neither the liturgy, the language of the liturgy, nor the sermons I heard seemed to have a vital connection with my daily life. (That is still true, alas.) I felt vaguely guilty about it but did not think of it as creating a crisis-situation for anyone but myself and for people like me.

Then came the day when I realized I no longer felt quite at home on Catholic campuses or at church-sponsored intellectual gatherings. Generally the style of thought there was different from that found in the intellectual world I actually inhabited; even the language was different from that used in the normal company I kept. Realizing this, I knew a discomfort I was long loathe to acknowledge.

When the time came for my eldest son to go to college, I found myself quite content that he did not choose a Catholic campus. I wondered why, and had to face up to the fact that I wanted him prepared for the wider world, even at the cost of missing much of the "classical culture" to which *I* had been exposed. Last June he got his degree from Harvard, and in certain ways he received a better education than I did at my Jesuit college. But I also know that from the point of view of the "classical culture" my son's father is still ahead. I have to admit, though, that he is more plugged into the intellectual currents of the times and into the world he will actually live in than I was at his age. It may be significant in this connection, incidentally, that my youthful idealism led me to the Catholic Worker movement, where we talked about an "apostolate"; my son and his young wife are now Peace Corps volunteers in a remote Indian village. They are no less idealistic than we were, but their concerns are strictly "secular."

Even last autumn, a visit to the Vatican seemed something like a visit to a museum. Waiting for an audience with the pope, surrounded by grown men in silken kneepants and monsignori decked out in their Renaissance finery, one begins to feel like a super in a grand opera. The opera, to be sure, is still colorful, still romantic, sometimes even exciting. But by 1966, even in Rome it had become disturbingly unreal. One knew that when the Swiss guards were out of sight, after the chorus of *Viva il Papa* had faded into silence, one was going to return to the reality of modernity, even though the pensione was less than five city blocks away from Saint Peter's.

Before the Vatican Council, I had been in Rome several times. I had seen elaborate ceremonies and stood with the crowds in Saint Peter's Square on high occasions. I had watched Pius XII, John XXIII, and finally Paul VI bless the crowds. All three popes used the telltale Constantinian formula *urbi et orbi.* In 1963 I had waited in the square for the white smoke to herald the election of a new Pontiff and heard Cardinal Ottaviani intone *"Habemus papam—Joannem Baptistam Montini."* I had watched the technicolor ceremonies connected with Pope Paul's coronation and joined in the applause when the triple tiara was placed upon his head. The tiara signified that Giovanni Battista Montini was now not only chief bishop of the Church, but the prince of princes, who exercised supreme jurisdiction over kings and emperors. What I did not fully realize until the council was well under way was that there simply was no contemporary reality behind much of this.

It finally dawned on me that Constantinianism had become one of the games Catholics play.

During the council, the idea became firmer. It became clear that most of the leading theologians and prelates in Rome were as modernized—or "secularized"—as I. When a Cardinal Ottaviani, a Cardinal Ruffini, or a Bishop Carli seemed to take seriously the presuppositions that would give substance to the rubrics, the elaborate ceremonials and rites carried out in St.

Peter's, they were thought to be a trifle absurd. It turned out that most of the fathers and *periti* were twentieth century men wearing fifteenth century clothes. Behind their verbal endorsement of outmoded formulas and forms was a modern mentality. By far, most of them had a contemporary man's understanding of secular reality. Many of them, it became clear, were as cut off from Bishop Wright's "classical culture" as I. Willynilly, they were as committed to modernity as I. Garbed in vestments that may have once been meaningful symbols of the prince-bishop (but are now sheer anachronistic display), they stumbled along in the universal tongue of the "classical culture" that has long since ceased to be universal. Most of the time, most of them did their best to give expression not so much to their classicism as to their modernity. It was significant that to state their real concerns, they had to find somewhat-less-than-classical Latin equivalents for such words as *airplane, space travel, birth control, nuclear weapons* and *developing nations.*

My earlier realization, i.e., that the classical culture had ceased to be a real factor in life, had not been without pain. It was some comfort, then, to realize in Rome that I was not alone.

I discovered, for example, that others also looked elsewhere than to the Church for their actual cultural values, political wisdom, social identification, and a personal link to the future. I learned that leading theologians and many of the best bishops in Rome thought the same way I did. The struggle between these men, the progressives, and the upholders of the romanticized version of modern Christian history—the royal guards of *Romanità*—was the underlying cause for the battle that raged throughout the council.

One group repudiated contemporary cultural values, contemporary political experiences, and the identity modernity confers, regarding them as expressions of rank secularism. The other argued for the end of what they believed to be illusion. One of the latter, Father Rahner, wrote that "we still have not awakened from our dream of a homogeneous Christian West."

On the books, the battle of the Vatican Council ended in a series of compromises between the two factions. That much will be evident to future historians who read the decrees of the council, the debates that preceded them, and the admonitions that followed them. In almost every paragraph in the council documents, one can hear the slamming of conservative brakes, bringing the logic of the dominant progressives to an abrupt halt.

The compromising spirit is also evident in almost every reform made by the council: vernacular in the liturgy—but a bit of Latin, too; a synod of bishops—but a synod with no legislative powers; abolition of the communion fast—except for one vestigial hour; married deacons—but no married priests; simplification of religious habits—but the garb, like the dress of feudal society, must be a "sign" and recognizably anachronistic; endorsement of responsible parenthood—but condemnation of contraception.

It *looks,* then, as if the struggle of Vatican II ended in a clean draw. We have episcopal collegiality *and* apostolic delegations. We have an episcopal synod *and* a sacred college of cardinals. We have a glowing endorsement of the significance of the simple priest and of the laity; but neither priest nor layman yet has a real voice in the nomination of bishops or pastors. Now we learn we may be given the choice of attending obligatory mass on Saturday or Sunday—but deliberately missing Mass is still a mortal sin, deserving of hell fire. Father Du Bay, forging ahead, was deprived of his priestly faculties; so was Father DePauw, holding back. Webster College went too far in becoming officially a secular institution. St. John's University, which justified its paternalism by appealing to its charter as a "Catholic" university, did not go far enough.

The ideal bishop is supposed to stand somewhere midway between Cardinal McIntyre and Archbishop Roberts. The ideal priest is supposed to stand midway between DePauw and Du Bay. The ideal editor is supposed to stand midway between Robert Hoyt of the *National Catholic Reporter* and Brent Bozell of *Triumph.* The ideal philosopher is supposed to stand midway between Teilhard de Chardin and the curial officials who prevented Chardin from publishing. After some contradictory orders, it was finally decided that the middle sound of the guitar might be a happy compromise between the organ and the jazz ensemble. One is reminded of Honor Tracy's Irish pastor who urged his flock to walk the straight and narrow path between truth and falsehood.

On the books right now, we Catholics are desirous of renewal and change, but we seem to prefer being just a little pregnant. In reality, however, I believe that the brakes will be released; the Church *in* the future will reflect the general orientation of the Council progressives. They will be clearly identifiable as the real victors, even though at the moment, to paraphrase St. Augustine's famous remark, we seem to be praying "Lord, give us modernity—but not yet." For the progressives of the council began the dismantling of the Constantinian facade, and we now see it for the Hollywood set it had become long before the council. Even the progressives did not go all the way, but they began removing the cultural freight the Church has carried for centuries. That weight, I am convinced, was an illusory burden, though even in its most solemn moments, as in the coronation of a pope, the Church acted as if it had no choice but to bear it.

But at long last, Catholics are being awakened from the "dream" that Father Rahner pointed out and are being recalled to reality. Like a patient who had lost contact with his true world and carried on as if reality were illusion and illusion reality, we are being drawn out of an unreal existence. The process is painful. Someone has said that the Catholic community is now acting like someone undergoing a nervous breakdown. This may be because the move from illusion to reality is so difficult. The ordeal is nerve-shattering, traumatic.

The illusion I have in mind was strikingly symbolized by that ill-fated triple tiara, with its three rungs indicating that the pope is head of a Church, of an imperium, and of a civilization. The reality, of course, is that the Church does not serve as the bearer of any actual living culture. Even if emperors and princes were still around, none of them would regard the sovereign pontiff as the supreme regent of the world. Politically, and philosophically and culturally too, the Church no longer has anything to give the world but memories. At least the world is not prepared to accept anything but memories when the Church moves beyond the boundary of what Father Rahner has called its "vital sphere" of revelation and religion. It is within this measurement of current reality that I place the future, or non-future, of the Catholic university.

In a now-famous dictum, George Bernard Shaw once said the words "Catholic university" are a contradiction in terms. Shaw seemed to be indicating that since a university of its nature is dedicated to the pursuit of truth and Catholics believe they already have The Truth—in uppercase splendor—Catholic universities exist only to transmit this Truth from one generation to the next. Therefore, the university in Catholic hands is reduced to a propaganda mill, a purveyor of dogma, where alien ideas are forbidden and honest, open-ended consideration of other than the accepted philosophy, the approved theology; and frozen tradition is outlawed.

That this paternalistic conception of the university's role did, and perhaps in some places still does, serve as a kind of presiding academic principle, I would not deny. But even in the distant days when I was attending a Catholic university, there were some who realized that the dogmatic slumbers of certain professors added up to a kind of betrayal of their own vocation and of the university itself. Our better teachers taught us enough about what a university should be to make us suspicious of the we-have-the-truth formula. We also learned enough about the faith to know that the Catholic university isn't the Church writ small. We knew even then that in many instances Shaw's remark was an accurate description of the way things actually were. But the contradiction was not intrinsic to the idea of a Catholic university as long as such universities were regarded as custodians of a specific culture.

I have now come to agree, however, that there is a sense in which the Shavian *mot* is meaningful. When one considers that the Church has ceased to preside over any actual culture, that Western Christianity has not only been splintered but in the past century has spread far beyond the bounds of the West; and that politics, philosophy, science, literature, the liberal arts, as well as theological speculation itself, are no longer tied to the ecclesiastical apron strings, Shaw's words make a certain kind of sense.

UNIVERSITIES CANNOT PLAY FAVORITES

I will try to put the case concretely. I think that today every university has a duty to teach its students what Freud had to say, *precisely as Freud wanted to be understood.* It also has the duty to teach its students what Freud's critics had to say, precisely as *they* wanted to be understood. The same goes for Marx, Neitszche, Hume, Spengler, Wittgenstein, Bertrand Russell, as well as for Saint Thomas, Niebuhr and Sartre. I do not believe that any university, precisely because it is a university, can play favorites among these giants. I do not believe that any university should indoctrinate its students in the teachings of any of them. By the same token, every university is obligated to expose its students to the thought of all of them and be committed institutionally to none. At the same time, exponents of all (not just critics) should be found on the same campus—scholastic with pragmatist, Protestant with Catholic, Christian with Jew, secularist with believer, existentialist with Thomist, as in an early day when Platonists coexisted with Aristotelians.

This demand can be made on all universities precisely because they are universities. I do not believe that today *any* university can be uncritically committed as an institution to a particular philosophy, political system, to any one religion or to anti-religion. By the same token, the university can not exclude from thoughful consideration any ideology, philosophy, political system or religion which living men of learning—by common agreement—deem worthy of consideration.

Obviously, this means theology belongs in every university—whether it be called Catholic, Protestant, or secular. In a certain sense, then, a "secular" university is as anomalous a term as "Catholic" university. Or as Miss Stein might have put it, a university is a university is a university.

It exists to bring all knowledge and respectable speculation under one roof. The university is not a church. It is not an arm of the Church. As Newman reminded us, it is not a seminary, a convent, or a monastery. It is not an extension of the pulpit or the parish. It is not a political club, not an ideological boot camp. It is a community of scholars with a purpose and meaning and end of its own—a center of independent criticism. It does not exist either to save souls or to send them to their eternal perdition. It does not exist to preserve society or to revolutionize it. It exists to feed minds, to acquaint students with the best thought of the best thinkers, with as much thoroughness, understanding and empathy as the exponents of those thinkers can summon, and to sponsor dialogue between these exponents. It exists not to strengthen its students' earlier commitments but to make meaningful, informed adult choices possible. In doing so, it does not play with loaded dice.

Obviously, some great minds have addressed themselves to the ultimate questions that are put under the heading of theology. Theology, then, belongs in every university as a recognized discipline. Consequently, to the extent that a "Catholic" university teaches theology, it is a better school than an institution that ignores theology. To the extent that any university either favors—over others—the particular theology of the Catholic Church, the Protestant Churches or Islam or does not give due weight to their rivals, it fails.

Theology faculties everywhere, then, should be genuinely pluralistic bodies. For the student considering ultimate questions has a right to know *all* the answers offered to these questions, without prejudgements about truth or falsehood on the part of the institution itself, whatever its teachers believe as individuals.

There are no special Catholic religious or philosophic questions; there are only special Catholic answers. They should be heard in every university. There are also Protestant answers, Jewish answers, Buddhist, and Muslim—as well as atheistic and agnostic—answers. They should be voiced in every university. When I attended Catholic universities I was not meaningfully exposed to other than Catholic answers—I was steered away from them. I heard them distorted: they were presented out of context; sometimes they were blandly ignored. I was "protected" by an Index of Forbidden Books and by a galaxy of forbidding professors. I think now that I was cheated. Certainly I was not prepared for the world I was going to live in. Other students attending "secular" schools may have been just as seriously defrauded because theology was denied them: secularism may have been their imperialism as much as Thomism was mine.

In the May, 1967 issue of *Harper's,* Father Theodore Hesburgh is quoted as saying that the Catholic university "touches the moral as well as intellectual dimension of all the questions it asks itself and its students; it must emphasize the rightful centrality of philosophy and theology among its intellectual concerns. . . . The Catholic university must be a witness to the wholeness of truth from all sources, both divine and human . . . [it] must reflect profoundly, and with full commitment, its belief in the existence of God and in God's total revelation to man." Another unnamed Notre Dame spokesman is quoted in the same article as holding that the goal of the university is "building bridges between the world and the wisdom of the Church."

These are thoughtful, serious statements from learned men deeply involved in a major Catholic university. It takes a certain amount of gall, then, for a journalist to disagree with them. But I do, or I could not anticipate with equanimity the demise of the "Catholic" university.

I could hardly disagree with Father Hesburgh's observation that the moral as well as intellectual dimensions of every question must be considered in the classroom. But in a university context, the statement strikes me as fairly meaningless. For in that context, the intellectual dimension *includes* the moral dimension. The distinction is logical, not substantive. I find a didactic moralism lurking in the educational goal set forth by Father Hesburgh—a moralism that does not seem to me to belong in an institution of higher learning. One's adult notions of wrong and right, good and evil, proper behavior and bad behavior, derive from one's total apprehension of the "questions" Father Hesburgh notes. The university's job is to make this apprehension possible. It is not the university's job to dictate the terms under which the apprehension is taking place. It is not the university's job to shape the questions in such a way that their "moral dimensions" can be isolated and *decreed* rather than intuited by the individual faced with making choices.

Then, I think that when Father Hesburgh speaks of the "wholeness of truth"—a proposition with which I personally agree—he is begging a central philosophical question of our time. As a university professor he has every right to hold to this position, as I would if I were a professor, and as I do with my colleagues at the Center for the Study of Democratic Institutions. I do not believe, however, that it should be a commitment of the university as such. At one time, to be sure, it was accepted dogma. Perhaps it gave rise to the very term *university*. But that time has passed: the "universe" of the university has expanded.

Furthermore, I do not believe it is within the competence of a university to "give witness" to any proposition currently debated by responsible men. For one thing, the university is simply not in the business of "giving witness" to anything but its own integrity as an institution where no controverted question is dogmatically foreclosed.

Then one must ask: Can the university-as-such believe in God? Are those who do not believe (or have ceased to), excluded from the university community? Moreover, should the university-as-such "reflect that belief in every aspect of its operation?" Here, I realize, is a difficult problem. But if one replies yes, what happens to agnosticism and atheism on such campuses? Should they be outlawed as unworthy of consideration? Are they to be triumphantly confuted? Is the argument settled before it begins?

Saint Thomas begins the Summa with the question: *An Deus Sit?* and takes the question seriously. If a university seriously asks its students the same question (and every university should), can it then carry on as if the question is not a real one, only one answer is intellectually tolerable? "The fool has said in his heart there is no God" is a biblical judgment. But, like Saint Thomas, the university can not carry on as if all who question God's existence are patently foolish and unworthy of consideration: even the scriptures are not self-evident.

Finally, Father Hesburgh is quoted as saying that the Catholic university is *"of* the Church but it is not the Church." A university that is *"of* the Church" strikes me as an anomalous concept. It suggests that the Church is the custodian not only of its own special (and limited) wisdom, but of all wisdom—that the Church has within its competence to confer on a university what it needs if it is to be a true university. It suggests that the Church is the bearer not only of revealed truth but the arbiter of all truth—that the Church can authoritatively determine the truth not only about what has been revealed but what is known from science, philosophy, and the social disciplines. I think this is nonsense both historically and logically. The Church's wisdom does not extend that far. Nor do I accept as authentic a university that derives its essential authority from any institution outside itself, including state or Church.

The *Harper's* article, it seems to me, makes painfully clear the basic difficulties of a Catholic university that is trying to be both a university and an institution *of* the Church. Today Notre Dame *is* the best Catholic university in the nation. But this is true precisely because, in a certain sense, Notre Dame is the least "Catholic" university, as the *Harper's* article indicates. Its difficulties may arise from the fact that it is stuck with the kind of leftover rationale attributed to Father Hesburgh.

If the rationale were carried to its logical conclusion, Notre Dame would not be a university in the modern sense at all but a seminary. The reason it is even in the running for university "greatness" is that the facts in South Bend do not match the rhetoric of South Bend. And this is becoming increasingly true wherever Catholic education is advancing toward "greatness." If one were to take Father Hesburgh's statements seriously, one might mentally construct an institution that looked more like St. John's of Brooklyn than Notre Dame. (I credit the Vincentian administrators of St. John's with a certain consistency in this regard.) But applying the Hesburgh statements to the task at hand will not, I believe, lead to the kind of university Notre Dame aspires to be.

NOT DISMANTLED EITHER

There *is* a sense in which a modern university can be "of the Church." Just as the individual Christian, rather than the Christian prince, is now seen as the link between Church and state, so the individual scholar is now the link between the world and the wisdom of the Church, as well as between the Church and the wisdom of the world. When I support the "universitizing" (not the "secularization") of the Catholic university, I do not mean, then, to suggest that places like Marquette should be closed down or that Jesuit scholars should be removed from the campus.

Marquette is a towering fact of life in Milwaukee and in the nation. So are a number of other Catholic universities in other communities throughout the land. Running a good university is *in itself* an admirable work. I see no reason, then, why Catholics, making a nonsectarian "secular" contribution to the total community, should not sponsor universities; not "Catholic" universities but universities, period. I see no reason why the Society of Jesus, the Congregation of Holy Cross, the Benedictines or any other religious order should not make a contribution to the common—not just the Catholic—welfare by conducting good universities.

The universities under Catholic auspices might take a special interest in Catholic affairs by sponsoring theological institutes emphasizing Catholic theology and theological research. But they should be basically universities, period. God knows, we need universities that are truly universities. Any group that adds to their number will have the nation in its debt.

Is it asking too much for Catholics to sponsor universities, period; without any overt apostolic or preservation-of-the-faith purposes, with no Revivals, Renascences, and Return-to-Tradition cultural imperialism in mind? Is it too much to ask the Society of Jesus or the Congregation of Holy Cross to lend their efforts to sponsoring the dialogue that a genuine university should embody in today's fractured world? The orders will have to answer that question for themselves. But I think that the first place for Catholics to show that they are in earnest about dialogue is in the universities under their control. A university, almost by definition, is a center of dialogue. The educational process at the reaches of higher learning is not didactic but dialogic. Dialogue means that intellectual confrontation is genuine. It is not a set-up, a fixed fight, in which one party or other is inevitably destined for victory. It is universal—all parties are present as equal partners. The dialogue is not an inter-institutional engagement—a kind of Fordham-versus-Columbia College Bowl; it has to take place within the same scholarly community if that community is a true reflection of the pluralistic intellectual society the student will enter as soon as he leaves the cheering gallery.

I want to make it clear then, that I am not hinting that either Marquette or Notre Dame should be dismantled. Nor am I urging that they should be "secularized," if secularization means that religion and theology are to be put outside the scope of their central interest. I am, rather, advocating that they should be pluralized, ecumenized, and universalized in order to be transformed into genuine universities in a pluralistic, ecumenical, and philosophically many-mansioned world.

In practice this would mean that there would be theologians of all persuasions on hand and anti-theologians as well—not to lend an appealing pluralistic coloring to what would otherwise be a depressingly sectarian institution, not to serve as ecumenical window-dressing, but to reflect the reality of the modern world and the bewildering choices open to the modern man when he asks his ultimate questions.

The change would not mean that the university Catholic chapel should be closed down. It would mean that Protestant and Jewish places of worship would be added. It would not mean that the religious orders should abdicate. It would mean that they might preside as administrators or serve as teachers in a university that as such is no more committed to the Order's view of life than Harvard is to the opinions of Nathan Pusey or the University of Chicago was to the ideas of Robert Maynard Hutchins or the University of California is to the views of Ronald Reagan.

Catholic Scholars Witness
To Freedom: A Symposium*

*Prompted by the dispute between the Board of Trustees
and the theological faculty of the Catholic University of
America in the spring of 1967,* Commonweal *magazine
invited a number of Catholic scholars and educators to
draft a model statement on academic freedom at a Catholic institution of higher learning. Each contributor was
limited to roughly 300 words and each statement was to
be formal, even if necessary, "legal." The question was
framed as follows:*

*Imagine that you are founding a new Catholic college.
The prospective faculty has asked you to draw up a succinct statement of the principles of academic freedom
which will be guaranteed in the college. They have also
asked that the statement refer specifically to the freedom
of research, publication and teaching as it bears on ecclesiastical authority and Catholic orthodoxy. What rights
will the faculty have, what are the limits of those rights?
Are any distinctions to be drawn between academic freedom in secular disciplines and academic freedom in areas
bearing on religion, the Church and Catholic doctrine?*

*Since the faculty would like the statement to be included
in a faculty handbook it should be short, formal, and
definitive. It is understood that any discussions or disagree-*

* Originally printed in *Commonweal,* June 2, 1967 (Commonweal Publishing
Co.). Copyright © 1967. Reprinted with permission.

ments concerning academic freedom will be resolved in the light of this statement.

MARY DALY

All members of the faculty have the right and the responsibility to contribute to the increase and the communication of knowledge within their respective fields of competency. These rights and responsibilities of the faculty imply that they are entitled to freedom in the work of research and in the publication of the results, and in the work of teaching. The common good of the college requires this academic freedom. It also requires the variety of methods, approaches, conclusions and opinions which such freedom engenders.

The right to academic freedom on the part of the faculty is grounded in demonstrated professional competency. Since this is the case, it would be an irresponsible act and an abuse of freedom if the professor habitually were to introduce into his teaching, matter which he is not competent to discuss.

In the event that a faculty member is seriously accused of introducing controversial material in an irresponsible manner, he is entitled to a hearing by his peers to determine his competency in the matter. This will also hold if the controversial material is theological. In all cases the only persons to be considered capable of passing judgment will be academic peers, not ecclesiastical authorities. The criterion for judging the faculty member will not be religious or political "orthodoxy," but scientific and historical accuracy.

It is understood that competency does not necessarily mean agreement with majority opinion, or with what are generally considered to be the safer, the more orthodox, or the more traditional views—either in theology or in any other academic field.

It is understood, moreover, that the college accepts as members of its faculty only those who have demonstrated their academic competency by the attainment of advanced degrees and/or by advanced research. Therefore, it is understood that this would not normally be called into question.

JOHN TRACY ELLIS

This extremely complex question can hardly be treated adequately in 300 words just as no theoretical statement of principles will ever succeed in avoiding all future tensions over the issue of academic freedom.

Concern about the amount of freedom the faculty will enjoy is altogether understandable, for in no area of life has the concept of the dignity of the human person, which in the words of Vatican Council II, "has been impressing itself more and more deeply on the consciousness of contemporary man," been more sensitively felt than in the world of learning. Furthermore, the history of this matter in Catholic institutions has not been particularly reassuring. Ours is a Catholic college and we accept, therefore, the obligation expressed in the 1940 "Statement of Principles on Academic Freedom and Tenure" of the AAUP that any limitations arising from the institution's religious commitment, "should be clearly stated in writing at the time of the appointment."

No college operates on the basis of absolute freedom. With our sister institutions we share the expectation that faculty members will speak and write—in and out of the college—with the accuracy that the norms of scholarship of their special discipline demands; and that they will reveal appropriate restraint, respect for the opinions of others, and a serious attempt to dissociate themselves from any identification as spokesmen for the college.

The ultimate purpose of every college is the pursuit of truth. As a Catholic institution we accept the defined doctrines of the Church. That is in no way intended to preclude, however, full and open discussion of the circumstances that surrounded their definition, as well as the new approaches and interpretations that have been advanced by reason of the findings of theologians in Newman's sense of the development of doctrine. Beyond that, this college sets no other limitation on academic freedom save that contained in the salutary admonition of the late Cardinal Suhard, that scholars "must not involve any consideration of interest be it even apologetical: you must seek only what is."

ANDREW GREELEY

In my judgment it would be a mistake to attempt to devise a statement of academic freedom for Catholic colleges any different from that contained in the classic statement on academic freedom of the American Association of University Professors. I see no reason why Catholic higher educational institutions cannot accept this statement of academic freedom as it stands, without any qualifications. To attempt any further elaboration on the nature of academic freedom in the Catholic college or university would be, in my judgment, to degrade the schools as American higher educational institutions.

I see no reason why even the teaching of theology cannot be covered by these principles, at least as long as theology is considered an academic discipline and not an attempt at indoctrination. The theological professor who, in the classroom, teaches the subject matter of his discipline accurately and gives an adequate account of the various solutions to controversial questions, has as much academic freedom—in my judgment—as any other college professor. I would think, however, that part of the problem at the present time is that some Catholic teachers have been inclined to inject their own personal doctrinal and ethical opinions into the academic environment. The theological classroom is no more a place for personal religious opinion than any other classroom, and some of the behavior which I have been informed is taking place at Catholic colleges and universities would not be tolerated at a university like the one with which I am affiliated. Repeated departure in the theology room from the responsible presentation of the subject matter to engage in attacks on the Catholic Church and ecclesiastical organization, or to present one's own personal religious opinion on controversial matters is irresponsible academic behavior. The personal opinions of the professor are not necessarily any concern of the university unless and until he uses the classroom as an occasion to present these personal opinions outside the framework of responsible scholarship. Similarly, the published research of a faculty member, as long as it is solidly documented research, need present no problem to any academic institution. However, if on pretext of scholarly research, a faculty member engages in the expression of personal opinion undocumented by evidence, then the educational institution could quite properly question whether he is the type of man who is worthy of promotion.

The point I want to make is that academic freedom is precisely academic. As long as the man is working within the limitations of this discipline in accordance with scholarly procedures and respecting the right of the student to the adequate presentation of the subject matter, he would be no more of a problem of the Catholic university than any other. If he steps out of his subject matter to engage in polemical activity within the classroom, then a Catholic university—as well as any other university—has every right to judge his behavior as irresponsible. The personal opinion of a professor is no particular business of the university as long as he does not try to impose it on his students in the classroom environment.

FRANCIS E. KEARNS

Given the Church's belief in the dignity and rationality of man and given the stress placed by Pope John's *Mater et Magistra* on the connection between the scholarly life and the life of involvement or social action, the duty of preserving academic freedom ought to be an especially serious one for a Catholic university.

It is not the function of a university to establish norms of orthodoxy or to regulate the public expressions or private conduct of its members. We assert our faith in the competence and good will of the community of scholars at large and believe that when the public expressions of a professor are inaccurate or unprincipled they will eventually be exposed as such through the unfettered exchange of views among his professional peers. Professorial abuse of freedom of expression in the classroom will best be left for correction to the opprobrium which such conduct will naturally incur in a genuinely free academic community, though flagrant abuse may become grounds for formal censure or impeachment by the university senate. Since the risk of tenuring a few mediocre professors is preferable to risking the freedom of younger faculty by attaching a probationary period of tenure, tenure will be conferred automatically and permanently on any scholar selected by the senate for membership in the faculty.

We believe that academic integrity and intellectual inquiry cannot be compartmentalized; therefore we recognize no distinction in the guarantees of academic freedom as applied to secular disciplines or to those dealing with religion and doctrine. Whether lay or religious, a professor owes his primary loyalty to freedom of intellectual inquiry. Should Church discipline or teaching conflict with such freedom, then it is the responsibility of ecclesiastical authority to accommodate the Church to the university, not the university to the Church.

Attempts to regulate or restrict conduct in a university community are justifiable only after authorization by the senate and only when such conduct interferes with the civil liberties or academic freedom of other members of the community. Any member of the university who feels that his academic freedom has been restricted shall have full access to academic due process, including assistance of the campus ombudsman, the right to a public hearing, and the right of appeal to the Academic Freedom Committee of the American Civil Liberties Union or to any other group recognized by the senate as an agency of binding arbitration.

ROSEMARY LAUER

St. Theophilus College, aware of its history as a Catholic institution and wishing to retain—insofar as sound academic policy and religious ecumenism warrant—the bonds of affection and mutual concern which have existed between the college and the Catholic Church, nevertheless acknowledges that no genuine academic freedom is possible in an institution of learning which does not enjoy autonomy in determining its educational policies. Accordingly, the Board of Trustees of St. Theophilus College, composed of civic leaders, professional educators and members of the faculty and administration of the college, is constituted as an independent body, subject only to the limitations of the college charter and the college statutes.

St. Theophilus College, since its reorganization in 1967, has no juridical ties with the Catholic Church; that is, it is not subject to any form of diocesan or curial ecclesiastical control and stands entirely outside the ambit of canon law. Members of the Society of St. Theophilus who serve as members of the board of trustees, as administrators, or as members of the faculty do so as individuals and not in any sense as representatives of the Society. Membership in the Society is not a requirement for holding any office in the college, nor is membership in the Catholic Church.

St. Theophilus College subscribes to the 1966 revision of the American Civil Liberties Union's "Statement of Principles Concerning the Civil Liberties and Obligations of Teachers and Desirable Procedures Involving Academic Freedom in Public and Private Colleges and Universities." Realizing that a truly vital academic atmosphere is not compatible with censorship, the college claims no exemptions from these principles in favor of its Catholic predilections. Recognizing the distinction between theological inquiry and evangelical preaching, and recognizing its own incompetence to distinguish between "orthodox" and "unorthodox" religious doctrine, the college guarantees to its department of theology all those freedoms which are assured to other departments. St. Theophilus College imposes no restrictions on the content of any teaching, whether theological, moral, or political.

Because the academic community by its very nature is society's critic, the college must expect, from time to time, to incur the disapprobation of the ecclesiastical, political, social, and economic establishments. St. Theophilus College accepts its role as social critic and pledges to faculty and students that all policy determinations will be made in accordance with the requirements of academic freedom and never in servile submission to anti-intellectual pressures. To act otherwise would be to undermine the college itself and to betray its faculty, its students, and the society which needs its criticism.

JUSTUS GEORGE LAWLER

General Norms. 1. At St. X, controversy relating to academic freedom will be regarded by the institution as a sign of intellectual health, and the teacher in question will be regarded, until judged otherwise by his peers, as having displayed by the very fact of his being controversial a commitment to his scholarly discipline.

2. No distinction is made between religious and secular disciplines.

3. Interference by externs, whether civil or ecclesiastical, in adjudicating conflicts over academic freedom will not be tolerated.

4. The accused will have the right to counsel.

5. The cost of all proceedings relating to the conflict will be borne by the institution.

Particular Norms. 1. We distinguish between (a) the role of instructor and scholar, and (b) the public role of a citizen. With regard to (a) further: (i) we distinguish between (a) speculation, and (b) advocacy; and (ii) we distinguish between (a) speech, and (b) conduct.

2. Alleged infringements relating to (b) in all three points fall within the scope of the ordinary regulations governing our society; they do not come under the rubric "academic freedom," and therefore are not subject to St. X jurisdiction.

Values to Be Maintained in Adjudicating Conflicts. 1. The right of the teacher. 2. The good of the intellectual community in general. 3. The good of St. X in particular. 4. The good of civil society as represented by the lay public. Finally, other things being equal, the right of the teacher is overriding.

Process of Adjudication. 1. Representatives of the intellectual community in general are the best judges.

2. Representatives of the St. X faculty are the next best judges.

3. The lay public is the least qualified to pass judgment.

4. This hierarchy flows directly from the preceding hierarchy of values to be maintained; it is based on the clear principle that though the right of the teacher is preeminent, no man can sit in judgment on his own case.

5. The secondary position given the St. X faculty seeks to diminish the effect of possible local prejudice.

Selection of Ten Judges. 1. Three specialists in the accused's own particular discipline shall be chosen from the faculties of three different universities; two specialists in two other disciplines shall be chosen from the faculties of two other universities.

2. Two members of the accused's department, and one member of another department shall be chosen from the faculty of St. X.

3. Two members of the board of trustees of St. X shall be chosen as representing the lay voice.

4. If representatives mutually acceptable to the accused and to the administration cannot be agreed upon, the determination shall be made by lot from a mutually acceptable list of names.

5. Administrators of St. X cannot be represented on this tribunal since they are acting as prosecutor.

6. The chairman of the tribunal shall be presiding officer, and shall be determined by simple majority vote.

Judgment. 1. Hearings shall be public or private as the accused requests.

2. A simple majority shall determine guilt and the penalties to be imposed.

3. In case of deadlock, the accused shall be assumed innocent.

4. No appeal from judgment can be made by the litigants to a superior tribunal.

NEIL G. McCLUSKEY

The privileges and responsibilities of scholarship belong to each discipline within the university structure, including theology. It is the prerogative and duty of the scholar to put forth the fruits of his scholarship into the academic marketplace to be examined, tested, modified, accepted, or rejected by his peer group. This body alone can appropriately challenge or approve because it has earned authority and competence in the same field of learning. The very justification for the *science* of theology in the curriculum as an academic discipline is precisely that it is not *catechesis* and, therefore, not directly subject to the *magisterium* or teaching authority of the Church.

Intelligent analysis and responsible discussion of Catholic dogma and official pronouncements of the Holy See on issues of faith and morals in the classroom are encouraged. However, part of the responsibility of the teacher is to be aware of the background and level of maturity of his auditors, so that opinions which call in question principles of Catholic faith and morals are to be presented with the same careful balance that is expected in the presentation of delicate and controversial questions in other academic disciplines. At least the same freedom for the professor is recognized in the case of scholarly publications. Allegations of serious and consistent departure from these norms on the part of a faculty member, lay or clerical, fall within the purview of the university's permanent Committee on Academic Freedom and will be judged according to the standards and procedures detailed in the faculty handbook.

The university finds no incompatibility between the above statements and its acknowledgement of and respect for the teaching authority of the Church, legitimately wielded by the local bishop who, by reason of his office, has a valid concern for the totality of Christian living. Yet because of its charismatic character, this authority is always exercised outside the formal structure of the university.

EDWARD MANIER

The responsibilities of the faculty member are such as to require full freedom in research, publication, and discussion of his subject in the classroom. His primary responsibility to his subject is to seek and state the truth as he sees it. His primary responsibility to his students is to present them with the methods, evidence and conclusions of his discipline and to

encourage them in the free pursuit of learning. His responsibility to his colleagues is to be accurate and respectful in the
open exchange of criticism and ideas. As an informed citizen
of the community, he has the duties of a citizen to speak and
act responsibly on issues of institutional and public policy
and morality.

These responsibilities require that the individual faculty
member be free from interference by political or ecclesiastical
authority, or by the administrative officers of this institution,
unless his methods are found incompetent or contrary to professional ethics after a hearing by members of his profession.

Tenure. After a probationary period not to exceed five years
(if the faculty member has had experience at another institution, the probationary period may be shortened or waived) the
faculty member has continuous tenure, and can be dismissed
only for serious cause. A probationary faculty member has the
same academic freedom as a tenured member of the faculty.

Dismissal for serious cause is defined as dismissal for one of
the following: professional incompetence or neglect of academic duties, conviction of a felony, or causing notorious and
public scandal.

A faculty member faced with formal charges which could
lead to his dismissal may request a hearing before a committee
of tenured members of the faculty, selected by the faculty.
The hearing committee, following procedures which protect
the rights of the accused, reports to the board of trustees. The
board ordinarily accepts the hearing committee report, and will
reject it only under unusual circumstances and for reasons
communicated to the faculty.

(The relation of teaching and research to Catholic orthodoxy
should not be allowed to complicate or specify the statement
of academic freedom. Nor is this problem to be evaded. It may
be met by a succinct prefatory statement of the general goals
of the institution: "In general, this university is guided by a
deep conviction of the worth and dignity of all knowledge, and
in particular that to be gained through the investigation of
man's relation to God, the cultivation of all religious studies,
and the examination and understanding of the Catholic faith

and the Judaeo-Christian tradition. The faculty, the administration, and the board of trustees share the responsibility for
a clear articulation of the particular educational goals of this
university.")

THOMAS MOLNAR

1. Academic freedom, like any other freedom, is not an absolute. The concept must include (a) the right of any group to
found an institution promoting and safeguarding the objectives of that group; (b) a reasonable assessment of the term in
the contemporary context.

2. The Catholic Church is not a "freak" in an otherwise
orderly and harmonious secular world but, on the contrary, she
is the chief inspirer of that world's best values. We need not
take any extra steps to "integrate" Catholic universities into
the world of higher education and scholarship; by being Catholic, a university may (or may not) be on the same level of competence as other universities; but its teaching of the Church's
doctrine and morality puts it by definition on a higher level
in *these* matters.

3. In addition to other courses, a Catholic university offers
those which are dictated by the teaching magisterium of the
Church. Professors who disagree with established Catholic dogmas, doctrine, morality, discipline, etc., have no place in a
Catholic university.

4. All other courses of the curriculum must also give a
prominent place to the Church's views on the matter. Yet the
professor should be free to present all pertinent views tested
by scholarship and research (excluding merely fashionable,
trivial, or obscene views). He should make every effort, however, to arrive at prudential judgments in the spirit of the
Church's teaching.

5. Today's youth is exposed to the confusing winds of many
ideologies. Freedom in a Catholic university does not consist in
offering youth a one-way ticket to the supermarket of ideas but
in leading this youth to at least a correct understanding of the
Catholic position on all matters.

6. In case of disagreement between the university authorities and the individual professor, the latter should be entitled to appear before a panel of ecclesiastical and lay officials of the university, as well as men competent in the particular field. Failure on the professor's part to conform to points (3), (4), and (5) should be considered as the equivalent of incompetence in courses such as geography, chemistry, etc., and may be cause for dismissal or removal from the teaching position. In judging the professor's conduct and teaching, the criterion next to scholarly competence should be his sincere effort to avoid causing scandal. Self-styled heroes and popularity seekers among impressionable youth are to be judged as severely as the incompetent scholar.

GORDON ZAHN

Any academic institution worthy of the name, Catholic as well as public, must be first and always a community of scholars in pursuit of knowledge. This means every guarantee of freedom must be provided in intellectual inquiry, in open exchange of ideas, and in research and publication efforts. The fact that an individual is admitted to a position of teaching or research responsibility within such a community should imply a judgment that he has established his worth in terms of scholarly competence, personal integrity, and sincere commitment to truth. Of course, the pursuit of knowledge being what it is, error will often be the product of the scholar's effort; that is a matter for others within his own discipline to discover and correct. Except where such errors are repeated or consistent enough to disprove the original assumption of competence, the only valid grounds for expelling a member of the academic community must relate to clearly established violations of integrity and scholarly commitment.

Unfortunately, human beings being what *they* are, this has occurred in the past and will undoubtedly continue to do so in the future. Medical science, for instance, has been known to ignore the limits set by respect for the physical and spiritual dignity of its subjects—often enough, and not altogether unrelated to this, to the debasement of the researcher and his science as well. Similarly, studies or writings deliberately designed to subvert the legitimate ends of the good society, or to destroy (or exploit) the religious faith of those exposed to them can result from improper use of the methods or techniques of the social sciences and the humanities. Where such things occur, they clearly constitute a violation of the responsibilities of the offender, not only as a scholar but also as a citizen and—even more—as a man.

In such cases, the offense can merit expulsion from the academic community; but such cases should be rare and, even then, subject to rigorous procedural limitations. The individual so charged must be informed of the precise nature of the charges and their source. He must be given the option of having the charges heard by a committee of scholars from outside his own academic community (with no more than a simple plurality drawn from his own discipline); and their decision must either be ratified or rejected by his faculty colleagues (at least the tenured faculty) before the university administrators act upon it. The action, when taken, should be final and irreversible, although subsequent reinstatement of the offender may be considered if circumstances warrant and appropriate safeguards can be introduced to lessen the likelihood of any recurrence of the offense. Beyond that, the only remaining appeals would be to some body outside the specific academic community—perhaps to the AAUP (in questions bearing upon procedural requirements), or to regular courts of law (if the substance of the charges themselves remains at issue).

No formula is perfect. Injustices would still occur, and offenses still go unchallenged and unpunished. However, should one be forced to choose, it is better that the risk be taken in the latter direction than that the scholar and his work become too vulnerable to the interests or whims of arbitrary authority, whether such abuse originate within the academic community itself or from some other agency or establishment on the outside.

Theological Research and the Magisterium

LADISLAS M. ORSY, S.J.

The need for academic freedom in the Catholic universities of the United States is affirmed repeatedly and strongly. This freedom is seen as an essential part of university life, and a necessary condition for recognition as a university. The absence of this freedom is considered as equivalent to sinking into mediocrity and to remaining an outcast in the field of higher education. The Catholic universities, if they want to take their full share in the intellectual and educational life of the nation, must cultivate academic freedom no less than other universities.

Yet in spite of firmness in stating the principle, a certain uneasiness remains within the Catholic community—in particular the academic community. It is felt consciously or unconsciously that the theoretical foundations for such an affirmation are missing and consequently the principle remains vulnerable. This paper is an attempt to clarify some of the theological foundations for academic freedom in theological research. It is not a complete survey of the problem of academic freedom: it is restricted to the issue of freedom in theological research. Yet, paradoxically, I feel that to restrict the investigations to theological research is to broaden the scope of the conclusions. Theological research is the most sensitive area in a Catholic university. It is there that the relationship of the work of the scholar to the power of the hierarchy comes into focus in the sharpest way. I shall try to show that this relationship need not be a legal one, entitled *The Theologian vs. the Bishop;* it can be a relationship of harmonious cooperation on the part of both parties, the theologian *and* the bishop. If harmony is possible in a field where the issues are the sharpest, surely it must be possible in other fields as well. My considerations will be mainly theoretical, but I shall complete them with some practical conclusions. I hope the doctrine I propose is a liberating one; if so, some liberating actions will be needed to bring about its practical realization.

The thesis that will emerge through the paper is that no school of theology incorporated into a university can function without academic freedom in the broadest and best sense of the expression as it is understood in American academic circles. The sources for demonstrating the validity of this thesis are mainly in both the theology of the revelation and the theology of the Church. I shall try to show that the work of the theologian is indispensable for receiving revelation today, and that his work is part of the dynamic life of the Church, the manifestation of the perpetual quest of God's pilgrims for a better knowledge and greater love of God's kingdom. This is the theologian's charism. It is not opposed to the charism of the bishop; both are God's gifts to the Church destined to complement each other in harmony. This paper is a search for this harmony.

ABOUT TERMINOLOGY

Since we try to bring clarity into a field that is notorious for its obscurity, it is more important than ever that I should give an account of the ways I am using various terms. This is the only way to lay a clear foundation for further construction.

The term *academic* in the expression *academic freedom* refers to an institute of higher learning or education; in concrete terms, to a college or a university. Within the structure of such an institution the so-called undergraduate and graduate levels have to be distinguished. As a rule, the undergraduate level stresses the acquisition of knowledge over creative research; at the graduate level, creative research takes priority over the acquisition of positive knowledge. My reflections will center more on problems that concern graduate schools, although many of the considerations and conclusions could be applied to undergraduate work as well.

Freedom means more the presence of an atmosphere in which an academic institution can pursue its own aim of higher learning or education than the absence of intervention or of constraint from an outside agent. Without such freedom, no university or college can be autonomous.

Authority is a term with many meanings but in all its meanings it implies a relationship of dependence. This relationship is usually associated with superior-and-subject type structures. This may be true in some cases, not true in others: I am not sure it will be true in our case. Let us say simply that authority means a relationship of dependence. Since the Church is a living and organic body, authority in the Church means a relationship of dependence between various members, organs, and their diversified functions. The source of authority in the Church can be either divine or human because both divine and human elements enter into its composition. Authority from a divine source always takes priority over any sort of human authority.

The source of divine authority in the Church is in the redeeming and sanctifying action of the Trinity. The first authority in the Church is *this* authority that is rooted in God. It can be expressed in various ways by speaking about the authority of the Father, the source of all power; the authority of the Spirit who is the life-giving principle in the Church. No human power could ever interfere with the authority of the divine persons. Their authority in the Church becomes manifest by the inspirations of the Holy Spirit and through the living word of God. There is a unity between the action of the Spirit and the word of God expressed in the Scriptures and in the very life of the Church.

Human persons can have authority in the Church only as far as they participate in divine authority, no more nor less. The children of God cannot be subject to any *mere* human authority. Only God has power over them, so that all relationships of dependence based on authority must have their sources in Christ.

But Christ can, and does, transfer his authority either directly or indirectly to human persons. It is our task to determine to what extent such a transfer has taken place, since for a Christian it is just as wrong to put God's authority where it does not exist as not to acknowledge it where it does exist. Let us add immediately that such transferred authority exists in a special way in the bishops who receive it through their consecration.

The teaching authority in the Church is destined to preserve the word of God through all ages from any substantial corruption—or better, it is destined to lead God's people towards the kingdom without letting them lose their way. This is another way of saying that the incarnation of the word of God (wisdom of God) is permanent and present through all ages. Although the word was given once for all, its understanding is a matter of progress. God revealed himself once for all, and he is revealing himself continually by giving new insights and understanding.

Theological research means an intellectual adventure into the realm of God's revelation in order to penetrate deeper into the mystery. This is the theologian's task. *Fides quaerens intellectum* is still a good description of his work and attitude. *Fides,* of course, is not enough for him; intelligence is indispensable. His research begins by the clarification of the *data* of revelation in history, by the clarification of words and events through which God saved his people. It continues by the usual methods of analysis and synthesis, of working hypothesis and its verification.

THE PROBLEM

The problem arises from seemingly conflicting interests and situations: the Church wants to remain faithful to God's revelation. (The term *revelation* should not be understood in a narrow sense here, it may include the development of doctrine as well.) Or, more correctly: the Church wants to be faithful to God who reveals himself through his word, his mighty deeds and the action of his Spirit in this world. This faithfulness of the Church to God is represented in a special way by the episcopate. The bishops have the authority to say whether or not a certain type of doctrine or teaching, a certain type of action bears the mark of fidelity. This power is given to the bishops through their consecration; it implies a special assistance of the Holy Spirit to them. They are much aware of this power and they want to use it by formulating judgments with authority over doctrines and actions.

The aim of a university—and of those engaged in theological research and teaching—is to be creative in the understanding of the faith, to represent the dynamic movement of the Church by attempting to penetrate deeper into the mystery revealed to us. Also, the university and the theologian within it stand at the point where the Church and the world meet. An academic institution is endowed (or so should be anyway) with a sensitivity to contemporary issues and needs. Being a *universitas studiorum,* a university of studies, its members are deeply involved in the study of the secular world and its problems. There is no better place for a theologian than a university to learn about such issues and to formulate the Christian response to them.

There should be no clash between the need of being faithful to God's revelation and the need to explore it more deeply, as there should be no conflict between the genuine Christian tradition and the Christian response to contemporary problems. Both attitudes and thrusts are necessary in the Church, and they are destined to operate harmoniously, completing each other. However, a clash may arise on a human level: the charism of the episcopate is primarily that of fidelity to the word of God; the charism of the theologian is that of searching for new questions and new answers. Every clash comes from men who are limited beings—even in the Church. No one has a comprehensive intuition of the truth, neither the bishop nor the theologian. No one has a horizon that would comprehend all conceivable aspects of the problem and every true solution. Apart from the situation in which infallibility operates (and they are rare situations), *all* are subject to error. The bishop may see danger or actual deviation where there is none. The theologian may push his search for truth so far that he transgresses the limits of fidelity. Then the conflict arises. Suspicions may begin to dominate on both sides: the bishop may manifest his distrust in the explorers, and the theologian will conceive the bishop as a person hampering progress.

The problem really has two aspects. The one is abstract, not too difficult to resolve in a theoretical way. It concerns the harmony between the charisms of the bishop and of the theologian; between the gift of stability and the gift of progress in the Church. The answer is that the two should work together and grow together in unity. The other is concrete, more difficult to resolve. It concerns the harmony between those who are in possession of the different charisms: the bishop and the hierarchy on the one side, the theologian and the university on the other. No one of these exists abstractly: they are all men of their own times, with all the limitations that concrete human existence entails. Any further step toward a solution postulates a more thorough discussion of the role of the sacramental episcopate and of the individual bishop, also the role of the university and of the theologian within the structure of the university.

DISCUSSION: EPISCOPATE AND THEOLOGY

The discussion could well start with the examination of the frequently heard of distinction between the teaching Church and the learning Church; between the *ecclesia docens* and *discens*. Although this distinction is widespread and can bear a good construction, it can be also a misrepresentation of the structure of the Church, an intellectual misrepresentation that may eventually lead to unfortunate actions. If the distinction assumes that in the Church the bishops—and the bishops *only* —are the ones to teach the content of faith, and all others have to remain on the learning side all the time, it is false.

The whole Church, no one excepted, is a teaching Church, under more than one aspect. The very concept of being a witness and of being sent by God to announce the good news involves the concept of *teaching* and there is no Christian who is exempt from the duty of witnessing and from carrying the good news, or a deeper understanding of it, to all men—to those who do not belong to the visible Church and to those who are members of it. Therefore, through this duty of being a witness, being a message bearer, every Christian *is* a teacher.

The apostles were the first witnesses of the kingdom. They had to tell others about their experience, and they had to explain Christ's message to all: the secrets of the kingdom were made open to them. Therefore, at the first Christian age they were teachers in the full and near exclusive sense, conveying a knowledge to others that the others simply did not have. However, once the gospel became the common possession of the whole Church, every Christian in his turn became a teacher too. Obvious examples can be quoted: a Christian mother taught the elements of faith to her children; a Christian sailor carried the good news to far away shores; a Christian slave announced a new doctrine of freedom to his fellow slaves. They *all* became part of the teaching Church—even if they did not have the charism of the bishops to teach with a particular authority.

It follows that every Christian is a teacher, since he is in possession of God's revelation and he is bound to announce it to all others. Facts bear out this statement: Very few of us were taught the Christian faith by bishops; most of us were instructed by lay persons or less frequently by priests.

At the same time, everyone is learning from everyone else. A mother can learn from the penetrating insights of a child into the faith. A sophisticated theologian can learn from the depths of the vision of St. Thérèse. The whole Church is teaching and being taught at the same time and everyone has to take his share of both.

The question remains though: What is the position of the bishops in this teaching and learning process? They have a unique position. Through their consecration as the shepherds of God's people they received the charism of speaking with authority in the matter of revelation; they have the charism of authenticating the Christian doctrine. Such a charism does not mean they are the *only* teachers. It does not mean they cannot learn from others, or that they should not learn from others. It does not mean that they have the deepest insights. It means that for the sake of the whole people of God the Holy Spirit

is assisting them in such a way that in their authoritative pronouncements they cannot betray the word of God, and that in
the important acts of their government they cannot mislead the
whole Church. It is a charism of *fidelity,* a charism given to the
whole episcopal body, not to each bishop taken individually.
The same charism is present also in its fullness in the head of
the episcopal college; i.e., in the pope. To identify such a
charism of fidelity with the exclusive right or duty to teach is
a mistake.

The charism of the theologian is that of an explorer. An
explorer ventures into a new land, into its valleys, mountains,
and forests, trying to draw a map of the unknown region and
to give a full description of it. The theologian is trying to
explore the deepest meaning of the mysteries of the faith; in
him the desire of the Church to penetrate deeper into the truth
of God is translated into action—an action inspired by grace
and intelligence. The duty of the episcopate is to create favorable circumstances for such research since it is an expression of
the vitality of the Church.

For this theological research, the conditions will not be very
different from conditions for research in other fields of
sciences. Some of them can be stated. First, an atmosphere of
trust and confidence is necessary. The theologian must be aware
that he is fulfilling an important function in the body of
Christ, and the members are relying on him and are with him.
The work of the theologian must have a community dimension.
Such trust acts as a powerful inspiration in the work of the
explorer. Secondly, an atmosphere of freedom is necessary. The
aim of the theologian is not to restate the facts of the revelation in traditional terms; his aim is to explore it deeper and
find new insights into it. This is possible only if he feels free
in his venture to push ahead in search of the truth even if it
means the possibility of a mistake. In other terms, there should
be freedom to make mistakes and errors in the pursuit of the
truth. A theologian by necessity will work through hypotheses
in the analysis of the revealed truth and in building a synthesis
among the data of revelation. A working hypothesis is not the
same as truth. It is an attempt to reach the truth, and eventually

when verification is possible, many or most of the working hypotheses will have to be discarded. With such hypotheses the theologian works and the ratio of mistakes in his work is not likely to be less than in any other science. In fact, it is likely to be higher: after all, he is exploring divine mysteries! Yet, while such a procedure is taken for granted in any and every branch of human science, in theology it is held suspect. Unrealistically, superhuman success is expected from the theologian; he is expected to find the truth immediately, which he cannot do.

In the person of the theologian the people of God are searching for a deeper understanding of the truth. This is good for the whole Church, in particular for the episcopal college. Therefore, the bishops should give as much confidence and freedom to the theologian as it is possible. Since the university is the primary place where this quest of the Church for the truth and understanding can be fulfilled, academic freedom at the universities should be jealously guarded by the bishops. A university does not compete with the episcopal office, it completes it.

A difficulty arises: what about the simple faith of those Christians who are not theologians? Will they not be disturbed by the speculation of the scholars? The answer is that they will be disturbed more than once. In fact, many *are* disturbed today. But this disorientation among the faithful is not simply the effect of the research of the theologians. It is caused just as much by the misleading training that our people received. The doctrine of the Church was presented to them as a neat set of propositions valid forever in all details. Few Christians have a sense of *mystery* that can be—has to be—expressed in many ways and that can never be well expressed in human terms. Therefore, the answer to the problem of confusion is not in suppressing theological research but in giving the faithful better information about its nature. Such a policy of enlightenment can go a long way, but it is good to recall that at final resort it will not reach everybody. Therefore, there will be always some persons in the Church who will be disturbed. No solution exists for them. All scandals at all times cannot be avoided. There will always be good people who will be shocked by good propositions. This is part of our human situation and we have to accept it and live with it. Further, all in the Church should be aware that it is part of our Christian condition that we do not live in full clarity, but in a great deal of obscurity. It is not clarity that Christ promised to his disciples, but the assistance of his Spirit in leading them through many obscurities to the light of the kingdom of God.

If it is correct to say that in a true sense the revelation of God is an unending process, the theologian is the person who helps the whole Church to discover and share this revelation. Most of the time the theologian will be the one who finds a new insight; the bishops will be the ones who authenticate it. The history of Vatican Council II is a splendid confirmation of this statement.

This leads to a short statement about the qualifications necessary for the theologian. He is entrusted by the whole Church to search for more light that eventually will lead to greater love. Therefore he has to be a dedicated man: a man of the Church. Not in the sense of being a speaker for the hierarchy, still less in the sense of seeking the favor of the highly placed in the external power structure of the Church, but in the sense of belonging to the whole Christian community (layfolk and bishops) and feeling a responsibility for all of them. The primary duty of the theologian is to discover a divine message in human history, then to interpret and illuminate it.

The mark of a good theologian is an awareness of both his vital mission in the Church and his real limitations. If he is unaware of either he will spoil or destroy his own work and the fine balance in the life of the Church will be affected. It is, however, not irresponsible for the theologian to publish his works or hypotheses for the criticism of his professional colleagues; it is a necessity. It would be irresponsible to publish unconfirmed hypotheses for all the faithful to read, especially if no warning is given that the writing represents an unconfirmed opinion and not the content of divine revelation.

TOWARD A SOLUTION

Freedom in theological research means the creation of an atmosphere of trust in which the theologian can best use all his creative faculties for promoting a deeper understanding of the revelation. It means also the absence of any constraint to prevent scholars from genuine adventure in exploring the divine mysteries. Such freedom for the theologians includes the possibility of formulating working hypotheses with responsibility but without undue anxiety and making them known to his colleagues for criticism and appraisal.

The teaching authority of the bishops means a charism attached to their office to authenticate the word of God revealed in this creation. Such authentication at the highest level supposes a prolonged research. The assistance of the Holy Spirit is not a miraculous divine intervention; the bishops themselves have to rely heavily on the work of the theologians. Therefore, the episcopate has the duty of helping and protecting places of research (such as the universities), and granting freedom of research to the theologians working there.

The university should be exempt from the jurisdiction of the local bishop since *one* bishop does not have the full charism of the authentication of the Christian doctrine. Moreover, if he is not a good theologian he would not have the required knowledge and capacity to judge with competence the results produced by the theologian. Episcopal conferences would be in a somewhat different position. There the collegial power of the episcopate would operate but not to its full extent. Obviously, the work of a theologian is subject to the judgment of the full episcopal college. But such judgment will be extremely rare, especially outside an ecumenical council. It would be subject to the judgment of the pope, too, since he is the head of the episcopal college and he is able to exercise the power vested in the college. But he is not able to delegate the charism of infallibility. Although the pope can be helped in his judgment by various persons and offices, neither the persons nor the offices are assisted in the same way as the episcopal college or the pope is. A judgment by an administrative authority in the Church cannot have a final value unless the episcopate or the pope makes it his own. A rare case, indeed.

Universities should be careful about the selection of those who are destined to be professional theologians. Their personal integrity and their devotion to the cause of truth should be ascertained in as far as possible. However, once they are appointed, trust should be given to them.

But a university is not a place of research only. It is also a place of teaching, especially at the undergraduate level. There, a certain practical policy should apply. Good theological knowledge and great pedagogical skill are necessary to convey to undergraduate students the sense of mystery and the desire to research into it in such a way that their faith should not suffer and at the same time their creative capacity should be awakened and encouraged. Details cannot be given here. They can be best worked out by the person who is actually on the spot, by the theologian who is teaching at the university.

There is a real practical problem. What if a theologian is appointed to a chair at the university, having all the qualifications and offering good evidence of a Christian dedication above any exception, and yet later he persistently professes and teaches a doctrine that cannot be accepted as one representing the Catholic tradition or its legitimate development.

Before any thought of condemning him, it is good to recall the pre-conciliar experience. Many statements that were considered suspect and dangerous before the Council are now incorporated into the achievements of Vatican II.

Yet, let us assume for the sake of hypothesis that the person concerned is definitely wrong, stubborn, and heretical. What will the relationship of the university to the episcopate be then?

The old solution was to condemn the person, and to remove him from his office. It would be difficult to contemplate such a solution today; it would do more harm than good. The best way of dealing with the problem would probably be in requesting professional criticism from other theologians. If that does not work, there would remain another possibility: the bishops could simply state that they believe that Catholic doctrine differs from the one professed and taught by the person concerned. This would clear the air, and both the position of the individual theologian and the position of the bishops would be known for what they are: the former as one of many private opinions, the latter the more or less official position of the

Church. Beyond this no one should go in offering general solutions for particular cases. Every case is unique and ultimately will have to be handled on a personal basis according to the local situation.

All that was said could be summed up imperfectly by recalling that the assistance of the Holy Spirit to the bishops means that they will be *prevented* from error; they receive a *negative* type of protection granted in virtue of the sacrament of order. The work of the theologian is part of the *positive* thrust of the Church to understand the kingdom; his gift can be a charism, but it is not the effect of a sacrament. The ideal situation would be to have bishops who are all theologians; there were many in the course of history and there are many today. But as this ideal situation does not exist everywhere, the problem of academic freedom in theological research will bother us and we have to search for a solution.

NOTE ON THE CANONICAL SITUATION

1. The part of the Code that refers to the office of the pope and of the bishop, and to the exercise of the magisterium has been either corrected or virtually suppressed by the Constitution on the Church and the Decree on the Bishop's Pastoral Office in the Church. The legal implications of the new theological vision of the council has not been worked out yet to any significant extent. Therefore, at present no simple and clear canonical statement is possible. Neither is it desirable since law is a practical science and to make a good law experience is necessary. The real problem for canonists today is to translate the theological principles of the council into some rules that are suitable for initiating reasonable experimentation. Eventually the experimentation should lead to more crystallized legal norms.

2. There exists already an effective movement of decentralization in the Church. The principle that helped to assert the central power of the popes in the Church—"Only the legislator can dispense from his own law"—has been partially revised; the bishops can dispense now from most of the universal laws of the Church. This gives them far greater power than it is

manifest just now. Eventually they will become more and more aware of their power, and the movement of decentralization will be strengthened and accelerated.

3. With the movement of decentralization the danger of fragmentation will emerge; some bishops may well be tempted to introduce strong papal power into their own dioceses. If this happens, the second evil will be worse than the first one. Therefore the holy see (presumably) and many bishops (certainly) are stressing the importance of the episcopal conferences and they want to see them develop into fairly well-structured bodies with genuine power of legislation, with executive and probably judicial offices.

4. In fact, a new balance is being worked out in the life of the Church. It is essential that while this search is going on and the situation is fairly fluid, the universities should take the initiative on themselves to work out theologically their place within the new structures. Then they should request legal provisions that are likely to help their development and protect them from undue interference. If they omit such planning, it is a reasonable prediction that laws will be imposed on them by those who have no university experience.

5. On a practical level it would be good to take the initiative and to suggest legal solutions to the episcopal conference. There is some urgency in taking this step. The Decree on the Bishop's Pastoral Office and the norm given for its implementation give power to the diocesan bishop over all apostolic works in his diocese. The texts are general enough to allow exceptions, some exceptions are even named; e.g., in connection with the apostolic work of religious communities. But universities are not mentioned, and a narrow interpretation could easily attribute to the bishop more power than what is due to him in virtue of his office. Since no individual bishop (apart from the bishop of Rome) has the charism of infallibility, no individual bishop should have full jurisdiction over Catholic universities in doctrinal matters. This was already realized in the Middle Ages, and various universities enjoyed various types of exemptions from the power of the local bishop. Similar exemptions

would be even more necessary today, and they should be part of the legal structure.

6. The idea has been debated of having a bishop for the pastoral care of the universities. All matters concerning the care of the souls (in the technical, canonical sense, i.e., appointing chaplains, blessing of marriages, etc.) would belong to such an *ordinariate*. If such a bishop would be a university man, many difficulties that arise today may well disappear.

7. On an even more practical level, the following canonical advice can be given: Catholic universities should be careful to preserve their right role in the Church. Such a role is more universal than the scope of the diocese would allow. Hence they should not unduly seek submission to the local bishop; they should be aware that they fulfill their purpose by having a more universal scope. Since there is no absolute law now, it is important that Catholic universities should contribute positively toward the evolution of a new legal system to be applied to academic institutions. Such a contribution can be done by initiating new customs—even at the price of some tension or possibly some reprehensions. At the same time, universities should try to build up a relationship with the episcopate at a level that is higher than the local diocese. This could be done in several ways: through liaison agencies with the episcopal conferences, through an ordinary for the universities—and through other means that only experience can reveal.

APPENDIX

LAND O'LAKES STATEMENT:
THE NATURE OF THE CONTEMPORARY CATHOLIC UNIVERSITY *

1. *The Catholic University: A True University with Distinctive Characteristics*

The Catholic University today must be a university in the full modern sense of the word, with a strong commitment to and concern for academic excellence. To perform its teaching and research functions effectively the Catholic university must have a true autonomy and academic freedom in the face of authority of whatever kind, lay or clerical, external to the academic community itself. To say

---

* Position paper adopted, July 20–23, 1967, at Land O'Lakes, Wisc., by the seminar participants: Gerard J. Campbell, S. J., President, Georgetown University; John Cogley, Center for the Study of Democratic Institutions, Santa Barbara, Calif.; Charles F. Donovan, S. J., Academic Vice President, Boston College; Most Rev. John J. Dougherty, Chairman, Episcopal Committee for Catholic Higher Education and President, Seton Hall University, South Orange, N. J.; Thomas R. Fitzgerald, S. J., Academic Vice President, Georgetown University; Rev. F. Raymond Fowerbaugh, Assistant to the President, Catholic University of America; Most Rev. Paul J. Hallinan, Archbishop of Atlanta; Robert J. Henle, S. J., Academic Vice President, Saint Louis University; Theodore M. Hesburgh, C.S.C., President, University of Notre Dame; Howard J. Kenna, C.S.C., Provincial, Indiana Province, Congregation of Holy Cross.

Robert D. Kidera, Vice President for University Relations, Fordham University; Germain-Marie Lalande, C.S.C., Superior General, Congregation of Holy Cross, Rome, Italy; Felipe E. MacGregor, S. J., Rector, Pontificia Universidad Catolica del Peru, Lima, Peru; Right Rev. Theodore E. McCarrick, President, Catholic University of Puerto Rico, Ponce; Neil G. McCluskey, S.J., Secretary of the Seminar, University of Notre Dame; Leo McLaughlin, S.J., President, Fordham University; Vincent T. O'Keefe, S.J., Assistant General, Society of Jesus, Rome, Italy; Right Rev. Alphonse-Marie Parent, Laval University, Quebec, Canada; Paul C. Reinert, S.J., President, Saint Louis University.

M. L'abbé Lorenzo Roy, Vice Rector, Laval University; Daniel L. Schlafly, Chairman, Board of Trustees, Saint Louis University; George N. Shuster, Assistant to the President, University of Notre Dame; Edmund A. Stephan, Chairman, Board of Trustees, University of Notre Dame; M. L'abbé Lucien Vachon, Dean, Faculty of Theology, University of Sherbrook, Canada; John E. Walsh, C.S.C., Vice President for Academic Affairs, University of Notre Dame; Michael P. Walsh, S.J., President, Boston College.

336

this is simply to assert that institutional autonomy and academic freedom are essential conditions of life and growth and indeed of survival for Catholic universities as for all universities.

The Catholic university participates in the total university life of our time, has the same functions as all other true universities and, in general, offers the same services to society. The Catholic university adds to the basic idea of a modern university distinctive characteristics which round out and fulfill that idea. Distinctively, then, the Catholic university must be an institution, a community of learners or a community of scholars, in which Catholicism is perceptibly present and effectively operative.

2. *The Theological Disciplines*

In the Catholic university this operative presence is effectively achieved first of all and distinctively by the presence of a group of scholars in all branches of theology. The disciplines represented by this theological group are recognized in the Catholic university, not only as legitimate intellectual disciplines, but as ones essential to the integrity of a university. Since the pursuit of the theological sciences is therefore a high priority for a Catholic university, academic excellence in these disciplines becomes a double obligation in a Catholic university.

3. *The Primary Task of the Theological Faculty*

The theological faculty must engage directly in exploring the depths of Christian tradition and the total religious heritage of the world, in order to come to the best possible intellectual understanding of religion and revelation, of man in all his varied relationships to God. Particularly important today is the theological exploration of all human relations and the elaboration of a Christian anthropology. Furthermore, theological investigation today must serve the ecumenical goals of collaboration and unity.

4. *Interdisciplinary Dialogue in the Catholic University*

To carry out this primary task properly there must be a constant discussion within the university community in which theology confronts all the rest of modern culture and all the areas of intellectual study which it includes.

Theology needs this dialogue in order:

A) To enrich itself from the other disciplines;

B) To bring its own insights to bear upon the problems of modern culture; and

C) To stimulate the internal development of the disciplines themselves.

In a Catholic university all recognized university areas of study are frankly and fully accepted and their internal autonomy affirmed and guaranteed. There must be no theological or philosophical imperialism; all scientific and disciplinary methods, and methodologies, must be given due honor and respect. However, there will necessarily result from the interdisciplinary discussions an awareness that there is a philosophical and theological dimension to most intellectual subjects when they are pursued far enough. Hence, in a Catholic university there will be a special interest in interdisciplinary problems and relationships.

This total dialogue can be eminently successful:

A) if the Catholic university has a broad range of basic university disciplines;

B) if the university has achieved considerable strength in these disciplines; and

C) if there are present in many or most of the non-theological areas Christian scholars who are not only interested in, and competent in their own fields, but also have a personal interest in the cross-disciplinary confrontation.

This creative dialogue will involve the entire university community, will inevitably influence and enliven classroom activities, and will be reflected in curriculum and in academic programs.

5. *The Catholic University as the Critical Reflective Intelligence of the Church*

Every university, Catholic or not, serves as the critical reflective intelligence of its society. In keeping with this general function, the Catholic university has the added obligation of performing this same service for the Church. Hence, the university should carry on a continual examination of all aspects and all activities of the Church and should objectively evaluate them. The Church would thus have the benefit of continual counsel from Catholic universities. Catholic universities in the recent past have hardly played this role at all. It may well be one of the most important functions of the Catholic university of the future.

6. *The Catholic University and Research*

The Catholic university will, of course, maintain and support broad programs of research. It will promote basic research in all university fields but, in addition, it will be prepared to undertake by preference, though not exclusively, such research as will deal with problems of greater human urgency or of greater Christian concern.

7. *The Catholic University and Public Service*

In common with other universities, and in accordance with given circumstances, the Catholic university is prepared to serve society and all its parts, e.g., the Federal Government, the inner-city, etc. However, it will have an added special obligation to carry on similar activities, appropriate to a university, in order to serve the Church and its component parts.

8. *Some Characteristics of Undergraduate Education*

The effective intellectual presence of the theological disciplines will affect the education and life of the students in ways distinctive of a Catholic university.

With regard to the undergraduate—the university should endeavor to present a collegiate education that is truly geared to modern society. The student must come to a basic understanding of the actual world in which he lives today. This means that the intellectual campus of a Catholic university has no boundaries and no barriers. It draws knowledge and understanding from all the traditions of mankind; it explores the insights and achievements of the great men of every age; it looks to the current frontiers of advancing knowledge and brings all the results to bear relevantly on man's life today. The whole world of knowledge and ideas must be open to the student; there must be no outlawed books or subjects. Thus the student will be able to develop his own capabilities and to fulfill himself by using the intellectual resources presented to him.

Along with this and integrated into it should be a competent presentation of relevant, living, Catholic thought.

This dual presentation is characterized by the following emphases:
A) A concern with ultimate questions; hence a concern with theological and philosophical questions;
B) A concern for the full human and spiritual development of the student; hence a humanistic and personalistic orientation

with special emphasis on the interpersonal relationships within the community of learners;

C) A concern with the particularly pressing problems of our era, e.g., civil rights, international development and peace, poverty, etc.

9. *Some Special Social Characteristics of the Catholic Community of Learners*

As a community of learners, the Catholic university has a social existence and an organizational form.

Within the university community the student should be able not simply to study theology and Christianity, but should find himself in a social situation in which he can express his Christianity in a variety of ways and live it experientially and experimentally. The students and faculty can explore together new forms of Christian living, of Christian witness, and of Christian service.

The students will be able to participate in and contribute to a variety of liturgical functions, at best, creatively contemporary and experimental. They will find the meaning of the sacraments for themselves by joining theoretical understanding to the lived experience of them. Thus the students will find and indeed create extraordinary opportunities for a full, meaningful liturgical and sacramental life.

The students will individually and in small groups carry on a warm personal dialogue with themselves and with faculty, both priests and laymen.

The students will experiment further in Christian service by undertaking activities embodying the Christian interest in all human problems—inner-city social action, personal aid to the educationally disadvantaged, and so forth.

Thus will arise within the Catholic university a self-developing and self-deepening society of students and faculty in which the consequences of Christian truth are taken seriously in person-to-person relationships, where the importance of religious commitment is accepted and constantly witnessed to, and where the students can learn by personal experience to consecrate their talent and learning to worthy social purposes.

All of this will display itself on the Catholic campus as a distinctive style of living, a perceptible quality in the university's life.

10. *Characteristics of Organization and Administration*

The total organization should reflect this same Christian spirit. The social organization should be such as to emphasize the university's concern for persons as individuals and for appropriate participation by all members of the community of learners in university decisions. University decisions and administrative actions should be appropriately guided by Christian ideas and ideals and should eminently display the respect and concern for persons.

The evolving nature of the Catholic university will necessitate basic reorganizations of structure in order not only to achieve a greater internal cooperation and participation, but also to share the responsibility of direction more broadly and to enlist wider support. A great deal of study and experimentation will be necessary to carry out these changes, but changes of this kind are essential for the future of the Catholic university.

In fine, the Catholic university of the future will be a true modern university but specifically Catholic in profound and creative ways for the service of society and the people of God.

The representatives of the Catholic universities of the world assembled at Lovanium University, Kinshasa, conscious of their responsibility to share in building a better and more human world, wish briefly to describe their specifically Catholic role in their fraternal collaboration with other institutions of higher learning.

In addition to the teaching, research and service common to all universities, by institutional commitment the Catholic university brings to its task the inspiration and illumination of the Christian

* Position paper adopted by the delegates to the Eighth Triennial Congress of the International Federation of Catholic Universities, held September 10–17, 1968, at the Lovanium University, Kinshasa, Democratic Republic of the Congo, The delegates and participants were: Cardinal Gabriel-Marie Garrone, Prefect, Sacred Congregation for Catholic Education; Vittorino Veronese, Pontifical Commission for Justice and Peace; Ch. Vieyra, Chief, UNESCO Mission to the Democratic Republic of the Congo. CANADA: Paul Berry, St. Francis Xavier University, Antigonish; Msgr. Albert Louis Vachon, Université Laval; R. Brosseau, S.S., Université de Montréal; Germain Lesage, O.M.I., Université St. Paul, Ottawa; Roger Bernier, Université de Sherbrooke. U.S.A.: Robert Drinan, S.J., Boston College; Leo McLaughlin, S.J., Fordham University; John Felice, S.J., Loyola University, Chicago; Theodore M. Hesburgh, C.S.C., Neil G. McCluskey, S.J., Edmund A. Stephan, John E. Walsh, C.S.C., University of Notre Dame; Paul E. Waldschmidt, C.S.C., Portland University; Robert J. Henle, S.J., Paul C. Reinert, S.J., Daniel L. Schlafly, St. Louis University; Edmund W. Morton, S.J., Seattle University; Msgr. Theodore E. McCarrick, Universidad Catolica de Puerto Rico, Ponce. ARGENTINA: Ismael Quiles, S.J., Universidad del Salvador, Buenos Aires; Msgr. Octavio N. Derisi, Pontificia Universidad Argentina, Buenos Aires; Fernando A. Storni, S.J., Universidad Catolica de Cordoba, Argentine. BRAZIL: Rev. Irmao José Otao-Stefani, J. Girotto, Pontificia Universidade Catolica de Rio Grande de Sul, Porto Alegre; Candido Mendes de Almeida, Pontificia Universidade Catolica de Rio de Janeiro. COLOMBIA: Antonio Osorio Isaza, Universidad Pontificia Bolivariana, Medillin. ECUADOR: Luis E. Orellana, S.J., Pontificia Universidad Catolica del Ecuador, Quito. NICARAGUA: Cardenal, S.J., Universidad Centro Americana, Managua. PARAGUAY: Msgr. Juan Moleon Andreu, Universidad Catolica, Asuncion. PERU: Felipe E. MacGregor, S.J., Pontificia Universidad Catolica del Peru, Lima. VENEZUELA: Carlos Plazza, S.J., Carlos Reyna, S.J., Universidad Catolica, Caracas. CONGO: Antoine Bala, Enseignement Supérieur et Universitaire, Kinshasa; P. Ekwa, S.J., President, Bureau de l'Enseignement

message. In the Catholic university, therefore, Catholic ideals, attitudes and principles penetrate and inform university activities in accordance with the nature and autonomy of these activities. Distinctively, then, the Catholic university must be an academic institution, a community of scholars, in which Catholicism is present and operative.

In the Catholic university, this operative presence is ideally and normally achieved first of all by the presence of a group of scholars in all branches of theology. The disciplines represented by this theologian group are recognized in the Catholic university, not only as legitimate intellectual disciplines, but as disciplines essential to the integrity of the Catholic university. Indeed, we believe that the science of religion by its very nature belongs to the task of any univer-

---

Catholique, Kinshasa; Louis-Paulin Mamanda, Ministère de l'Education Nationale, Kinshasa; Msgr. Tharcisse Tshibangu, Alphonse Elungu, Maurice Plevoets, Albert Mpase, Msgr. Luc Gillon, Université Lovanium. ETHIOPIA: Mother Maria Nora Onnis, Sister El Forces Berardi, University of Asmara. IRAQ; Richard J. McCarthy, S.J., Al-Hikma University, Bagdad. LEBANON: Abdallah Dagher, S.J., Université St. Joseph, Beyrouth. JAPAN: F. X. Oizumi, S.J., Sophia University, Tokyo. PHILIPPINES: James J. Meany, S.J., President, Philippine Accrediting Association of Schools, Colleges and Universities; John Doherty, S.J., P. Ortiz, S.J., Ateneo de Manila University; Sylver Verhaeghe, Rev. Paul Zwaenepoel, St. Louis University, Baguio City; Rudolf Rahmann, S.V.D., University of San Carlos, Cebu City; Jesus Diaz, O.P., S. Molina, University of Santo Tomas, Manila; Luis F. Torralba, S.J., Xavier University, Cagayan de Oro City. BELGIUM: Msgr. A. Descamps, Rev. P. Lagrain, M. Vinck, M. Van Vindekens, Université Catholique de Louvain; Camille Joset, S.J., Facultés Universitaires, Namur. FRANCE: Msgr. Jean Honoré, M. l'Abbé Ecole, Melle Tremoulet, Université Catholique de l'Ouest, Angers; Msgr. Michel Descamps, President, Bureau International de l'Enseignement Catholique, Paris; Francois Russo, S.J., International Catholic Center of Coordination with UNESCO, Paris; Msgr. Pierre Haubtmann, M. L'Abbé Latour, Gilbert Olivier, Institut Catholique de Paris; Michel Falise, Msgr. Georges Leclercq, Canon Gerard Lepoutre, Facultés Catholiques de Lille. HOLLAND: J. Lammers, Katholieke Universitat Te Nijmegen, Nijmegen. ITALY: Sante Graciotti, Università Cattolica del Sacro Cuore, Milano; John E. Blewett, S.J., Paolo Dezza, S.J., Jesuit Generalate, Rome; Hervé Carrier, S.J., Pontificia Università Gregoriana, Rome; Stanislas Morawski, Università Internazionale Pro Deo, Rome. POLAND: Stanislas Nagy, Katolicki Uniwersitet Lubelski, Lublin. SPAIN: Luis A. Sobreroca, S.J., Escuela Superior de Administracion y Direccion de Empressas, Barcelona; Rev. Jaime Loring, Escuela Superior de Tecnica Empresarial de Cordoba; Francisco Ponz, Universidad de Navarra, Pamplona; Tomas Garcia Barberena, Francisco Martin, José Rodriquez Medina, Universidad Pontificia de Salamanca. SWITZERLAND: Norbert A. Luyten, O.P., Université de Fribourg.

sity. Since the pursuit of the theological sciences is, therefore, a high priority for a Catholic university, academic excellence in these disciplines become a double obligation.

At this period of social change when the mind questions the role of the university in society, when the Christian community itself is uncertain of the future of the Catholic university, we deem it essential to recall the reasons which justify in regard to society in general and to the Christian community in particular the objective which Catholic institutions of higher learning have to fulfill in the present time.

In practice there is a variety of activities proper to a Catholic university, which would include such endeavors as the following:

1. To contribute as much as possible to the integration of all knowledge in the light of the wisdom of Christian revelation, in accord with the university's mission of universality.

2. To make theology relevant to all human knowledge and all human knowledge relevant to theology itself.

3. To put at the disposal of the people of God and especially of those with responsibility for making serious decisions in the Church the discoveries of knowledge in every field.

4. To study and research problems of high Christian and human priority. For example:
    — Respect for students' freedom during their formative years
    — Enriching of culture and its profound human meaning
    — The problem of faith in a pluralistic society
    — The dignity of love and the stability of family life in an age where these values are being eroded.

5. To create a Christian community of learning, in which, because of its authentic universality, non-Catholics as well as Catholics may participate and cooperate thus bringing to the Catholic university the ideas and values of many traditions.

6. To create a true university community in which all members whether professors, students or administrators, whether clerical or lay, participate authentically in its total life.

7. To promote ecumenism by forming thinkers fully equipped for dialogue through ecumenical studies at the highest level.

8. To serve society in general with dedication, in a Christian perspective, which especially focuses on the needs of the emerging nations and on the new world civilization now forming. To assist Catholic universities in the developing areas in the formulation of a theology suited to their cultures and ways of life.

9. To prepare graduates who can participate with all men in the continual development of every sector of our pluralistic society, especially in the achievement of social justice.

To these special tasks, Catholic universities are dedicated by an institutional commitment which includes a respect for and voluntary acceptance of the Church's teaching authority.

Thus, the Catholic university both in theory and in fact presents a rich potential of forms, modes and activities. The Catholic universities of the world judge, therefore, that they have a specific contribution to make to university activity in general, and that they should respond in rich and creative ways to the needs of contemporary society.

To achieve any significant influence in contemporary society, an institution of higher learning must possess a certain quality of excellence recognizable throughout the academic world. Accordingly the International Federation of Catholic Universities urges careful planning before the foundation of universities and university colleges under Catholic sponsorship. Moreover, the Federation wishes to encourage the movement among Catholic institutions to affiliate both among themselves and with other private and state institutions of learning, as well as the movement toward sharing of resources.

The Catholic universities desire to be of service to their local communities as well as to the larger society, national and international. They feel, consequently that to achieve these goals they merit wide support not only from the general public, and philanthropic institutions, but also from governmental sources.

All are agreed that the essential note of a Catholic university consists, as Pope Paul VI has noted, in its existence as "a community of persons who are diverse in experience and in function, equal in dignity, occupied with scientific research and the integral formation of man, and who, whatever their task, draw inspiration from the light of revealed truth," rendering it therefore "a center for development and diffusion of an authentic Christian culture."

SECTION I

A. *Essential Characteristics of a Catholic University*

Since the objective of the Catholic university, precisely as Catholic, is to assure in an institutional manner a Christian presence in the university world confronting the great problems of contemporary society, the following are its essential characteristics:

1. A Christian inspiration not only of individuals but of the community as well.
2. A continuing reflection in the light of Christian faith upon the growing treasure of human knowledge.
3. Fidelity to the Christian message as it comes to us through the Church.
4. An institutional commitment to the service of Christian thought and education.

All universities that realize these conditions are Catholic universities, whether canonically erected or not. The purposes of the

---

* *Position paper adopted at the close of the congress of Catholic universities which met at the Vatican from April 25 to May 1. The elected delegates were:* Guillermo Alba-Lopez, F.S.C., Universidad "LaSalle," Mexico; John E. Blewett, S.J., Sophia University, Tokyo; Msgr. Octavio N. Derisi, Pontificia Universidad Catolica Argentina, Buenos Aires; Msgr. Albert-Louis Descamps, l'Université Catholique de Louvain, Belgium; Herbert DeSouza, S.J., St. Xavier's College, Ahmedabad, India; Laercio Dias de Moura, S.J., Pontifica Universidad Catolica do Rio de Janeiro, Brazil; Jesus Diaz, O.P., Santo Tomas University, Manila, Philippines; Rev. Clarence W. Friedman, National Catholic Educational Association, Washington, D.C.; Msgr. Luc Gillon, l'Université de Lovanium, Kinshasa, Congo; Msgr. Pierre Hauptmann, l'Institut Catholique de Paris; Robert J. Henle, S.J., St. Louis University. Also: Theodore M. Hesburgh, C.S.C., International Federation of Catholic Universities; Maria-Joseph Heuts, l'Université Catholique de Louvain; Msgr. Georges LeClercq, International Federation of Catholic Universities; Felipe E. MacGregor, S.J., Universidad Catolica del Peru, Lima; Neil G. McCluskey, S.J., University of Notre Dame, U.S.A.; Msgr. John J. McGrath, St. Mary's College, Notre Dame, U.S.A.; Rev. Jeremiah Newman, St. Patricks College, Maynooth, Ireland; Rev. Simon Nguyen Van Lap, Catholic University of Dalat, Vietnam; Br. Gregory Nugent, F.S.C., Manhattan College, River-

Catholic university can be pursued by different means and modalities according to diverse situations of time and place, and taking seriously into account the different natures of the disciplines taught in the university.

B. *The Different Kinds of Catholic Universities*

Given the different stages of development of higher education under Catholic auspices in various parts of the world, and even of institutions within the same country, it would be futile to attempt a univocal approach to the contemporary challenges and problems of our institutions of higher learning. Accordingly, the responses to the questionnaire of the Congregation are simply the efforts of each institution to describe what it understands itself to be, how it understands its mission, and how it tries to achieve its objectives as a Catholic institution.

Since the meaning of the term "Catholic university" has been historically determined and conditioned by each historical and national situation, different institutions will have different relations to ecclesiastical authority relative to the magisterium, pastoral concern, and governance. As the following list indicates, there are various categories into which fall Catholic institutions of higher learning. Two basic categories can immediately be discerned: those institutions

---

dale, N.Y.; José Stefani-Otao, Pontificia Universidad Catolica Rio Grande do Sul, Brazil. Also: Most Rev. Candido Padin, Pontifica Universidad de Sao Paulo, Brazil; Leon Pallais, Universidad Centroamericana, Nicaragua; Rev. Marian Rechowicz, Catholic University of Lublin, Poland; Xavier Scheifler, S.J., Universidad Iberamericana, Mexico; Daniel L. Schlafly, St. Louis University, U.S.A., Rev. Laurence K. Shook, Institute of Medieval Studies, Toronto; Jean Sonet, S.J., Universidad Catolica, Cordoba, Argentina; Aloysius Torralba, S.J., Xavier University, Cagayan de Oro, Philippines; Richard Tremblay, O.P., Laval University, Canada; Andreas G.M. Van Lelsen, Nijmegen University, Holland; Rev. Pietro Zerbi, University of the Sacred Heart, Milano, Italy; Michael P. Walsh, S.J., Fordham University, New York; Most Rev. Roque Adames, Universidad Catolica, Santiago, Dominican Republic.

The following were official observers and periti: José Bacelar e Oliveira, S.J., Universitas Catholica Lusitana, Lisbon; Florentino Idoate, S.J., Universidad José Canas, San Salvador, El Salvador; Nicanor Lana, University of San Augustine, Iloilo, Philippines; Edoardo Miras, Pontificia Universidad Catolica, Buenos Aires; Thomas Pak, S.J., Sogang College, Seoul, Korea; Eugenio Veiga, Universidade Catolica San Salvador, Brazil; Rev. Umberto Betti, Pontificio Ateneo Antoniano, Rome; Rev. Luigi Calonghi, Pontificio Ateneo Salesiano, Rome; Paola Dezza, S.J., Curia Generalizia S.J., Rome.

which have a juridical bond to Church authority in one form or another and those which do not.

According to the most reliable estimate, there are nearly 600 institutions of higher education in the world which are "Catholic" in some way or other.[1] Included in this figure are 143 universities; 240 separately organized university colleges; 86 separate faculties on a university level; over 80 university colleges which are constituent elements of state universities.

These institutions may be classified according to:

1. kind of instruction and research; e.g., almost exclusively theological-religious or not;
2. level of instruction and research and degrees conferred;
3. institutional complexity; i.e., one, several, many faculties, schools, departments, or institutes;
4. type of institutional governance; e.g., relative position of faculty, administration, students, and others in policy-making and executive work;
5. relationship to authority ecclesiastical or civil, whether expressed or not.

C. *The Autonomy of the Catholic University and Its Relationships to Ecclesiastical Authority*

The Catholic university today must be a university in the full modern sense of the word, with a strong commitment to and concern for academic excellence. To perform its teaching and research functions effectively the Catholic university must have a true autonomy and academic freedom. Nor is this to imply that the university is beyond the law: the university has its own laws which flow from its proper nature and finality. The following are the philosophical and theological principles which bear upon the meaning of autonomy in the university.

D. *Philosophical and Theological Principles Relating to the Autonomy of the University*

1. Since the university is an institution for research and teaching at the center of society, it exists to serve the community which cre-

[1] Edward B. Rooney, S.J., "The Present Factual Situation of Catholic Universities in the World and What It Means," a paper prepared for the Eighth General Assembly of the International Federation of Catholic Universities at Kinshasa, Congo, September 1968, p. 14.

ated and sustains it. This community can be the civil state, the Church, or a private group of persons. Rightfully then the university will depend upon its social sponsorship and cannot be completely autonomous but remains subject to the legitimate exigencies of the society which sustains it. For example, the preparation of civil servants or research in fields of high priority, etc.

2. However, this service to the community is valid only if the university is able without restrictions to follow the imperatives which flow from its very nature: pursuit of the truth without conditions. From hence flows its autonomy: freedom of research and of teaching. In other words, it is limited by no other factor than the truth it pursues. Every limitation imposed on the university which would clash with this unconditioned attitude for pursuing truth would be intolerable and contrary to the very nature of the university.

3. Because the universities themselves are best qualified to judge what is needed to pursue the truth, academic autonomy normally entails administrative autonomy in such things as the selection of faculty, the planning of academic programs, organization of teaching and research, the establishment of chairs, etc.

4. There is here a delicate balance which must be established between the self-government of the university and the right of accountability which belongs to the society from which the university takes its origin and exists. Public interest can make itself felt here in a way which does limit self-government provided that imperatives of unconditioned research for the truth are respected.

5. In the Catholic university there is a special element in the domain of academic autonomy including freedom of teaching and research. Though all natural truth is directly accessible to us through the exercise of our innate ability to grasp and to understand reality, the authentic Christian message is not available to us except with a guarantee of doctrinal authority, which is the magisterium of the Church. The datum from which theological reflection arises is not a datum of reality fully accessible to the human intelligence, but a revealed message entrusted to the Church. The freedom of the theological researcher, at the risk of basic self-destruction, rests on the foundation of revelation.

6. It follows from this that the magisterium as such can intervene only in a situation where the truth of the revealed message is at stake. Within these limitations, this means complete freedom of research and of teaching must be guaranteed. In every case the intervention of the competent ecclesiastical authority should respect the

statutes of the institution as well as the academic procedures and customs of the particular country.

E. *Practical Considerations*

With the foregoing principles in mind the following considerations should be stressed.

1. The Church has the right and the responsibility to determine Catholic belief and to define Catholic moral principles. To this authority all Catholics are subject, whether lay or cleric, preacher or theological scholar.

2. The theological scholar in taking his place in the university, must be able to pursue his discipline in the same manner as other research scholars. He must be allowed to question, to develop new hypotheses, to work toward new understandings and formulations, to publish and defend his views, and to approach the theological sources, including pronouncements of the teaching Church, with the free and full play of modern scholarship. His work should normally be reviewed and evaluated by his scholarly peers as is the case in other disciplines.

3. History teaches us how much the influence of the Church has been limited because of certain ecclesiastical or religious authorities who, overzealous to defend certain established positions, have precipitously and arbitrarily blocked the diffusion of scholarly research.

4. In teaching theology in the university, the theologian must of course present the authentic teaching of the Church, but he may and should form his students to an intelligent and critical understanding of the faith, prudent account being taken of the maturity and previous preparation of the students. As an individual he is bound to accept the authentic teaching of the Church and to submit to its legitimately exercised authority. As a theological scholar he is bound by the nature of his discipline to take into proper account the pronouncements of the Church. However, his relationship to ecclesiastical and religious authorities will vary in accordance with the types of Catholic universities.

5. In a university without statutory relationships with ecclesiascal or religious superiors, these authorities may deal with the theologian as an individual member of the Church. If they can make representation to the institutional authorities, any juridical intervention in university affairs must be excluded. In other institutions provision is made for appropriate action by designated eccle-

siastical or religious superiors. In all cases, however, any action taken by ecclesiastical or religious superiors should conform exactly to their authority as established in the university statutes and should be carried out according to those procedures of due process established in the statutes and recognized as general university common law in the geographical region of the particular university.

F. *Pastoral Concern*

The members of the community of a Catholic university constitute a special sort of community in which Christian professors and students are encouraged to live the Christian life together. Obviously, the ecclesial aspects of this common life—the Word, the sacraments, the eucharist liturgy—are subject to episcopal authority in the same way as any parish.

However, since the members of this community and its common interests are different, the style of Christian living should be appropriately different. Hence it is important that the relevant episcopal authority recognize this difference and not only allow for it but encourage it. The university community is especially appropriate for authorized experimentation, particularly concerning ways to make Christianity more relevant to their lives.

Since a university usually transcends the limits, the needs, and the conditions of a single diocese, it might be well to establish a bishop or a group of bishops for the university ministries—as is often done for the military chaplaincy. In any case the designated episcopal authority in directing the university ministries, both in Catholic and other type institutions, should rely on the advice of men trained in universities and experienced in the university ministry.

The relationship of university chaplains to episcopal authority and to religious superiors will vary according to the different constitutions of universities and the different agreements between universities and the episcopal or religious authorities.

SECTION II

A. *The Contribution of the University to the Common Good of Society*

1. *Objectives*

a) The Catholic university, as a university, has an obligation to promote the progress of knowledge through scientific research, to assure its dissemination for the good of the society, and to form men of intelligence and action who will be able to serve society constructively.

Furthermore, as a Catholic university, it is a "public, stable and universal institution of Christian ideas within the total, intellectual effort to promote a superior culture" in a Christian manner (*Gaudium et Spes,* 10). It is also a center for scientific study and for the dissemination of the Christian message.

b) Since the Catholic university is being integrated in local, regional, national, and international societies at a given time in history, this prospect for service ought to stimulate the university to be, through means within its competence, an instrument of progress for these diverse societies. The university should promote cultural values proper to the society in which it is located and it should concern itself with problems of developing countries which require a combined effort for their scientific, technological and cultural progress.

c) The Catholic university's faithfulness to its scientific character and its objective search for truth render it particularly suitable for efficaciously influencing the changes of structure which existing political regimes require for both more human and more spiritual progress. The idea of "objectivity" is not incompatible with the idea of "service."

d) Although the Catholic university is dedicated to the service of society, it wishes to transcend the fluctuations of politics. It cannot link its activities to those of present or future political parties. Nor is it possible or desirable for the university to serve as the tool of any political party. It must in total independence propose and defend approaches to truth that seem most adequate to it, and it must be involved in current problems that lie within its competence.

2. Means

a) In carrying out its objectives, the Catholic university is convinced that the progress of society and the improvement of structures can only result through the efforts of groups of men who are well formed intellectually, spiritually and morally, who are capable of influencing social structures and of becoming "eminent men of the faith in the world."

b) The university's admission policy should give preference to students who, because of their academic ability and other talents, are capable of making significant contributions to society. The admissions policy should help provide for the able student with financial difficulties.

c) The university should give its students the opportunity to become competent men in the exercise of their private or public profession; men capable of contributing to the progress of society by their presence and action; men of science, qualified to take responsibility in theoretical or applied scientific research or in teaching on different levels; men of moral integrity who are enlightened by their faith. The university should give to its Catholic students in particular the potential of becoming men who are capable of thoroughly examining and spreading the Christian faith at the university level in the context of the basic problems of the modern world.

d) In the choice of careers of teaching, research or the social activities of its members, the university should present ideas for the progress of and service to contemporary society. Specifically, it should:

—Give its students factual information about the cultural, social and economic realities of their milieu in its present condition, its foreseeable developments in its human and spiritual context, and information about the doctrines of the Church. This will help them in choosing their professions or acquaint them with the research needed for the development of their area of society.

—Propose to diverse societies observations, solutions or partial solutions to obstacles to their progress. This is especially necessary in developing countries in regard to the problems of hunger, culture, the birthrate, housing, labor, and social legislation.

—Encourage its professors and students, to the fullest extent compatible with their academic functions, to engage in direct and specific social action resulting from scientific studies and research. Such action should be directed primarily toward the education of the underprivileged in the areas of culture, technology, health, and religion.

B. *The Autonomy of a Catholic university in Regard to Civil and Economic Organizations*

The importance of the autonomy of universities in relation to other authorities—especially political authority—is generally recognized in all universities, particularly among the faculty and academic authorities.

At the Fourth General Conference of the International Association of Universities, held in Tokyo in 1965, delegates clearly expressed their desire for a greater degree of university autonomy. This was not done from an attitude of self-defense or a reflex of auto-defense, nor from the standpoint of a quest for power, but in the sole conviction that through its autonomous nature a university is more capable of rendering to society the services that it should.

Catholic universities share the same viewpoint on autonomy, according to the differing circumstances of each university. The Tokyo Conference advocated full university autonomy in regard to these five specific points: selection of academic staff; freedom in its student admission policy; freedom in curriculum planning; freedom in research projects; and great freedom in apportioning its budget.

These objectives are similar to those of Catholic universities and they are restated here in a more general manner:

1) Juridical autonomy: The right to confer academic degrees and to set up programs of study which lead to these degrees. This autonomy is limited and subject to laws pertaining to certain civil and professional diplomas. It is desirable, however, that even these legal rules be as flexible as possible, so that the universities may have real freedom of action, mainly to permit them to adapt their programs in accordance with scientific advancement.

2) Academic autonomy: Freedom in its student admission policy and in appointment of personnel; freedom in regard to subjects taught; and freedom of opinion in teaching, often referred to as academic freedom.

3) Administrative autonomy: The university must govern itself freely, especially in regard to the apportionment and the administration of its budgets, both regular and special.

4) Financial autonomy: This more properly can be called financial viability. It means that the Catholic university of today and tomorrow will often have to appeal for public financial support. It is not unreasonable to envision a process whereby, in regard to the preceding points, university autonomy will affirm itself increasingly while public financial aid continues to grow. The latter can certainly be doubled through proper supervision in the use of funds, but this supervision should not obstruct the university in the planning of its budget, and it should not have any influence on the exercise of the various forms of autonomy mentioned above.

The exercise of parallel autonomy clearly entails special obligations as the Tokyo report notes. It presupposes a high degree of responsibility on the part of all university personnel: its officials, teaching and administrative personnel, and students.

The autonomy of the universities is founded, in short, on the autonomy of knowledge. The latter is sovereign in its discipline. It is necessary, moreover, to distinguish it formally from all that does not pertain to it, political power included.

C. *Relations with Other Universities and Cultural Organizations*

The Catholic university has an obligation to associate itself with other public and private universities in order to participate in the scholarly life of the modern world. Active membership in local, regional and international associations of universities widens the intellectual horizons of administrators, faculty and students.

Collaboration with other universities in fields of common interest and research should be encouraged. The mutual exchange of professors, students and academic credits between universities should be fostered so as to furnish the best academic experience for all. The larger and more experienced universities should lend their personnel, resources, experience and guidance to newer universities whenever possible.

In like manner, the Catholic university should work with cultural organizations such as UNESCO, OAS and other groups with whom the university shares a common commitment to serve the people of the world.

D. *The Relationship of the University with Society.*

The relationships of the university with the society of which it forms a part are multiple. The main one may be described as the cultural stimulation that society needs for its dynamism and progress.

The university fulfills this function of stimulation by promoting knowledge, by forming the men that society needs, and by assisting in various tasks of research that the state or particular societies propose to it or that they themselves bring forth. An important part of cultural stimulation is the critical function in the light of scientific knowledge that the university exerts upon the environment in which it exists and upon the culture in which it grows. Catholic universities are able to play an important role in this context because they are not directly dependent on the state or a political regime.

By its nature the Catholic university favors a diversified system of higher education which is not made up exclusively of the state system of education but rather is enriched by the various systems and modes of organization of the nonofficial educational system. This is conducive to a climate of liberty and competition among various types of universities.

Besides its relationship with the state and political powers, the university is related to other organized societies in the national or international political community. Its relationship must always stem from its function as a useful institution within an autonomy and freedom that are irrevocable. Especially in regard to groups with economic power, the universities must maintain this close and yet remote relationship, leaving them free to fulfill their proper mission.

Universities today are regarded often as poles of economic development and local progress. It is for this reason that communities claim them more and more as avenues leading to cultural and social maturity. Catholic universities are civil institutions integrated within the society to which they belong. They live and grow according to the laws of each of the countries they serve. They must resist, therefore, any tendency to present them as parts of the supranational society that the Church is.

Finally, pontifical universities should take into account the needs of the society or community which they serve.

E. *The External Activity of the University under the Aspect of Its Religious Dimension*

It is probably impossible to propose a precise series of actions to be undertaken by all Catholic universities, since conditions differ from country to country, region to region, and institution to institution. Thus ways and means of reaching essential purposes within these varied environments must remain completely open and relative to a specific institution at a specific time in its history.

It is imperative, however, that the Catholic university have competent Catholic administrators, scholars, and scientists as members of its staff. If the university has such competent people, they will study the environment within which the university is located; they will be aware of the essential purposes of the Catholic university; and they will then, through examination and study, devise and try ways and means to reach these purposes in their own particular religious environment.

The Catholic university, like any other university, is called to serve society in general in many different ways. As Catholic, it surely has a unique role to play for religious society in general and for Catholic and Christian society in particular—but this role cannot easily be defined a priori. The Catholic university undoubtedly also has a special role with respect to nonbelievers by making religion—including Catholicism—both a plausible and positive force for the world itself. Yet the specific means of doing this can only be worked out by starting from the exigencies of the university itself in its particular social setting.

The university community must endeavor to succeed in being witness to Christ. Although the Catholic university should not, properly speaking, be a center for indoctrination, yet its Catholic atmosphere should be such a living, palpable reality as to invite attention from non-Catholics and even nonbelievers. Possible forms of this witness might include the following:

1. With respect to religious sciences, the Catholic university should deepen its understanding and provide for the diffusion of commentaries on the doctrine of the Church. Beyond its primary academic obligation for an appropriate curriculum for its regular students, the Catholic university must make itself available for the service of people in general. Its undertaking continuing education programs, particularly in religious sciences will give proof of its interest in and concern for basic religious needs of all men.

2. The Catholic university is an ideal setting for dialogue with nonbelievers and for ecumenical contacts of a high level. In its openness to collaboration in a vast array of cooperative programs with universities that are either non-Catholic or nonsectarian, as well as in its participation in interdenominational activities within the community, the Catholic university can give ecumenical leadership that will have profound influence on all men of good will.

3. The Catholic university should serve as a laboratory to help the Church and the hierarchy by doing that type of research for which the university is particularly equipped, whether it be in the field of religious sciences or in allied fields of interest, such as education, sociology, etc.

4. The Catholic university must accept seriously its obligation to give testimony to the world around it. It must demonstrate that there is no incompatibility between science and faith. When given at the level of individuals, such testimony is not exclusive to the Catholic institution, since there are individual Catholic scholars in nonsectarian universities. When given at the level of a group, through the community of teachers and scholars in a Catholic university, such testimony is a unique contribution of Catholic higher education and, as such, it has special value. The most positive testimony of the

Catholic university is in its being present to the world and giving a vision of life that has inner form and conviction.

Finally, in considering the essential purposes of a Catholic university in respect to its external religious milieu, it must be emphasized that the basic purpose of any university revolves around learning. The greatest liberty and freedom in the pursuit of truth must always be there, together with the responsibilities such a task involves. Professional competence must be the basis of all activity. The university pursues truth, inculcates basic respect for the dignity of man, and encourages a way of life consistent with this concept.

F. *Long-Range Planning of the Universities in Today's Society*

1. Catholic universities should be conscious of the need for expert long-range planning if they are to develop as their responsible authorities hope they will, and if they are to be properly understood in the contemporary world. Modern methods of long-range planning are indispensable for probing the strengths and weaknesses of modern institutions.

2. Long-range planning is the projection, through diagnosis and prognostication of the reasonable aims and means by which an institution can fulfill its service to God and society. Such long-range planning should employ, in the case of Catholic universities, the advanced and more or less proven techniques and strategies utilized by knowledgeable and expanding governments, corporations and academic institutions. This means that each institution must have a diagnosis and prognostication of its own. It must ask itself exactly what kind of university it wants to become; the rate at which it can and should develop; the amount of duplication and competition with other universities and with itself which is justifiable; and where the revenues it requires are to be found.

If it is agreed that there can be expansion, and that this expansion will take the form of serving more students and establishing more faculties, centers, institutes, then planners must ask further what kind of students they are looking for. Such questions should be whether they are searching for paying or scholarship students, merely adequately or well prepared, socially predisposed for higher education or not. They should ask where they are going to get competent staff to teach them, how they are going to communicate their plans with their staff and students, with their constituency and with the general public. They should inquire how their project is going to be affected by changes already in progress, e.g., loss of contributed services, student activism, attitude of society toward universities and their support. It should be asked how exactly the revenue is to be found to pay for them, whether from fees, contributed services, gifts from alumni, private benefactors, corporations, government, or Church sources. In every case, the projection must be based on publicly known figures so that all can determine who has and who has not been supporting the university, and what requires changing here if the planning is to be effective.

3. There should be collaboration and coordination among existing universities in a given region. Before deciding on a new university, already existing universities should be taken into account and competent authorities should be consulted. It may sometimes be best to consider the possibility of integrating available resources into a non-Catholic university. The development committee of the International Federation of Catholic Universities (IFCU) may eventually be helpful in the long-range planning of universities.

SECTION III

A. *Introduction*

The university world of today is characterized by a general and profound dissatisfaction with its professed functions and goals: the pursuit and communication of truth.

The reasons for this dissatisfaction, and the manner of its expression, may vary from university to university. Among the alleged causes of this state of affairs, the following deserve mention.

1) The tendency toward overspecialization. This has resulted in a feeling that knowledge has become too fragmented, and that truth has been dissociated from other values. In addition, there is an assumption that truth must be sought in ways that are not necessarily cognitive or rational.

2) The greater awareness and maturity that today's students bring with them to the university. Modern methods of telecommunication give every viewer an immediate and vivid realization of the world around him, especially of its injustices and horrors; and this engenders, particularly among the young, a sense of the irrelevance and futility of what is supposed to absorb them at their universities.

3) There is a keener sense of competitiveness among university students today. Higher education is no longer the privilege of the

affluent. Everyone wants a university degree today, to prepare him for a better living. A fear that the university is failing him in this regard often finds expression in violent disapproval of its goals.

4) Everywhere, but especially in developing countries, there is a feeling that a new age has begun. The age of unquestioning subservience, of colonial dependence, has passed. The times demand the assertion of individuality, the development of personality, the exercise of an inalienable right to equality of opportunity and status. From the obstruction of these ambitions there develops among some students a conviction that the universities are outdated embodiments of traditions which ignored these ambitions in the past, and that they are still too closely allied today with forms of government, or structures of society, that are violations of democracy in practice.

The malaise in university life today is obviously not peculiar to Catholic universities. We cannot therefore isolate the problems of a Catholic university from those of other universities. Our task is rather to grapple with the basic problems of the university in order to provide solutions for them in the light of our Christian faith, and to put them into practice first of all in our own universities.

B. *Teacher-Student Relationship in the Classroom*

The commission takes it for granted that a Catholic university should, in every respect, meet the requirements of a modern institution of higher learning for the pursuit and transmission of truth at all levels; that is to say, its faculty members should be of high competence, and that its structures should provide opportunities for the kind of team work rendered necessary today by the wide diversification of methods of investigation. Secondly, the commission interprets this part of the question as bearing on such relationships which belong intrinsically to the discovery and diffusion of knowledge.

The commission expresses its conviction that these relationships should be inspired by the following principles:

1) That although today's students demand from their universities, and from the individual staff members, a social, or even a political commitment, the pursuit of objectivity in the transmission of knowledge should at all costs be maintained.

This objectivity should be viewed by the university, and by its student body not only as the testimony of the primary and profound commitment of universities to truth as such, but also, as the only possible guarantee on behalf of the university of its respect for the individual commitments, along different subjective parts, that may possibly be made by the individual members of the university community.

However, the pursuit of objectivity is not enough. The university should continually reexamine its curricular and research programs, to ensure their relevance both to the progress of knowledge and the practical needs of mankind.

2) That as producers of knowledge, universities are highly organized centers for the creation of culture. In all its aspects culture is created by communities through a process of intersubjective communication. Consequently, at the university, the organic units involved in the on-going process of creating knowledge, should be composed of teams of professors and students, or of directors and collaborators, involved in reciprocally creative activity. This is another way of saying that knowledge, if it is to be universal, should also be universal in its becoming.

Therefore the university should, on the one hand, provide the organic structures that permit the effective participation of all its members at their specific levels of contribution; and on the other, reduce to a minimum the one-way transmission of readymade knowledge, which can so easily degenerate into dogmatism, thus setting up another psychological barrier between professors and students. The foregoing is not intended as a general repudiation of the lecture method.

3) That Catholic universities should excel in the practical application of the above-mentioned principles; for objectivity and universality, rightly understood, are the forms which charity assumes in the intellectual sphere, thereby placing the highest value on the potential contribution of every human personality to the growth of knowledge, and to its integration with other values.

In this way, higher education at Catholic universities becomes the instrument of a truly self-controlled transformation and liberation of mankind.

C. *Concern for Human Development*

1) The root causes of student unrest should be carefully examined with the students themselves.

2) The university should create special institutes, if advisable, that will undertake to provide satisfactory solutions to the social problems that exert such a powerful impact on the psychological

attitudes and behavior of students. The success of this attempt will be greatly enhanced by the collaboration of economists, sociologists, psychologists, moralists, etc., who would contribute their knowlege and experience to a correct enunciation and solution of the problem under study.

The Catholic university will especially examine the ethical dimensions of the social problems confronting mankind, such as poverty, discrimination, particularly in so far as they affect the students. Through the study of these moral issues, in the light of the gospel and of our Christian heritage, the students will have the opportunity to justify or modify their own moral stand or position on these issues.

The university that neglects this course of action in the face of the many problems that exercise the youth of our times, betrays one of its most serious responsibilities and sets itself up at odds with society, which it is its mission to serve.

3) The university must also endeavor to discover and identify the universal values that are present in the different national cultures, on the principle that the values of each culture complement one another.

4) The university is under a special obligation to initiate students in the correct methods of scientific research in the different areas of knowledge, according to their own personal aptitudes.

The university is also urged to provide opportunities to students to exercise academic and social responsibility. One way to achieve this objective would to be provide them with facilities to organize themselves into working teams to pursue their own research projects with the cooperation of the faculty.

D. *The Governance of the University*

The forms of governance of Catholic universities must be adaptive to their wide diversities, to the laws of the various states and to local conditions, and, therefore, no rigid patterns should be established. On the contrary, workable patterns will have to be determined according to specific needs. With this principle in mind, the commission recommends:

1) that the governance of the university be exercised within the just laws of the state;

2) that provisions be made in the structure of the university for all the members of the university community to participate, one

way or another, according to the level and potentialities of each member, in the formulation of policy and in the decision-making process. It should be understood that such participation does not mean that all the members necessarily have a deliberative power in decisions and policy-making actions of the university;

3) that the rights and obligations of all the members of the university community be clearly stated; and that a procedure for recourse be set up in case of conflicts regarding these rights;

4) that all the members of the university community have a right to be informed of the reasons for decisions made by the governance of the university, with due respect, however, for confidentiality and charity;

5) that a spirit of charity characterize the relationships within the university community, made especially manifest in a willingness on the part of all its members to engage in sincere dialogue. This dialogue will be ensured by the establishment of open, specific and clearly defined channels of communication between the governance and all the members of the university community.

E. *The Dialogue of the Academic Disciplines with Philosophy and Theology*

The commission has not considered it its task to discuss the differences and analogies between the different types of positive sciences: mathematics, physics, chemistry, biology, sociology, history, philology, etc. Nor has the commission thought it necessary to discuss profoundly the theoretical aspects of the dialogue between the positive sciences on the one hand and philosophy and theology on the other hand. The commission has confined itself to some general observations regarding the theoretical aspect of this dialogue. It has concentrated its efforts on indicating practical ways favoring this dialogue. By following this policy the commission has taken for granted that a Catholic university is the *locus naturalis* for such a dialogue.

1) The first principle governing the dialogue between science and theology is that if man wants to understand reality, it is necessary for him to make use of the methods and of the results of all types of knowledge available to him. History has taught us that there is not just one intellectual method, but several; not just one approach to reality, but several.

Using several methods to reach the truth does not imply that a real synthesis of knowledge is readily possible. The best we can hope for is perhaps a global vision, in which one type of knowlege complements another one. Much would be gained if we could prevent the trespassing of one discipline into the field of another. The mutual purification of theology, philosophy and positive science is a condition for a sound dialogue. For without regard for the data of science and philosophy, theology cannot really be theology. Without criticism of theology and of philosophy, science is in danger of extrapolating its results into fields which are not its proper domain.

2) It would be wrong to see the dialogue between science and theology only in the perspective of "concordism" and of cheap apologetics. "Truth will liberate us," but only if we give it the chance to show itself to us.

3) An effective way in which science, philosophy and theology can cooperate will be found in a concentration upon the concrete problems which confront mankind today. Each discipline as a specific approach to reality has the tendency to isolate itself, concentrating on the abstract problems as they appear in the perspective of the methodology of the science involved. The needs of mankind, however, are concrete. They invite an interdisciplinary approach in which each science can show its intrinsic value.

F. *Concrete Recommendations*

1) A dialogue is only possible when the participants know each other and are prepared to accept each other as they really are. This also applies to the dialogue between the different disciplines. For this reason it is necessary that the students of the different disciplines have the opportunity to get acquainted with the methodology of other disciplines. This is also a prerequisite for the reflection upon the methodology of one's own discipline. Without this reflection no correct view of the way in which a discipline approaches the truth is possible. Without this reflection no representative of a certain discipline can be a valuable participant in the dialogue. It must be stressed, however, that the acquaintance with the different methodologies of one's own discipline and of that of other participants, is not only a matter of the theory of knowledge. It is as important that each participant has a clear view of the different ways in which the different disciplines are able to contribute to the solutions of the practical needs of mankind. In sum, in each Catholic university opportunities should be provided for an introduction to the different disciplines and their methodologies. They should be available to students of each discipline.

2) It is already common practice in many countries that students of philosophy combine their studies with that of another discipline. Special curricula for such combined studies exist. As far as the commission knows, there is, however, hardly any opportunity to combine the study of theology with that of a positive science. Yet theologians prepared in this way are needed for a serious dialogue.

3) If there are philosophers or theologians who are acquainted with certain positive disciplines, it is of great importance that these philosophers or theologians are not only members of their respective faculties, but are also associated with the faculty or department of the positive discipline involved.

4) When a Catholic university grows in a quantitative and a qualitative sense, the danger exists that it is so preoccupied with teaching and research in the different disciplines that it has hardly any time and energy left for those interdisciplinary problems which are of the greatest value for mankind. Nevertheless these problems ought to be of the greatest concern for each university that calls itself a Catholic university.

In this situation it may be a good policy for a university to create a special instrumentality, consisting of both faculty members and students. The instrumentality could be a "higher institute," a commission or whatever may be best according to local circumstances. The important point is that this mechanism should have the specific task of stimulating and organizing interdisciplinary research in all these problems in which a Catholic university ought to be interested.

INDEX